# TRUE CONSERVATISM

# TRUE CONSERVATISM

## Reclaiming Our Humanity in an Arrogant Age

ANTHONY T. KRONMAN

Yale

**UNIVERSITY PRESS**

New Haven and London

Yale University Press books may be purchased in quantity for
educational, business, or promotional use. For information, please
e-mail sales.press@yale.edu (U.S. office) or sales@yaleup.co.uk
(U.K. office).

Set in Janson type by IDS Infotech Ltd.
Printed in the United States of America.

Library of Congress Control Number: 2024943863
ISBN 978-0-300-27703-6 (hardcover : alk. paper)

A catalogue record for this book is available from the
British Library.

This paper meets the requirements of ANSI/NISO Z39.48-1992
(Permanence of Paper).

10 9 8 7 6 5 4 3 2 1

*For Nancy*
*My contrarian muse*

It is necessary for all those who are interested in the future of democratic societies to unite, and for all in concert to make continuous efforts to spread within these societies a taste for the infinite, a sentiment of greatness, and a love of immaterial pleasures.

—ALEXIS DE TOCQUEVILLE, *Democracy in America*

# Contents

# Preface

Modern conservativism begins with the French Revolution. It starts with Edmund Burke's rousing defense of the ancestral loyalties that give our lives meaning and weight. The inhuman radicalism he despised has remained a force in Western culture since the days of the sans-culottes. It has had its ups and downs, its periods of decline and renewal. Today, in our colleges and universities, and on the left more generally, the leveling program of the French Revolution is having a revival. This has provoked a ferocious reply from its conservative critics who view the contemporary version of Robespierre's egalitarian auto-da-fé as a form of moral madness enforced by a regime of compelled belief that terrifies the timid like the shadow of a guillotine.

As the party of the left has grown more strident and self-assured, its conservative opponents have responded in kind, with louder voices and less respect for the hard-won achievements of our enlightened civilization. Each year they do a poorer job of defending their position as a citadel of human values without lapsing into an angry assault on ideals that progressives and conservatives share. Each year it becomes harder to see the appeal of conservatism as a morally and intellectually compelling philosophy of life. The conservative cause has lost its way. A truer conservatism is needed to remind us of the worth of custom and inheritance; the splendor of what is excellent and rare; the expansive solidarity of our friendship for the dead; and the dignity, indeed necessity, of the human longing for a connection to the eternal and divine—and to persuade us that these timeless goods are compatible with the modern ideals of liberty, toleration, and reasoned argument.

My conservatism takes these ideals for granted but is on guard against allowing them to become prejudices that compromise vital aspects of human fulfillment. It rests on a view of the human condition that is partly shaped by my attraction to the extravagance of human desire—to the boundlessness of our yearning to know and our unquenchable appetite for brilliance and glory—and partly by my conviction that this extravagance itself demands a compensating modesty in our relations with others and even with ourselves. The result is a portrait of humanity that puts excellence first and insists the world is divine but emphasizes the importance of caution and humility in political and personal life.

It is the product of many years reading and teaching old books of great power and beauty in a humanistic program devoted to the study of literary, philosophical, and historical works of lasting value. Among the works I have read and taught, those of Thucydides, Aristotle, Cicero, Tacitus, Montaigne, Spinoza, Burke, Hume, Gibbon, Madison, Tocqueville, Lincoln, Mill, Nietzsche, Tolstoy, Chesterton, Oakeshott, Arendt, Strauss, and Heidegger are a few of the ones that have shaped my thoughts and feelings. It is a motley crew. The only connection among them is the one I have made for myself. Through a process of metabolism as natural to the mind as to the body, I have digested some ideas and discarded others. The philosophical result is as distinctive as my physical self and, like it, has changed over time.

Mine is the conservatism of a child of the enlightenment, grateful to have been born when he was yet not entirely at home in his enlightened world. I have written this book for others who share my division of feelings, however they experience or express it. I hope it helps to clarify our points of agreement and disagreement. Mostly, though, it is a book for those who believe that human dignity demands a progressive view of life and feel no attraction to conservative values. For them, especially, I hope to show that humanism *is* conservatism, not at all times and places, perhaps, but under the aegis of the prejudices that surreptitiously accompany our enlightened ideals and, drawing false authority from them, do so much harm in our moral, political, and spiritual lives.

# TRUE CONSERVATISM

# CHAPTER ONE

# Our Prejudices

## I

The rich and enlightened societies of the modern West are the most prosperous, tolerant, and democratic the world has ever known. Liberties are broadly defined and well protected. Equality is acknowledged in theory and honored in practice. The idea that all human beings have a number of basic civil and political rights is widely accepted. Opportunities abound; never have those with pluck been less confined by the accidents of birth. The freedom to worship as one chooses is taken for granted. Diversity is valued, not suppressed on account of superstition or fear. Science flourishes. We understand the world better than ever before. New time- and energy-saving inventions appear every day. Generous systems of welfare provide help for those who need it.

There are dramatic exceptions, of course. Even in the most enlightened societies, millions remain trapped by poverty and bias. Rights are denied or abused, regularly in some places. Wealth is distributed unequally; the benefits of technology are unevenly shared. On top of this, our ingenious inventions bring new dangers of their own. For the better part of a century, we have lived with the mixed blessings of atomic power. Today, we confront the Frankensteinian prospect of computers with minds exponentially more powerful than our own. Who will rule whom?

Still, even with all these failures and dangers, a sober observer may be forgiven for thinking that ours is the most brilliant civilization that has ever existed—because it is.

To many, it seems obvious that our remaining problems are mainly due to the half-hearted application of our enlightened ideals. Where discrimination persists, we need to uncover its causes and attack them with greater resolve. If the gap between rich and poor tears at the social fabric, we must reduce it through taxes and transfer payments. Better technology will clean the air, cool the climate, and help us live healthier lives without forsaking the benefits of industrialization. What we need is more justice, greater equality, and better science, not less.

This is the essence of progressivism. Progressivism is not a specific set of prescriptions or policy positions. It is an attitude or disposition. It comes in varying strengths, from the meliorist to the revolutionary, and is compatible with a wide range of different programs. But the shades of progressive belief share one fundamental feature in common. They all rest on the conviction that our basic values are sound, our problems the result of imperfect devotion to them.

There is much to be said for this view. Even if we could turn the clock back to the unenlightened world of scripture and tradition, of priests and landed lords, we would never do it. We value the separation of church and state, the guarantee of equality before the law, and the freedom to move, work, and marry as we choose too much to give them up.

We have no choice but to go forward, more or less in the same path, and no wish to do anything else. In this sense, we are all progressives by default. The only question, it seems, is what kind of progressive to be. Which reforms should we support, and with what degree of zeal? There is room for debate at a practical level, but within the limits of a confident consensus that the only cure for our imperfect state of enlightenment is more of the same.

Yet this sensible-seeming conclusion misses something vital. Our broad ideals of equality and toleration, individual freedom and scientific advancement, are accompanied by three prejudices about the nature of human beings and the conditions of human fulfillment. These are so widely shared and casually accepted that we barely notice them. They are affirmed with an arrogant self-confidence that puts them beyond the range of debatable propositions. They appear to belong to our ideals themselves—to be part of them and to possess the same authority.

But this is an illusion. Our prejudices have a life of their own. They are not required to support a culture of enlightenment. Nor are they innocent mistakes of modest importance. Each obscures an essential dimension of human experience and depreciates one of our defining spiritual needs. This is more than a cost to be counted against the benefits of enlightenment. It strikes at something deeper. It wounds the humanity of those for whom all costs and benefits are weighed.

The first of these prejudices concerns the value of equality. It insists that equality is not merely *a* good but the very *highest*, sovereign over every other—the measure by which we assign all other goods their relative value. This makes it difficult to justify the place of institutions of high culture, which honor excellence and promote the enjoyment of beauty, in a society based on the principle that every human being is entitled to equal respect. More fundamentally, it breaks the link between equality of opportunity and brilliance of achievement, which alone explains why the first is worth having at all. That everyone has the same political and civil rights is an axiom of modern democratic life. It is a precious and hard-won ideal. That equality comes first in the explanatory order of values is a dogma that denies the ancient truth that freedom is for the sake of excellence, not the other way around.

The second prejudice enthrones a particular view of the past. It asserts that the past is only a storehouse of resources to be used for present needs. It urges us to disregard the past when it fails to serve our interests or conflicts with the values we now hold. "The earth belongs in usufruct to the living."[1]

Jefferson's dictum expresses one of the basic assumptions of modern scientific research. It also captures the thrilling forward rush of democratic life—its love of innovation and impatience with the dead hand of the past. But it has an inhuman aspect too. A people that sees its past in this light, unburdened by piety, tradition, and the love of those to whom they are related by descent, is free but homeless. The same is true of individuals. The challenge in each case is to reach the right relation between freedom and inheritance. If the past has no claim to our loyalty except as it conforms to what we need and believe, the challenge disappears. But so does a vital component of human fulfillment. Without a loving connection to the dead, we cannot love our living friends or those who are unborn. We cannot even be good friends to ourselves.

The third prejudice concerns the existence of God. Some say God exists; others deny it. Toleration means letting each person decide for him- or herself. This is a very good thing. But toleration encourages the false belief that the existence of God is a matter of private opinion. The separation of church and state does not depend upon this belief, nor must one accept the truth of any of the Abrahamic religions to explain why it is false. Moreover, like our other prejudices, it misrepresents the human condition. It belittles the longing for a connection to eternity that is part of any recognizably human existence, including that of the enlightened atheist whose aggressively godless vision of life cannot be explained except by reference to what Aristotle calls "the eternal and divine."[2]

In each case, we need to separate the prejudice from the ideal to which it seems so closely joined and diagnose the damage it does to our humanity. This is more difficult than it seems. Our prejudices are masked by the appeal of the enlightened ideals in whose company they travel. They are hidden by the glare of our brilliant achievements. Yet the pride we properly take in our ideals blinds us to the ways in which our prejudices make the humane age in which we live so strangely inhuman.

Franz Kafka caught this ambiguity in a striking parable. There was once a man who wished to move the world to a new location. He was sure he could, if only he had a lever long enough. But where must he stand in order to dislodge the earth from its ancient orbit? The answer was revealed to him. "He found the Archimedean point," Kafka says. "But he used it against himself. It seems that he was permitted to find it only under this condition."[3]

Kafka's parable of triumph and self-defeat reminds us that amid the moral and material wonders of our enlightened world, we must be alert to the dimensions of human fulfillment that our prejudices blithely discount. We need to *conserve* the humanity they disguise and insult against the enthusiasms of a one-sided progressivism that sees the virtues of our ideals but not the vices of the prejudices they conceal.

## II

When the young French nobleman Alexis de Tocqueville visited the United States in the early 1830s, he was astonished by the extreme "equality of conditions" he observed.[4] He was struck by the fluidity of wealth and social standing that made America a scene of constant motion. What most impressed him, though, was the supreme importance that many of those he met, both rich and poor, assigned to the ideal of human equality.[5] They recognized, as anyone must, that there are grades of achievement in almost every human pursuit—that some are better farmers, doctors, mechanics, traders, and teachers than others. But they emphatically denied the existence of a rank order among human beings in general and insisted that all men and women are entitled to a meaningful measure of equal respect. This seemed to Tocqueville the moral and political cornerstone of the new civilization aborning in America.

There were, of course, striking exceptions. Many considered blacks and Indians less than fully human. The position of women was equivocal, at once exalted and unseen. Tocqueville was sensitive to the condition of all three groups and wrote about each at length.[6] But the new American ideal of equality was more important, he thought, than the exceptions to it—in part because it armed critics with a norm to challenge these exceptions.

The ideal of equality that inspired the fight against slavery and later for women's rights sprang from the same belief that lay at the heart of American democracy in the 1830s. It rested on the conviction that there is no class or caste of human beings that is superior to others simply and without qualification—no group that is better on account of its overall condition or status. That such a class or caste exists and is entitled to the obedience and respect of lesser men and women was the premise of the aristocratic societies of nineteenth-century Europe, of their feudal predecessors, and of the civilizations of classical antiquity.[7] The new order of values that Tocqueville discovered in America begins with the repudiation of this age-old belief.

Tocqueville saw America as the leading edge of a global revolution. He prophesied that its ideal of human equality would transform the older societies of Europe and, in time, the rest of the world.[8] Events have largely borne him out. There have been convulsive, bloody campaigns to restore the idea of inequality to a commanding position in the order of human values. The Confederacy fought for it in the American Civil War; the Nazis nearly destroyed Europe for its sake. But these great reactionary movements, and many lesser ones, have been defeated, if at immense cost.

The restoration of a social order based on the belief that some human beings are indelibly inferior to others, not in this or that particular respect but altogether, is logically conceivable. We can imagine it happening, though today the prospect seems remote. Even the populist movements that have roiled American and European politics in recent years affirm the ideal of human equality. They merely interpret it differently from the liberal elites whose cultural values they angrily challenge.[9] The fight between them is over the meaning of equality, not its authority as a value. The ideal of human equality is here to stay.

Its most important practical corollary is that every adult ought to have an equal say in the political affairs of his or her community. We now take the principle of universal suffrage for granted. In America and elsewhere, constitutional arrangements slow and deflect the immediate expression of popular will.[10] The practice of judicial review is a striking example. But none of these devices challenge the fundamental assumption that, whatever their level of ability in other respects, all citizens are equally competent to form and express their views about matters of public concern and entitled to have their votes weighed equally with others'.

It is common, of course, to grumble about the ignorance and venality of those with whom one disagrees. But few openly say that some should be deprived of the right to vote because of their lack of intelligence or virtue. Those who want to restrict the franchise always fly under a different flag. Whatever their secret motive, they give lip service, at least, to the ideal of human equality, whose authority is at a maximum in the area of political and civil rights, including, most importantly, the right to vote.[11]

Here, the ideal does a great deal of good. It is a counterweight to privilege and an antidote to pretension. It protects against abuse and exploitation. It honors our sense of solidarity with all who share the human condition. As a practical matter, the principle of universal suffrage is the only one on which a large and diverse society can approach, even distantly, the goal of democratic self-rule.

All of this belongs on the positive side of the ledger. But Tocqueville worried that the principle of human equality has a destructive aspect too. Even as he applauded the spirit of egalitarianism that had given birth to a society "more just" than the aristocracies of Europe, he protested against the extension of the principle of equality beyond the realm of politics and law to that of cultural fabrication and enjoyment.[12] Here, Tocqueville insists, the belief that no human being is superior to any other encourages a leveling of appraisal and appreciation in which distinctions of beauty and character become more difficult to acknowledge and perhaps even to see.[13]

People often disagree about what constitutes excellence in a particular pursuit—fly-fishing, for example, or welding or the practice of law—but there is no moral awkwardness in praising it. Achievement of this sort is what distinguishes experts from incompetents and beginners. If there is even a modest tension between the judgment of rank implied by such distinctions and the principle of universal equality, it is dulled by the limited nature of the first, which always exists within a circumscribed field.

The ideal of human equality is more directly challenged by the belief that some men and women stand out on account of the superiority of their character or the splendor of their lives as a whole—of the closeness with which they approach a state of human greatness or realized power. The judgment that they do has an aristocratic look.[14] Less controversially, one might say that it expresses a "perfectionist" ideal. However one describes it, the affirmation of superiority in this sense assumes the existence of a hierarchy among human beings that reflects their differing success not in this or that particular activity but in what Aristotle calls the "work" of being human.[15] Collaterally, it assumes a similar order in their literary and artistic works, the beauty of art differing from the utility of a tool in the same way that nobility of character differs from expertise—as a kind of splendor that rises above the demands of all local pursuits to reveal something general and lasting about ourselves and the world.

Tocqueville believed in the existence of this hierarchy among persons and things. He believed that its denial or suppression can only produce a world that is thin, banal, unfulfilling—inhuman in an elementary sense.[16] He shared this belief with many others, then and since, some of whom have been the sworn enemies of the new egalitarian order he admired.[17]

What sets Tocqueville apart is his qualified verdict. When it comes to voting and the law and perhaps even the distribution of resources—though this is more controversial—the principle of equality takes precedence. It is not the only principle at work even here, but it comes before every other. It is the first and highest of political values.

In the realm of culture, though, it has a destructive effect. It devalues what ought to be honored and invites a spirit of plebiscitarian rule where judgments of rank should prevail. In the moral realm, which stands between that of culture and politics, of beauty and justice, the principle of universal equality simplifies the work of judgment by reducing all questions of proper behavior to those of duty and right, draining the notion of character (which bears a resemblance to the idea of beauty) of much of its ethical force.[18]

Tocqueville worried that the sweeping egalitarianism he encountered in America was likely to encourage a casual and often mindless extension of the principle of equality from the realm of politics, where it belongs, to that of culture, where it does not. The extension happens when equality is asserted to be the highest of all values, not in this or that domain but absolutely, universally, in every human pursuit. The abstractness of the idea invites the extension. If we accept the priority of equality in one sphere, why not in every other?[19] The burden shifts to those who would resist it.

In a democratic society, the belief that equality is the value that justifies and explains every other has a hydraulic force that promotes its authority in all departments of life. To many this belief is a "self-evident" truth, but in reality it is a prejudice. A commitment to full equality before the law and to greater equality in the distribution of resources does not entail it. It is perfectly possible to be an enthusiastic egalitarian in these respects but reject the idea that equality is first among goods in the realm of culture and the only or even principal one in the sphere of moral judgment. Neither logic nor duty compels it. This is not, moreover, an unimportant confusion. The belief that equality occupies the highest rung in the explanatory order of values is a threat to human fulfillment. This was Tocqueville's somber, at times despairing, judgment.[20] Many readers of *Democracy in America* may wish to forget it, but if they do they miss the most unsettling truth of his wise and balanced book.

Tocqueville was particularly concerned about the fate of institutions of high culture—those devoted to knowledge, taste, connoisseurship, and refinement.[21] These depend on the acceptance of an order of perfection among works and personalities. Can the appreciation of this order survive in a society that puts equality before all other values? Tocqueville feared that the coming age would be one of more and better-protected rights but of mediocrity too, an age in which the splendid and rare are reduced to a level with the undistinguished and common.[22]

There is an obvious response to Tocqueville's anxiety. So long as culture remains a realm of personal pursuits and private enjoyments, no problem arises. Trouble begins only when exaltation and splendor assert their authority in public life. This leads to subordination, enslavement, or worse.[23] To prevent this, the claims of high culture and the values of political life must be kept strictly apart. Even within the realm of high culture, we need to remind ourselves from time to time that equality is the highest of all values. Doing so is a kind of preventive medicine.

This sounds reasonable, but it contains a poison pill. The moment judgments of excellence are subjected to this kind of egalitarian supervision, the realm of culture, instead of being tolerantly indulged, becomes a venue for the vindication of the principle of equality itself. It becomes ripe for colonization in the name of equality. The judgment "She is an outstanding human being and he an ordinary one" or "This work is beautiful and that one coarse or kitschy" loses its authority and is met with the morally devastating reply, "That is your opinion; you are entitled to it; I feel otherwise; we should agree to disagree." In this way, the principle of equality extends its sway over the dominion of beauty and truth, sapping them of their power to command our admiration and deference—as it should, say those for whom the value of equality is the measure by which every other must be judged.

Tocqueville rightly saw that institutions of high culture are jeopardized by an over-extension of the principle of human equality, driven by the prejudice that equality is not merely a good but the highest one, sovereign among values. But he failed to see that even where equality comes first in practical terms (as it does in law and politics), it never comes first in the order of explanation. If equality is good, here or anywhere else, that is because it is good for the pursuit of some other, higher good on whose account we assign equality the derivative value we do. The only way to unseat the prejudice that equality is the highest of all values is to install excellence on the throne of sovereignty instead.[24]

Rather than allowing equality to put excellence in its place, the order must be reversed. This leaves plenty of room for the enthusiastic endorsement of most forms of legal and political equality and a commitment to greater fairness in the distribution of wealth and opportunity but blocks the hegemonic extension of the principle of equality to other dimensions of life on the grounds that it is the highest of all values in the order of justification. The suggestion sounds extravagant, but nothing less will do. More half-hearted measures are too weak to counter the reduction of culture to politics that is the most destructive effect of the first of the three prejudices that darken our enlightened ideals.

## III

Every society progresses and conserves. We move forward, adapting as circumstances require. We try to make the best of things under continually changing conditions. In the process, we ourselves change. Yet every new departure draws on whatever resources we already possess. These have to be conserved to be of any use at all. No society stands still or starts from nothing.

In this elementary sense, we are all progressives and conservatives, not by choice but by necessity. Before we have begun to reflect on the meaning of these terms, or to ask where our allegiance lies, human nature has enrolled us in both parties. Many eventually do ask, though. The question arises in a natural way.

Even our most primitive plans employ the power of reason. A plan is a reflective strategy for using the inheritance of the past to attain some future result. It is a common if not irresistible extension of this power to ask how the future is related to the past, not in this or that particular case but in general. The answers we give begin to divide us into the parties we conventionally call "progressive" and "conservative."

Progressives say that yesterday exists for the sake of today and tomorrow.[25] Where the past is a help, we should exploit it; where it stands in the way, we must discard it. Where its values differ from our own, we should ignore or repudiate them. No one thinks we can live wholly free of the past. From a progressive point of view, though, the practical value of our inheritance depends on its availability as a resource for our present and future needs and its moral value on the degree to which it anticipates the enlightened ideals we now embrace.

The resource may be material—an accumulation of physical capital. It may be intellectual—the storehouse of knowledge built up by earlier workers and thinkers. It may be moral—the ideals of duty and decency to which previous generations subscribed. Whatever the nature of the resource, though, the progressive attitude toward it is one not of reverence but of use, and this must always be decided from the standpoint of our current needs and values.

What reason can we have, the progressive asks, to be loyal to the past for its own sake? The past has no dignity or authority of its own. We have no duty to conserve the past or honor the dead unless doing so serves our present purposes. All our moral and practical energies should be directed toward the future. This is the only attitude that makes sense from a progressive point of view.

We need not go far back to find a very different idea of the past. All forms of traditional authority rest on the belief that we should act today as our ancestors did, because they did, and for no other reason.[26] This is the cornerstone of every archaic system of ancestor worship and of the religions of revelation that displaced them, which, whatever their revolutionary potential, begin with the demand that their followers honor the word of God, regardless of its present or future utility, because he spoke it at a decisive moment in the past.[27]

In broad historical terms, the displacement of all such views by the progressive belief that the past has value only as a moral and practical stepping stone to the future is a relative novelty. Its triumph is a consequence, in part, of the rise of modern science, which is a novelty too.

The modern science of nature is only four hundred years old. In this short time, it has reshaped our understanding of the meaning of truth and of the methods for discovering it. Today, the principles of scientific verification are accepted by all. They represent a universally acknowledged standard of objectivity—one that transcends our moral, political, and religious differences. The president of the United States and the supreme leader of Iran may be prepared to take their countries to war because they disagree about democracy and God. But neither doubts the truth of the laws of atomic physics.

One of the premises of scientific research is that the past is valuable only as an aid to the future. We must reject its lessons the minute they are experimentally disproven. A participant in Galileo's *Dialogue concerning the Two Chief World Systems* tells the story of a friend who, after having been shown by an anatomist that the nerves originate in the brain rather than the heart, as he had supposed, declares that he would believe what he has seen "if Aristotle's text were not contrary to it."[28] The anecdote is meant to illustrate the absurdity of assigning the past any authority of its own in a serious scientific inquiry.

In this sense, modern science is progressive by definition. Today, its assumptions enjoy an unrivaled prestige, largely on account of their astonishing success. The practical and intellectual triumph of scientific research has in turn given the progressive view of the past greater credibility in other realms of human action, including that of politics, where until recently the authority of tradition always carried greater weight.

In the second half of the nineteenth and early part of the twentieth centuries, many European and American reformers, inspired by Enlightenment thinkers as diverse as Condorcet, Bentham, and Marx, insisted on a more scientific approach to the solution of social, economic, and political problems.[29] They envisioned different futures and proposed different strategies for reaching them, but agreed that an enlightened society must be governed by deliberate planning for tomorrow rather than blind obedience to the "eternal yesterday" of traditional norms.[30]

The past, they said, is a catalogue of moral, cultural, and economic experiments. It shows that some work and others do not. But this exhausts its value as a source of inspiration and instruction. Custom and tradition must yield to the rational design of administrative programs and objective methods of review, analogous to those used in a laboratory.

This was the heart of Western liberal progressivism, which in this respect at least resembled the Bolshevism that many of its advocates despised.[31] In the West, progressivism meant a qualified deference to the market and the benefits of competitive pricing. In the Soviet Union, it meant centralized planning. This was a difference of historic importance.

But it rested on a shared belief in the need for a scientific approach to the problems of political life—one that treats the past as a stockpile or "standing reserve" whose contents have value only as moral, cultural, intellectual, and physical material to be used or discarded, as reason demands, in the pursuit of a fairer and more prosperous future.[32]

This view draws seemingly irrefutable support from the norms of scientific research, whose authority can be felt in every corner of life. It also makes practical sense. When faced with a political problem, what choice do we have other than to decide what we currently want and believe, and which course will bring us closer to our moral and material goals? In most policy debates, the progressive view of the past is not an option but a necessity. This is true even when progressives say that the satisfaction of our present needs requires the conservation of something from the past, for in that case too, the value of the past is fixed from the standpoint of current requirements. That it seems impossible to proceed in any other way gives the reduction of the past to a storehouse of utilities the appearance of a self-evident truth.

But it is not, at least not when this view of the past, which science commands and the challenges of practical decision-making appear to confirm, is taken to be a general truth about the human condition. That is a prejudice. The belief that we have no reason to honor the past for its own sake may be unavoidable in the precincts of science and policy, but its extension to the whole of human life is required neither by reason nor experience. Like the belief that equality is sovereign among values, it illegitimately elevates an idea that makes sense in certain settings to the status of a universal truth. In the process, it discounts an essential dimension of human fulfillment, which depends on our capacity for friendship with the dead as much as with the living, and on a tempered piety toward their achievements.

A measured friendship of this kind is a condition of family loyalty. It is a part—though only a part—of patriotic devotion. Progressives deride these attachments or redescribe them in ways that strip them of the implication that affection for the dead is ever a proper emotion.[33] But their deracinated portraits show how inhumanly thin the world becomes when we eliminate this feeling from our view of the past and reduce it to what we can use and approve.

Friends take an interest in one another's well-being for the friend's sake, not their own. Living friendships fit the pattern. So do our relations with the dead. Any feeling of loyalty to them, however qualified, depends on the friendly assumption that their lives matter to us apart from their serviceability and rectitude as measured by our current needs and values. Even the weakest form of patriotism, constrained by the strongest moral commitments, rests on this assumption.

There is a personal analogue. Integrity is partly a matter of living up to one's chosen principles, but only partly. It is also a matter of honoring those elements of character that fall on the side of destiny rather than choice—that constitute one's inheritance. "Honoring" does not mean blind obedience in a personal setting any more than in a political one. Reflection and selection are always involved. But it does mean, in the one case as in the other, an attitude of friendly care for the fate that befalls us. No fully human life is possible without it, for individuals and political communities alike.

The belief that we should approach all the problems of life, as the scientist and policymaker do, in a liberated spirit free from the gratuitous entanglements of fate is a prejudice that works like acid on this attitude of care. It mocks and demeans the instinct of piety, which even in our enlightened age has something to teach us about the conditions of human fulfillment.

# IV

The first of our prejudices is that equality is the highest of all values. The second is that we have no reason to honor the past for its own sake. The third is that religion is a matter of personal opinion. This is one of the causes (or symptoms) of what Max Weber calls the "disenchantment" of the world—the relegation of religion to the sphere of private belief and the disestablishment of every public institution whose authority depends on its claim to preserve and teach the truth about God.[34]

This is a spur to toleration. The members of a multi-confessional society are more likely to tolerate one another's religious views if they agree that belief and disbelief are personal choices the state may neither command nor forbid. There is, of course, room for debate. What exactly does the separation of church and state require? The British believe it is compatible with the existence of a national church. The French believe it is incompatible with the wearing of head scarves in public schools. Americans believe it compels the opposite conclusion in both cases.[35] Yet despite these disagreements, there is a broad consensus in the enlightened societies of the modern West that the existence of God is a question of conscience that we must each be left free to answer on our own.

For many, agreement on this point is part of the definition of enlightenment itself. There are still a few defiantly theocratic regimes, like Iran and Saudi Arabia, that reject this consensus. They continue to fight to uphold the public truth of religion in a world increasingly united by an ethic of personal choice. But they are battling against the tide of enlightenment. In the end, they cannot prevail.

This does not mean that religion is bound to disappear as enlightenment spreads. Even in the world's most progressive societies, churches and believers exist in very large numbers. They are likely to continue to do so for the foreseeable future. Their numbers may even grow, if more seek the comforts of religion as an antidote to the anomie of modern life.[36]

What it *does* mean is that religion is destined to decline to the status of a private opinion, which society ought to honor for moral and practical reasons, but only as a choice to be indulged outside the realm of public life—from which, as Weber famously remarked, the process of scientific rationalization and the morality of individual freedom have chased the old gods once and for all.[37] The world's enlightened societies have reached this point already. Its few remaining theocracies are being carried along toward it, loudly protesting.

That toleration is a great good few will deny. That its achievement on a historically unprecedented scale is one of the outstanding triumphs of enlightened thought is uncontroversial. That it depends on the separation of church and state seems obvious.

It does not follow, though, that the existence of God is a matter of personal opinion. The process of disenchantment may have proceeded on this assumption and been hastened by it. But the belief that the assumption is *true* is a prejudice, closely associated with the enlightened ideal of toleration but neither necessary to nor justified by it.

There are other justifications for religious toleration than this one. The most obvious is that people are often so attached to their beliefs about God that they are willing to spill blood in their defense. Treating belief as a matter of private opinion helps to curb religious violence.

But the utility of this assumption does not entail its truth as a proposition. Those who insist that God exists understand this. They are happy to take advantage of the protections the separation of church and state affords. But the idea that the existence of God is a private belief is in their eyes a blasphemy. God is not an opinion. He is the truth about the world. From a religious point of view, the enlightened assumption that the question of God's existence must be settled in the tribunal of individual conscience is itself an expression of the disenchanted secularism that is the cause of our spiritual woes.[38]

Disbelievers respectfully respond that this is merely an opinion too, to which the religious are entitled. That is the enlightened position. Those who defend it occupy the high ground in these interminable debates. But in one crucial respect they are wrong.

It may be impossible to establish the truth of any religious doctrine beyond dispute. But every religion is a response to the universal human longing for a connection to eternity. The longing is not an opinion. It is part of our makeup. Reason itself confirms this, if we follow its path to the end. Immanuel Kant (who went far along the path) puts it well. It is obvious to every observer, he says, that no finite rational being, like ourselves, can ever be satisfied with the merely temporal.[39] We long for what cannot be found within the horizon of time. That we do is an essential component of our human being. To deny it is degrading.

The assumption that belief in the existence of God is a private opinion obscures this basic truth. It encourages the idea that our longing for eternity is as dependent on personal choice as the decision to become a Roman Catholic or an Orthodox Jew. No one need become either. But we are all driven by an irrepressible desire to reach what Kant calls the "unconditioned," his synonym for God.[40] The drive takes many different forms. The desire itself, though, is not an option. The belief that religion is a matter of individual conscience and a choice like any other is a prejudice that leads from toleration, which is a virtue, to the depreciation of an essential dimension of human fulfillment, which is a terrible loss.

This is the third of the prejudices that make our humane and enlightened world so inhospitable to the human beings who live in it. Accredited by the enlightened ideals with which they are often associated, our prejudices enjoy an ersatz authority that gives them the appearance of solid truths. In reality, they are groundless and harmful. True enlightenment means freeing ourselves from their grip.

By this measure, it is not the progressive who is enlightened. He rightly insists that our ideals are precious and worth preserving. But he cannot see the prejudices that accompany them and underestimates the damage they do. The truly enlightened person is the one who recognizes our prejudices and feels the need to conserve the human goods they threaten. She loves what is splendid and rare, rising above the mediocre and banal; feels a friendship for the dead and a loyalty to her inheritance;

and longs to come closer to the eternity we all seek by different names. For her, these feelings are not embarrassing or criminal. They are not a blow to human dignity but elaborations of it. Nor are they incompatible with the love of democracy, science, and toleration. If she is an enlightened conservative, she loves all these things and sees no contradiction in doing so. Today, the balance of enlightenment lies with her view of life. She is the one, in Tocqueville's memorable phrase, who sees "not differently, but further."[41]

# V

I call her view "conservative" in the simplest sense of the word. It is motivated by a desire to save or conserve something of value against diminution or loss.

This is not the only meaning of the word. It is an elastic term with no agreed-upon definition. As a practical matter, we often use it as a shorthand to describe a person who holds certain positions on specific matters of law and social policy. A conservative in this sense is someone, say, who opposes government regulation, gun control, open borders, restrictions on prayer in public schools, and an expansive right to abortion. This topical use of the word, though, is not of much value. It shifts with the focus of public debate; what is conservative one year may not be the next. More important, at any given moment there are likely to be self-proclaimed conservatives on both (or various) sides of the issues. Some conservatives support a woman's right to choose; others oppose it. Some favor free trade; others condemn the market as a corrosive force that undermines our national and local attachments. Some want to lower the wall between church and state; others would raise it higher.[42]

These differences exist because the positions a person supports depend on his or her reasons for doing so. Different reasons produce different groupings. If a set of policies is not a mindless jumble but has any coherence at all, there must be some organizing conviction that joins them. A collection of policies is conservative only if the principle that unites them is.

And what principle is that?

To answer this question, it is useful to distinguish three different traditions of conservative thought. Each has a long and honorable history and offers a set of ideas with which to construct an organized response to the perceived shortcomings of progressivism. One is libertarian. Another is traditionalist. The third has a religious tenor. There are others, but most are compounds of these. They are the building blocks of conservative argument, and while they can be combined in various ways, there are also abiding tensions among them.

For enlightened conservatives who embrace the ideals of our free and tolerant civilization but reject the arrogant prejudices that hide in their shadow, these three traditions provide a place to begin. They offer a wealth of arguments with which to test the limits of progressive belief. None, though, has the resources to break the spell of the prejudices that blind us to the inhuman side of our egalitarian, scientific, and secular civilization. For that, we need to dig deeper—to attack these prejudices at their root from a humanistic point of view. Still, it is useful and respectful to start by reviewing the strengths and weaknesses of the three familiar lines of thought that inspire most conservative criticism today.

The first is the libertarian conservatism of Adam Smith and his followers.[43] They oppose big government, favor the invisible hand of the market, are hostile to collectivism, and deride the pretentions of rational planning. They stress the material benefits of spontaneous order and the moral value of individual freedom.

Some may dispute whether this is a conservative view at all. It grows out of and remains tied to the ideals of classical liberalism long associated with enlightened reform. Still, many who today call themselves conservatives defend their position in libertarian terms. They do not reject the principles of enlightened thinking in general but only their illegitimate and self-defeating extension—for example, the destructive dogma (as they see it) that centralized control is the best way to protect individual liberty and increase social wealth. In this respect, the libertarian position resembles my own, which also rests on a distinction between sound ideals and insupportable prejudices. The resemblance is close enough to justify asking whether the libertarian branch of conservative thought is able to explain why the ruling prejudices of our age are so harmful to the human spirit. The answer is no.

The libertarian is first and foremost a defender of free markets. These have two advantages. One is practical, the other moral. The practical advantage is the way markets make use of the information dispersed among the countless individuals participating in them as buyers, sellers, lenders, and speculators.[44] Much of this information is lost or neglected in a centrally planned economy where the planners must predict what producers and consumers want and how they will behave. Better, says the libertarian, to let individuals speak and act for themselves. The result is a price system that utilizes the information they possess about their own preferences and powers.

The moral advantage of a market is that it allows us to chart our own course in life. We all have an interest in being able to choose how to live rather than having our occupations, roles, and relations thrust upon us by a third party, however beneficent. We have the right to make these choices for ourselves. To deny it is demeaning. It renders the life of the person whose freedom has been taken away less worthy of respect, whatever our estimate of the wisdom of the choices he or she makes.[45]

These practical and moral advantages apply to the law as well. Friedrich Hayek is the best-known exponent of this view.[46] Decentralized adjudication of the kind embodied in the common law has, he says, the same informational advantage as a free market. Many judges deciding many cases according to their assessment of the facts is superior to a uniform system of statutory regulation, which inevitably leaves much of this information behind. It also allows for a finer calibration of the relation between action and effect and thereby fosters an ethic of individual responsibility rather than blurring the consequences of personal conduct in an administrative collectivism which, at the limit, treats individuals as vehicles for the pursuit of some common good.

These are the strengths of libertarian conservatism. They are always worth keeping in mind. Depending on the issue at hand, they may carry the day. Sometimes markets are superior to centralized administration—perhaps in many cases. But the libertarian's commitment to free markets does not attack or even challenge our deepest prejudices. It intensifies them.

To begin with, free markets reinforce the idea that there is no disputing about taste. They reward expertise of all sorts but discourage the belief that there is such a thing as excellence in living overall. Or rather, they treat this belief as just another preference that some share and others do not, with no firmer foundation in human nature than a taste for peaches instead of bananas.

Markets liquidate all ideals of excellence. They do this, in part, by multiplying the goods that buyers and sellers are able to trade. More fundamentally, they do it by elevating individual freedom to a position of supreme moral value, from whose vantage point every law-abiding choice is equally dignified simply because it is the choice of the person who makes it. In this way, libertarian conservatism seconds our prejudice in favor of equality rather than resisting it.

The same is true of religion. The transformation of objective values into personal preferences hastens the reduction of religion to a private opinion. Free markets may be practically and morally superior to planned economies, but they are the most powerful engine of disenchantment the world has ever known. Nothing dissolves the old truths and subverts the ancient hierarchies of religion as quickly and effectively as a system of free exchange.[47] One can view this in a positive or negative light—as an aid to toleration or an engine of corruption—but the fact is that nothing has done as much to diminish the authority of religion as the libertarian ethic of choice.[48]

Finally, on a libertarian view of life, the past is drained of inherent value. Friedrich Hayek stresses the importance of the past as an inventory of experiments, the most successful of which have survived and should be respected on account of the wisdom they presumptively embody. This leads him to a form of traditionalism. But Hayek's affection for tradition is strictly utilitarian. We should respect the past because doing so is useful, not because it has any authority of its own.

The latter view is incompatible with the libertarian's insistence on the supreme value of choice. The only way these can be reconciled is on instrumental grounds. Deference to the past may be the most sensible course, given our epistemic limitations. At most, we can identify and modestly correct them—among other ways, by training ourselves to respect the past instead of jumping to the conclusion that we always know better than our ancestors did. Perhaps this is wise counsel. But it is only a clever refinement of the progressive view that the past is merely a storehouse of utilities, not a challenge to it.

# VI

The second branch of modern conservative thought descends from Edmund Burke.[49] Burke's followers attach great importance to precedent and the traditions of the past. They celebrate prudence or practical wisdom, which they consider the greatest of all political virtues. They affirm the value of social hierarchy and organized religion. Their views differ sharply from those of libertarians. They are traditionalists, not individualists.

Does Burke's conservatism give us what we need to understand and arraign the prejudices of our age? With respect to our attitude toward the past, the prospect seems bright.

Burke's view of the past is not narrowly utilitarian. He writes about it in reverential terms. He speaks of his British ancestors with pious respect. Their works have dignity and authority. They are not to be rummaged through for useful bits as one might sift a pile of debris.

Burke never satisfactorily explains, though, why reverence is a good of such importance. The closest he comes is the famous passage in his *Reflections on the Revolution in France* in which he describes the living, dead, and unborn as parties to a compact that forbids the living to "waste" their inheritance and obliges them to conserve it for their descendants instead.[50]

It is a striking image. But the language of contract, which Burke employs to great rhetorical effect, is incapable of explaining the value of piety except in self-interested terms—as an attitude we ought to adopt so that our successors do not treat our works with the same cavalier disregard that we treat those of our ancestors. This is a motive for piety perhaps. But it cannot explain the spirit of devotion in which the pious serve the dead regardless of the good it does them. Friendship toward the dead as much as toward the living goes beyond the self-serving limitations that the self-imposed restrictions of contractual obligation place on those who voluntarily assume them. One searches Burke's writings in vain for a better explanation than this.

Burke's attitude toward religion is similarly disappointing. For Burke, the value of religion lies in its unique power as a source of social cohesion. Religion must be shielded against the assaults of skeptics and atheists because without it we are cast adrift to trade on our own "private stock of reason," bereft of the comfort and direction that only an established religion provides.[51] This may be so—the question is debatable—but Burke's defense of religion is that it is useful, not that it is true.[52] Even among the disenchanted, there are many who concede the point. The prejudice that God is only a belief cannot be refuted on Burkean grounds. To do that, we must venture into metaphysical depths that Burke was loathe to explore.

Against the doctrine of universal equality and the associated idea of the "rights of man," Burke offers a spirited defense of rank. He hated the leveling implications of the slogan "All men are created equal" and emphasized the virtues of distinction, hierarchy, and privilege.[53] Even for those who share Burke's sentiments, though, his attack on the dogma of equality is a dubious resource.

That is because Burke blurs the distinction between what he and others call a "natural" aristocracy and an "artificial" one.[54] He identifies more closely than his American counterparts did the privileged position of the noble and well-born, with their greater virtue and wisdom. Like Burke, Thomas Jefferson and John Adams believed that a natural aristocracy of talent really exists. They agreed that those who belong to it ought to play a leading role in their new republic. But both rejected (in Jefferson's case, with spitting contempt) Burke's association of this natural aristocracy with the artificial one of wealth and social status.[55]

It is essential, they said, to create an educational and institutional milieu in which the first can be separated from the second. Anyone who today hopes to restore greater authority to the idea of human excellence in a democracy far more egalitarian than Jefferson and Adams imagined has no choice but to follow their lead. Burke's conflation of moral and intellectual rank with the superficial distinctions of money and title is a fatal confusion that makes it easy for those who are suspicious of elitism in any form to dismiss him as a reactionary crank.

Finally, Burke's celebrated paean to prudence is not very useful as a maxim of conservative thought.[56] The reason is simple. Prudence is indeed a political virtue. But this is true regardless of the program one hopes to advance. Burke's caution against undue abstraction, reckless inattention to history and facts, blind pride in ideas, and utopian disregard for the stubborn realities of human nature is good advice for all politicians, regardless of the party to which they belong.

Prudence is an empty vessel. Anything can be poured into it. Those who support the most progressive programs are well advised to act by increments. So are those who resist them. But prudence itself is of little help in isolating the prejudices with which our enlightened ideals are closely entangled or diagnosing the damage they do.

## VII

The third tradition of thought to which conservatives often look for inspiration has multiple sources and many representatives. There is no single figure who stands at its head in the way Smith and Burke do of theirs. Its defenders are united only by their shared belief that religion is true, and that its truths are an essential anchor against the dislocations of modern life. There are Jewish, Christian, and Muslim versions of this religious strain of conservatism, which neither libertarians nor traditionalists wholeheartedly endorse.

Religious conservatives insist that those who turn away from God lose something very great—contentment and joy, a unique sense of purpose and meaning, release from the terrors of death, eternal life beyond the grave. The substance of this truth is a matter of dispute. There are conflicting interpretations of it. But the conviction that there is such a truth and that nothing matters more than finding and affirming it unites this otherwise diverse group of conservative thinkers.[57]

This sets them apart from those who believe that religion is a matter of private choice, as libertarians do. Many who deny the existence of God subscribe to the latter position, which undergirds the separation of church and state. The faithful recognize the practical advantages of keeping religion out of politics and vice versa. But they deny that religion is an option, a preference, a matter of conviction alone. It is the truth about the world and humankind. Those who fail to see it are lost.

The same judgment distinguishes religious conservatives from prudential ones, for whom the principal if not exclusive good of religion is its power to sustain a spirit of social solidarity. This was Machiavelli's view, more or less, and Hobbes's too.[58] Burke shared it as well, although he was more ambivalent than either Machiavelli or Hobbes about the truth of the Christian religion.[59] None of them, though, puts religion at the center of the human condition or makes it the pivot of the soul's immortal career. For all three, the highest goods are worldly ones.

Religious conservatives acknowledge these but contemplate a higher good beyond the range of finite concerns. G. K. Chesterton, C. S. Lewis, and Jacques Maritain are examples of the type.[60] There are important differences among them. But all use the words *eternity* and *God* to describe a dimension of reality without which, they say, human life is withered and barren.

This is not a casual usage. It directly challenges the central prejudice of modern secularism—that God is a discretionary feature of human fulfillment that we are free to embrace or reject as we choose. It confronts the phenomenon of disenchantment head-on in a way that libertarians and traditionalists do not. This is the great appeal of religious conservatism for those who believe that something of inestimable value has been lost as a result of the privatization of religion without being able to agree on an alternative or perhaps even to conceive one.

The question is whether religious conservativism, as it now stands, is able to account for this loss in terms that cannot be dismissed by enlightened unbelievers as just another opinion whose expression is protected but whose truth is indemonstrable. The answer is no, so long as the account is tied to the teachings of the Abrahamic religions.

These differ in striking ways but are united by their belief in a transcendent God who brings the world into being from nothing through an act of divine creation. The Christian version of this belief played a crucial role in the development of the scientific worldview that, beginning in the thirteenth century, displaced the Aristotelian naturalism that had dominated Western physics and astrophysics since the High Middle Ages.[61]

The idea of creation was particularly influential in this process. If everything in the world is the work of an intelligent creator, then it may—indeed, must—be assumed to be intelligible, in principle at least, even if we can understand only a fraction of it and only in a hypothetical or provisional way. This assumption shattered the limits of Aristotelian cosmology and prepared the way for an aspirational rationalism of boundless reach—the foundation of modern research science.

Over time, the creator God who had inspired this development was pushed farther and farther into the background and eventually expelled from the new world picture that science had constructed on wholly naturalistic grounds. He came to be seen as an obstacle to science and was eventually dismissed as an irrational superstition. In this sense, one might say that the theology of creation was responsible for its own loss of authority in a scientific civilization whose credentials it helped to establish through a long process of intellectual and cosmological rationalization that runs, roughly speaking, from the Condemnation of Paris in 1277 to the publication of Newton's *Principia* four hundred years later.[62]

Anyone who hopes to draw on this theology, in any of its Abrahamic variants, to mount a defense against the forces of disenchantment faces an insuperable difficulty. It is not merely that the doctrine of creation must be accepted on faith. The problem lies deeper. Divine creation is inherently irrational. A creator God whose acts are in principle fully intelligible, even if we shall never understand them, is no longer free. To be intelligible, they must be guided by reason—and therefore constrained by it, though it is impossible for us to see exactly how. God's freedom requires (more precisely, it consists in) a spontaneity that defies all understanding.[63] This puts the idea of creation on a collision course with the rationalism of modern science.

There have been many attempts to reconcile the two.[64] But they cannot succeed without sacrificing one to the other, which is no reconciliation at all. Either the spirit of science, with its disenchanting commitment to the endless expansion of reason, must prevail. Or we have to accept the mystery of creation as a final, irrational limit to human inquiry, in which case the ambitions of scientific research are not merely unfulfillable—as every scientist concedes—but an expression of blasphemous pride, like the one that moved our parents in Eden to seek a knowledge above their human station.

So long as religious conservatism remains tied to the creationist theology of the Abrahamic religions, this clash cannot be avoided. Those who embrace it may find solace in its teachings. They may discover a source of cosmic and personal meaning that insulates them against the specter of pointlessness that haunts our godless world. But they cannot answer the question that the enlightened defenders of this world put to them with such serene superiority: "What reason do you have to believe in the existence of the God to whom you pray? You have the right to your opinion but no rational basis for it."

The authority of reason is the measure and meaning of disenchantment. It may be resisted from the outside in the name of a theology that denies what it accepts. But this can never be more than a holding action, and a losing one at that, so long as the dominion of reason continues to grow in a civilization founded on the belief that the truth is preeminently what science declares it to be.

For religion to be an effective force in combating the prejudice that the existence of God is just a belief, and a credible source of opposition to the disenchantment of the world, it must free itself from the Abrahamic assumptions that underlie the most familiar and widely accepted forms of religious conservatism today. It has to make its case for the eternal and divine from within the precincts of reason, not as an irrational challenger from without. Relying as it does on the creationist metaphysics to which Jews, Christians, and Muslims all subscribe, religious conservatism of the conventional kind has little to offer those who agree that we live in a spiritual desert yet dismiss the idea of creation as an irrational myth.

## VIII

The religious branch of conservative thought, like the libertarian and traditionalist strains, has impressive strengths and recalls essential truths. But like them too, it lacks the resources to explain why the prejudices of our age inflict such harm on the human soul while honoring the ideals of our egalitarian, scientific, and tolerant civilization. None of the familiar forms of conservatism, either alone or in combination with the others, offers a compelling alternative to a self-assured yet half-blind progressivism that affirms these ideals but ignores the prejudices that travel in their shadows, turning triumph to self-defeat.

We need to make a fresh start.

The essays that follow are connected by a thread of arguments that attack our prejudices at the root without denying the worthiness of the enlightened ideals that clothe them with unearned prestige. They illustrate a style of thought distinct from the older ones I have surveyed, whose arguments must be refreshed to explain the meaning of the predicament that Kafka's parable describes. My arguments belong to the same family of ideas but have a different center of gravity, from which, I hope, the perennial attraction of the conservative view of life can be felt with renewed force. They express the spirit of a true conservatism, distinct not only from the respectable if limited varieties of conservative thought we have inherited from the past but from the raucous and intemperate sorts that crowd the public stage today, whose contemptuous dismissal of liberal values is a mirror of the arrogance with which the champions of progressivism strive to impose their inhuman prejudices on us all.

CHAPTER TWO

# Bullied Pulpit

## I

The word *culture* has two very different meanings. One implies elevation, refinement, and taste: a superiority of perception, judgment, and feeling. We owe the Western version of this idea of culture to the Romans, who invented it in admiration of the Greeks and then bequeathed it to their successors, first Christian and later Enlightened. We still invoke this older idea of culture when we say, for example, that Virginia Woolf and Vladimir Nabokov were cultured human beings.

The second idea is a modern invention. It means something like "mores," "habits," or "conventions." This is the sense in which we use the word when we speak of "American culture" or describe Kim Kardashian as a "cultural icon." Refinement and elevation have little to do with culture in this sense. There are glimmerings of this modern usage in the writings of classical authors like Herodotus and Tacitus.[1] But the systematic elaboration of the idea of culture as a set of widely shared habits or norms begins only in the eighteenth and nineteenth centuries, in the sociological treatises of Montesquieu, Vico, Tocqueville, Ferguson, Herder, and others.[2]

The older Roman idea of culture has not vanished. It has not been violently suppressed. Yet it no longer possesses the authority it once did. Those who consciously defend it now sometimes do so with a blush.

The decline in the authority of culture in the Roman sense has accompanied the triumph of democratic culture in the second, modern one. Indeed, it is a part of this triumph itself—of the unstoppable spread of the democratic mores that Tocqueville made the subject of his monumental study of American life. The increasing uneasiness many feel about the Roman idea of culture reflects the awkwardness of a hierarchical ideal of human refinement in an age defined by a belief in the equality of all human beings.

What does this uneasiness imply about the proper place of institutions of high culture in a democratic civilization whose expansive egalitarianism seems, on the surface, hostile to notions of cultivation, distinction, and connoisseurship? What does it mean for our colleges, universities, museums, libraries, orchestras, theaters, and dance companies, which profess to be especially devoted to these values, and whose authority depends on their commitment to them?

No one interested in the fate of these institutions can afford to ignore this question. Nor, for that matter, can anyone interested in the promise of democratic life.

## II

When Virgil died in the port town of Brundisium in 19 BCE, he had just returned from a trip to Athens, the home of "the immortal Plato." Hermann Broch tells the story of the poet's homecoming in his novel *The Death of Virgil*.[3] Its central episode captures the Romans' abiding sense of inferiority to the Greeks in all matters pertaining to what today we call the "fine arts," including poetry and philosophy.

On his deathbed (as the novelist imagines him), Virgil has resolved to burn the manuscript of the *Aeneid*. The emperor Augustus, who has just returned from Athens too, pleads with the poet not to destroy his work. He tells him the poem is a national treasure—that it now belongs to the Roman people and is no longer his to destroy.[4]

In his memorable reply, Virgil explains that the *Aeneid* lacks the power and vitality of Homer's epics. It is only a faulty copy of a Greek original. The same is true, he says, of every Roman effort in the realms of philosophy and art. These can never be more than weak imitations of what the Greeks accomplished in a more authentic way. All the most original Roman achievements lie in the sphere of politics and administration—in their roads and laws and armies. So far as high culture is concerned, the Romans can only copy the Greeks, whose works remain the standard of excellence in painting, sculpture, architecture, poetry, philosophy, and drama. Virgil insists that his own poem is a second-rate piece of work. It deserves to be destroyed.[5]

The self-deprecatory words that Broch puts in the mouth of the greatest of all Roman poets are not as eccentric as they sound. They reflect an enduring attitude toward the Greeks, whom the Romans saw as their permanent superiors in the realms of beauty and thought.

A good example is Cicero's most ambitious work of philosophy, *De Finibus* ("On Ultimate Ends"), composed in 41 BCE, two years before his death.[6] It is written in the form of a dialogue. The participants review several different systems of philosophy, each associated with a particular school of Greek thought. There is no suggestion that the Latin-speaking participants in the dialogue have anything original to contribute. The real challenge, one of them remarks, is to find or invent Latin terms that accurately convey to a Roman audience the substance of arguments that already exist in a complete and polished form. The problem is one of translation.[7]

The principal speaker (Brutus) does not despair of the Romans' ability to do this. Their language, he says, is rich and flexible. It is well suited to the work of translation. Strikingly, he associates translation with tradition—literally, the "handing on" of something valuable, in this case an existing body of philosophical wisdom.

Every craft, Brutus says, requires its own specialized vocabulary to do this. Even "agriculture itself, a subject entirely unsusceptible of literary refinement," needs technical terms to pass along the accumulated knowledge of the past.[8] Sometimes these terms must be invented. This is especially true in philosophy, which is filled with neologisms. For Roman philosophy to proceed, it needs Latin neologisms to replace the Greek originals. This requires considerable creativity. But it is creation in the service of tradition—of faithfully preserving what the Romans inherited from their Greek predecessors in an already finished form.

The Roman contribution to philosophy is one of conservation: the construction of a linguistic home in which the treasures of the past can be safely housed and transmitted to later generations. The whole of Roman philosophy is an act of piety, not unlike that of Aeneas, who "translates" his ancestral fire from the ruins of Troy to a new Italian shore in order to save the memory of the dead who still live in its embers.[9] The most famous example is Lucretius's *De Rerum Natura*, which "saved" the philosophy of Epicurus in a poem that became a foundational text for modern thought.[10]

In certain disciplines, the Romans created novel works greater than any the Greeks left behind: law, administration, and civil and military engineering are examples.[11] In all these fields the Romans were the first in the West to do what had never been done before, or done on such a scale. But in the realm of art and philosophy, the Romans saw themselves as copyists and custodians who preserved and passed along the exemplary achievements of their Greek forebears.

"Preserved and passed along" sounds submissive and pliant. There is certainly something deferential about it. But it has an active meaning too. There is a positive side to the Roman work of conservation. Cicero understood this with particular clarity and saw how inheritance and "translation" are connected to the ideal of culture as refinement.

## III

"It seems it was Cicero," Hannah Arendt writes in a probing essay on the subject, "who first used the [Latin word *cultura*] for matters of spirit and mind. He speaks of *excolere animum*, of cultivating the mind, and of *cultura animi* in the same sense in which we speak even today of a cultured mind, only that we are no longer aware of the full metaphorical content of the usage."[12]

The word *cultura* originally referred to the cultivation of the land, the work of clearing, pruning, and tending required to turn a tract of unproductive ground into a fertile garden. It was later extended to include the establishment and maintenance of religious sites and the practices associated with them. (Our word *cults* captures this meaning.) By extending its use to include the cultivation of the mind or soul, Cicero gave the word an amplified significance that outlived the disappearance of the agricultural and religious practices in which it was literally rooted.

The goal of cultivating the land is long-lasting fertility—a well-tended plot that will sustain the bodies of those who live on it for an indefinite time. The goal of cultivating the mind is the production of steady spiritual rewards. We describe this with a term that has its origin in the physical work of agriculture and the metabolic routines it supports. We say that a cultured mind is one that possesses "good taste"— the ability to discriminate between what is fine and what is commonplace or shoddy in works of philosophy and art, together with an appetite for the first and distaste for the second.

Good taste is not something we possess by nature. It must be trimmed and trained like the plants in a garden. The process presupposes primitive pleasures and aversions that may be shaped into something more refined. In this way, it resembles the cultivation of the land, which begins with the spontaneous fertility of the earth and directs it toward human ends. Each process makes use of natural materials but arranges them into a carefully constructed order that in a revealing phrase Aristotle calls a "second" nature.[13]

This takes time. In the case of the land, it requires years of labor and great patience too, as the planter waits for the seasons to turn. Time is also needed to create a cultured mind that knows the pleasures of good taste. A young person must be shown many fine things, and with the guidance of a teacher helped to see what makes them fine: to recognize the master's touch in a well-wrought poem or painting or philosophical argument. He must be taught to tell the difference between what is fine and what is not. And he must be led, through example and encouragement, to enjoy the first with special relish, much as a child learns to take pleasure in foods with stronger flavors.

Recognition and enjoyment are not the same. But they tend to go together. An apprentice who learns to make a sturdy and attractive piece of furniture not only acquires a discriminating eye for better and worse chairs and tables. She is increasingly likely to take pleasure in the first and feel disappointment or even disgust at the second. A cultured soul (in Cicero's sense) experiences something similar. The hallmark of such experiences is a union of discrimination and pleasure. The heightening of both is what we mean by good taste.

There is a difference, though, between cultivating one's soul and tending a garden or developing an artisanal skill like furniture making. No bright line separates these activities. Nor is it wrong to say that a gardener or furniture maker can be spiritually fulfilled by his or her work. Still, there is something distinctive about the process through which one acquires the special kind of intellectual and aesthetic culture that Cicero has in mind. Or rather, there are two things. One concerns the objects toward which the process is directed. The other has to do with the quality as opposed to length of time that must be devoted to it.

Objects of literary and philosophical taste belong to a special realm of works that stand apart from the prosaic world of ordinary things. It is conventional to describe this as the realm of "fine art," though neither Cicero nor other ancient writers use the term.[14]

What counts as fine art is a subject of endless debate. Today, many believe that any ordinary object or experience can be a subject of artistic or literary attention. Marcel Duchamp's urinal is a famous example; James Joyce's *Ulysses* is another.[15] A belief in the beauty of ordinary things is one of the elementary assumptions of modern art. It is the result of a two-thousand-year process of moral and intellectual adjustment inspired in part by the Christian elevation of the individuality of every human being to a position of supreme worth.[16] Cicero would not have understood it.

Still, the idea (which Cicero takes for granted) that the cultivation of good taste is peculiarly concerned with a domain of special objects distinct from those we encounter in the ordinary course of life remains essentially valid. We do not value the works that belong to this domain because they satisfy a practical need. The pleasure they arouse is detached from what is merely useful.[17] Human beings have a longing for this pleasure because—to put it paradoxically—we need the needlessness of beauty. That a useful object (even a urinal) may be removed from its context and placed in an exhibit so that it becomes an object of aesthetic contemplation does not contradict this uniquely human longing but demonstrates its strength and universality.

A person who wants to acquire good taste, in Cicero's sense, must spend a great deal of time in the company of objects of this kind—those that are useless for every purpose but the refinement of aesthetic judgment and pleasure. The time involved therefore has a special quality too. It must, in a literal sense, be time "out"—time away from every activity concerned with doing or producing something useful. So long as one is attending to use and the satisfaction of need, the detached enjoyment that accompanies the study of beautiful things for the sake of their beauty alone can at most be an intermittent experience in an activity dominated by purposes and pleasures of a different kind.

We say that those who are momentarily free from the demands their needs impose on them are "at leisure."[18] The freedom of being at leisure is a necessary condition for the cultivation of good taste. It is not, however, a sufficient one. Leisure can be spent in other ways too—in the pursuit of entertainment, for example. There is nothing wrong with entertainment. We all like to be entertained. Moreover, the line between what is beautiful and what is entertaining is blurred and shifting. But if those who are fortunate enough to have intervals of leisure time do nothing with it but entertain themselves, they will never experience the special pleasures of a cultivated soul.[19]

This takes discipline and concentration, though not the kind involved in the effort to do or make something useful. Only a few are prepared to invest so much in an enterprise so useless. By contrast, the pleasures of entertainment come easily and are widely shared. Again, the distinction is not sharp but it is well understood. It is the difference between sitting in the stands at a football game on Saturday afternoon and in a philosophy class the day before.

The latter promises pleasure too, but of a sort that takes determination and long practice to discover. The person who succeeds is on her way to becoming a cultured person. To reach her goal, she must devote a meaningful portion of her leisure time to something other than entertainment. Nor can she reach it by herself. She needs a teacher to enforce the discipline it takes to recognize the difference between truth and banality, poetry and doggerel, beauty and kitsch, and to enjoy the disinterested pleasure in things and ideas that is the mark of a refined human being.

We call such a person a *connoisseur*.[20] The word no longer has much ethical power. We tend to associate it with snobs and condescending elitists. But it captures the meaning of Cicero's ideal of *cultura animi*. His man of good taste is a connoisseur.

This is a Roman ideal, not a Greek one. In the *Nicomachean Ethics*, Aristotle identifies two exemplary ways of living. They represent contrasting, perhaps competing, ideals of human fulfillment. One is the life of action—of political engagement.[21] The other is the life of the mind. Connoisseurship is something different from both.

The connoisseur is neither a statesman nor a philosopher. He is not engaged like the one or self-reliant like the other. The connoisseur is a private person, not a public citizen. He has little interest in legislatures and courts. He is chiefly concerned with his personal self-development. In this respect, he resembles the philosopher, but only up to a point. The latter refuses to take anything on mere authority. He insists on reasoning things out for himself. (Socrates is the most famous example.)[22] The connoisseur, by contrast, devotes himself to the study of what he has received by way of tradition and defers to it, not slavishly but respectfully, with the sense that he has a duty to conserve the best, and a love of the best, that he has inherited from the past. (John Ruskin comes to mind.)[23] The connoisseur is a conservative at heart. The Greeks were too original, too inventive, too radical, too careless, and perhaps even too self-destructive to be conservative in the sense that Cicero's ideal of connoisseurship implies.

Cicero knew the Romans could never rival the Greeks in the realm of philosophy and art. But he believed that the Greeks' achievements would cease to be known and enjoyed without a tradition devoted to the cultivation of a taste for what they had thought and made. The Roman ideal of connoisseurship was therefore parasitic on the brilliant inventions of an earlier civilization. Yet in its own way it represented an original contribution to the storehouse of Western values—one that has come down to us, battered and bruised, perhaps, but recognizable even today, whenever we use the word *culture* to describe a condition of spiritual refinement.

That good taste is a virtue; that its cultivation demands freedom from need; that it starts with tradition and cannot be acquired except though long and closely supervised study; that only a few possess it: all these Roman assumptions were still taken for granted by eighteenth-century writers on the nature of taste, including Shaftesbury, Burke, and Kant.[24] Many now think of taste in a very different way. They view it as a spontaneous and purely subjective preference that requires no training and provides no basis for criticizing anyone else's taste since each has his or her own. Even now, though, from time to time, we still hear a distant echo of the old Ciceronian ideal—in the realm of higher education, for example.

Colleges and universities that claim to be loyal to the tradition of liberal learning that Cicero helped to define still feel compelled to declare, with ritual regularity, that they aim to do more than equip their students with useful vocational skills. They insist that they exist, in part, at least, to help their students enrich their enjoyment of thought and beauty for their own sake—as pleasures detached from need.[25] Many fail in practice. But the fact that they feel bound even to announce it as an aspiration suggests how strong the connection remains between their own sense of authority and the old Roman belief that the purpose of a program of liberal education is to enhance the student's ability to take pleasure in what used to be called, with less embarrassment, "the finer things of life."[26]

Few college presidents today have the courage to put things so directly. The elitism of the Roman ideal of culture and its conservative temper put it at odds with the egalitarian ethos of our democratic civilization. The same is true of many other cultural institutions as well—of our museums, libraries, opera houses, and theater companies. They too are devoted, in part, at least, to the cultivation and enjoyment of a taste for the useless pleasures of beauty and truth. Their authority also depends on a commitment to conservation and refinement. Unless it is to be relinquished altogether, these institutions too must ask how their commitment to connoisseurship can be justified in a democratic culture—to use the word now in its modern sense—that puts innovation, equality, and material well-being ahead of other values, especially that of *cultura animi*, the elevation of the spirit.

## IV

Tocqueville begins his monumental survey of American life with a brief description of the country's geography, history, and system of government. He then proceeds to examine in marvelous detail the distinctive "habits," "opinions," and "mores" of the American people. "My principal goal," he writes, is to make "the reader feel the importance" of these habits to the "maintenance" of social and legal order in the "altogether new" kind of democracy that America represents.[27]

The mores that Tocqueville identifies include a respect for practical skill and a correlative impatience with philosophy; a love of "material enjoyments"; an insistence on one's own experience as a measure of truth, coupled with a passion for joining groups of all kinds; a contempt for aristocratic pretensions and a lack of reverence for old traditions and great works; a love of change, movement, novelty; a love of freedom and independent-mindedness—and, in profound tension with these, an embrace of equality and the comforting anonymity of "majority opinion." Tocqueville weaves all this and a great deal more into a study of American culture in which even today American readers are astonished to find a more or less accurate portrait of their national character.[28]

In broad terms, Tocqueville's idea of culture differs from Cicero's in two respects. First, it is popular by definition. The culture of a people is an ensemble of habits widely shared by the members of some group as a whole. Culture, in Cicero's sense, is always and only the possession of a few. They alone have the leisure to acquire it. From a Ciceronian point of view, it is incoherent to say, "Our culture is debased." What is refined may be denounced, neglected, or forgotten. But it cannot itself be something crude, vulgar, or ignoble. By contrast, a culture in Tocqueville's sense may be high, low, or both at once. When we use the word in this way, the phrase "popular culture" is perfectly intelligible. It is a pleonasm, not an oxymoron.

Second, the perpetuation of a people's mores does not demand the same degree of strenuous attention as the cultivation of good taste. Connoisseurship requires a purposeful devotion to the task. The culture of a people has a life of its own. One acquires it by breathing the air. The un-thinking assimilation of cultural values may, of course, be supplemented by deliberate rituals and routines. Learning to say the Pledge of Allegiance is an example. But even where cultural habits are consciously taught, the teaching must be simple enough to allow the least patient and gifted to absorb its lessons. Its goal is acculturation, not refinement.

These two differences distinguish popular cultures of all sorts, ancient as well as modern, from the elevation of the spirit that Cicero has in mind when he speaks of *cultura animi*. Still, it is possible for his ideal of connoisseurship to exist alongside the widely diffused and untaught values of many popular cultures without contradiction or even conflict. But modern democratic culture presents a special case. Between it and the Ciceronian ideal there is a unique and pointed tension.

This has several sources, of which three are worth mentioning. The first has to do with the democratic preference for change; the second, its hostility to rank; and the third, its encouragement of material values.

Democratic politics is constantly in motion. Parties, leaders, and programs succeed one another with lightning speed. The same is true of the economy, where nothing ever stands still. The realm of culture is changeable and turbulent too. One style predominates and then is quickly pushed aside by another. The result is a succession of tastes, techniques, themes, and motifs that follow one another with dizzying speed. In the rapidity with which they change and evolve, even the fine arts approach the mutability of what we loosely call "fashion."

This is not just a fact but a valued characteristic of democratic life. As much as anything, Tocqueville thought, Americans appreciate invention, initiative, and creativity, not despite but because of the unrest they produce. They have a passion for movement and change—one that contrasts in the sharpest possible way with the rigid canon of taste and fixed standards of judgment that characterized the old European world of aristocratic values.[29]

Tocqueville found much to admire in the democratic preference for change over order, for restlessness and innovation over impassivity and routine. He approved the democratic spirit of individual initiative; its greater openness to social and economic advancement; its freedom from inherited and inflexible measures of taste. He valued the American spirit of invention, unfazed by the belief that what has been done a certain way in the past must continue to be done that way forever.[30] He admired the spirit of experimentation in political, economic, and cultural life to which later

American writers like John Dewey and Louis Brandeis attach such great importance.[31]

Still, the passion for change and improvement puts democratic culture at odds with the conservative instincts of those who follow the old Roman path to the refinement of their spiritual powers. Their way starts with the study of tradition and the gradual development of a capacity to understand and enjoy it. It begins with a respect for the past and a sense of custodial responsibility toward it. There is room, of course, for creative work that imaginatively advances the tradition one has inherited, but except for the rare genius, meaningful creativity is possible only after years of disciplined work and the patient refinement of feeling.[32]

The Ciceronian ideal of connoisseurship strikes the balance between inheritance and invention in favor of the former. It recognizes the second but ties its value to the first. The democratic love of novelty reverses the order. It turns the relative value of conservation and creation upside down. It actively opposes tradition as an obstacle to cultural progress and favors avant-garde experimentation instead.

Modern democratic culture challenges the Ciceronian ideal in a second way by endowing the principle of universal human equality with irresistible moral force. Tocqueville looked with favor on the American commitment to equality. He endorsed the idea that every citizen has an equal right (and responsibility) to participate in the public life of his community. He applauded the countless ways that Americans prepare for and practice the art of self-government in the institutions that occupy the kaleidoscopic realm of civil society.[33] He had a positive view of what he calls the "mildness" of American manners; the breadth of fellow feeling for those in different economic, social, and occupational circumstances; and the relatively stronger spirit of religious toleration.[34] He admired the buoyancy, optimism, and neighborliness of the Americans he met. But he believed that the democratic passion for equality can be carried too far and that when it is, new dangers arise.

The first is that of conformism—a collective state of mind that Nietzsche colorfully described as one in which "everybody wants the same, everybody is the same" and "whoever feels different goes voluntarily into a madhouse."[35] Tocqueville feared that the "tyranny of majority opinion" would become the nursery bed for a novel species of despotism based on the acquiescence of what today we call the "masses."[36]

A second danger is the triumph of mediocrity. Tocqueville believed that, carried to an extreme, an insistence on the equality of all human beings casts a pall of moral disrepute over judgments of intellectual and aesthetic superiority. As a personal matter, he subscribed to the Ciceronian ideal of *cultura animi* and deplored the democratic tendency to reduce grades of spiritual refinement to a uniform level and to deny the intrinsic worth of greatness in learning and the arts.

Good taste is discriminatory by definition. It judges some things to be finer than others and places a higher value on the enjoyment of what is excellent and rare. Judgments of this kind pose no challenge to the democratic belief in universal equality so long as they are confined to a particular activity with internal standards of its own—playing a sport, building a house, or writing a newspaper article. These all require discrimination. Each offers an opportunity for the exercise of judgment. Some people do better than others, but the recognition that they do puts no pressure on the democratic belief that all human beings are equal by nature.

The Ciceronian ideal of refinement does. It values the superiority of some men and women not in this or that particular pursuit but in the comprehensive work of being human. It recommends the cultivation of the soul and judges those who acquire a discriminating taste for what is noble in matters of beauty and truth to be more complete human beings. This puts the ideal in direct conflict with the democratic commitment to equality.

Among other things, the latter strongly implies that no one can authoritatively claim that his or her judgment is superior to anyone else's where the fine arts are concerned. These are not technical works useful to those in specific fields with their own distinct criteria of success. They are portraits of humanity, and no assessment of them should be accorded greater respect on the grounds that the person offering it has a better understanding of the human condition than those who judge the same works from a different point of view or pay no attention to them at all. The judgment that some novels and paintings are better than others ceases to be anti-democratic only when it is viewed as a benign expression of expertise—that of a trained art historian, for example.

This view is reinforced by the belief that disagreements about the beauty and truth of different works of art are no more meaningful than disputes about the superiority of different flavors of ice cream. Who can say whether a taste for chocolate is better than one for vanilla? Conflicting judgments express divergent preferences, nothing more.[37] If the same is true of arguments about the relative worth of different works of literature, architecture, philosophy, music, and painting, then the Ciceronian ideal of connoisseurship falls to the ground. Some have always thought it should, but in a modern democratic society the ideal is especially vulnerable. That is because the love of equality converts the age-old suspicion of those who agree with Cicero into a moral complaint. It transfers the ethical advantage from the cultured few to those who challenge their claim to superiority as spiritually advanced human beings.

The third way in which democratic culture contradicts the Roman ideal of connoisseurship is a consequence of what Tocqueville calls its "materialism." "In America," he writes, "the passion for material well-being is not always exclusive, but it is general; if all do not experience it in the same manner, all do feel it. The care of satisfying the least needs of the body and of providing the smallest comforts of life preoccupies minds universally."[38]

This "care," of course, is timeless. Human beings have always been compelled to meet the needs of their bodies. In America, though, the "passion for material well-being" has been carried to an extreme and acquired a prestige unknown before. It is one thing to be interested in material goods. It is something else to put this interest ahead of every other in the order of values.

By the time Tocqueville made his visit, the richness of America's natural resources and the spirit of enterprise had already produced the rudiments of an economy that promised an unprecedented level of comfort for more human beings than ever before. America was becoming a land of plenty. When Tocqueville speaks of the American preoccupation with comfort, though, he has in mind not a fact but a value: the elevation of material concerns to a position of overriding importance.

There is an affinity between materialism in this normative sense and the democratic reverence for equality. In no respect are human beings more equal than in their need to attend to the demands of bodily life. The promotion of the latter to superiority in the hierarchy of values is a way of recognizing and honoring the universal equality of all human beings.

American materialism has an appealing side. It draws attention to the needs of those with less. It makes their deprivation more obvious and distressing. The inventive search for new ways to satisfy the needs of the body results in a growing economy that works to the benefit of all—the rising tide that proverbially lifts all boats. It gives a greater number of men and women the opportunity to raise themselves out of the poverty that has swallowed the lives of most human beings in anonymous obscurity since the beginning of time.

At the same time, though, materialism is a threat to the cultivation of the spirit as Cicero conceives it. True, the would-be connoisseur can find what she wants in the market too. There are sellers prepared to satisfy her taste for art and literature, like that for food and clothing or any other good.[39] But the principle on which the market rests is in conflict with her aims. The market is an engine for the satisfaction of need. It is only in a trivial sense, however, that an interest in beauty and truth for their own sake can be described as a need like any other, addressed to the "comforts of life." There is indeed a human appetite for beauty and truth, but to put it on a par with all our other desires masks its distinctive character and demeans its special value.

This is the way the appetite looks from the standpoint of a market economy based on the principle that the value of a thing is a function of its utility as determined by the needs of those who buy and sell it and revealed in the price on which they agree. Within the realm of exchange, no other principle makes sense. But the further its authority extends beyond this realm—the more deeply it penetrates into the mental habits that guide what people do with the things they buy and the spirit in which they use and enjoy them—the more difficult it becomes for those who value beauty and truth despite their lack of usefulness to sustain an outlook so deeply at odds with the ethic of the market.

The materialistic reduction of value to need puts the Ciceronian ideal of a life devoted to the cultivation of a refined taste for the uselessly beautiful on the defensive to a degree it has never been before. It compounds the difficulties created by the democratic love of novelty and hostility to judgments of rank in all pursuits that purport to engage the whole human being. Together, these three—passion for change, all-conquering belief in the equal worth of every human being, and preoccupation with the satisfaction of material need—have produced a civilization uniquely inhospitable to the cultivation of the soul as Cicero conceived it.

## V

This worried Tocqueville deeply. Late in his long book he writes, "It is necessary for all those who are interested in the future of democratic societies to unite, and for all in concert to make continuous efforts to spread within these societies a taste for the infinite, a sentiment of greatness, and a love of immaterial pleasures."[40] Tocqueville was an aristocrat but not a surly or mean-tempered one.[41] His own refined taste did not prevent him from appreciating many of the admirable features of American democracy to which others of his class were blind. But it sharpened his awareness of cultural loss and caused him to wonder how "a sentiment of greatness" might be preserved, in some measure at least, in a society whose habits are so hostile to it.

This led Tocqueville to emphasize the role of religion as a broad tempering force that anchors a concern with spiritual matters in the everyday lives of ordinary people.[42] It also moved him to praise the constructive contribution of philanthropic organizations devoted, in more focused ways, to the cultivation of learning and the arts.[43] Through their benign influence, Tocqueville hoped, the best features of American democracy might be preserved and its worst ones allayed.

Tocqueville's balanced judgment distinguishes his view from that of reactionaries who hate everything about modern democracy and yearn to restore the world of church and privilege. It also sets him apart from the uncritical champions of egalitarianism who look with contempt on every vestige of aristocratic feeling. There are two different ways, though, of interpreting Tocqueville's more nuanced verdict. They strike the balance between democracy and aristocracy at different points.

The first assumes that in a democratic society the "love of immaterial pleasures" is bound to vanish for all but a few. The role of cultural institutions is to preserve a privileged sanctuary of taste and refinement. They are islands of a sort—a refuge from the rising tide of egalitarian beliefs that refuse to acknowledge hierarchies of beauty and taste. Their responsibility is to save what can be saved from destruction.

The second suggests a different role for these institutions. Tocqueville only hints at it but later writers develop it more fully. Until recently, it might even have been called the "orthodox" view of the relation between the egalitarian norms of American democracy and the elevated ideals of its colleges, universities, museums, libraries, and other organs of high culture.

On this second view, these institutions are not a refuge *from* democracy but a component *of* it. They contribute to the fulfillment of the promise of democratic life. They are founded on the assumption that the relation between democracy and culture, in the Ciceronian sense, is not an external and antagonistic one—not necessarily, at least—but potentially an internal and positive relation instead.

For a very long time this second view was widely accepted by those who established and supported our great cultural institutions and by the general public that took advantage of the opportunities they offer.[44] It is presently out of favor—so much so that few of those now leading these institutions have the courage to defend it. But it is more than a historical curiosity—an outdated way of thinking that has little relevance today. It is the only view that explains why we should ever acknowledge the authority of any institution devoted to the conservation of beauty and truth, and the cultivation of a discriminating taste for them, in a democratic society based on the recognition of universal human equality.

Let us return for a moment to Cicero. Cicero believed that the pleasures of connoisseurship are only for a few. Partly this was for material reasons. Most human beings, he thought, are condemned to lives of toil that give them no leisure to attend to useless things. Partly it was for philosophical reasons. Like Plato and Aristotle, Cicero believed that the human soul contains a hierarchy of distinct powers; that the higher ought to lead the lower; that only a few are capable of such self-control; and that without it, they are destined to lead the life of an animal.[45] Most never rise above their animal passions. However leisured, they remain slaves to their appetites. They live without the *cultura animi* that is the mark of a fulfilled human being.

For those who believe in the promise of democracy, Cicero's assumptions are no longer compelling. To begin with, modern democratic societies rest on the conviction that every human being is equally competent to rule him- or herself and to participate in the processes of collective self-government. All possess the reason required to form and express their views in an intelligible manner. No one is obliged to defer to the judgments of those who by nature are superior to them—because none are. Decisions are not to be left to the rational or virtuous few.

The freedom and equality that define the spirit of democratic politics are reflected in the fluidity and openness of the economy. Individuals move up and down, free to an unprecedented degree of the constraints that once bound both the high and low to their family, class, and place of birth. The result is an economy, characterized by mobility, initiative, entrepreneurial energy, and ever-increasing abundance, that liberates a growing number of human beings from the exhausting demands of labor and allows them some meaningful measure of leisure.

This is only an ideal, of course, like that of equal participation in the affairs of government. No actual democratic society fully achieves either (or perhaps even comes close). But the shortfall can only be measured and criticized—in a fundamental sense, it only *exists*—because the ideals of political and material freedom are central to the life of every such society. They make it the society it is: democratic rather than tribal or feudal.

What, if anything, remains of Cicero's ideal of connoisseurship in a society that from his classical perspective rests on assumptions so remote from his own?

The answer is a great deal.

What Tocqueville calls "a taste for the infinite" and "love of immaterial pleasures" are not peculiar to the classical conception of human fulfillment. They are perennial features of the human condition. They remain a part of our humanity under all social conditions, including modern democratic ones. Their satisfaction is essential to a full and rewarding life, today as in the past. Democracy changes many things, including the way we see our responsibilities toward others in light of this basic fact. But it does not change the fact itself.

The "taste" and "love" of which Tocqueville speaks are the products of a power so elementary that we often overlook it. It is the root of all religion and art. The cave paintings made forty thousand years ago by unknown artists show this power at work. Its emergence out of the nearly 4-billion-year prequel of life on earth marks the debut of the human adventure.

Those who made these paintings used images to represent different objects in the world—other human beings and animals, mostly. To do this, they had to be able to see an image *as* an image, whose essential function is to depict something distinct from the image itself—something the image is *not*.[46] What could be more obvious? And yet so far as we can tell, this peculiar way of seeing is a power that resides in human eyes alone.

It might be described as a kind of detachment. The artist looks at the lines he has drawn on the wall of the cave but his vision is not confined to them. In his mind's eye he looks beyond these lines to the animal they represent. His imagination roams abroad. There are no limits to how far it can go. Without the freedom this entails there could be no art, no poetry, no philosophy. These are uniquely human creations because the power of imaginative detachment from which they and the whole world of culture springs is one that we alone possess.

The paintings tell us something else about the artist. We surmise that they were meant to serve some useful purpose—perhaps to summon or placate or thank the spirits of the animals drawn on the wall. But there is something gratuitous about them. They are more beautiful than they need to be. We cannot help but think the artist saw them in this light too. And this makes sense only if we believe that for him or her, as for us, beauty is a source of pleasure in its own right apart from any practical ends it serves.

Here, then, in the Neolithic cave paintings with which modern surveys of art history often begin, we already find two of the most striking characteristics of the human condition.[47] One is the power of detachment that liberates us from the flowing succession of images in which other living things are forever trapped, that enables us to see them from an imaginative distance and thus eventually to conceive of time itself as an object of interest and speculation. The other is the love of beauty for its own sake, independent of any use to which it may be put. So essential are these to our human being that it might be more accurate to say they are not so much *characteristics* of our humanity as *the thing itself*—the attitude or orientation that distinguishes us in the most primordial way from other animals and opens a chasm between their world(s) and ours.

From the first comes the philosophical longing to know, first about particular things and then about the world as a whole, about time and its relation to eternity.[48] From the second springs the yearning to beautify the world with artifacts and words. Together they constitute the spiritual side of human existence. Some people have greater opportunity to explore it and some, of course, do more with the chance. The Greeks and Romans were impressed by the fact that some human beings are more refined than others. But no one is shut out from the life of the spirit, for that is what makes us distinctively human and renders our lives different from those of flies and dogs.

More important, every one of us has an interest in the development of this side of our nature. It may have to be postponed until we have met our animal needs. But it is no more conceivable that, given the opportunity, a human being can be uninterested in the life of the spirit than that he or she could be human without such a life at all. The ubiquity of religion and of the longing to beautify, which survive even under conditions of extreme deprivation, testifies to the strength and universality of our interest in spiritual matters.[49]

It follows that a life in which there is no encouragement or opportunity to fulfill the need for truth and beauty is less human overall. It is impoverished too—like the lives of those consumed by bodily need. This simple observation is the inspiration for the once widely accepted view that institutions of high culture devoted to the refinement of taste are not privileged oases for a few but vital components of a civilization that seeks to realize the full promise of human equality.

The material abundance of a modern democratic society gives more of its citizens the leisure to pursue beauty and truth for their own sake as essential spiritual goods. The principle of equality guarantees that none are disqualified on account of their social position or psychological endowment. For those who see things in this light, the result is a kind of spiritual solidarity. They are struck by our shared participation in the love of what goes beyond material need; by the interest we all have in the development of our spiritual powers; and by the obligation to help others get as far as their leisure allows.

From their perspective, Cicero's aristocratic hauteur seems selfish and obtuse. How can he blithely write so many out of a share in the pursuit of a fully human existence? He takes as little notice of them as (in Broch's telling) Virgil does of the crowd that fills the "street of Misery" up which his litter is carried from the harbor to the palace where he will die.[50]

A democrat feels differently. Her attitude toward other people is characterized by sympathy and hope—not the indifference of those who look down from a position of privilege to the unimaginably distant lives of their inferiors, whose fates interest them only as an object of curious study. This is the sentimental basis of democratic egalitarianism. It is the fruit of the revolution in feeling wrought by the Christian religion, which destroyed the world of pagan values and prepared the way for our own.

The fellowship of all human beings gives the democrat a reason to care about the suffering of others and (within limits) to help relieve it. This applies most obviously and urgently to material suffering. But it has a spiritual dimension as well. Those who are well fed but incurious about the useless pleasures of beauty and truth or have had little exposure to them or whose powers of enjoyment are undeveloped or unrefined are proper objects of democratic sympathy too. They are doing less with their humanity than they might. This is not as poignant or pressing a loss as that of food or shelter, but it ought to move those with greater cultural advantages to share them with those who are culturally less well-off: a motive no more patronizing than the desire to see the homeless housed and the poor properly fed and as consistent with the sentiment of solidarity on which the spirit of democratic life depends.

Democracy means than Cicero's *cultura animi* is open to all. None are barred because they are female, dark-skinned, or poor; engaged in a menial occupation; or from an undistinguished family. Everyone is invited.

Greater leisure allows many more to accept. Some, of course, decline—
they would rather be entertained—and some of those who take up the invitation develop an especially keen taste for beauty and truth. Their
powers of observation and enjoyment become more refined. This is not a
technical achievement or form of expertise. The enrichment of these powers represents a development of the whole human being, an enhancement
of the spiritual side of human nature that is reflected in our unquenchable
curiosity about questions no expert can answer and our attraction to the
gratuitous excesses of beauty that go beyond mere function and use.

This much of Cicero's ideal of connoisseurship remains even under
democratic conditions, with the proviso that it is now open to all and accessible to many, and that those with more have a duty to help those with
less approach it as far as they can. For a very long time, this seemed an
appropriate—indeed, inspiring—way for the custodians of high culture
in America to think about their responsibilities and to take pride in the
contribution their institutions make to the enrichment of democratic life.

# VI

In a democracy like ours, institutions of high culture face in two directions. Looking outward, they say: "This is a place for the rich and poor
alike; the newly arrived and long established; for those who have been
raised in families that value the life of the spirit as well as those who have
not; for the curious and committed whatever their gender or color. Our
doors are open to all. We will do our best to see that you are able to
enjoy the treasures within." Their external posture is enthusiastically
egalitarian.

Looking in the other direction, though, their attitude is very different.
It is one of conscious discrimination among works, ideas, and experiences,
based on their power to awaken and enrich the human spirit. Facing inward, our institutions of high culture say, "When you walk through our
doors, you will find yourself in a place whose values are different from
those of the democratic society outside. Here, we do not think the worth
of a thing is its price. We reject the idea that there is no disputing about
taste. We are devoted to the recognition and celebration of excellence in
art and thought; to connoisseurship and the refinement of judgment; to
the conservation of what is beautiful and true against the tide of fashion
that sweeps in and out every day. Here, you will be invited and helped to
develop your powers of discrimination—to direct them toward finer

things. All of this is for the sake of your spiritual enrichment. This comes after material want in the order of need. But it is essential to your fulfillment as human beings. Our democratic society opens the prospect to all."

Consider the Metropolitan Museum of Art in New York City. The museum serves many different purposes. It gathers and shares information about the works in its collection. It promotes philanthropy. It trains young people who want to work in the art world as curators, administrators, and restorers. Its first responsibility, though, is to share the works it has saved and restored with the millions of visitors who come to the museum each year.[51]

Why do they come? What do they find when they do? What do they experience during their visit? There is no single answer, of course. Visitors come from all over the world for countless reasons. Still, it is possible to sketch an answer.

Those who walk through the doors of the museum and wander through its rooms find themselves in the presence of a vast number of precious objects from different times and cultures. Many are centuries old. They have been rescued from loss and defacement, in some cases against astonishing odds.

The museum is first of all a place where extraordinary works are conserved. Every visitor is bound to be impressed, to some degree at least, by the rarity and beauty of the objects in its collection and the conscious effort of collectors, donors, and curators to protect them over generations of time. For many, this is the reason they have come: to see some exceptionally beautiful things that have been rescued from loss and decay. It is why they are there rather than sitting in a café or fixing a leaky faucet at home.

The contrast with the world outside its doors could not be sharper. The Metropolitan Museum of Art sits in the heart of one of the most vibrant, restless cities in the greatest democracy on earth. Its streets have a thrilling energy. Walt Whitman made it the subject of several of his most memorable poems.[52] But the city's energy flows from a different source.

In the streets outside the museum, objects of all sorts are jumbled together, the ordinary and the exceptional. This is the everyday world we inhabit most of the time. It is a world of common things and turbulent change. Here and there one notices efforts at conservation. But conservation is no more the rule outside the museum than are works of beauty. Outside, they are exceptions. Inside, they predominate. They define the purpose for which the museum exists. It is for the sake of an encounter with beauty, saved from the whirlpool of change, that millions come to the museum each year.

What can we say about the nature of their encounter? Again, experiences differ so widely that it may seem impossible to generalize. But some common elements stand out. The first is that most visitors hope to enjoy the experience. This demands a degree of disciplined attention. In this respect, it is a little like school. But few expect their visit to be painful, like a trip to the dentist, which must be endured for the sake of some other good. Most assume that the experience of looking at the works in the museum's collections will be enjoyable for its own sake.

What kind of enjoyment is this? It is not like the pleasure of lunching at a café after a visit to the museum. That involves the consumption of things—a sandwich and a glass of wine. The pleasure and the consumption are entwined; in a sense, they are the same.

By contrast, the pleasure of looking, for example, at Jacob van Ruisdael's *Landscape with a Village in the Distance* (1646) demands an abstention from consumption. Obviously, a visitor cannot touch the painting. She must observe it from a distance. But the physical space between her and the painting is only the outward sign of an inward detachment that the painting invites and rewards. To experience its beauty, the visitor must see the painting in a particular light: as an object exempted from the world of consumable things whose value consists in their being used, and used up, like the sandwich and wine.

The beauty of the painting is completely useless. It comes to light only when the painting is released from the subjective pull of my needs and allowed to stand on its own—to be an object of aesthetic contemplation. When this happens, I am in the grip of its attractive force, not the other way around.

The viewer who values the painting because it gives her a chance to impress her companion with her knowledge of Dutch art, or offers a clue to some historical puzzle about seventeenth-century village life, or is on a list of paintings to see during her visit to New York, does not (yet) see its beauty. The fact that visitors to the museum have a mixture of motives; that they disagree about which works are beautiful; that they debate which ought to be in the collection at all: none of this alters the distinctiveness of the experience of beauty itself, which always involves the suspension of need and submission for a time, however brief, to the commanding presence of an object that has been exempted from the torrent of need so that it may be enjoyed without being used.

This experience is unusual in several respects. First, it contrasts with the perpetual search for useful things. We spend most of our time engaged in this search—even when we are at ease. It is what we are doing when we look for entertainment. The detachment that beauty demands in order to be seen at all is something different. It is not relaxation but leisure, which begins only where need, including the need to be entertained, ends.

Second, the works that serve as the occasion for this experience—the ones that we call "beautiful"—are by definition as rare as leisure itself. Beauty only exists by contrast with what is common or coarse. An ordinary object may be made beautiful. It can be converted from an article of use to one of aesthetic appreciation. Sometimes this is done simply by removing it from one context to another.[53] But when this happens, the object ceases to be ordinary. It now stands out from the banality of the background to which it belonged. The rarity of leisure and the rarity of beauty belong together. The disengagement from need that defines the first creates the space that allows the second to be seen.

Third, the enjoyment of beauty, which we experience only in moments of leisure, can be greater or less. It is not of equal intensity or durability for all. The love of beauty is a universal human disposition. It is the raw material of all aesthetic appreciation. But its refinement takes effort and time and its growth brings increasing pleasure.

That the rewards of this experience are always equal for everyone is plausible only if we think of the experience as being like those that take up nearly all our time in the busy world of need that awaits us in the streets. Here the rule is "There is no disputing about taste."[54] To apply this rule to what happens in the museum conflates preference with connoisseurship. The distinction between them is imperfect but must be preserved if the rarity of the leisurely appreciation of beauty is not to be absorbed by the commonplace ethics of consumption and the purpose of a visit to the museum lost by being assimilated to the countless other activities we pursue for the sake of need.

This sounds farfetched. Can a visit to the museum really imply all this? Surely, the experience of most visitors is not nearly so complicated. They come because the museum is famous. They want to see it for themselves. They spend an hour or two, walk through a few of the galleries, and perhaps visit one of the current exhibits. They see some objects that please them and many that leave them cold. Some leave thinking they ought to come back. For others, one visit is enough. How many recall their experience in the way I have described it, as an encounter with beauty in a place consecrated to the conservation of extraordinary works saved from the ravenous demands of consumption and need?

Perhaps only a few. But that is beside the point. This is the experience the museum promises those who walk through its doors, whatever their reasons for coming or feelings after.

It offers the experience to all on equal terms. Everyone is invited; no one is excluded; the museum belongs to the people. It is a democratic institution. Yet the experience for whose sake the museum exists is not democratic at all. It honors the value of conservation in a world of change; of the exceptional in a society hostile to rank; and of the immaterial good of beauty in a market defined by the pursuit of useful things. It exists for the nourishment of the human spirit—for the sake of *cultura animi*, the aristocratic ideal that Cicero made a standard of human fulfillment, now freed from the confines of classical prejudice and offered on equal terms to all the citizens of a great democratic civilization. The authority of the museum as a custodian of culture depends on its fidelity to this ideal under conditions that Cicero never imagined and would not have approved.

## VII

The Metropolitan Museum of Art is not alone in this respect. The same can be said of many other institutions that are devoted to the collection, display, and enjoyment of art, including the performing arts. They too serve a number of different purposes but have an important one in common. They offer those who come to see an exhibit, hear a concert, or watch a play the chance to experience the pleasure of beauty in an environment shielded from the distractions of need and to discover that the pleasure can be enhanced by looking or listening more closely, with the eyes or ears of a connoisseur.

The category is large and diverse. It includes established institutions like the Met and more experimental ones like the La Mama Theatre in Greenwich Village. A coffeehouse that has amateur poetry readings every Friday is a place of culture too. So is the New York Public Library. Its main reading room on Fifth Avenue is a contemplative space dedicated, in part at least, to the cultivation of the spirit. These are all institutions of high culture in the older sense of the word. Some that are cultural in the newer sense straddle the line. A jazz club or blues bar may be a haven for connoisseurs even if many are there to be entertained—and of course the line between connoisseurship and entertainment, here or anywhere else, is never a sharp one.

Among our institutions of high culture, colleges and universities occupy a special place. They inspire and train the leaders of many others. They promote a spirit of philanthropy in the arts. Historically, they have sought to nurture in their students an appetite for culture that will last for the rest of their lives.[55]

Today, of course, much of the work of our colleges and universities has little to do with the cultivation of a taste for beauty and truth. They are places of vocational training, dedicated to preparing their students for useful careers. They are also in large part devoted to the production of new knowledge in the many different specialties into which a modern campus is divided.

Still, where the tradition of liberal education survives, if only in an abbreviated form, the refinement of the human spirit remains a goal of higher learning. Those who feel even a lingering loyalty to this tradition insist that a college or university is more than a place to equip oneself for a job or to pursue productive research. It is also a school in the original sense of the word: a place of leisure exempt from the demands of life, where students and faculty can practice together the arts of looking, listening, and reading for their own sake—for the pleasure of advancement in the recognition and enjoyment of what is beautiful and true, regardless of practical interest or immediate need. In this sense, a four-year liberal education has the same goal as an hour at the Met, though many fewer have the resources or inclination to pursue it.

For a long time, our liberal arts colleges and universities lived comfortably with their divided responsibilities as the custodians of high culture in a democracy inspired by a belief in human equality. Beginning in the second half of the twentieth century, they worked with increasing determination to assess their applicants in a more equitable way on the basis of individual merit. They used standardized tests, scholarships, and affirmative action to achieve this goal.[56] Looking outward, they acted on the egalitarian impulse to open their doors more widely to qualified students, regardless of race, religion, or social class. That they did so imperfectly and sometimes hypocritically confirms rather than indicts their commitment to the ideal.

Looking inward, they continued to view themselves, as they had from the beginning, as the caretakers of works and traditions devoted to the uplift of the human soul. They offered courses in art, philosophy, history, literature, music, and mathematics that convey useful information about the world but in addition ennoble the hearts and minds of students by deepening their appreciation and strengthening their enjoyment of the finest achievements of the human spirit in all these different fields. They saw themselves as the curators of an ideal of spiritual cultivation that is discriminatory by nature—one that responds to a universal and uniquely human need but whose refinement only a few have the time, money, and desire to pursue for four years in an organized program of study.

The democratic temper of the first, outward-facing attitude and the aristocratic tenor of the second, inward-facing one were not thought to be in contradiction. Quite the opposite: for the colleges and universities that took this view of their responsibilities, the second looked more like a component of the first than a challenge to it. It seemed to be a part of the promise of democratic life rather than an assault upon it.

The same could be said of the other institutions of high culture whose leaders were inspired and trained in college and graduate programs. This double-sided way of seeing things did more than give them a convenient excuse to indulge their spiritual elitism in a society devoted to the ideal of human equality—as a cynic might suggest. It justified their work as a vital part of the egalitarian revolution that Tocqueville describes, which for the first time in human history gave all a chance to share in the privileged pleasures of *cultura animi*.

Today, many institutions of high culture have lost the confidence to maintain the balance this double perspective requires. Pressured to conform to the egalitarian norms of society at large, they have redefined their inner purpose, and reformed their inner practice, in ways that bring them into closer alignment with the axiom of universal equality but impede the unembarrassed acknowledgment of connoisseurship and spiritual refinement as valued goals. The result has been a massive and sometimes shamefaced retreat from their earlier open recognition of a responsibility to guard these values, not against our democratic world but for it.

The authority of our institutions of high culture depends on their willingness to affirm this responsibility—to embrace their duty to conserve an older ideal of culture in a modern democratic civilization whose mores are in many ways hostile to it, so that the spiritual joys of *cultura animi* may be made available to a larger number on fairer terms. When those who lead these institutions lose the confidence to say this for fear of appearing elitist; adjust their internal norms along more egalitarian lines; and redefine their primary goal to be the advancement of social justice in the world at large, the authority of these institutions begins to slip away. Their power remains. They still raise money, wield influence, and determine careers. But their legitimacy becomes harder to define and defend.

The resulting loss of authority is a consequence of the *politicization* of high culture. The process has proceeded furthest in the realm of higher education. It began there and from there has spread to other institutions.

Today, the drive for ever-greater equality in the hiring of faculty, design of curricula, and distribution of academic prestige goes under the name of "Diversity, Equity, and Inclusion." This has become a baggy slogan but its meaning is clear. Older judgments of intellectual and aesthetic quality; distinctions of rank in scholarly achievement as measured by objective norms of accuracy, truth, elegance, and imaginative subtlety; traditional Western-oriented courses and programs; the behavior of teachers and the needs of students: all of these are now to be reviewed and revised from the standpoint of the value of equality, imported from the democratic world outside our colleges and universities to their internal and once-autonomous operations.[57] Along the way, our institutions of higher education have arguably become more egalitarian—though the point is debatable. But the distinctive contribution they make to our democracy as the guardians of an ancient and still vital ideal of human fulfillment has been obscured and devalued.

Something similar is happening in our museums, libraries, opera houses, and theater companies. They are being aggressively politicized too.

For the egalitarian bent on putting these institutions to use in the service of a political ideal, they can only seem to be the smug protectors of an anti-democratic prejudice whose preoccupation with the "exceptional" and "refined" ignores the needs and interests of ordinary people and blithely discounts the suffering and abuse of power on which the very existence of any putative realm of "high" culture depends. It is not enough, the egalitarian says, to make the experience of a visit to the museum more accessible: to advertise the opportunity; subsidize the cost of entry; hire special guides for those whose knowledge and sensibilities have been stunted by poverty and ignorance. These are important first steps, but they fail to address the root problem of elitism itself.

However many pass through the turnstile, if the message they encounter when they enter a museum or music hall is, "Here what matters is the conservation of outstanding works and the refinement of the capacity to enjoy them," the internal culture of the place remains, in the eyes of the reformer, a standing insult to the democratic idea of equality. Further steps must be taken to ensure that those who enter its "privileged" space are not offended by the thought that some works are greater than others and some human beings more refined. Things must be arranged so that those who walk through their doors have a cultural experience on the inside that confirms their democratic belief on the outside that all human beings are worthy of equal respect—a political commitment of historic importance but one whose watchword is parity, not splendor and distinction.

This sentiment was expressed with shocking clarity a few years ago by the president of the Ford Foundation. He described America's art museums as "guardians of a fading social and demographic order" and called on them to "resist reinforcing biases, hierarchies and inequalities" by (among other things) staging exhibits that depict "people whom the system excludes and exploits."[58] An art critic for the *New York Times* echoed the thought in an over-the-top review of a show at the Met entitled *The African Origin of Civilization*. He criticized the museum as "profoundly conservative," urged it to "politicize the art historical narrative," and called on it to free itself from "antiquated, racist Western distinctions" in deciding what to collect, what to display, and what to say about the works in its galleries.[59]

The Pierpont Morgan Library has promised to "strive to amplify at every opportunity the voices of women, artists of color, and people from other underrepresented groups"; to "diversify acquisitions with regard to race, gender identity and expression, and sexual orientation"; and to "alert users to offensive material by acknowledging and identifying instances of racism, sexism, ableism and other forms of discrimination and biases."[60] The president of the Art Institute of Chicago describes museums as "contested sites." "We are not neutral," he says. "This is a time for self-reflection, a time for us to thoughtfully understand the best ways to advance racial justice. . . . As we reflect on our past, we are accountable for our museum's legacy of white privilege and exclusion, not only in the representation of artists of color in our collection but also of those in our community who have historically felt unwelcome in our spaces."[61]

In 2020, the chief classical music critic for the *New York Times* urged the abandonment of the practice of auditioning orchestral musicians behind a screen. Their identities should be visible so that weight can be given to race in hiring candidates. "Hanging on to a system that has impeded diversity is particularly conspicuous at a moment when the country has been galvanized by revulsion to police brutality against Black Americans." "If the musicians onstage are going to better reflect the diversity of the communities they serve, the audition process has to be altered to take into fuller account artists' backgrounds and experiences. Removing the screen is a crucial step." The critic compared the abandonment of blind auditions to affirmative action in higher education. "It's like an elite college facing a sea of applicants with straight A's and perfect test scores," he said. "Such a school can move past those marks, embrace diversity as a social virtue and assemble a freshman class that advances other values along with academic achievement."[62]

My examples are selective but representative. They reflect a widely shared and influential view of what our universities, museums, libraries, symphonies, and theaters ought to do with the resources they command. The number of those who share this view is growing. They are disproportionately represented among those who lead these institutions and sit on their boards of directors. They seek to draft the institutions they govern into a political program whose goal is to puncture the aristocratic pretensions of art and learning by demonstrating that every appeal to excellence is a feint meant to distract us from the racism, sexism, colonialism, patriarchy, and heteronormativity that lie behind it. They believe their main responsibility is to draw our attention to these injustices, over and over again, until *we* see that *our* main responsibility is to get to work curing them rather than sitting on our self-satisfied bottoms, pretending to be connoisseurs of beauty when the rest of the world is drowning in inequality.

Shame on our colleges and universities, they say, on our museums and orchestras and theater companies, for having been for so long the defenders of an elitist ideal of cultured refinement! The only way for them to make amends is to renounce their elitism for the sake of social justice. Penance is long overdue, and reparative steps toward greater equality urgently needed. This is the message one hears, monotonously repeated with sanctimonious assurance, in all our institutions of high culture today. "The past is nothing but a record of injustice and works of proclaimed beauty only propaganda for the prejudices of a privileged few. The enjoyment of beauty and truth for their own sake is a reactionary conceit." Those to whom the message is addressed—students in the classroom, visitors to the museum, listeners in the symphony hall—are urged to be good democrats and to subordinate the self-indulgent pleasures of connoisseurship to the demands of the oppressed.

No doubt those who teach this didactic and censorious lesson feel more in tune with the values of the egalitarian society to which they belong. These values are inspiring. In law and politics, they rank highest of all. But when the leaders of our cultural institutions rush to legitimate their role in the moral vocabulary of an ever-more aggressive and less conditional ideal of equality, they discredit themselves. They make it impossible to explain how institutions like those on whose behalf they speak can be both democratic and elitist at once, and throw away the only lasting source of authority available to them as the protectors of an ideal of spiritual refinement in an age of human equality.

With this, the tense but productive balance on which the authority of these institutions depends, poised between equality and excellence, is lost. It is replaced by a single, more uniform, righteous, and democratically correct but less ennobling commitment to equality and nothing else. This is a loss for them. It puts their legitimacy in doubt. More important, it is a loss for democracy itself, the grandeur of whose promise is measured by the breadth of the conception of human fulfillment it offers to all.

# VIII

"In the United States," Tocqueville observes, "when the seventh day of each week arrives, the commercial and industrial life of the nation seems suspended; all noise ceases. A deep repose, or rather a sort of solemn meditation, follows; the soul finally comes back into possession of itself and contemplates itself. During this day, places of commerce are deserted; each citizen, surrounded by his children, goes to a church; there strange discourses are held for him that hardly seem made for his ears."[63]

Tocqueville approved the American attachment to religion precisely because it is so out of step with the country's materialism and restless, selfish bustle. In church, he writes, "each citizen" hears from the pulpit "each week" a lesson meant to draw his attention from material things to spiritual ones; from the transient to the everlasting; from the equality of human beings to their smallness in relation to the greatness of God. In this way, the deepest tendencies of democratic life are resisted, or at least suspended, and their worst effects tempered in a small but regular way.

Tocqueville was not blindly hopeful in this regard. He saw that the tendency to recast all values in utilitarian terms and to reduce all interests to needs is as strong in church as outside it. Americans tend, he says, to think of God and eternal life as they do other business prospects—as an advantage to be gained through hard work and self-sacrifice, pursued in the spirit of what he calls "self-interest rightly understood."[64] This is antithetical, in Tocqueville's view, to the true spirit of religion, which rises above the self into regions of timeless grandeur. But he was cautiously optimistic that, on balance, the spirit of religion would continue to have a modest leavening effect on the self-centered materialism of American life.

What Tocqueville did not fully anticipate, despite his nearly superhuman foresight, was the long, slow, now seemingly irreversible decline of religion in America. Punctuated at intervals by evangelical revivals of one kind or another, religion has for some time been losing ground, as measured by church attendance and the way individuals describe their religious beliefs.[65] But he also did not guess that through private philanthropy and state support, a vast web of institutions would grow up devoted to the cultivation of the spirit by means of what we call "the arts and letters"—to the nourishment of an interest in the "great," the "infinite," and the "sublime," like that once provided by our churches.

The American landscape is dotted with colleges and universities. Our cities and towns are filled with museums of art, theater companies, and music halls founded by philanthropists for the benefit of the people at large.[66] These institutions exist to elevate the hearts and minds of those who make use of their resources—to lift them up into regions where the distinction between the great and the ordinary, the lasting and the perishable, the beautiful and the useful is preserved and honored. In this respect, they serve as a replacement of sorts for the churches whose pews have been emptying for years. They do not teach an orthodoxy or offer rituals of sanctification. But they do provide a sanctuary from the leveling materialism of democratic life, as our churches once did, and play a countercultural role similar to the one Tocqueville approved in the case of religion.

There may be fewer Americans in church on Sunday morning. But the lines outside the Metropolitan Museum of Art are long. Those who come are hoping for an experience analogous to that of churchgoers listening to a sermon from the pulpit. They have taken time out of their distracted, restless lives, swept along by the current of fashion and need, for the sake of a moment of contemplative repose in which they can glimpse a higher and more lasting order of values.

They are there to see beautiful works saved from the debris of time and to be reminded, by their greatness and uselessness, of values that can never be captured in egalitarian or utilitarian terms. This is the lesson they hope to hear from the pulpit of the Metropolitan Museum of Art and all the other institutions of high culture that exist for the sake of reminding those who pay them a visit of eternal truths without which there can be no progress in the work of being human, no perfection of the human soul: a perfection we are now all free to seek, thanks to the democratic revolutions of the last three centuries.

But when what they hear instead is that greatness is a fabrication of political power; that beauty is a trick to distract us from oppression; that the past is only a repository of crime and subjugation; that there are no privileged points of view from which one work, idea, or performance can be judged objectively superior to another; that all are equal in this regard; that high culture is in the eye of the beholder; that there is no disputing about taste; that no spiritual achievement ever escapes the gravitational field of its material circumstances; that every style is replaced in a twinkling by another with the same claim to our respect: when the museumgoer and theater viewer and college student hear *this* message preached, over and over again, from the pulpit of all the institutions of high culture that are the secular successors to the churches whose work Tocqueville thought essential to maintaining the right balance between the good and bad of democracy, then they are deprived of the very thing they came to enjoy.

This is a misfortune for them. It is a misfortune for their democracy, whose promise of human fulfillment is whittled down to something less inspiring and complete. And it is a misfortune for these institutions themselves, whose authority vanishes when they cannot in good conscience explain their own commitment to excellence and refinement in a democratic culture—even if, for a time at least, their power survives. Bullied by an aggressive and unsubtle egalitarianism, those who today preach from these secular pulpits have forsaken their responsibilities and done massive damage to themselves, to the men and women who rely on them, and to their country.

CHAPTER THREE

# The Sovereignty of Excellence

## I

Which is more important, freedom or equality? On one side are libertarians who put freedom first. They oppose the forcible redistribution of wealth and related programs like affirmative action.[1] On the other are egalitarians who tolerate or endorse restrictions on individual freedom for the sake of greater equality.[2] There are degrees of enthusiasm on both sides, and each draws on the other. The libertarian favors an equal freedom for all; the egalitarian puts freedom at the head of the list of goods that a fair society distributes equally. Still, the distinction is clear enough. It is one of the main fault lines in American politics. Red states favor liberty, blue states equality. The tension between them is perennial. Tocqueville diagnosed it two centuries ago.[3]

But is either freedom or equality the highest good in the realm of values? One may rank the first above the second or vice versa. There are countless ways to balance and combine them. But is there some other value that is superior to both? The answer is yes. Excellence is sovereign among values. It is distinct from freedom and equality—even, in certain respects, opposed to them. Yet excellence alone explains why we care about these other goods and pursue them with such passion.

*Excellence* is the central term in a complex of ideas that lie at the heart of the classical view of human nature and political life. *Fulfillment* and *perfection* belong to this complex too. Freedom and equality each has a place in this tradition but only a subordinate one. They are good because they make excellence possible and only insofar as they do.

That freedom and equality are supreme goods and excellence a derivative one is a characteristically modern belief—one that turns the classical ideal on its head. It is reflected in Kant's famous statement that every excellence of character (amiability, courage, prudence, and the like) is good or bad depending on what one chooses to do with it: good only if it is accompanied by a "good will" whose value is not derivative but self-contained, like a "jewel shining in the night."[4]

The difference between these two traditions of thought reflects a disagreement about what I shall call the explanatory order of values. That one thing is good is often explained by the fact that something else is good in a different and superior way. This is generally true, for example, of means and ends. Exercise and diet are good as means to health. Health is good in itself. It is that for the sake of which we go to the gym and avoid dessert. It is a good of a higher order than the good of the means by which we secure it. The same is true of parts and wholes. A sauce is good because of the way it complements the other ingredients in the dish. On its own, it would be less good or perhaps not good at all. Being good as a part and good as a whole are not the same thing. The second explains the first. It occupies a higher position in the explanatory order of values.

This is not the only way in which goods can be ranked. There is often a temporal priority among them as well, one that is frequently the reverse of their explanatory order. Suppose I enjoy reading on my porch. Reading is, for me, an intrinsically worthwhile activity. But I have no chair on which to sit and read. Buying or building one comes first in the order of time, though last in the order of explanation—first, a trip to the store or the labor of construction so that I can then read in comfort on my porch.

If I am dying of thirst, a drink of water comes before everything else. It is first in the order of time. But the value of the drink is explained by something more important. I drink water in order to live, not the other way around. Philosophers in the classical tradition believed that the search for explanations can be carried even further. If drinking is for the sake of life, they said, life is for the sake of living well.

Freedom and equality often come first in the order of time, before the pursuit of excellence. They have an immediate claim on our attention. Yet however urgent their temporal priority, freedom and equality are always subordinate to excellence in the explanatory order of values. This is the classical view, which I endorse with certain modifications. The modern view reverses the relation. It encourages us to view freedom and equality as values of the highest order in all respects, including the explanatory. This promotes a kind of fetishism. It discourages us from asking *why* they are good at all. If we did, we would discover that the best answer is that we value freedom and equality for the sake of something higher, which is neither free nor equal but compulsory and discriminating in ways I shall explain later on.

## II

Equality is a principle of distribution. It asserts that the members of some group ought to receive the same share of some resource, privilege, or opportunity. This is an abstract formulation. It leaves many blanks to be filled in. Which group, exactly, and what resource or opportunity?

Most of the practical and philosophical controversies that surround the principle of equality concern questions of this kind. Does it violate the principle of equality if black and white children are required to attend separate but equally well-equipped schools? If citizens have an unrestricted right to enter and leave their country but foreigners do not? If some make $1 million a year and others less than $30,000? I assume the answer to the first question is yes, the second one no, and that we have divided views about the third. I pass all such questions by. Mine is a different one. Whatever the group and regardless of the nature of the good (education, mobility, or money), is there any reason to think that equality has an intrinsic value of its own? Harry Frankfurt explored this question thirty-five years ago in an article entitled "Equality as a Moral Ideal."[5]

Frankfurt was concerned with the distribution of material goods—food, clothes, medicine, housing, and the like. More specifically, he was concerned with the distribution of money. Money is a multipurpose good that allows one to purchase these other ones. There are some things money cannot or perhaps should not be allowed to buy (the right to vote, for example). But in thinking about the good of equality, money is a reasonable place to begin. Is there a morally compelling case, Frankfurt asks, for distributing money equally—for ensuring that everyone gets the same amount as everyone else? His answer is no.

Frankfurt starts by observing that money is not good in itself. It is "for" something else. Money is good because it allows us to satisfy our needs. This is an intrinsic good. The satisfaction of a need is "for" something else only when it is a step toward the satisfaction of some other, higher need.

People disagree about the exact hierarchy of needs. There is broad agreement, however, that some are universal and pressing. We all need a certain caloric intake to survive and function effectively. If money is so unequally distributed that some people do not have enough to eat and meet their other basic needs, they have a moral claim on those with more than enough to a share of their greater wealth.

This amounts to a (limited) demand for equal treatment. To satisfy the demand, some redistribution of wealth is almost surely required—more or less depending on how we define the category of basic needs and the community of those with a duty to share. (Does it include all human beings or only all Americans?)

Still, whatever the degree of equality sought, Frankfurt says, its moral value depends on that of satisfying the needs that are considered "basic." If no one should have less than anyone else so far as the satisfaction of these needs is concerned, that is because everyone ought to have enough to satisfy them. The moral goodness of having an equal amount of money, or of the things that money can buy, is parasitic on the moral goodness of having enough.[6]

Only when equality in the distribution of money is declared to be good for its own sake are we tempted to think that everyone ought to have the same amount of it. This may seem extravagant, but more than a few philosophers have defended some version of the idea.[7] Frankfurt's point is that this view becomes plausible only when we lose sight of the explanatory dependence of equality as a moral good on the higher-order good of having enough.

One might object, of course, that it is impossible to distinguish basic needs from other, optional ones in a way that will command widespread agreement. One person's necessity is another's luxury. But this sidesteps Frankfurt's argument. Even if a perfectly equal distribution of money were practically feasible (which seems incredible), a boundless equality of this kind would still not be good for its own sake. It would be good because of what it enables those with an equal share of money to do. Having the same amount of money as everyone else is never good in itself.

Frankfurt's view bears some resemblance to a principle of distributive fairness that Amartya Sen and Martha Nussbaum have developed in recent years. They call it the "capabilities" approach.[8] Their basic idea is that a flourishing human life requires the secure possession of various freedoms and resources without which the power to exercise our capacities for association, expression, and self-development will be blocked or stunted.

Nussbaum has attempted to describe these capacities with some precision.[9] She emphasizes the redistributive implications of her approach, which, she claims, if taken seriously, would require a dramatic reallocation of wealth on a global scale.[10] In her view, the capabilities approach has strongly egalitarian implications. The justification for it, though, depends on the intrinsic value of satisfying our most important human needs, including the political and spiritual needs for self-expression as well as the animal need for bodily health. In this respect, her view, like Frankfurt's, explains the value of having an equal share of various goods in terms of the higher value of having enough.

But the comparison is not exact. There is an important difference between these two accounts—one that puts Frankfurt's conclusion in doubt.

Nussbaum's capabilities approach applies not only to economic resources but to rights as well—including the right to vote, speak, move, and marry. It may be extravagant to think that morality requires that everyone have exactly the same amount of money. So long as we all have enough, there is no moral harm if some have more than others. But the only morally acceptable distribution of rights, it seems, is one of strict equality. Here, surely, equality is good in itself.

The right to vote, to own property, to be protected in one's person is not a good, like money, whose magnitude can vary from one person to the next. One either has the right or doesn't. We often debate whether to extend a particular right to a given class of persons. Should female minors have the right to an abortion without parental notification? Some may think the answer is no, but if it is yes, then every woman in the group possesses the right to the same degree. Where rights are concerned, the idea of "degree" makes little sense.

One might, of course, attempt to extend Frankfurt's argument to rights as well. Rights, like money, are good because they are good for something. The right to vote, for example, gives one a say in collective decisions. It confers a power that those without the right (minors and citizens of other countries) do not possess. The right to own property empowers property owners to use and dispose of their assets with the active support of the state. The right to control one's body does the same in the most intimate realm of life.

In each case, the assignment of a right increases a person's power in the same way that putting money in her pocket does. It enables one to do more things in more ways.[11] The good of a power is transitive. It is explained by the good of the outcomes it "empowers" one to achieve. This is easy to see in the case of money. If we view the good of having a right as a form of empowerment too, the same argument appears to apply. The moral case for conferring a right equally on the members of a particular group seems ultimately to depend on the good of what they can do with it when they put the right to use.

This misses something important, though. Rights are valuable not just as instruments of power—as means to the achievement of a goal. The conferral of a right is also an acknowledgment of the worthiness of the person who receives it. It is a public recognition of the status of its recipient as one deserving of respect—the same respect accorded to everyone else with the right in question. If someone has a moral claim to such respect, the bestowal of a right that confirms it is good in itself, independent of the good of whatever goal the right empowers its possessor to pursue.

The same can be said about the distribution of money. The good of money is dependent on that of the things it allows one to buy. But if we are morally entitled to have enough money to meet our basic needs, that is because our status as human beings with needs of this kind is one that is deserving of equal respect.

In the case of money, the argument for the intrinsic good of equality may not extend beyond the amount required to assure a certain threshold of well-being. It does not justify a perfect equality in the distribution of wealth—unlike the distribution of rights. Still, Frankfurt's contention that where money is concerned the morally relevant consideration is having enough, implicitly rests on the assumption that we are all equally entitled to some specified level of support because of the respect we are due as human beings.

If this is true, then making sure that we have enough money to satisfy our basic needs has value in its own right, in the same way that granting everyone over a certain age the right to vote does. It is not wholly dependent, as Frankfurt says, on the good of what one does with the money one has.

Still, even on this revised account, equality (of money or rights) is good only because something else is. The good of equality is explained by our regard for the worth of every human being as a free and responsible agent. Our agency gives us the moral standing to demand that we be treated as equals. The first justifies the second, not the other way around. Freedom stands higher than equality in the explanatory order of values.

But is freedom the highest value of all? Or is its value in turn explained by a still higher one? If we pursue this question even a short way, we find ourselves entangled in a metaphysical thicket that many might wish to avoid. But there is no way around it. We are in the position of the man who, having jumped into a bramble bush and scratched his eyes out, has no choice but to jump in a second time and scratch them in again.[12]

## III

Kant is the most formidable philosopher of freedom. He defined it as "autonomy" and gave the concept the prestige it now enjoys. In the moral realm, Kant says, autonomy occupies the highest position in the explanatory order of values. It is the supreme good for whose sake we pursue all others.[13]

All living things seek nourishment on their own. They incline in this direction without having to be forced to do so. This is a kind of self-direction—Aristotle was greatly impressed by it—but it is not the special sort that Kant has in mind when he speaks of freedom or autonomy.[14] This rests on a power of reflection that among all the animals on earth, human beings alone possess.

Kant defines this power in a cryptic passage in *The Groundwork of the Metaphysics of Morals*. "Everything in nature," he writes, "works according to laws. Only a rational being has the power to act according to his conception of laws, i.e., according to principles, and thereby has a will. Since the derivation of actions from laws requires reason, the will is nothing but practical reason."[15] These few words contain a great deal.

We may start with the simple observation that a law of any kind is a rule. It is a generalization or abstraction. It therefore has a different kind of reality from that of the items the law covers or describes. It follows that only a being with the power of abstraction can form an idea or "conception" of a law, as distinct from merely conforming to one. Squirrels behave in a regular way. Their behavior exhibits identifiable patterns. But squirrels cannot account for their actions in the way a biologist does when she abstracts these patterns from what she observes and uses them to explain and predict the behavior she sees.

The power she employs in doing this is at once familiar and mysterious. To begin with, it is the unnoticed ground of all human science. Other animals acquire habits, some quite complex, and we of course do the same. Their lives and ours display a great deal of regularity. But only we are able to explain what they and we are doing when we act in a regular way. Only we ask "Why?" and attempt to answer the question by identifying the laws that account for what we apprehend with our senses. We could not even start unless we already possessed the power of abstracting laws from the welter of experience.

The same power has what Kant calls a "practical" employment. Because we are able to "conceive" laws, we are in a position to ask which of them we ought to follow and why. Other animals cannot do this. They are therefore not accountable for their actions in the same way we are. We may praise or blame a dog if it is well or poorly behaved, but the vocabulary of moral judgment ("deceitful," "prudent," "disgraceful," "public-spirited," and the like) has no application to what the dog does or fails to do. Moral responsibility assumes a capacity to assess one's actions from the vantage point of a rule that is detached from the actions themselves in the same way the laws that govern the behavior of squirrels are detached in the biologist's mind from the things squirrels actually do.[16]

Our scientific explanations are often wrong and always incomplete. Our moral failings are even more glaring. But this only highlights the aspirations that define these two branches of human experience, whose very existence depends on the power of abstraction that enables us to think and act in accordance with a "conception of laws" in the first place.

This power may be defined in still more elementary terms as that of time-consciousness. Kant attempts to demonstrate this in a section of *Critique of Pure Reason* entitled "On the Schematism of the Pure Concepts of the Understanding."[17] His argument is notoriously difficult, but its main point is easily stated.

Like everything else, we exist in time. Yet we alone know that we do. We are not merely time-bound but conscious of time too. Time is for us an object of reflection. We are *in* it but not wholly *of* it.

Our unique if limited detachment from time defines the human scene—the world of mortal beings who possess what Pope calls "the useless knowledge of their end."[18] It is the ground (source, cause, explanation) of the power of abstraction that both science and morality presuppose. We are able to form the concept of a rule that connects the different moments of our experience in scientific terms ("What happened yesterday is the cause of what is happening now") or in moral ones ("To-morrow I will keep the promise I made today") only because we have the ability to step aside from our experience as it unfolds in time and to "see" it from a stable point of view that is independent of the endless, restless flow of transient happenings.

John Rawls makes the same point in a more intuitive way in *A Theory of Justice*. To ensure that all "persons" deliberating about the best structure of society are treated with equal respect, he imagines them positioned behind what he calls a "veil of ignorance."[19] And who or what is a person—the kind of being the veil is meant to respect? One who is capable, Rawls says, of forming a "rational plan of life."[20] To have such a plan one must be able to conceive the time from birth to death (or any lesser portion of it) as a single unit. This is possible only if one is sufficiently detached from the "time of one's life" to take it as an object of deliberation. All and only human beings possess this power of planning. That is why there are no nonhuman beings in Rawls's "original position." In whatever other ways his moral and political philosophy may or may not resemble Kant's, Rawls and Kant agree that what makes one a person with the special dignity that free and rational beings alone have the right to expect is the ordinary yet astounding power to conceive of time as a series of passing events.[21]

Kant was, of course, not the first to notice this power. It is hardly a modern discovery. Plato and Aristotle were fully aware of it too, and their philosophies, like Kant's, are built upon it. One might even describe each of the three as an elaboration of the nature and implications of the power in question.

In his Parable of the Cave, Plato assumes that the prisoners chained to their bench in a cavern beneath the earth possess the power to predict the order in which the shadows before them appear.[22] They could not do this if they were not already sufficiently detached from the passage of time to watch it from a distance. Their liberation from time is the springboard from which a few of them are able to achieve the greater liberation that leads to a knowledge of the Form of the Good and the culminating rapture of philosophical ecstasy.[23]

In Aristotle's case, our ability to grasp the changeless forms that shape and guide the careers of natural things rests on the same power to observe movement and change from a perspective not imprisoned by it.[24] This presupposes a freedom from time that is at once the source and motive of the desire to know whether there is anything that is exempt from time altogether—a longing fulfilled by the knowledge of what Aristotle calls "the unmoved mover," his counterpart to Plato's Form of the Good.[25]

Like Kant and Rawls, these ancient writers recognized the phenomenon of human transcendence. They appreciated the significance of the detachment from time that allows us to think and plan in ways other animals cannot. Who could fail to note it? There is a fundamental distinction, though, between the ancient and modern views of human transcendence—one that has vast implications for our understanding of the explanatory order of values and the character of the highest good within it.

## IV

The fact of transcendence is a manifest feature of the human condition. Yet interpretations of it differ. Broadly speaking, two have played a defining role in the history of Western philosophy. The first may be called "rationalist." It associates transcendence with the experience of thinking and identifies it with the faculty of reason. This is how Plato and Aristotle saw it. The second is "voluntarist." It identifies transcendence with the act of choosing and the faculty of will. Augustine is the first and most important defender of this view in the Western tradition. The difference between these two views is the crux of the conflict between classical and Christian thought. It reflects the intercession of biblical beliefs, which transformed the world of ancient philosophy by giving the wholly unclassical idea of creation a central place in our understanding of the nature and meaning of human transcendence.

On a rationalist view, transcendence is a kind of discernment. It is the capacity to see and understand the truth. Its exercise has an independent measure of success. Some thinking falls short of the truth. It is feeble or misguided and misses the goal that reason strives to reach. It follows that thinking can be better or worse. The mere exercise of the power of thought is no guarantee of its worth. That depends on whether it succeeds in doing its work well. Thinking is valuable as an activity only because the discovery of the truth is valuable. The latter has an explanatory priority over the former. It is that for the sake of which one thinks.

Thinking can therefore be graded as better or worse depending on what it achieves. Moreover, if thinking is the quintessential human activity—the locus of human transcendence—then success in thinking means success in being human. Gradations in the first correspond to those in the second. This explains Aristotle's confident judgment (shocking to many today) that some human beings are so deficient in thought that they need to be directed by others whose thinking is of a higher grade.[26]

On a voluntarist view, by contrast, the essence of transcendence is not thinking but willing. The will is a power of affirmation or dissent—the ability to say yes or no.[27] Of course, it must always say yes or no *to something*. On Augustine's view, a good will says yes to God's commands; on Kant's, to the moral law. This may seem to make willing like thinking, since in each case the goodness of the act depends on its success in reaching a goal that exists independently of the act itself. But there is a crucial difference.

Truth has a compulsory power that reason cannot resist. In the presence of the truth, reason has no choice but to submit. The truth is like light; it floods the eye willy-nilly. This is the meaning of Socrates' famous dictum that to know the good is to do the good.[28] Aristotle allowed room for what he calls "incontinence," the all-too-familiar fact that a person can know what is best yet follow a self-destructive path instead.[29] But even for Aristotle, failures of this kind are not failures of will, in Kant's sense or ours. They are the product of bad habits and the resulting inability to control one's desires—of poor education and training.

The picture Augustine paints in his *Confessions* is radically different. The will he describes is not compelled to act by reason or anything else. There is nothing to which it must submit. Even in the glaring presence of the truth, it remains free to acquiesce or not. Over its own acquiescence, the will retains untrammeled control. So far as its own distinctive "work" is concerned, Augustine's will is completely autonomous. It defers to nothing but itself—unlike the power of reason, whose defining experience is one of submission. To illustrate the autonomy of willing, Augustine chooses an example from his own experience: his decision, as a boy, to steal his neighbor's pears just because stealing them was wrong.[30]

Two things follow. The first is that what makes a will good *as a will*—as a power distinct from that of reason—is its choosing to do the right thing regardless of how one defines it. A person may be faulted for not grasping the standard that ought to guide his conduct. But that is a failure of intelligence or character, not of will. If he understands the correct standard and refuses to obey it, then and only then, like Augustine's boyhood theft, is his failure one of willing. Likewise, if he follows the right standard but only because it is conventional and urged on him by others, his failure is one of willing as well.

A person wills as she should only if she knows the right standard and commits herself to it. In this case, though, the dimension of her success that is attributable to her will—rather than experience or education or anything else—is the result of commitment alone. Whether a will succeeds or fails *as a will* is therefore entirely within its control. This is part of what Kant means when he says that the goodness of a good will is wholly self-contained.[31]

Second, a will cannot be partly free or free only to a certain degree. It is either entirely free or not free at all. The grades and shades of accomplishment so prominent in thinking have no analogue in willing.

Success in thinking depends on one's proximity to truths that are independent of the mind. I may be fully committed to the venture and have the best intentions in the world and still get only so far. By contrast, success in willing does not depend on anything outside the will, whose power is complete at every moment. Our intentions, which are always fully under our control, decide the question of success or failure, even if external events prevent us from reaching our goal.

This was emphatically Kant's view.[32] When, under the influence of Christian ideas, he reinterpreted the phenomenon of human transcendence in rigorously voluntarist terms, the idea of a hierarchy of achievement in the work of being human, which seemed so obvious to the Greek philosophers who took thinking rather than willing as their clue to the human condition, lost its prestige and fell under a shadow of disrepute on account of the conviction that the essence of our humanity is the possession of a power of assent that is complete at every moment and able on its own to decide whether one succeeds in living up to the defining demand of our God-given potential.

# V

If equality is good in itself and not on account of something else, that is because it expresses an equal respect for those who deserve it. And who deserves it? Kant's answer is every human being, on account of his or her autonomy, which he ascribes to all who possess the power of acting in accordance with "a conception of laws" or "will."

This formula reflects an epochal reinterpretation of the phenomenon of human transcendence. It marks the metaphysical divide between the culture of classical antiquity and the Christian civilization that followed. It reflects the demotion of excellence—which in classical thought stood at the pinnacle of the explanatory order of values—to a subordinate position in Augustine's philosophy and in that of Kant, who followed the path Augustine scouted.[33]

Plato and Aristotle believed that other goods are pursued for the sake of excellence. Some get farther than others; the classical view of human life is unavoidably hierarchical. When Augustine reimagined human transcendence as a power not of thinking but willing, the belief that excellence is the highest of all goods lost its footing. If the will fails, its failure is its own. One can no longer say, "Even with all the good will in the world, you failed to fulfill your human potential." The idea of the will as a bimodal power of assent or denial—a kind of "on" or "off" switch—reinforces this conclusion. It leaves little or no room for the judgments of rank that in Plato and Aristotle's view define the work of thinking.

In these and countless other ways—cultural, aesthetic, and political—the Christian reinterpretation of transcendence as willing undercut the classical conviction that some human beings are better than others, not just in particular respects but altogether, in their overall degree of flourishing. In place of the idea of an encompassing hierarchy of achievement, it installed a sweeping egalitarianism instead. As a result, the idea that dignity is a status one may possess to a greater or lesser degree gave way to the conviction that it is a universal condition shared equally by all. In time, it came to seem obvious that human dignity presupposes no special measure of knowledge or refinement of character, but reflects the respect to which every being endowed with a will is entitled—even the criminal who wills wrongly.[34]

In Augustine's view, wisdom and prudence are helpful to those who want to protect their wills against the deforming power of ignorance and desire. But these intellectual and practical virtues are only enabling conditions. They are for the sake of something higher that education and character do not guarantee—something equally available to the ignorant and lowborn, the whores and tax farmers of the gospels.[35]

Still, if other goods are for the sake of willing, willing is not, in Augustine's view, the very highest good of all. Willing is for the sake of our reconciliation with God, from whom we have been estranged since the Fall.[36] For an orthodox Christian like Augustine, reunion with God is the supreme good in the explanatory order of values. Kant's view is more ambiguous, though there is reason to think that he held a similar belief, albeit in an attenuated and highly rationalized form.[37]

Since Kant, we have drifted away from this defining Christian conviction. Many today embrace his idea of autonomy but with no religious presuppositions at all. In their view, autonomy is not for the sake of anything else. Its supremacy is unconditioned. These godless Kantians (of whom Rawls is an example) understand autonomy in the way that Kant and Augustine did—as a power of voluntary self-direction that each of us possesses to an identical degree. But for them the value of autonomy has been unchained from any higher goal. This is already implied by Kant's redefinition of success in willing as a kind of self-referential consistency. For Kant, a good will is one that makes the very power of willing the standard by which its acts are to be judged. If there is any substance to this idea—if a good will wills some things and not others (honesty and philanthropy, for example, instead of theft and avarice)—the moral value of willing them, for Kant, lies in the noncontradictory *form* of the agent's affirmations, not in the objective *content* of what he or she affirms.[38]

Rawls's *Theory of Justice* carries the process further. The last trace of theology has disappeared from it. For Kant, God still retains some vestigial importance. He continues to function as what Kant calls "a regulative ideal."[39] For Rawls, God has ceased to be even this. Many thoughtful men and women in the enlightened West now subscribe to a similar view. Like Rawls, they embrace the idea of freedom, choice, or self-direction as the highest of all values, for whose sake we pursue every other. They enthusiastically endorse its egalitarian implications, which have become steadily more demanding since will replaced reason as the paradigm of human transcendence. Whether or not one accepts the details of Rawls's artful construction, *A Theory of Justice* reflects the now-conventional metaphysical beliefs of an entire civilization.

These are strengthened by the various relativisms that, exploiting Kant's self-proclaimed "Copernican Revolution" in philosophy, characterize his putatively objective measure of moral judgment as only one cultural possibility among many, with no anchor in the world apart from the personal or collective acts of endorsement that assign a value to it.[40] With this, the separation of freedom from excellence is complete. The position of autonomy as the highest of all possible goods is stably secured. For many today, the suggestion that the value of a free life depends on the higher value of living well is refuted by the reply, "That is just your view. You are entitled to it. I respect it as an expression of your autonomy but deny that it is true. Indeed, it cannot be true because the value of autonomy and that of other goods is asymmetrical. They all depend on it and it on none of them."

In political terms, this is sometimes expressed by saying that the state ought not to distinguish among its citizens on the basis of their "conceptions of the good."[41] Perhaps this is sound policy, but it is philosophically debatable. Its authority depends on an acceptance of the most fundamental result of the Christian reinterpretation of transcendence as will, a revolution in thought whose convulsions continue to reverberate through our personal and public lives.

# VI

Like all living things, we are carried along by the stream of time. Yet we transcend it in thought and imagination. Transcendence is the hallmark of human experience. It makes science and morality possible, and not just these. Every aspect of human life is touched and transformed—"humanized"—by our consciousness of time and consequent knowledge of death. Freud's account of sex is a striking example.[42]

Transcendence is given to us as a fate. We did not invent it and cannot escape it. It is a "fact of life"—the phenomenological reality from which every account of the human condition takes its start. Willing and thinking—and the faculties of choice and thought in which we imaginatively embed them—are interpretations of it.[43]

Each construes its object from a particular point of view. It is a partial account of something more fundamental and less confined than the explanatory scheme it imposes upon its object. If autonomy seems to many today a fact about human existence rather than an interpretation of it, that is because Christian and post-Christian attitudes have triumphed so completely over classical ones that they obscure the partiality of the view that now thoroughly colors our picture of the human condition.[44]

Like any interpretation, the Christian explanation of transcendence as will has both strengths and limitations. It brings certain features of the human condition into focus and ignores or suppresses others. How should the balance be struck? Let us begin by exploring its limitations, which are harder for us to see. The best way to do this is to consider again the archaic force of the interpretation it displaced.

The Greek understanding of transcendence begins not with choosing but thinking and the experience of wonder that sets it in motion.[45] That we are wondering beings with a desire to know that cannot be satisfied until we know everything that can be known was for both Plato and Aristotle the most striking fact about us. In their view, the value of the power that unleashes the wonderstruck longing to know is the good of the knowledge in which the exercise of the power finally comes to rest. Nothing seemed more obvious to these otherwise very different philosophers—nor plainer than the fact that different human beings realize their potential for knowledge to different degrees.

What most impressed the Greeks was the outstanding achievement of those who rise farthest toward the world we all encounter in our ecstatic release from the closed circle of animal life. This was true from the start of the tradition. It is the *splendor* (*kleos*) of the great warriors, fighting and dying, that holds Homer's attention.[46] Aristotle celebrates a sublimated version of the same phenomenon. It is the *actuality* (*energeia*) of the statesman and philosopher he holds up as a benchmark of human achievement.[47]

Those who fall below these great figures are negligible by comparison. They are less than fully human. Aristotle's natural slave hovers in a kind of twilight, human enough to follow orders yet so lacking in self-control that he needs another to direct his life. In the second book of the *Iliad*, the lowly figure of Thersites has the nerve to challenge Agamemnon in open session before the entire Greek army. He is a physical and mental wreck of a man: "bandy-legged and lame in one foot," his shoulders "rounded, stooping together over his chest," his mind "a great store of disorderly words." He barely qualifies as human by comparison with the great ones who greet his intervention with derisive laughter, like that of the gods.[48]

These judgments of rank are pervasive in classical literature and philosophy. The Greeks and Romans accepted them without a hint of moral disapproval. One cannot read a page of Homer, Sophocles, Thucydides, Plato, Aristotle, Ovid, Virgil, or Tacitus without being struck by their easy acknowledgment of the rank order of men.[49] It is what most profoundly separates the classical world from ours. It is the essence of classicism.

The classical acceptance of the excellence of some human beings and deficiency of others rested on two assumptions that seemed so blindingly obvious as not to require a defense. The first is that the actualization of a power is always prior to the power itself in the order of explanation. It is what one does with the power that explains why we value, use, and honor it. What is the value of the power of sight? Plato asks.[50] That it enables us to experience and enjoy the act of seeing. A person who can see but does not derives nothing of value from the power. This is the condition of those in Socrates' Cave.[51]

To explain why the capacity to do something has the value it does, one must always appeal, Plato thought, to the actual doing itself, and while the capacity may be equally distributed (like the power of sight), its realization is not. Some see farther, better, and more clearly than others. The same is true of the power of thought. This led Plato to conclude that the philosopher, who sees most clearly and thinks most deeply, is not only superior to those he leaves behind in the Cave but has a duty to lead them up to a higher level of fulfillment than their blinkered vision allows.[52]

Aristotle shares Plato's conviction about the relation between power and activity, though he expresses it more abstractly. To exercise a power we must first possess it. What Aristotle calls potential (*dunamis*) always precedes its realization in time. But the value of the power—what it is for and why it is worth having—can only be explained by what he terms the "active-being-at-work" or "fulfillment" of the power.[53]

Aristotle acknowledges that there are other ways to explain why something possesses the power it does, for example, by appealing to its material makeup. We explain how an eye works by describing the arrangement of its physical parts. But among all the possible explanations, the one that ranks highest, on which every other depends, is the explanation that reminds us of what the power is *for*—of the state or condition of fulfillment for whose sake we employ it. This condition completes the work of striving toward it. It gives the work its direction and meaning and explains the value of having the power that "enables" one to begin.[54]

A power may be widely, even universally, shared among beings of a certain kind. Its fulfillment, though, is a matter of degree and therefore of rank. Some birds realize their power of flight; others fall flightless from the nest. The first are more fully bird-like. The same is true of men. In Aristotle's view, a man whose distinctive human powers—above all, those of thought and political action—are more developed that those of others ranks higher as a human being.

The second assumption underlying Plato and Aristotle's easy acceptance of the rank order of men is that living well is a meaningful and supremely important task. No one denies that some people excel at certain pursuits. There are outstanding doctors, confectioners, and horse trainers. (These are Plato's examples.)[55] They are masters of their respective crafts. We are untroubled by such judgments because each craft is a circumscribed activity. Failure in one is compatible with success in another.

This is not true of life as a whole. There is nothing outside it; it covers the entire field. Here failure is not a local shortcoming; it is a kind of catastrophe. Yet living well, Plato thought, is an art or craft too.[56] It is the craft—as he puts it in the *Republic*—of properly ordering the parts of one's soul.[57] This is the supreme craft; it explains the purpose and value of every other. Some do especially well at it. Their souls are distinguished by their greater harmony and beauty, just as the candies of a master confectioner are distinguished by their superior decoration and taste.

Aristotle agrees and puts the point in his characteristically matter-of-fact way. The principal subject of his lectures on ethics is the nature of *eudaimonia*, or human flourishing. He offers a homely analogy to explain what he means. We all acknowledge that some play the flute better than others. They realize the power of flute-playing to a higher degree. Are we then to say, Aristotle asks rhetorically, that there is a power of flute-playing but no such thing as the power of being human? The question answers itself. And if there is such a power, then some must achieve a higher degree of success in the all-encompassing work of being human, just as some do in the limited work of playing the flute.[58]

That the fulfillment of a power always ranks higher in the explanation of its value than the mere possession of it, and that being human is itself a "craft" (*techne*) or "work" (*ergon*) in which the power of working is realized to different degrees, are the two unstated and mostly unnoticed assumptions on which the classical acceptance of the sovereignty of excellence in the realm of values and endorsement of the rank order of men rest so securely. The reinterpretation of human transcendence as will discredited both assumptions. It reconceived transcendence as a power whose value is self-contained (Kant's "jewel in the night") and therefore precedes and explains that of its achievements—reversing the classical equation, which puts fulfillment ahead of potential in the explanatory order of values. And it demolished the idea that life is an art or craft in which, as Aristotle might have put it, "practice makes perfect," substituting for this the belief that every life is equally eligible for salvation, up to its very last moment, if the person whose life it is makes the right choice.

The Christian reinterpretation of the phenomenon of transcendence not only hides these assumptions from view, it devalues them and makes them seem wicked, a self-serving justification for the despicable regime of pride that Augustine condemned so ferociously in his blistering survey of pagan vices.[59] It converts them to blasphemies—an offense against God himself, who made us all in his image by endowing each of us with an equal measure of the same freedom that he exercised at the moment of creation.

But the interpretive devaluation of these assumptions does not make them false. Even beginning students, reading Plato and Aristotle for the first time, are struck by the intuitive force of their ideas. The students' instinctive egalitarianism makes it difficult for them to embrace the idea of a rank order of excellence in living. Still, their first and often positive reaction to the power of these texts is some evidence that the explanatory priority of fulfillment over potential and the application of this priority to the work of life as a whole are ideas of lasting appeal that can never completely lose their authority.

To the extent they still possess it, these classical ideas invite—indeed, compel—us to put excellence before autonomy in the explanatory order of values. If the value of autonomy (like that of any power) depends on the good of what one does with it, above all in the comprehensive enterprise of life, and if some get farther than others in this supremely important assignment, then it follows that excellence is sovereign among goods, prior to freedom and equality alike.

Why is this conclusion so difficult for us to accept? One reason is that the reinterpretation of human transcendence as will has acquired such immense authority in the modern West that it makes any flirtation with the classical view appear vaguely criminal. A deeper reason, though, is that the latter view, like its Christian successor, highlights certain things about the human condition and ignores others. What it obscures, moreover, is an aspect of our humanity that the voluntarist view brings to light. In this sense, Christian voluntarism is an antidote to the limitations of classical thought. It is a complement and corrective. This is the other side of the coin.

# VII

The Greeks were riveted by the phenomenon of human greatness—of words and deeds that stand out on account of their brilliance, bravery, or reckless indifference to concerns that occupy most of us most of the time. It filled them with amazement. They called it *deinos*: inspiring, terrifying, "awful" in both senses of the word.[60] The reaction that greatness provoked in the Greeks and later the Romans was not one of moral approval, at least not necessarily and always. It was closer to astonishment. Even today, reading the ancient texts that record their response, we can feel something of the same sense of amazement and danger in the presence of memorably great human beings.

Achilles produces this reaction. Slashing through the Trojan ranks, he fills us with wonder and dread. So does Odysseus, as he scourges the suitors who have infested his palace and block the way to his great-rooted bed.[61] The Athenians' terrible, truthful ultimatum to the inhabitants of Melos shocks the conscience but arouses a feeling of stupefied wonder.[62] The philosopher who has achieved an indifference to death is great in a different way. But his greatness too is a cause of astonishment and disquiet. Plato's account of the trial of Socrates may or may not be convincing in philosophical terms, but its readers can never forget the unnerving calm of the man who stands in the dock.[63]

The brilliance of the great is overpowering. They cast a blinding light on those around them—the undistinguished run of human beings who in the light of the great can barely be seen at all. The latter fall outside the range of interest and care. Their obscurity testifies to their insignificance.

This indifference to ordinary people is a kind of blindness—a loss of vision caused by the spectacle of the great, like the blindness that results from looking too long at the sun. It explains the cruel ridicule Homer heaps on the plebian figure of Thersites and Aristotle's casual affirmation that some men are slaves by nature. More generally, it is the premise of every aristocratic culture, from Homer's blood-soaked warrior camps to the cerebral calm of Aristotle's lecture hall. Nietzsche understood this more viscerally than any other modern thinker. Too viscerally, perhaps.[64]

But the overwhelming impression that human greatness makes upon us does more than deflect our attention from the low and insignificant. It blinds us to the antecedent condition that allows greatness to appear in the first place. This condition itself is something astonishing, though we easily lose sight of it. Martin Heidegger employs an image to help us recover our lost sense of amazement. All human words and deeds appear, he says, in a "clearing."[65] What does Heidegger mean by this?

The world is a dense and impenetrable forest. Its inhabitants have no vantage point from which to observe and represent it. Like the clearing a woodsman cuts in the middle of the forest, which brings light into the woods and makes it visible for the first time, the human being—Heidegger's term is *Dasein*—is himself a clearing in the midst of Being. His detachment from the world establishes a perspective on it and thereby brings the surrounding reality into view.[66]

The clearing allows for detachment. It *is* a kind of detachment. It is an ecstatic space—not in the ordinary sense of joyful transportation but the etymologically primitive one of "standing out from": in this case, standing out from the world, or transcending it.[67] The clearing is Heidegger's way of visualizing the phenomenon of transcendence that sets human beings apart from other animals. It allows for what he calls the "projection" of the world as an object of detached observation and care.[68] It is the ecstatic space of speech and reason, of thinking, planning, depicting, remembering, honoring, and everything else that only human beings do.

Like every other human act, great ones appear only within the lighted field of the clearing. Human greatness may be astonishing, but to be astonished by it we must first see it. It must be visible to us as a *human* achievement. Other animals do extraordinary things, but the greatness of Achilles, Odysseus, Socrates, and the Athenian ambassadors to Melos lies beyond their power.[69] The greatness of human striving—whether it succeeds or fails—is a function of ambitions that human beings alone experience. Modifying the metaphor a bit, one might say that the clearing is a theater in which the greatness of the actors on the stage first comes to light. This was Hannah Arendt's way of describing the nature of political action as the Greeks originally understood it, in the spirit of her own Heideggerian education.[70]

Before the astonishment we feel in the presence of greatness, we have reason to be amazed at the existence of the clearing in which greatness can be seen. We have reason to be astonished at the possibility of our astonishment— to regard it with reverent awe. That there *is* a clearing, that we *do* transcend the world, that we stand out from it and rise up toward the world in ordinary and remarkable ways—what could be more wonderful that *that*? It is easy to forget this—as easy as forgetting that the world is visible only because it is bathed in light. In the *Republic*, Socrates reminds us of this primordial sense of wonder when he observes that his companions, in searching for the truth, have forgotten that in addition to the truth, and minds with which to grasp it, they need light to see at all.[71]

The clearing is a metaphor for the human condition. Admission is granted to all who are conscious of time and not mindlessly swept along by it—who possess what Kant calls the power of acting in accordance with "the conception of a law." How far any human being goes in putting this power to work is a matter of circumstance and ability. Some get farther than others. The power itself, though, is distributed equally among all who share the clearing with the spectacularly brave, noble, wise, and foolhardy.

In this sense we are all companions of the clearing, the anonymous along with the memorable. Thersites, too, is a human being. He speaks—poorly, perhaps—but he is not a pack animal or mute object, like a shield or spear. The same is true of Aristotle's natural slave. He is a "talking tool" who hears and understands words.[72] Like Thersites, the slave also belongs to the ecstatic community of speech. His equal membership in it is the premise of Hegel's famous account of the struggle between lord and bondsman.[73]

This equality of membership precedes the distinctions of rank that first appear in the lit space of speech. The first (to put it as Kant might) is the precondition necessary for the possibility of the second. Blinded by the brilliance of the performance of the few who excel, the Greeks and those who followed them in the classical tradition lost sight of this precedent condition. This is the blind spot of classical thought, the dark side of aristocratic radiance, in which Homer, Plato, Aristotle, and Thucydides stand in thrall. It weakens the grounds of companionate affection that all human beings ought to feel for one another as inhabitants of the clearing whose existence is the most astounding thing of all.

The Christian religion is a needed corrective. Christianity is a religion of charity. It teaches humility and concern for others—for all others, since each of us is made in the image of God.[74] This is the theological way of expressing the equality of all human beings as creatures endowed with the same God-like power that since Augustine has been interpreted as "will." But if we understand this power as transcendence, without interpreting it more specifically as will or reason or anything else, the equality that Christianity celebrates, and to which it attaches so many ethical duties, may be defined as that of all who share the experience of standing out from the world in the ecstatic awareness of time that is the root of every human endeavor.

That this happens at all is cause for wonder. How can it be that there is a clearing in the world? Is this the world's own doing? The wonder arises every time we see a human being, if we have eyes to look. It is no less wonderful in the lives of the least than of the great. It is there in the eyes of every child. Those who reflect even for a moment on the wonder of the clearing in which we find ourselves joined by fate in the common adventure that we call the human condition are bound to be struck by the thought that every human being possesses what Kant calls a "worth" beyond "price."[75]

The Christian religion protects us against the blindness that afflicted the poets and philosophers of Greece, who wrote Thersites and his lowly tribe out of the human family. It discredits the terrible doctrine of natural slavery and reinforces the amazement we properly feel in the presence of all who share this power with us. Kant captures this sentiment in his famous exclamation that "the moral law" fills the mind with "admiration and awe" the more we reflect upon it.[76] Christianity accentuates this feeling and develops a system of obligations based upon it.

Two are of special importance. The first is the duty we owe our companions of the clearing to make sure they remain within its luminous space—that we neither force them out by denying their humanity nor allow their human powers to be extinguished by poverty and neglect. The denial or destruction of a person's humanity, by force or inattention, is the extinction of a light whose existence is a wonder that surpasses understanding. Christianity conceives it as a crime against God. This is an interpretation of something more fundamental: of the disregard for what, if we turn our attention to it, ought to stop us all in our tracks. It is the worst kind of forgetfulness—not of some small and replaceable thing, but of our human being, in whose light all things are found and lost.

The second duty is to keep our clearing in good repair. It is always in danger of being overgrown. The existence of the clearing is inexplicable, but it *does* exist and to allow it to be swallowed again by the forest—though this is not to destroy the world, which is beyond our power—is to put out the light that allows the world to appear at all. The Christian religion interprets this as a repudiation of God's gift. Again, this is an interpretive gloss on a more primitive duty: our shared custodial responsibility as companions of the clearing to keep it open so that the world can be seen (known, celebrated, and adorned). Today, it lies in our power to close the clearing. That would be more than irresponsible. It would destroy the ground of responsibility itself.[77]

What do these two duties imply? What do they require of us? I pass all such questions by. The important point is that the duties exist. The classical tradition obscures or denies them. Its fascination with human greatness encourages a forgetfulness of the condition on which the recognition of greatness depends. This condition is one of equality. It is also one of freedom. The detachment that allows for this uniquely human form of recognition is a liberation, a release, a "freeing-from" the closed routines of animal life.[78] The equality and freedom of all human beings is the precondition necessary for the possibility of the greatness of some.

The first is prior to the second in the way that every precondition comes before the achievement it makes possible. The Christian religion reminds us of this priority and of the duties it entails. This is its lasting contribution to Western thought—the corrective it provides to the myopia of classical values.

But the value of this corrective is compromised by the Christian reinterpretation of transcendence as will. The reinterpretation does more than remind us that the freedom and equality of transcendence come before the greatness of what some do with it, in the way that potential always precedes fulfillment. It conceives this potential as a self-contained good whose worth is secured by willing to do the right thing, even if the effort entirely fails, and elevates this good to a position of supremacy in the realm of values. It discredits the classical assumption that the good of any power can in the end be explained only by the realization of what it empowers its possessor to do—by the good of the power at work. And it undermines the conviction, which Plato and Aristotle shared, that the explanatory priority of achievement over potential applies with the same if not greater force to the inclusive work of being human as to every lesser task.

This is a consequence not of Christian humility and its inspiring ethic of charity but of the voluntarist metaphysics that Augustine and Kant employ to reinterpret the fact of human transcendence in cosmic terms that invert the classical order of values. Christianity does more than correct the blindness caused by the classical obsession with greatness. It substitutes a symmetrical blindness that has clouded our vision for centuries.

## VIII

What is transcendence for? For whose sake does the clearing exist? For that of the world? For its human occupants? Perhaps it exists so that the world will be lit and we experience an enlightenment inaccessible to those who dwell outside its light. This may be true, but it is not very helpful. It only redescribes the phenomenon of transcendence itself. There is a better answer.

We cannot say what the clearing is for. To do that, we would have to be able to see it from a vantage point beyond the clearing itself—to transcend our transcendence, which we are unable to do. Transcendence liberates us from the world but not completely. It is at once a release and a restraint—a freedom and a fate. This is what Kant means when he says, in his characteristically compressed way, that our condition is that of "finite rational beings."[79]

Still, even if we have no way of knowing why there is such a thing as transcendence at all, we can answer the more modest question of what the human striving that takes place within its open space is for. Transcendence is a form of empowerment, and the value of this most remarkable power, like that of any other, is explained by the good of the goal it allows us to reach.

The end or aim of transcendence is that of "putting the world into words," as Aristotle says.[80] In the clearing that lights the world, we reach up to know, portray, and love it. Some do this more successfully and inspiringly than others, though none ever succeeds completely. There are also the astonishing failures—the larger-than-life careers that arouse fear and pity rather than admiration.

We distinguish between the remarkable and the admirable, the extraordinary and the excellent, and debate about the meaning of excellence itself. Which achievements and lives display it? But the ferocity of our disagreements about the nature of excellence confirms its importance rather than the reverse, and suggests that this increases as we move from limited activities to the all-embracing one of being human. They remind us that the good of a power is measured by the degree of its realization and that this applies above all to the most elementary power we possess, the one that makes us human in the first place—the ecstatic power of transcendence that enables us to stretch out toward a world that beckons from a distance with a reality greater than our own. They remind us that however contestable the meaning of excellence may be, we need it as an explanatory benchmark to account for the good of the power that sets us apart from our animal friends.

The Greek poets and philosophers understood this. They knew that the value of our humanity is explained by what one does with it. They put excellence first in the explanatory order of values because they understood that the power of being human, like any other, exists for the sake of its fulfillment, not the other way around.

They were so impressed with the brilliance of human achievement that they lost sight of the existence of the power that enables those who rise so high to rise at all. This power is shared equally by every human being. It dictates a care and concern for all who possess it. The classical tradition is deformed by its lack of respect for our common humanity. But respect is only a prelude to an appreciation of the order of excellence in human attainment. The power comes before its fulfillment in the order of time, but the order of explanation is the reverse. This is the abiding truth of the classical tradition.

The Christian religion corrected the Greeks' inhuman blindness to the wretched of the earth. But it obscured—indeed, ruthlessly suppressed—the explanatory priority of excellence by interpreting freedom and equality in metaphysical terms as properties of the will and describing autonomy as the highest of all human values. This is the harm the Christian religion continues to do in its post-Christian and secularized forms, even as its still-inspiring ethic of charity reminds us of the obligations we owe our companions of the clearing.

Softened by a due measure of humility, the classical insistence on the sovereignty of excellence remains as persuasive as ever. Only it can explain, in a satisfying way, why we assign the value we do to freedom and equality. These are good but not good in themselves—any more than a power that lies dormant or achieves but little is of such intrinsic value that its realization is irrelevant to its worth. This enduring truth applies to powers of all kinds but most forcefully to the power of transcendence that is our humanity itself. And it applies despite our disagreements about the meaning of excellence in art or politics or anything else— indeed, it is what gives these disagreements their liveliness and interest.

The Christian revaluation of values is an antidote to the Greeks' belittling contempt for weakly developed or underperforming human beings. But the reinterpretation of transcendence as will distorts the explanatory order of values and impoverishes our lives by discrediting the idea of excellence as a standard of judgment except in circumscribed pursuits, where it is always subject to the overriding claims of equality. The distortion is clearest, perhaps, in the philosophies of those disenchanted heirs of Christian belief who today aggressively defend the priority of autonomy in strictly secular terms and wear their contempt for the sovereignty of excellence as a badge of anti-pride.[81] Their systems of thought express our settled beliefs. They reflect the mood of the times. Yet how weightless they seem in comparison with a single page of Homer or Plato!

## IX

I conclude with three loosely connected observations.

The first concerns the definition of excellence. I have defended its explanatory priority on the grounds that a power has value because of what it enables its possessor to do; that the more one does with it, the more valuable the power becomes; that this applies not only to particular arts and skills, like the art of cooking and the skill of reading, but to the art of being human as well, which can be thought of as the exercise of the elementary power of transcendence that defines the human condition and creates the space for every other pursuit of a distinctively human kind (the building of cities, writing of symphonies, discovery of laws of nature, and the like). This is the classical view, broadly defined, which puts excellence at the summit of the explanatory order of values. But what *is* the excellence I put there, following Plato and Aristotle? I have not answered or even asked this question. My silence invites a familiar objection.

"Judgments of excellence vary. They are highly subjective. There is no objective benchmark by which to assess them—as Plato and Aristotle wrongly assumed. We must each be left free to define excellence as we choose. Our choices fix its meaning. This is obviously true in circumscribed pursuits like cooking and painting. It is even truer when it comes to what some call the 'work' or 'art' of living. Whatever meaning excellence may have elsewhere, it has none here. What matters is the freedom to live as one chooses, not the undefined excellence that you insist distinguishes some lives from others. When it comes to life as a whole, the value of choice is sovereign."

I am unpersuaded.

The variety and complexity of factors that bear on judgments of excellence in any setting often require that some selection be made among them. This may be described as a kind of "choice." Literary critics choose what to praise in a poem. The judges at an ice-skating contest choose what to emphasize in the skaters' performance.

But their choices do not make the poem or performance excellent. A choice may be controversial and when it is, it must be defended. In defending it, though, it is never enough to say, "The justification for my choice is the fact that I made it." This is sufficient to explain some preferences (for spicy food, for example) but not to justify a judgment of excellence. This typically demand distinctions, discriminations, and choices, but the choice is explained by the excellence of what it purports to pick out, not the other way around. That a choice is debatable does not disprove but confirms this.

Some judgments of excellence appear to be straightforward. The criteria seem relatively clear; there is not much room for debate. Doctors in a particular field, for example, are often ranked or graded. There are standardized reports that do this. They identify a few at the top—the really outstanding radiologists and neurosurgeons.

By contrast, asking which of the paintings in the Metropolitan Museum of Art are the best ones looks like a pointless inquiry. How can one possibly answer? Yet even in a collection so vast and varied, viewers are likely to judge some works of higher rank on account of their exceptional beauty and greater historical influence. Any selection is bound to be controversial, as are the criteria on which it is based. The selection must be explained by appealing to some idea of excellence. But saying that this idea is justified by the fact that one endorses it is no justification at all.

The difference between the seemingly easy and difficult cases is in reality one of degree. The practice of medicine is a form of artistry too. Regardless of their complexity, or the contentiousness of the criteria on which they are based, judgments of excellence in any discipline or activity assume that it is meaningful to ask which works and acts, within that field, are most worthy of admiration and esteem. If excellence were in the eye of the beholder and a matter of choice alone, these questions would have less interest and meaning, if any at all.

When it comes to excellent *lives*, however, serious doubts remain. Works and acts can perhaps be ranked, but only in the context of a specific activity or institution that has its own internal standards. Lives are different. Living is not one activity among many. It is the sum of all activities or, better, their encompassing whole—the boundless horizon of all our bounded pursuits. By what standard is excellence in living to be judged? Here, it seems, choice decides the matter because nothing else can. I live this way, you live that. There are as many lifestyles as there are individuals who choose them. Who is to say that one is better than another—that some human beings excel in the art or activity of living?

Aristotle's view was the opposite. If it makes sense, he said, to ask what excellence means in a pursuit like playing the flute, it makes far more sense to ask what constitutes excellence in the work of being human. Is Aristotle's verdict still credible? Or has the metaphysics of autonomy, with its emphasis on the supreme value of commitment and choice, washed it away?

Aristotle believed there are only two ways to live an outstanding life. One is the life of a statesman, active in the affairs of his city. The other is that of a philosopher, devoted to understanding the nature of being. These came to be called the *vita activa* and *vita contemplativa*. In Aristotle's view, these are the two supremely fulfilling forms of human achievement.[82]

His selection is clearly too narrow. There are other forms of human greatness. There is the greatness of the artist, for example, and that of the saint. The first Aristotle considers a mere craftsman; the second he does not consider at all. Their inclusion among the eligible forms of human greatness belongs to a later age. Each is shaped by Christian values.[83]

How many forms are there? Certainly more than Aristotle thought. There are also tensions—indeed, contradictions—among them. Some demand the avoidance or active suppression of values that others exalt. (Gauguin is a famous example. Gandhi is another.)[84] But however diverse or even contradictory the ways of living an outstanding human life, excellence is not displaced by choice as the first among values. We do not say of those who lead extraordinary lives, in any of the various ways human beings do, that their greatness is explained by the decision to pursue the life in question. It is the other way around. The men and women who live these lives choose them for the sake of whatever they put at the pinnacle of human fulfillment.

In doing so they show what human beings are capable of when their powers are deployed in a certain direction—when they are concentrated on knowledge, beauty, public action, physical courage, self-sacrifice, connoisseurship, or some other admired goal. They reveal a dimension of human greatness. It demeans the value of their achievements to ascribe it to their having chosen to live one way rather than another. In every line of human greatness, there are countless aspirants who stand below those at the top—weak thinkers, banal artists, incompetent politicians, and distracted saints. If choice explained the splendor of the greatest lives, it is hard to see why it would not confer equal value on the lesser achievements of those who choose the same goal but fail to reach it.

"What an unfeeling judgment! What patronizing disregard for the dignity of the lives of those who fall below what you presumptuously call 'the top.' Do you not see that their lives are just as worthy as those you single out as 'great,' 'extraordinary,' and 'splendid'—as if these words conveyed anything more than your own personal taste? Have you no sympathy for the hardships under which so many labor—all the roadblocks to human fulfillment in any line of endeavor? Have you no respect for the choices people make to live as they do, and for the value these choices themselves confer on their lives?"

Here all the objections to what I have been saying come crashing down at once. My answer is as follows.

The point of doing most things is doing them well. This gives success its meaning and value. It even gives failure meaning and value. "If something is worth doing, it is worth doing poorly."[85] Why do people learn to play the flute, dribble a basketball, plant a spring garden, cook lasagna, or make a budget, if not for the sake of doing it well?

Those who invest their time and energy in these and countless other activities are not indifferent to excellence. They care about it and measure their work by it. The work may be a means to a higher end. We make budgets for the sake of financial security. But regardless of its position in the hierarchy of a person's needs and ambitions, the quality of the work almost always matters. If the distinction between "better" and "worse" has no application to it, we may still go through the motions, but the work itself will not command our interest and attention to the same degree.

These increase as we move up the hierarchy of activities from limited to more inclusive ones. Doing well becomes more important. Excellence has greater salience and authority. How preposterous to think that we strive for excellence in lesser pursuits but not in the activity of being human—in the exercise of the power of transcendence that gives *all* the pursuits that set us apart from other animals their uniquely human character, even though as finite beings we must always deploy the power in some specific direction. Aristotle's judgment is still valid today. It is not discredited by his narrow view of the varieties of human greatness. Nor does our acknowledgment of other forms, to which his metaphysical prejudices blinded him, make excellence a function of choice, as if doing well were simply a matter of choosing or willing to do it.

Some never have a fair chance to try to live well. Poverty, ignorance, and disease keep them shut within terrible limits. It is a moral disgrace. Everyone ought to have enough to try to be an outstanding human being. Those with more owe it to those with less to see that they have the wherewithal to try.

But among those who are adequately empowered—even those who are rich and highly educated—only a few reach the summit of human greatness in any of its recognized departments. A few are utter failures; most are mediocrities of middling attainment; the greatness of some is unnoticed at the time—it only comes to light later.[86] This may seem a harsh judgment, but those who reject it in the name of freedom and equality confuse the obligation to ensure our companions of the clearing a fair shot at realizing their human potential with the fulfillment of this potential itself. The latter alone explains why the power of being human has any value at all. Its realization or enactment comes in grades of splendor. To say that a person's achievements have the value they do because they reflect her authentic affirmation of the way of life she has chosen reduces all accomplishments to a uniform dimness and discredits the idea of excellence that makes human living, as distinct from bare survival, worthwhile for the great and modest alike.

This brings me to my second observation. Excellence is not only prior to freedom in the order of explanation. It is in tension with it.

The experience of pursuing excellence in any direction is one of constraint. It is the experience of submitting to a discipline. The discipline directs the work and confines it. Every interesting discipline leaves room for improvisation, but the freedom it affords is won only through hard work. Neither the discipline itself nor its creative possibilities are variable at the discretion of the person who enters upon it.[87] Subjection, not freedom, is the initial condition of mastery in all human pursuits that offer meaningful opportunities for self-development and self-expression. Freedom comes later, and when it does is often experienced as an increasingly intimate form of subjection in which one is more and more attuned to the demands of the work. Progress is toward greater deference, not discretion. Excellence means less freedom, not more.

Nietzsche understood this. Many think of him as a champion of freedom. This is a common mistake. Nietzsche saw with particular acuity the essential relation between discipline and greatness and knew from his own experience that those with gifts are slaves to them.[88] Spinoza expresses a similar thought at the end of the *Ethics*. "All things excellent," he says, "are as difficult as they are rare."[89] This is true of excellence in every pursuit and above all in the work of being human—the subject of Spinoza's book, whose born-again paganism restates a classical ideal in modern terms.[90]

My last observation concerns justice and beauty.

Equality and freedom belong to the sphere of justice. They have an immediate and pressing claim on our attention. "Justice," Rawls says, "is the first virtue of social institutions."[91] A society may be prosperous, pious, or cultured, but if it is not just, it is a failure. Before a society can pursue other goals, it must first secure the conditions of justice.

This priority, though, is only a temporal one. Justice comes first in time but not in the order of explanation. It is merely a gating condition. Justice is *for* something else. It is for the sake of excellence.

Questions of justice are often exceedingly complex. They have many different dimensions. Philosophers and lawyers debate them endlessly.

When justice becomes an end in itself, though, these questions are detached from what gives them their final importance. They lose their connection to much of what fascinates us about human beings and the astonishing things they do with their powers. The debate becomes boring.

*Boring* is an aesthetic term.[92] It is bound to seem misplaced—immoral, even—to those who put justice first in all respects. So long as there is one drop of injustice left in the world, how can it possibly matter that its definition and eradication are tedious topics?

The answer is that we do many tedious things because we must but ought never to lose sight of why we do them or forget what the tedium is for. If freedom and equality belong to the sphere of justice, excellence in all its manifestations belongs to the realm of beauty—of what stands out from the commonplace on account of its greater power to disclose some truth about the world, large or small.[93] Justice is for the sake of beauty, not the other way around. Kant had it backwards. Beauty is the "jewel shining in the night." Rilke calls beauty a kind of "terror" that "we are barely able to endure." It "amazes us so," he says, "because it serenely disdains to destroy us."[94] With these words, this most modern of poets sought to convey some sense of what struck the Greeks ages ago: the awful power of beauty, which stuns us into appreciative speech and artistic emulation.[95]

Today this is a heterodox view, but it is not un-American. The poet who immortalized the song of America knew perfectly well that justice comes first in the order of practical tasks. He championed abolition and worshipped Abraham Lincoln.[96] But he believed with equal fervor that fairness and equality are for the sake of a poetic ideal that, however remote, alone gives our struggle to reach it meaning and value. Beauty stands on the highest peak of what Walt Whitman calls our "democratic vistas."[97]

Justice is equality. Equal things are on a par. Beauty shines forth. It commands our attention. Beauty is another name for excellence, sovereign among goods in the realm of human values.

# CHAPTER FOUR

# Can We Be Friends with the Dead?

## I

In 1513, Niccolò Machiavelli was living on his farm nine miles south of Florence. On a clear day a visitor can see the dome of the city's great cathedral from the front steps of his home. The city seems close—almost within reach.

Not for Machiavelli, though, who had been exiled to the country earlier that year after being tortured on suspicion of participating in a plot against the new government of Florence, again in the hands of the Medici after eighteen years of popular rule. It must have been another kind of torture for this intensely political man to see from his own doorstep the most striking monument of the city he loved but was now forbidden to enter.[1]

Yet exile had a compensating advantage. It gave him the freedom to write. Here, away from the distractions and demands of the city, he composed his two most famous works, *The Prince* and *Discourses on Livy*.[2]

In the dedicatory letter he sent to Lorenzo de' Medici with a copy of *The Prince*, Machiavelli compares himself to a landscape painter who sets up his easel "down in the plain" in order "to consider the nature of mountains and high places."[3] He hopes, he says, to illuminate from his humble point of view the practical problems that leaders like Lorenzo face every day but are more clearly seen from a distance. Machiavelli the rustic offers his essay to Lorenzo the urban prince as a handbook of detached wisdom regarding the affairs of a city the writer can better describe because of his forced separation from it.

Machiavelli was hardly a rustic in the ordinary sense, though. He was a supremely cultured man with an immense literary appetite. Books were at the center of his life. He reminds us of this in a letter he wrote to his friend Francesco Vettori a few months after being exiled to his farm.[4]

After recounting in amusing detail his morning round of chores, Machiavelli describes the pleasant distractions of arguing with his country neighbors over cards in the local inn. But then, he says, "on the coming of evening, I return to my house and enter my study."

> At the door I take off the day's clothing, covered with mud and dust, and put on garments regal and courtly; and re-clothed appropriately, I enter the ancient courts of ancient men, where, received by them with affection, I feed on that food which only is mine and which I was born for, where I am not ashamed to speak with them and to ask them the reason for their actions; and they in their kindness answer me; and for four hours of time I do not feel boredom, I forget every trouble, I do not dread poverty, I am not frightened by death; entirely I give myself over to them. And because Dante says it does not produce knowledge when we hear but do not remember, I have noted everything in their conversation which has profited me.

In what spirit does Machiavelli enter his study and resume his dialogue with the dead? Is it curiosity? The desire for self-improvement that an eager student brings to class? Yes, undoubtedly, but also something more.

Machiavelli crosses the threshold to his study in a spirit of reverent attention. He approaches his long-dead interlocutors hoping not only to learn from them but to save their wisdom from the oblivion of time—to conserve what they have bequeathed him. His attitude is one of affectionate devotion, of friendly attention—almost, one might say, of pious care.

For the Romans, whom Machiavelli studied closely, piety was perhaps the greatest virtue of all. Their veneration for the dead had archaic roots. These reach back beyond the light of history to the ancestral worship of the ancient family, gathered around its sacred hearth. We glimpse them only in the form in which they survived and were later recorded, long after groups of families had gathered in those larger "civic" or "political" associations whose religious practices were shaped by the age-old habits of familial piety that preceded them.[5]

The durability of these habits and their lasting influence on Roman ideals is the central theme of the great poem of the Augustan age that sought to define once and for all the distinctiveness of the Roman venture and its sustaining values. The poet of *The Aeneid* repeatedly describes its hero as "*pius Aeneas*," "pious Aeneas," whose flight from Troy and search for a new home is driven by the longing to keep the fire of his ancestral hearth from going out—by a reverence for the dead, whose fate is in his hands.[6]

The heroes of the *Iliad* and the *Odyssey* possess many remarkable traits—great courage and cunning, for example. But piety is not among them. No one would call Achilles or Odysseus a "pious" man. Aeneas has a number of these other qualities too, but his outstanding virtue is piety. It is what makes him a uniquely Roman hero.

A century after Machiavelli wrote his letter to Vettori, the sculptor Gian Lorenzo Bernini caught the idea of Aeneas's piety in his masterpiece, *Aeneas, Anchises, and Ascanius*. You can see it today in the Borghese Gallery in Rome.[7] There, frozen in stone, is Aeneas with his son Ascanius by his side and his aged father Anchises on his back, fleeing the ruins of Troy. In his hands Anchises carries the household gods that he himself will soon join. It is a fine expression of the Roman reverence for the dead and the continuity of tradition in general—for everything the word *piety* conveyed to the Roman imagination.[8]

Machiavelli is not a Roman *pater familias*. When he enters his study dressed as an ambassador from the present, he does not come to worship those who have long since died—to sprinkle incense at an altar. Yet his relation to them is not a selfish one either. Yes, he hopes to gain from the encounter, but he wishes to give something in return. He wants to learn from the ancient authors he admires but also to rescue their ideas from the shallow misunderstandings of contemporary readers—to bring their genius back to life in his own much-altered world, just as Aeneas hopes to give his ancestors a new life in their transplanted home.

Machiavelli's relation to the dead is best described as a form of friendship. Like all friendships, it is motivated by a wish that one's friends live and flourish. We know this wish from our friendships with the living. Nothing is more familiar. Few things are more important. But can we be friends with the dead?

The idea is puzzling, paradoxical even. It also seems suspiciously close to an older form of traditionalism that more enlightened views have swept away. Is it possible at this late date for us, the children of enlightenment, to be friends with the dead, as Machiavelli—that most irreverent of thinkers—seems to have been? Or is the idea just a ghost from the past?

# II

The essence of friendship is a concern for the friend's well-being. We want this for the friend's sake, not our own.[9] The concern engenders responsibilities. But what can it mean to care for the dead for their own sake? The suggestion seems incoherent and dangerous to boot. It distracts us from our only real obligations, which are to the living and the unborn. Thomas Jefferson puts the point bluntly. "The earth," he says, "belongs in usufruct to the living. . . . The dead have neither powers nor rights over it."[10] If we accept Jefferson's view, as many today do, the question of what it means to befriend the dead hardly seems intelligible at all.

The modern thinker who most passionately defended the idea of such a friendship and most enthusiastically approved the duties it implies was Edmund Burke. Burke believed that even we, the inhabitants of a liberal and enlightened age, have reason to treat our ancestors with the solicitude we show our living friends. He defended this belief against the progressive ideals of the French Revolution and the deeper currents of thought it represented.[11]

This was the heart of Burke's conservatism. Some remain sympathetic to it. For them, the idea that we owe the dead our affectionate care still has resonance and appeal. A growing number, though, side with Jefferson. They consider Burke's views deeply suspect. His sharpest critics regard Burke's friendship for the dead with something approaching moral disgust.

The now-ubiquitous debate over "monumentalization" illustrates this clash of views.[12] To whom among our ancestors should monuments be raised or allowed to stand? What are the standards by which we ought to distribute honor in the land of the dead? Every iteration of the question has its own specific context and raises issues peculiar to it. But there is a division of sentiment that runs through them all. How one weighs the facts in any particular setting depends on the mood in which one approaches them.

Some do so in a Burkean spirit. They incline to the view that the dead have a prima facie claim to our loyalty and affection. They do not approve every monument to every soldier, politician, or poet just because it happens to exist. No reasonable person refuses to recognize the distinction between those who are worthy of honor and those who are not, among the dead as well as the living. But the sense that we owe the dead some measure of selfless care, as we do our living friends, even when they are compromised and imperfect, defines a tone that distinguishes these latter-day Burkeans from their enlightened critics who see little value in such an attitude and think it morally confused.

In the critics' view, our relations with the dead depend on their moral performance alone. They are to be judged by the principles of justice and virtue we use to weigh all human acts and aspirations. No special significance should be attached to the accidental position they occupy in the sequence of generations. The mere fact of being dead has no moral meaning of its own.

Whatever other disagreements separate the defenders of memorials from those who would replace or tear them down, a general inclination to the Burkean view, on the one hand, and an enlightened contempt for it, on the other, reflects a difference of orientation that shapes the more particular judgments that disputes of this kind necessarily involve. The authority of the latter view is growing. Many powerful philosophical arguments can be mustered on its behalf. Is there anything to be said on the other side?

Not, I think, in the stern old Roman spirit of the *Aeneid*. We long ago ceased to be Roman. If we are still moved by the Roman idea of piety, it is as a literary invention. Virgil's poem and Bernini's statue thrill us as works of art. But Aeneas's reverence for his ancestors is remote from modern values. We enjoy it aesthetically but reject it morally, as we do the murderous rage of Achilles.

Burke's devotion to the dead at times has a Roman look. Loyalty, reverence, and tradition are important values in his political imagination. Still, they fall far short of the worshipful determination that Aeneas represents. Burke's conservatism is not an ancestor cult. He believed that friendship toward the dead is compatible with an enlightened ideal of constitutional self-rule and what he calls a "rational and manly freedom."[13]

Yet many find even Burke's more tempered piety indefensible. Loyalty to the dead? Obliged to look after them as we do our living friends? The analogy seems strained—and morally dubious. Machiavelli's friendly concern for the ancient authors who await him in his study seems questionable too. His ambassadorial robes look like an affectation. Yes, we can learn from the dead—their lives and works are a repository of useful experiments. We owe them an impartial hearing before the tribunal of justice. But do we owe them anything more?

Burke has an answer to this question. In the end, though, it falls short. The path to a better answer begins by identifying the deficiency of the one that Burke suggests.

## III

We share the world with other living human beings near and far. We owe them many things, depending on the nature and proximity of our relation to them. We have duties to the unborn as well. We owe them a world in good repair. More basically, we owe them a *world*. Today it is in our power to make the planet uninhabitable—to ensure that it will never again be a home for human beings.

There are endless difficulties in defining with precision our obligations to the living and the unborn. There are also complex trade-offs between them. Are the living morally required to make sacrifices so that their descendants will have better lives?[14] But the question of what we owe those in both groups makes sense only because we can *do something* to make them better off. We can improve the lives of the living and prepare a cleaner, saner, more welcoming world for those who will succeed us.

The dead are different. Their lives are finished. However disgraceful the conditions under which they lived, however regrettable their suffering, the dead are beyond our power to help or heal. We are only witnesses to what they did and suffered. It is meaningless to speak of obligations to the dead—whether of friendship or anything else.

Or so it might appear. A famous passage in Burke's *Reflections on the Revolution in France* suggests another view.[15]

One of the first and most leading principles on which the commonwealth and the laws are consecrated is lest the temporary possessors and life-renters in it, unmindful of what they have received from their ancestors, or of what is due to their posterity, should act as if they were the entire masters; that they should not think it amongst their rights to cut off the entail, or commit waste on the inheritance, by destroying at their pleasure the whole original fabric of their society; hazarding to leave to those who come after them, a ruin instead of an habitation—and teaching these successors as little to respect their contrivances, as they had themselves respected the institutions of their forefathers. By this unprincipled facility of changing the state as often, and as much, and in as many ways as there are floating fancies or fashions, the whole chain and continuity of the commonwealth would be broken. No one generation could link with the other. Men would become little better than the flies of a summer.

"Society," Burke says a little later on, is "a contract ... between those who are dead, those who are living, and those who are to be born."[16]

The terms of the contract are easy to state. The living, who at any given moment occupy the world, depend on their successors to protect and perfect the projects they have begun. A woman has spent years saving to buy a house on a lake and more years renovating and furnishing it. She wants to leave it to her children and makes a provision to that effect in her will. The prospect of their enjoying the house after she is gone is a source of present satisfaction that depends on the belief that her bequest will be honored. This in turn rests on her assumption that the legal order will remain intact—that her successors, including those who are not yet alive, will respect and obey the law. Her present fulfillment depends on the fidelity of the unborn.

This is even more obviously true when an undertaking cannot be completed in a single lifetime but depends on the efforts of others yet to come. Building a cathedral is a famous example; interpreting the words of a written constitution is another.[17] Science is like this as well. So too, perhaps, is art.

The investments of the living do not become completely worthless if they know or believe that their successors will not honor or add to them. Even if she is convinced that the world will descend into anarchy shortly after she dies, the woman with the lakeside home has reason to buy and improve it. She wants to get as much enjoyment out of it as she can while she is alive. It will be less than she experiences sitting on the deck, imagining her grandchildren watching sunsets she no longer sees. But it will not be nothing. Similarly, even if I believe that no one will pick up my research when I am gone, I have reason to pursue it for the sake of my own understanding, though the pleasure is sharply reduced.

The point may be expressed in economic terms. The return the living make on their investments is increased if they can count on the support of the unborn. To get as large a return as possible, they must be able to rely on their successors to respect and protect what they have done. This is the forward-looking side of Burke's contract among the generations. The backward-looking side follows directly.

There is little we can do to bind the unborn. If they choose to disregard us, we have no power of enforcement. We can try to constrain them in all sorts of ways, but they are free to ignore these constraints as well. What we can do is set a good example by treating our predecessors with the same respect we hope our successors will show us. As an economist might say, this sends a strong *signal*.[18] By limiting their own freedom to deny their duties to the dead, the living show, in the most compelling way they can, that the preservation of the human world from one generation to the next is a condition of maximizing whatever satisfaction any generation is able to extract from it.

In this way, the contract becomes self-enforcing. It can never be strictly so because each generation is free to disregard it. There is no power standing above the generations that is in a position to punish defectors. Signaling to the unborn that we depend on their support by providing our own to the dead is the best that we can do.

The second is not "consideration" for the first, in the technical sense we use the term in the law of contracts.[19] It is better, perhaps, to call it a pledge or a form of security, though even this is not entirely accurate since the pledge cannot be redeemed. Still, despite its insecurity, Burke thinks the pledge supremely important—a condition of any life even remotely human, as distinct from the lives of flies that live only for a summer and, never advancing, begin each generation at exactly the same point.

This is a reasonable argument. But it does not answer the question of whether we can be friends with the dead. It does not show that our relations with them can or ought to rest on a spirit of affectionate care. That is because like all economic arguments, this one relies on self-interest alone. If friendship figures in it, it does so only in a derivative way, as an attitude we ought to cultivate for our own well-being and not someone else's—which contradicts the spirit of friendship itself.

One person makes a contract with another not because he is directly concerned with the other's welfare. Each seeks to advance his or her own and uses the other's symmetrical motive as a means to do so. A contract is a collaboration among self-interested parties. It makes no difference if they also happen to be friends or work to foster friendly relations as a means of strengthening their contractual ties.

The same is true even if we imagine the contract to be one among the generations. At any given moment, only the living are in a position to affirm the contract and act on it. They also have the strongest motive for doing so. But their motive (on the account I have given of Burke's views) is entirely self-serving. The living pay the price of respecting the plans and projects of the dead *in order that* the unborn will respect theirs in turn. It is for their own benefit that they honor those who went before them.

If friendship with the dead means anything at all, it must mean more than this. It must mean helping the dead for their sake, not ours—in the way our friendships with the living do. But how can we possibly help the dead? Self-interest seems to be the only basis for our relation with those who have passed beyond our power to help or hurt. Perhaps Burke's contractual explanation of our responsibilities to the dead is the only one we have.

# IV

Burke's belief that we owe the dead our friendly care rests on a sound intuition, but his use of the idea of a contract to explain it is incomplete and unsatisfying. Is there a better explanation? We can start by considering more closely the conditions of friendship in general.

Sometimes we choose our friends. Often we stumble upon them. People become friends for countless reasons. Broadly speaking, though, there are two conditions on which every friendship depends. The first is that one's friend be an individual human being. One may be passionately devoted to a principle or program. This is a kind of partiality too, but not the sort that friendship implies.

The second is that friends have something in common. What they share may be an interest, an experience, a history, a feeling, or a belief. The possibilities are endless. But the less two people share, the less likely they are to be friends.[20]

Among the living, these two conditions are satisfied on a very wide scale. The challenge is to find or make a few friends among the many who might be. Where the conditions are not met, though, friendship is impossible. This becomes important when we turn from the living to the unborn and the dead. Here a striking asymmetry emerges.

"The unborn" is an abstraction. It comprises all those who might be. None has yet emerged into the concreteness of existence. None has a distinct identity. We have duties toward the unborn but not the sort of tangible relation on which friendly affection depends (and loathing or hatred as well). Nor do we share much in common with them. The unborn might never be born at all, in which case we will share with them no more than we do with those whose existence is merely hypothetical.

"The dead" is not an abstraction in the same way. The dead have lived and carry with them the vividness of the living. It fades but never disappears. The land of the dead is filled with personalities. Each has, or had, a name, unknown to us, perhaps, but assignable, marking a specific place on the ever-lengthening register of those who have preceded us in the business of living.

We also share more in common with them than we do with the unborn. We live in the shadow of death. All we do derives its meaning from the mortal frame that encloses our lives and gives them a significance they would not have if life went on forever or we were unaware that death is coming. The dead had this experience too. They knew what it means to know that one will die. They knew what it means to be human. The unborn will as well, if they are ever born, but the humanity we share with them is strictly conjectural.

The dead, by contrast, have left us a record of their mortality—of their hopes and regrets, their fulfillments and defeats, their ambitions and disappointments, in the form that human beings alone experience these things. The dead are our real, if departed, companions in the venture of life. The concreteness of their lives reminds us of what we have in common with them. When we turn our eyes ahead to the legions of the unborn, this sense of commonality vanishes into the thinness of an idea, separated from the conditions on which all human friendship depends.

Among the living, we have more in common with some than with others. They are special candidates for friendship, whether we befriend them or not. The same is true of the dead. Here another asymmetry between the dead and the unborn becomes apparent.

In the first place, there are our ancestors—our parents, our parents' parents, and so on back in time. We generally take a particular interest in them. As a rule, we are more warmly disposed toward our ancestors than to others to whom we have no family connection. We feel we ought to look after them with special care—to remember them and make the most of what they did or left undone. The feeling may fail. Some children hate their parents and want to forget them. They are disgraced by their family past. But we do not begin from a point of neutrality as we do with strangers. Where our ancestors are concerned, we generally start with a feeling of care. We may lose or reject it, but it serves as a kind of default.

The feeling is not limited to family. We experience it, in a weakened form, for those who went before us in the political communities to which we belong. We no more choose them than we do our parents. They are given to us, as a kind of fate, along with life itself. Care is a default here as well.

It is more easily overcome in the case of our political ancestors, though how easily is a matter of dispute. Choice certainly plays a larger role here. We can choose a new country more easily than we can a new family. Still, among all the human beings in the world, those who built and sustained the way of life we have inherited have a special claim on our affection, even if in the end we conclude they do not deserve it.

The same is true of our institutional ancestors: those who labored to create and protect the institutions we voluntarily join as adults. I did not inherit my predecessors on the Yale faculty the way I did my great-grandparents or the Framers of the Constitution. I acquired them wholly by choice. Still, I had no power to decide who they would be. They also were given to me as a destiny of sorts. I do not feel affection for them all or believe I ought to honor each one's memory. Yet affection and care are presumptions in this setting too. Those who belonged to the Yale faculty a hundred years ago lie for me in the penumbra of ancestry, whose densest zone is that of family life. They have a rebuttable claim to my friendly attention. The same is true, even more remotely, of all the long-dead philosophers, poets, and historians who built the civilization of the West, which is part of my inheritance too—the authors of the books in Machiavelli's study.

The unborn are different. We certainly have responsibilities toward them, but they are not (yet) concrete men and women. Nor do we (yet) share with them the pathos of mortality. With the dead, the conditions of friendship are met. That is why it is possible for us to view a few of them with friendly care. When we look ahead to the unborn, these conditions vanish and it becomes harder to pick out those for whom we feel a special affection.

In *A Theory of Justice*, John Rawls raises the question of what the living owe the unborn. Do we have a duty to share the resources of the earth with them? Like every question of distributive fairness, this one must be settled, Rawls says, by asking what those behind his fictional "veil of ignorance" would say about it.[21]

To ensure they have a motive to care about the welfare of later generations, he suggests that each of those behind the veil think of him- or herself as the head of a long family line, stretching far into the future, with an obligation to represent its interests in the imaginary congress that has gathered to choose lasting principles of justice.[22] It is a revealing proposal. It recognizes our human partiality toward those close to us in blood and the psychological need to clothe the unborn with some semblance of intimacy in order to make our duties to them vivid and compelling. But the special loyalty we feel toward the unborn members of our families (if we do indeed feel it) lacks the individuality of the affection we feel for their living and dead counterparts. It is not clear that it can be called a form of friendship at all.

The minute she was born, my youngest granddaughter became a candidate for friendship. She became an individual who shares my mortal condition. This is the meaning of the old saw that birth is the beginning of dying.

Perhaps this happened a bit before, when she was still in utero, and a sonogram allowed me to see the features of her face. Perhaps it happened at conception, though "friendship" is an odd word to describe my feelings at that stage. But before conception there is no possibility of friendship at all, even if (as Rawls assumes) I feel a general partiality toward my descendants.

Birth is the threshold of friendship. It marks the moment at which the conditions of friendship are met, though it takes time for friendship to ripen and evolve. And what of death? Does it erase these conditions? Those who are dead still have an individual identity. They bear the mark of mortal experience—the one we are now having. Even after death we share this experience with them. If birth creates the conditions of friendship, death does not extinguish them or eliminate the special ties we have to some among the many who have ever lived.

Still, this only shows that it is *possible* to be friends with the dead. It says nothing about the nature of this friendship or its value. "Friendship with the dead": the phrase has a suggestive ring. It touches what Lincoln called the "mystic chords of memory."[23] But perhaps it is only a rhetorical flourish. Readers of Burke, in particular, may be forgiven for being suspicious. Few have written with so many flourishes.

Yet Burke's insight was sound. Without our friendship for those who have already died, we are indeed the "flies of a summer." Friendship with the dead is more than a posture that serves our present needs or a signal we send to the future. It is part of what it takes—of what it means—to live a human life. It is an element of our humanity.

## V

To see why, we must distinguish the idea of friendship with the dead from two other attitudes toward them. Both are more familiar. Each is easier to define. But neither is consistent with the experience of friendship or capable of sustaining the special human values that friendships of every kind honor and protect.

The first attitude is that of devotion. The dead have bequeathed to us the world we inhabit and enjoy. This is enough, in the view of some, to hallow the dead. It entitles them to our loyalty and obliges us to conserve their memory. Gratitude and piety belong in this orbit. Aeneas is its classical representative.

The second is moral approval, or, more often today, disapproval. The respect we owe the dead depends on the values they held and the actions they performed. The values *we* hold are the benchmark by which we make this judgment. This is not a choice but a necessity. What other values could we possibly use to weigh the beliefs and conduct of the dead than the ones we now embrace?

According to those who take this second view, whether our ancestors deserve loyalty and affection depends on their moral standing. Only the dead who did the right thing, or suffered at the hands of those who did the wrong one, are worthy of being remembered with care. It is to them alone that we owe anything at all.

Neither of these attitudes is compatible with the idea of friendship or expresses what is most distinctive about it. If they were the only ways we have of relating to the dead, we could never be friends with them. Our friendships with the living make this clear.

These are generally constrained by the belief that our friends are decent human beings. When this belief falters, friendship may as well. By contrast, Aeneas's piety is unconditional. It can never be weakened or destroyed. Our living friendships are subject to moral review. They are not founded on a spirit of reverence. This is the (limited) truth of the second, morally judgmental point of view.

By the same token, though, we do not hold our friends to the meticulous moral accounting to which some believe we ought to hold the dead. We forgive our friends their minor transgressions and often continue to hope that major ones will be corrected. Most of the time we do not view our friends in a moral light at all. We share an endless variety of interests and worries with them—in-laws, careers, vacation plans, diets, illnesses, feelings, the state of the world—but are less often concerned with the moral propriety of their behavior. Certain acts are beyond the pale. But when moral judgment becomes the steady, dominant attitude in a relationship, friendship is often at an end. Moral censoriousness destroys it. This is the (limited) truth of the first point of view—of the belief that loyalty and affection depend on something other than the friend's compliance with our moral judgments.

These are negative conclusions. They remind us of what friendship is *not*. But our friendships with the living have a positive dimension as well—one that throws light on what it means to befriend the dead and explains why this peculiar form of friendship is important to our fulfillment as human beings.

Our friends have various goals; there are things they hope or want to do. One hopes to go on a cruise; she has never been to sea. Another wants to learn to play the piano; it is a lifelong dream. I am eager for them to succeed. I may have no interest in these things myself—perhaps I get seasick or find piano music boring—but this makes no difference. It is not *my* interests that matter but my friends'. I hope they succeed because it will make *them* happy.

Many of my friends' goals are attainable. They may be challenging and take time. Accidents sometimes spoil their plans. But there is no reason why, in principle, they cannot succeed. Going on a cruise is an example. Mastering the piano well enough to play a few tunes is another.

Some of my friends' goals, though, are not attainable even in principle. Fully mastering a complex subject—any subject—is a goal of this kind. Even for a master, there is always more to learn. When he was eighty-three, Pablo Casals was asked why he continued to practice the cello four hours a day. "Because I think I am making progress," he answered.[24] The most that we can hope for friends engaged in such pursuits is that their power and competence continue to grow.

Among these unattainable goals, one is of particular importance, not because it always takes precedence over others (generally it does not) but because it reflects a longing that human beings of the greatest diversity share, whatever specific aims and interests set them apart. It is a universal human yearning. It is the longing to know oneself.

Self-knowledge is not the same as consistency, harmony, or balance. Consistency is a condition of self-knowledge. A person who acts with no consistency at all—who does one thing one day and the opposite the next—may lack the minimal psychic coherence that the pursuit of self-knowledge requires. His condition is unstable, perhaps even diseased. But consistency is not a guarantee of self-knowledge. It cannot be, because no human being is ever perfectly consistent.

We all contain multitudes. We each have conflicting wishes, desires, and fears and continually contradict ourselves.[25] To be rid of my conflicts and contradictions, I would have to be someone else—or no one at all. My conflicts make me who I am. They define my individuality as one human being among countless many. Without consistency, I have no identity. With too much, I have none that is distinctively mine.

I can settle the conflicts in my soul only by ceasing to be who I am. Still, it is possible to hope for a better understanding of them—for a deeper knowledge of myself, not as a human being in general, but as an individual unlike any other in the world. This is a lifelong pursuit that no one ever completes. We are always on the way and die with loose ends.

Every bit of progress we make toward a knowledge of ourselves, though, is an important good. Other things often take precedence—caring for our children, for example, or our country. These demand immediate attention. But the good of knowing who we are never disappears. It is always there, waiting for the right moment. In a calm hour, if we are lucky enough to have one, we recall it.

This is a distinctively modern ideal. It has no counterpart in the ethical systems of pagan antiquity. For Plato and Aristotle, fulfillment means conformity to a type. In their view, the self-knowing human being is one who fits a model—who possesses certain general traits. Before self-knowledge in the modern sense can become a value, individuality must emerge from the formalism of Greek metaphysics as something real and worthy in its own right. We stand at the end of this long and complex development and today live in a world that values the uniqueness of individuals—ethically, politically, and aesthetically—in a way that Plato and Aristotle would have found incomprehensible. The meaning and worth of self-knowledge have been radically reconceived as a result.[26]

This has important implications for the ethics of friendship. If self-knowledge is a good for me, it is for my friend too. I want her to make progress toward a fuller understanding of who *she* is. I wish my friend to have the self-understanding that suits *her*, in the way I wish her success in reaching other goals that are inspired by interests I do not share.

Yet even if my friend must find the way to self-knowledge for herself, I can help her along it, just as I can help her reach other, more mundane goals. I can listen, question, urge, warn, challenge, and encourage in a spirit meant to help her on the way—for her sake, not mine. This is part of what being a friend means.

Friendship is more than this, of course. It involves many less elusive forms of support (finding a reputable cruise line or a good piano teacher; visiting the hospital; sharing a meal; watching a movie together). But help in the pursuit of self-knowledge is a dimension of friendship too—one whose value is obscured but not refuted by the infrequency and indirectness with which help of this kind is needed and offered.

# VI

This is an abstract conclusion. To better understand it, we might consider a special form of friendship in which the pursuit of self-knowledge is the principal motive for the friendship itself. I am thinking of the relation between psychoanalyst and patient.

Their friendship is oddly constrained. It does not exist outside the analytic hour. Even within that rigidly demarcated period, their relation does not have the free-ranging and bilateral character of most friendships. The focus is on the patient alone, and while the analyst and patient may discuss all sorts of things, every exchange between them is directed by an exclusive concern with the patient's well-being. It is also bought. The patient pays for the analyst's time.

Still, the relation is a friendly one. The patient is suffering. His life is troubled; it is not going as well as he wishes and he has come to the analyst for help. He has agreed to pay the analyst but expects more than expert advice. He wants sympathy and concern. If these are missing, the relation will fail. The analyst's friendship is a condition of success. For the patient to make any progress toward a more satisfying life, he must believe that the analyst is on his side—that she takes an interest in his welfare. And for him to believe this, she must really care for the patient for the patient's own sake. She has to be his friend.

The patient's anxieties, phobias, and compulsions, his sense of inner turmoil and outward failure, have, Freud says, a common cause. They are all the result of repression. The patient has had experiences earlier in his life that he has chosen to forget. He has pushed them below the threshold of conscious memory.[27] Their effects have not disappeared—nothing disappears from our mental life—but they have been cut off, isolated, surrounded with the protective apparatus of forgetfulness.[28] The result is a lack of self-knowledge.

The analyst helps the patient achieve a greater measure of it. This is the point of their relation. It is what the relation is *for.* She does this by guiding the patient in a process of recollection whose goal is restoring to memory what the patient has repressed. The result is not some simple, well-adjusted harmony—a calm and unruffled uniformity of feeling that has no tensions or dissensions within it. This is not only unattainable, it is undesirable. The wish for such harmony is itself a childish fantasy. The self-knowledge toward which the analyst helps her patient is something more mature: the patient's increasing understanding and acceptance of the peculiar course of suffering and disappointment and the many adjustments he has made to it that makes him who he is—one individual among others, responding in his own idiosyncratic way to the vicissitudes of the human condition.

The analyst helps the patient toward greater self-knowledge by allowing him to reenact in their relation the buried traumas of his life and slowly, patiently, in an affectionate way, bringing these reenactments to his conscious attention so that he can experience again, in the friendly milieu of the analytic hour, what for a long time has been too disturbing to recall. Freud calls this "acting out."[29] It enables the patient to transfer to his relation with the analyst the patterns of avoidance and adaptation that formed in response to feelings the patient has repressed, and, by bringing these to light in this present relation, to see his life in a way he could not before.

This is the secret of what Freud calls "transference"—the mechanism by which the special friendship between analyst and patient promotes the latter's self-knowledge.[30] Other friendships do this in a more episodic, bilateral, and less deliberate way. The psychoanalytic relation that Freud discovered, or rather invented, is of particular interest because it highlights this feature of friendship in a dramatic fashion.

In a remarkable essay elaborating on a brief remark in *The Interpretation of Dreams*, the psychoanalyst Hans Loewald likens the process of reenactment and transference that takes place in the analyst's office to the experience of Odysseus in book XI of the *Odyssey*.[31] Odysseus has been told by the enchantress Circe that he must visit the world of the dead to seek advice from the prophet Tiresias about his journey home. When he arrives in the underworld, Odysseus finds himself surrounded by mute shades. To get them to speak, he makes a blood sacrifice. The dead taste life again; they find their voices and can speak for a short while. This resembles the analytic relation, Loewald says. The patient's real, present relation with his analyst is the blood he needs to make the ghosts of his past speak—to bring his dead and buried feelings back to life.

The transaction between living and dead with which analyst and patient are concerned is one that exists within the patient's own soul. To illustrate this intrapsychic relation, Loewald employs a story about an exchange between a man from the land of the living and those who dwell below the earth in the realm of shades. What is the meaning of this story for our relations with those who are really dead? This is the question toward which we have been moving all along.

To answer it, we must try to see how the pursuit of self-knowledge, which lies at the heart of the psychoanalytic relation, bears on our connection not just to the dead within us but to others who are no longer alive. The proposal seems strange. How can we help the dead to a better understanding of themselves? Yet the ambition is more familiar and appealing than it looks. It is the inspiration for the work of biography, which is defined neither by piety nor moral judgment but a species of friendship instead.

# VII

Every living human being is someone's child, parent, friend, neighbor, or acquaintance. While we live, we are never completely anonymous. That comes only after death. Most of the dead are invisible in a special and permanent way.

Even among our ancestors, most are lost from view. Few can trace their families back five generations; none can trace them fifty. The Americans who lived in Boston in 1675; who fought at Antietam; the Jews and Italians huddled in Gilded Age slums; the black slaves who lived and labored and died on the plantations of the South: I know they all existed, but most are nameless blanks. And these are just my American ancestors! Beyond them the dead stretch out in an endless, faceless crowd.

Here and there a few stand out because they did something remarkable. Their lives are like flashes of lightning in the night. These are the great ones, the riveting exceptions. Sometimes, not always, their greatness is worth honoring. We consider them paragons of excellence or virtue. We do more than remember their lives; we celebrate them as models of human achievement.

None of us can do without models of this kind in our personal lives. No community can survive for long without them. But honoring is not the same as befriending, in our relations with the dead any more than in our relations with the living.

Among the living, it is neither a condition nor a consequence of friendship that we regard our friends as outstanding examples of excellence or virtue. We are more likely to confuse friendship and moral esteem in our relations with the dead. That is because the role a few of them play as aspirational models of achievement or virtue is often the main and sometimes the only reason we remember them at all. Even in the land of the dead, though, veneration and friendship are not the same. Biography highlights the difference between them.

There are, of course, biographies of monsters and saints. These mark the boundaries of the genre. Even here, though, a good biographer's aim is not wholly or even mainly moralistic. It is less to condemn or honor than to understand. How did Hitler—a man with common phobias and longings—become the uncommon tyrant he was?[32] How did Gandhi, who struggled with ordinary human desires, rise to levels of superhuman self-control?[33] Even here, at the limits of human failure and success, the biographer is neither a hagiographer nor a hamartographer (a cataloguer of error and sin) but something else.

This is clearest in intermediate cases—in the biographies of those who may command our attention because of the extraordinary things they did or said, but whose personalities reflect the mixture of virtue and vice, folly and wisdom, loyalty and betrayal, self-sacrifice and self-absorption that are typical of less remarkable lives, including our own. What is the biographer of such a life hoping to accomplish?

Robert Caro's still-unfinished biography of Lyndon Johnson is a good example.[34] Here he is: the ambitious young schoolteacher, the rising politician, then master of the Senate; warmhearted, cruel, empathetic, bigoted, unprincipled, charming, loyal, manipulative, and in the end, a great and tragic president. What is the point of this astonishingly complex portrait that sees all, ignores nothing, and refuses to arrange Johnson's contradictions in a neater scheme than his life allows?

It is neither adulation nor condemnation. Caro offers moral judgments along the way, both favorable and not, but judging Johnson is not his principal aim. Nor is his goal to present his subject's life with scientific sangfroid, as a kind of specimen, in the way an entomologist might describe an exotic bug.

Caro's biography is disciplined and detached. It is not motivated by partisan passion, but neither is it indifferent. It is animated by palpable affection for its subject. Caro is not dazzled or deluded by Johnson, as many of his acquaintances were. But he cares for Johnson, as a friend might, in the peculiarly one-sided way that, among the living, a psychoanalyst cares for her patient.

An analyst seeks to help her patient better understand his life as a whole—as more of a whole, at least, since none of us ever sees him- or herself completely. The biographer's subject is beyond help of this kind. Still, his goal is not dissimilar.

"As a whole" does not mean "without contradictions." There is no human wholeness of that kind. Nor does it mean "in the best light"—as a life imagined in accordance with its most attractive features, struggling, as it were, to break free of its limitations and disabilities, so that, conceived in this way, the life of the subject becomes in retrospect a faulty realization of something more perfect than itself.

Viewed "as a whole" means as a singular adventure, with more complexity than can be captured in any simple theme—a life punctuated by experiences of indecision, betrayal, and self-doubt—self-loathing, even—that are devalued or denied when the life is redescribed in the light of a guiding ideal, whether it be the biographer's own or what he imagines to have been the ideal his subject was imperfectly striving to reach.

The best biographies do not leave the contradictions out. They do not polish the rough edges away and leave an ideal in its place, like the schoolbook portraits of Abraham Lincoln and Martin Luther King that we are taught to admire. This is hero worship. It has a place in every civic culture, but it is not good biography or even biography at all.

Examples abound. I have mentioned Robert Caro's biography of Lyndon Johnson. Another is Ray Monk's life of Robert Oppenheimer—brilliant, inventive, narcissistic, insecure.[35] An older one is Gibbon's unforgettable portrait of Julian the Apostate—wise, pious, learned, impetuous, doomed.[36] A third is the biography of Muhammad Asad, born Leopold Weiss—the Polish Jew who converted to Islam, translated the Quran, and inspired the radical Islamism of Sayyid Qutb and others: a life of spiritual depth, determined fidelity, rootlessness, and betrayal.[37] I mention these because I have been thinking about them lately. The difficulty is not finding examples. It is explaining what they mean.

Unlike a psychoanalyst, a biographer who wants to write the life of a person who has died cannot put questions to his subject and wait for a reply. There can be no conversation like the one that takes place in the analyst's office. The biographer "questions" the material his subject leaves behind, but he has to provide the answers as well. The relation between biographer and subject is even more one-sided than that between analyst and patient. Yet writing a biography is an act of friendship too.

We want to succeed; we want to reach our goals and live up to our ideals. But we also want to know who we are. We want to see ourselves clearly, through the mist of illusion and self-serving invention. We want this not (just) as an aid to reform but in part, at least, because honesty is something we prize for itself.[38]

The forms of dishonesty are legion. None of us escapes them completely. They all lead away from the complex being one *is* to something simpler, cleaner, easier to understand and accept. This always entails a loss of reality. We accept it as a condition of life. But there is a kind of deadening in it—a turning away from what is objectionable, disturbing, and obscure in oneself.

The psychoanalyst helps her patient bring the dead parts of his soul back to life. She helps the patient be more *real*. This is the gift of honesty the analyst brings to their relation. It is a gift of friendship because the motive for it is the patient's welfare, not the analyst's own.

Something similar is true of biography. Here, the familiar concerns that one friend typically has for another have vanished completely: the wish for prosperity and success; for physical health and intimate happiness; for the teasing, relaxed, serious, and lighthearted pleasure of each other's company. All that remains is the wish that the subject be real—and here, as on the analyst's couch, the gift that fulfills the wish, to the limited extent it can, is that of honest speech.

But for whom is the gift made? For the subject? How can that be? It seems more reasonable to say that the gift is made for the benefit of everyone *but* the subject—for the biographer himself and his reading public. Yet this is not entirely true.

Life demands dishonesty. We need our fictions in order to live. In any case, death terminates with implacable finality our limited power to be honest with ourselves.

But it does not change the fact that while we live, we long to know ourselves, however compromised or mutilated the longing may be. The biographer surveys his subject's life from beyond the grave. He is in a position to see it as a finished whole—a perspective the analyst lacks. This is an important distinction. Still, like the analyst's questions, the biographer's researches serve the human longing to be real. In the case of the analyst's patient, the longing is blocked or repressed. For the biographer's subject, it is buried once and for all. Yet, like the analyst, the biographer gives his subject something he wanted and could not find on his own.

A woman visits her unconscious friend in the hospital. She sits for hours reading quietly, then goes home. She brings the gift of her company, not for her sake alone, though it may increase her peace of mind, but for her friend's as well.

When his subject is dead, a biographer's gift is less obvious. It has no exact counterpart in the land of the living. It is a gift the living can *only* make to the dead. But the friendly concern for another that inspires the biographer's work is as real as that of the woman who sits by the hospital bed.

Who are we, really? We wonder but never know. Only our successors are in a position to say. They extend our search for wholeness, honesty, *reality* when we no longer can. They extend our lives, not as prototypes to be admired and copied but as individuals, "no two alike and every one good."[39] This is the biographer's gift of life. He and his readers draw satisfaction from it. It is not a selfish satisfaction but the pleasure of joining in a special act of friendship that is possible only because its beneficiary is no longer alive.

When the frenzy of life is over; when the need for fantasy and fiction is gone; after the quiet of death descends, there is finally time for honesty. Some think they want to be remembered for the good they did. A few are. But the desire for fame corrupts honesty while we live and nearly always clouds it after we die.

Honesty is what we get if we are lucky; freed from the passion for admiration, it remains as the quieter longing to know who we are. It cannot be fulfilled while we live, so we depend on those who come after us for help. In their biographies we live again, a more honest and real existence than we can achieve by ourselves. How paradoxical that sounds! That we become more real after we die? Yet it is so, for those fortunate enough to attract a biographer's attention and receive the friendly gift of being seen as a whole, living on not as abstractions, as august figures raised above "the fury and the mire of human veins," but as individual human beings with unique careers of their own.[40]

Generally speaking, only those who stand out from the crowd attract such attention. The biographer's gift of an honest afterlife is something rare. Good biographies are rarer still. The spirit of biography, though, is not limited to the writing of biographies in the narrow sense.

A woman who remembers her dead parents as whole human beings, or strives to; who neither blames them for their faults nor reveres them for their virtues; who feels the need to preserve the memory of their lives, with all their contradictions, not in a spirit of clinical detachment, as a vivisectionist might, but with friendship tempered by distance, bringing to her parents' grave the gift of an honest appraisal that none of us can ever achieve while we live—dissembling, pretending, and polishing our selves into something simpler and better—a woman who thinks about her parents in this way does so in the spirit of biography. And while biographies are exceptional, her attitude is not.

Many of us strive to see our parents in this light and, to the extent we are able, more remote ancestors too. This takes time and effort and materials to study. These may be largely or completely missing. But those who undertake a study of this sort are generally motivated by more than curiosity. They wish that the dead be remembered as human beings who once were mortal like us, once felt the turmoil we now do, and whose lives were no more of a piece than our own.

This is a friendly wish. Everyone who has tried to construct a family genealogy knows it. The greatest biographies exemplify it to a striking degree. But the wish itself covers a wider territory. At the limit, it extends, in a diluted way, to the whole of the land of the dead. All those who have ever lived deserve a great biography, even if few receive one. They deserve the honest afterlife that only their successors can give them.

## VIII

"What do we owe the dead?" It is an old question. I propose the following answer, in the spirit of Freud and Burke.

We do not owe the dead our pious devotion. They were human beings, not gods. But neither do we owe them merely the right to appear before the bar of our better-informed moral judgments and be found guilty or innocent according to prevailing norms. We owe them our friendship, nothing more, but also nothing less. We owe the dead our affectionate companionship as fellow human beings who, like us, were once perplexed by life's contrary passions and now, in the stillness of death, can with our help find the honesty and self-knowledge that no living man or woman can attain or even afford.

We live in an age that sneers at the Roman reverence for the past. That is gone forever. Few today think it can or should be revived. But the loss of reverence has swept away with it the different and defensible belief that we can and must be friends with the dead. This has been discredited in the rush to convert the past to a storehouse of utilities that we are free to treat without affection or care as we rummage through it in search of whatever we need to accomplish whatever we choose to pursue.

This is the view expressed by Jefferson's declaration that "the earth belongs in usufruct to the living." Burke fought against it with all his intellectual and expressive powers. He was persuaded that when our affectionate connection to the dead is lost, our humanity is diminished. He was right about this, though his use of the language of contract to explain the nature and importance of the loss is a forced and in some ways misleading way of describing the bond of friendship that joins us to the dead.

Friendship for the dead may not be a precondition of friendship with the living. But it is not unconnected to it either. Those who say that the dead must be piously worshipped and those who insist they be summoned before the court of prevailing opinion acquire habits of mind that in opposing ways are uncongenial to the spirit of friendship in general. Their capacity for friendship declines—not just with the dead but with other living human beings and, strange as it may sound, themselves as well.

These latter sorts of friendship depend on a combination of honesty and generosity that reverence and censoriousness rule out. The person who either worships her friends or holds them to unflagging moral account withholds the gift that only a friend can bestow. If she proudly exalts her own perfection or ruthlessly condemns herself because she believes she has never once done anything right, she withholds the same gift from herself.[41] Because it is so easy to disparage or blindly revere the dead—because they are so completely in our power to befriend or not—the failure of friendly feeling looking back in their direction spreads with greater ease over the world of the living and the one we dimly discern ahead. It becomes the general disposition Burke feared.

Without friendship for the dead, our living friendships and the experience they afford of solidarity in the joyful and anguished work of self-knowing that lies at the heart of the human condition become less secure, less durable, less fulfilling, and our lives more like those of Burke's flies. This is not the loss of an asset or opportunity. It is the corruption of a condition. Who would call a life without friends fully human?[42]

We cannot help but see the world from our present point of view. But the Jeffersonians who elevate the present to a position of blinding authority and invite us to sever our affective ties to the past deride our friendship with the dead and reduce us in our own eyes to something less interesting, complex, difficult, rewarding, and ultimately less human. The work of memory is an act of friendship, not of reverent devotion, sanctimonious judgment, or self-centered exchange. If we view it in this light, we have reason to join Machiavelli as he crosses the threshold of his study and resumes his friendly dialogue with those who have long since died. We have reason to bring to the land of the dead the gift of friendship that allows them to speak, not so that we shall be well treated by our descendants in turn but because, as Burke understood, there is no "we," no human world, in the absence of an abiding care for the shades who once called it their home.

# CHAPTER FIVE

# Character and Country

## I

At the beginning of Plato's *Republic*, Socrates and his young friend Glaucon are on their way back to Athens from the harbor at Piraeus, where they had gone to see a new festival in honor of the Thracian goddess Bendis. They are intercepted by a group of acquaintances who insist they stay to see the torch-lit horseback race later that night. Together, they all go to the home of the father of one of them, a retired merchant named Cephalus, where they spend the evening in talk. It is the most famous conversation in the history of Western philosophy.[1]

After a few pleasantries, the discussion turns to the nature of justice. What does it mean to be a just person? Several answers are considered and rejected. Then one of the participants, a volatile young man named Thrasymachus, explodes with frustration and tells the others that they are all misguided idealists. Justice, he exclaims, is whatever the strong say it is.[2]

To determine whether Thrasymachus is right, Socrates makes a dramatic proposal. Let us shift our attention, he says, from justice as a quality of individuals to its nature as a property of cities. Justice is hard to see in the soul of a single person. Perhaps it will be easier to discern on a larger scale—in the arrangements of an entire community.[3] The rest of the *Republic* proceeds on the assumption that these two kinds of justice— the political and psychological—are sufficiently alike that the first can serve as a useful guide to the second.

The analogy seems plausible. Both souls and cities have different parts that inevitably clash. The challenge in each case is to fashion a durable whole out of discordant elements. The question is what kind of whole shall this be. Socrates' answer is that the best arrangement in each is one that assigns the leading role to its rational part—to the thinking part of the soul and its political analogue, a class of enlightened guardians led by a philosopher-king.[4]

It has often been observed that Socrates' argument rests on a false premise. Yes, both cities and souls have internal conflicts that must be settled or softened. But a city is composed of individuals with separate lives of their own. Its parts are independent of one another in a way those of a soul are not.[5]

Respect for the independence of individuals is an axiom of modern liberal thought. It explains the hostility to every argument that denies it—Aristotle's doctrine of natural slavery, Rousseau's theory of the "general will," and those versions of utilitarianism that treat individuals as mere vehicles for the advancement of some collective good.[6] Socrates' analogy collapses because it fails, in John Rawls's words, to "take seriously the distinction between persons."[7]

Yet many who take this distinction very seriously nevertheless believe, as Socrates did, that there is a parallel between good order in a city and in an individual soul, though they conceive the parallel in radically different terms. For Socrates, the principal conflict in our psychological and political lives is that between reason and passion. Unity is possible in either, he says, only if the intellect directs our appetites and feelings. For us, the defining tension in both is between freedom and necessity. This resembles the conflict between reason and passion but is different from it. Reason is the mind's deference to the truth—to the laws of an independently existing reality. Freedom is a power of spontaneous self-direction. It obeys only its own laws and defers to nothing but itself.[8] The idea that human beings possess a power of this kind is a by-product of biblical theology. It accompanies the belief in a God who brings the world into being from nothing in a spontaneous act of creation and endows his human creatures with a power similar to his own. Following Augustine, we conventionally call this power the *will* and distinguish it from both rational thought and bodily desire.[9]

The idea of the will as a power of spontaneous affirmation or denial lay beyond the horizon of Plato's metaphysical imagination. Greek philosophy has no place for it. The emergence and eventual triumph of this idea made it necessary to rethink every important philosophical question, including that of what constitutes a worthy and sustainable order in both cities and souls. The post-Augustinian answer is, only an order that has been freely willed by the individual or community whose order it is.

A person may give greater weight to thought than feeling or vice versa. She may care more for her country than her friends or the other way around. Perhaps she attaches greater importance to work than play or the reverse. Her preferences and habits give her life a distinctive order. But to have any value from a Christian point of view, the order must be one she freely chooses. This alone makes her life "authentic."[10] A person who simply drifts along, or allows others to chart a course for her—whose soul is guided by rules and habits she has not chosen for herself—is a moral and spiritual disappointment.

The same is true in politics. Whatever their content, the laws of a political community are legitimate only if its members can trace them back to a creative act of founding in which they or their forebears deliberately established the regime that governs them. An association that mindlessly defers to what Max Weber calls "the eternal yesterday" of tradition no more deserves our political loyalty than an inauthentic individual commands our moral respect.[11]

The idea of the will undermines Socrates' analogy between cities and souls. The autonomy of individuals means that their political associations can never be organic wholes with mutually dependent parts. Yet the same idea suggests a new and wholly un-Greek definition of good order in both. It also raises a novel question regarding the nature and source of the goodness involved.

The question arises on account of what is perhaps the most striking feature of the human condition. We may make the will our measure of value, but human freedom is plainly confined. We cannot be or do whatever we wish simply by willing to be or do it. Much of who or what we are, personally and politically, is given, not chosen. Unlike God's will, our human ones are condemned to work on an inheritance of some kind. What, in the resulting amalgam, deserves our admiration and respect? Only what is attributable to the choices we freely make? Or does inheritance have a value too, and if so, of what sort? Is it valuable merely as a condition of freedom—because it supplies the material on which our finite human wills are required to work? Or is it good in itself?

In the case of souls, the question is that of character. Is a person's character to be judged strictly by what he chooses to do with his accidental endowment of interests and feelings? Or do these have some value of their own? In the case of cities, it is the question of patriotism. Is devotion to the history and culture of one's country for their own sake ever worthy of respect? Or only its commitment to universal human values? These questions may look different but at bottom are the same.

## II

Many factors contribute to the development of a person's character. One is native endowment. We come into the world with different physical and mental powers and—it seems—distinctive likes and dislikes. These are the building blocks of character. So is the training we receive early in life. That we have the endowments we do and are cared for by particular adults with their own distinctive characters is a piece of fate. So is the fact that we are born into a community with specific traditions and beliefs. Choice of course plays an essential role too—first the choices of our parents and teachers and eventually our own. The result is always a combination of inheritance and design. A person's character is never either the inevitable product of inexorable tendencies or the free creation of a sovereign will with the power to be whatever it chooses. It is something in between, a blend of freedom and necessity, like any work of human craftsmanship that begins with materials the builder finds on hand and fashions according to a plan.

This is how Aristotle thought of character. He likens its formation to the construction of a table whose success or failure must be judged as a whole. The value of a table is as much due to the materials of which it is composed as the choices that have shaped it.[12] The same is true, in Aristotle's view, of a person's character. Its strengths and weaknesses cannot be ascribed to inheritance or choice alone.

For Aristotle, acquiring a good character is an especially important kind of success. A single action may be good or bad, but its effects can often be repaired by other actions. A person's character is less easily changed. It is a durable framework of sentiment and judgment—a settled disposition to feel and behave in certain ways.[13] We admire those with good characters not as skilled technicians with a limited expertise but as accomplished human beings. They have succeeded in what Aristotle calls the "work" of being human.[14]

Success in this work is vastly more important than making a good table. Yet the two processes are alike. A carpenter selects lumber from his storeroom and imposes a form on it. The lumber is something given, but the selection and the design are both choices the carpenter makes. The result is a synthetic union of matter and form whose elements cannot be disaggregated except in thought. It is good or bad overall—as an artful combination of the two. The same is true of a person's character. It is admirable or disreputable not just because those who had a hand in shaping it made good or bad choices and not just because the materials with which they began were promising or resistant, but altogether, as a composite whose virtue and beauty cannot be explained by either element alone. It follows that the worth or worthlessness of a person's character is always to some degree due to luck or fate since the materials of which it is composed are given at the start.

This was Aristotle's conclusion. It marks a sharp departure from the more one-sided judgment of his teacher Plato. Plato's relentless rationalism led him to denigrate the value of the given in every branch of philosophical inquiry. In metaphysics, the result was the doctrine of the Forms and the devaluation of appearances. In ethics, it was the conviction, boldly stated by Socrates in the earliest of Plato's dialogues, that "to know the good is to do the good"—a claim that Aristotle emphatically rejects.[15]

Plato's elevation of the power of decision—illustrated by the hopeful message of the *Republic*, which encourages us to believe we have the power to be happy even in the worst regimes—was not (yet) supported by the theological idea of a sovereign and spontaneous will.[16] It remained tied to the notion of an eternal order of objective truths. But Plato's celebration of choice and assault on the value of the given were stepping stones toward the full-blown voluntarism of Christian belief and away from Aristotle's more authentically pagan conviction that in our appraisal of character, the value of what we admire is partly due to what is fateful in it.[17] It is Kant who presents the alternative view in its most rigorous form.

Kant recognizes, as anyone must, that different people have different character traits. Some are generous and just, others the opposite. The first incline toward philanthropy and honesty, the second toward misanthropy and theft, when they can get away with it. These inclinations, though, have no value in themselves. They may be deeply rooted and pervasive—unlike the desire for a peach, which arises and passes away in a moment. But their durability gives them no greater intrinsic worth than my most short-lived appetites. According to Kant, my moral respectability depends entirely on what I choose to do with my inclinations, the lasting as much as the transient.[18]

Thus, a philanthropist is worthy of respect only if he freely wills to use his inclination to help others, in accordance with a rule or "maxim" that comports with what Kant calls "the moral law."[19] Similarly, a person inclined to steal deserves our respect only if she abstains not from fear of getting caught but because she wills to treat others as ends and to refrain from exploiting their vulnerability by stealing from them.

In either case, the moral value of the act is solely a function of the rule one adopts as a guide, and this is always a matter of choice. None of us is ever constrained, even by our most entrenched habits, to choose one rule rather than another. We are free to make the right or wrong decision because we each possess a spontaneous power of choice that transcends the whole of the given world, our characters included, and are able to decide what weight to assign and how to employ our character traits.

The will we exercise in making this choice is, for Kant, the only conceivable source of value in the realm of moral life, and while it necessarily works on material that has been given to us, this material itself has no worth of its own. What worth it has it acquires from the outside, as it were: from the free choices we make to confer whatever value we do upon it. Nothing could be farther from Aristotle's judgment that a good character is admirable in its own right as an integrated whole. The same disagreement is recapitulated at a political level.

# III

Political communities do not grow by nature, the way a tree grows from a seed. They are works of foresight and planning. What Aristotle calls the "constitution" of a city—its distribution of powers, rules of enfranchisement, and the like—is a product of conscious design.[20] Cities belongs to the category of "made" things, whose organizing principles are conceived in thought before they are realized in practice, unlike the complex order of a beehive, which emerges "on its own."[21]

Like any artifact, a city has both form and matter. The first is deliberate. It is chosen by those who construct it. The choice is often the result of discussion and debate. Frequently, it reflects a compromise among competing interests. This distinguishes the process of founding a city from that of making a table, which may require compromises too but not of the same kind. Still, a fundamental similarity remains. The constitution of a city, like the design of a table, is imposed on materials that are given in advance. The carpenter must use the wood he finds in his workshop. In a similar way, those who found a city are constrained to work with the historical, cultural, physical, and other characteristics of the men and women who are already there. The founders inherit these characteristics. They are reflected in the final product, just as the grain of the craftsman's wood can be seen in the table.

The result in both cases is a hybrid of form and matter, the one freely chosen, the other given and only partly amenable to change. It is a blend of freedom and necessity, like the character of an individual person. The resemblance is reflected in the fact that we often speak of political communities as having different characters (the French and German, for example), even though they are governed by the same ruling principle (democratic self-government constrained by a respect for individual rights). Aristotle's way of thinking about the act of founding a regime seems intuitive. It has a commonsensical appeal. Yet to many today it looks misguided and morally obtuse. That is because they understand the act of founding in light of the revolutions of the modern age—the American, French, and Russian above all.[22]

Aristotle thought of revolution as a change of form—the sort of thing that happens when one political system replaces another through violence or drift. He believed the number of forms to be limited. Replacements occur within a narrow field and perhaps in a predictable order (an idea that Polybius later developed at great length).[23] In politics, as in the heavens, there is nothing new under the sun, only the same few regimes revolving in a course as steady as that of the planets.

This pagan idea of revolution is antithetical to the modern one. The American, French, and Russian revolutions were inspired by the belief that human beings have the power to bring something entirely new into the world—a regime never before seen or even imagined.[24] We are able to do this because, like God, we possess a creativity that is morally and metaphysically incompatible with Aristotle's conception of the political art as a species of craftsmanship or making.[25]

In one respect, Aristotle's ancient view remains valid. Our power of political invention may resemble God's *fiat lux*, as Hobbes says at the beginning of *Leviathan*, but it is obviously constrained.[26] Even the most sweeping revolution starts from a particular place. It begins with traditions, prejudices, class relations, religious beliefs, and a history uniquely its own. These cannot help but give every revolution a local complexion, even if, like the American, French, and Russian, it is committed to principles of universal application. But the modern idea of revolution, coupled with the fact that no human political creation is ever *ex nihilo*, compels us to ask a question that Aristotle never confronted.[27] In a nation that begins with a revolutionary founding, do the inherited materials on which the founders impose their will possess any value of their own? As with individual character, there are two competing answers. One is broadly Aristotelian and the other Kantian in spirit.

The first acknowledges the importance of the principles freely chosen at the moment of founding. In America, these include the moral and political ideals of the Declaration of Independence and the axioms of government enshrined in the Constitution. But the identity of a people (say those who give the first answer) is no more wholly a matter of free election than the character of an individual person. It is a composite of choice and inheritance whose value cannot be assigned to either alone. In the case of America, this inheritance includes language and laws; history and habits of address; music, food, and geography; folktales, films, poems, sports, heroes and villains of many kinds. It is not all of a piece. There are tensions and contradictions within it. No inventory—not even Walt Whitman's famous catalogues (or H. L. Mencken's)—can do it justice.[18]

Anne Hutchinson; Hester Prynne; the Newport furniture maker John Townsend; Denmark Vesey; the Merrimack River; Jim Bridger; Cassius Clay (both of them); John Calhoun; Frederick Douglass; Emily Dickinson; Tom Watson; Audie Murphy; Phillis Wheatley; Jim Crow, Lou Gehrig, and Eudora Welty all have their place in it. So do Bob Moses and the Freedom Riders; the bayous and storms of the Gulf Coast; Elvis Presley and the Staple Singers; the Erie Canal; the Thanksgiving table; Joe Hill; the bogs of Rhode Island and front range of the Rockies; John W. Davis; the Japanese internment camps; John Paul Jones; Sacagawea; Jimmy Buffett; Hugo Black; Amelia Earhart; Humphrey Bogart; the Golden Gate Bridge; and the writ of habeas corpus.

Americans make choices about this inheritance. They repudiate some elements and embrace others. Different Americans make different choices. But even after it has been subjected to critical scrutiny and the good separated from the bad, the meaning and value of an inheritance— including this one—are not explained by choice alone.

Loyalty to the good in an inheritance always owes something to the fact that it is one's own, like the family into which one is born. Even newcomers who freely choose to make it theirs are not free to substitute a different inheritance. Together with the decision to affirm the ideal of human equality and to adopt a scheme of government intended to secure the principle of popular rule for ages to come, the worthy elements of this inheritance belong to a compound of freedom and fate whose value cannot be exclusively assigned to either alone—as, in opposing ways, both cosmopolitans and ethno-nationalists invite us to do.[29]

This is the first answer to the question. The second is inspired by the political theology that undergirds the modern understanding of revolution.[30]

Every revolution is motivated by specific grievances and exploits opportunities peculiar to it. These constitute the material on which the revolutionaries work. But their "work" is not an act of production in Aristotle's sense. It is a free creation. The government they spontaneously bring into being owes its authority to their will and nothing else. In this respect, it resembles its divine original. The power of human beings may be limited in ways that God's is not, but the legitimacy of the political order they create is exclusively a function of their will, as the authority of God's commands is of his. God's laws bind their human subjects because God declares them to be binding—not on account of their conformity to some antecedent norm. In a similar way, the authority of every modern revolutionary regime flows from the act of founding with which it begins. The revolutionaries may appeal to the past to explain what they have done and why. They may invoke the idea of "natural law" or "natural right" to justify their actions. But these have only rhetorical meaning. The sole source of the authority of the laws to which they commit themselves at the founding is their commitment itself.

Every moral maxim, Kant says, has both matter and form.[31] The first derives from what he calls our "inclinations"—our interests, appetites, and passions.[32] The latter owes its existence to the will alone. It reflects the choice we make to affirm, reject, or reform the inclinations we have. In Kant's view, only the form of a maxim has any moral value at all.

The political morality of revolution reflects a similar judgment. Every human society has both form and matter too. The second is an inheritance. The first comes to be in a spontaneous act of founding. The act must, of course, have some content. It has to establish a particular political system in the same way that every maxim of personal conduct must enjoin, forbid, or permit some concrete action. But to be worthy of respect, the laws of the regime need to echo or reflect the axiomatic principle that the authority of the regime as a whole derives entirely from the freedom with which it is founded. A private maxim deserves respect only if it affirms the need to treat oneself and others as autonomous agents. Similarly, a revolutionary founding binds its successors only if it makes the freedom and equality of all the basic law of the order it creates.[33] A maxim that endorses the moral superiority of those with certain natural gifts is as much a contradiction as a revolution that celebrates a pious reverence for tradition or affirms the legitimacy of slavery.

A commitment to freedom as the sole ground of authority cannot be made once and for all, either by individuals or communities. It must be constantly reaffirmed. In politics this means that a country that begins with the declaration that all men are created equal deserves the loyalty of its citizens only if it strives to live up to its commitment in circumstances those who first made it never imagined. Their successors may feel a sentimental attachment to many other things—to the culture, history, and language of their homeland—but these have no intrinsic value. They are an arbitrary bit of fate. What is given at the moment of founding and later suffered in the course of history has value only insofar as it illustrates the resolute will of a people committed to the principle of universal equality and determined to meet its unending demands.

To think that Americans or any other people owe their loyalty to an amalgam of choice and inheritance, one must view it in an Aristotelian light: as a whole whose value cannot be reduced to choice alone. The modern political theology of revolution condemns this view as an illegitimate concession to self-proclaimed patriots who seditiously distract their fellow citizens with comforting appeals to memories and traditions that have no worth except as the record of a people fitfully striving to abide by "the proposition that all men are created equal."[34] This is the post-Christian view of political loyalty. It is widely shared today. Kant offers a rigorous and admired defense. The Aristotelian view seems vaguely treasonous by comparison.[35]

# IV

In part, we choose our characters; in part, we inherit them. They are amalgams of freedom and fate. Countries are like this too. Their political order is partly chosen and partly determined by history and culture.

What, in these fusions of choice and inheritance, is the proper object of our affection and loyalty? Logically, there are three possibilities. We may put it wholly on the side of inheritance, wholly that of freedom, or in the union of the two.

The first view has few defenders today. One must go back to Homer to find a conception of life in which destiny plays a near-exclusive role in determining the significance and worth of human actions.[36] The other two views have had powerful champions from the start of the Western philosophical tradition.

Plato insists that the value of every union of form and matter is attributable to its form alone. He elevates the soul's power of detachment from the given circumstances of life to a position of solitary authority. Kant radicalizes Plato's demotion of fate with his teaching that only a will can ever be good or bad in itself.

For Aristotle, the value of a whole formed with given materials cannot be assigned to its form or matter alone. It lies in the integration of the two. The irreducible value of wholes is a leitmotif in Aristotle's philosophy.[37] It connects his writings on ethics and politics with his treatises on life, nature, and stellar motion.

Edmund Burke belongs in a distant way to the philosophical tradition that Aristotle inaugurated. He too believes that the union of what we inherit and choose to make of it deserves praise or blame as a whole. Its value cannot be reduced to either element apart from the other. As the mention of Burke suggests, those who follow in the Aristotelian line often see themselves or are seen by others as conservatives. Those who follow Kant's lead frequently think of themselves as progressives. The distinction is crude but accurate enough and broadly familiar.

On the progressive view, the matter with which we are constrained to work in shaping our characters and countries is an essentially negative presence. It is an obstacle to be overcome.

Consider, again, our carpenter and her table. She first goes to the lumberyard or perhaps the forest to select wood well suited to her design. Some pieces may be better than others. But any wood she selects will have peculiar characteristics that make it less than perfectly adaptable to her plan. To build the table of her dreams, she must accept these imperfections and work around them. Yet she need not assign them any positive value.

Like the table, no character or country is built from scratch. Those who build it always start with given materials—in the first case, with the passions, aptitudes, and family relations that are for each of us a kind of natal fate; in the second, with the history that precedes every act of constitution-making. In each case we are condemned to exercise our freedom on an inheritance that constrains our range of invention. That is a consequence of the finitude of all our human powers regardless of the scale on which we employ them. Still, we are not compelled to dignify these limitations. They are the knots in our wood. They impede the adequate expression of who or what we choose to be. The proper attitude toward them may be one of resignation, resentment, or angry defiance, but never of positive endorsement.

This is the progressive view. It is inspired by the frustrations we all experience in the most prosaic acts of making. The conservative view takes its start from another aspect of the same experience.

Suppose, after careful deliberation, our carpenter chooses her wood. It has irregularities like no other. To some extent, these are an obstacle. She must make an effort to ensure they do not spoil her plan. But they are also an invitation. She sees that if she tries to bring out the grain of the wood instead of straining to disguise it, the finished table will have a distinctive look that sets it apart from other executions of the same design.

This requires careful attention and many deliberate choices, but the value of the final product cannot be ascribed to these choices alone. The wood's irregularities constrain her creativity. Yet they also enable it. They establish a concrete field of opportunities within which it is possible for her to be free. The same is true of a poet working in the language he was taught as a child or in an established genre, like haiku or sonnet. These constitute an arena of creativity at the same time and for the same reason they confine it.

On the progressive view, a person's inheritance has nothing to do with his "true" self, which is wholly attributable to those aspects of his personality that he freely affirms. He wears his inheritance like a cumbersome coat that cannot be discarded but is no part of who he truly is. Revolutionaries who regard the past as a deadweight with no value of its own and believe that the identity of a political community is exclusively defined by the principles to which it commits itself at the moment of founding see things in a similar light.

By contrast, those like Burke who adopt the conservative view see the relation between inheritance and choice in a different light. For them, the given circumstances within which characters and countries unfold are not just an obstacle to be overcome or indifferent stuff with no value apart from the form we impose upon it. They are the indispensable framework of freedom—a potential whose peculiar limitations at once restrict and liberate the effort to realize it. The result is an indivisible whole whose value is attributable to both its matter and form, between which it is impossible to draw a rigorous distinction.[38]

I have traced the difference between these two views to a metaphysical dispute between Plato and Aristotle, but it has considerable practical importance. The conflict between them has existed in an especially sharp form for centuries now, since the progressive view acquired a commanding authority under the influence of Christian theology and precipitated a more conscious formulation of the conservative view in response. Much else, of course, inflames the partisans on both sides of this divide, but their quarrel cannot be fully understood apart from the ancient dispute over whether wholes composed of choice and inheritance have an irreducible value or deserve our admiration and respect on account of the first alone.

There is, however, a third view distinct from these other two. It is harder to define and defend. It is related to the conservative view and might perhaps be seen as an extension of it but goes beyond the modest affirmation that inheritance is the enabling framework of freedom and not simply an impediment to it. The third view is that our personal and political fate is something to be cherished, not without qualification, but not merely as a constitutive condition of choice that might be equally well satisfied by any other inheritance as well. The third view of the relation between freedom and fate is that their integration is a labor of love.

This is the view that attracts me. It used to be associated with the idea of piety. Among progressives, piety is no longer a respected value. Many contemporary conservatives are wary of it too. But it is the inspiration for a strand of conservative thought that is worth preserving (or reviving) because it reminds us of a dimension of human fulfillment that we recognize but have lost the words to describe.

# V

The political version of this third view is what some mean by patriotism. They say they love their countries partly, at least, as communities of fate. Their love is defeasible. It can be disappointed or destroyed. But they insist that their inheritance is more than a necessary condition of freedom. It is an object of love, worthy of affection and loyalty in its own right.[39] The personal counterpart might be called the feeling of patriotism toward oneself, or pride.

*Patriotism* and *pride* are freighted words. Many insist that the first is justified only if a country subscribes to the right ideals and the second only when one lives according to the moral law, in which case the proper word is not pride but self-respect.[40] From this familiar and widely accepted point of view, those who love their political heritage or personal destiny for its own sake are confused and perhaps even criminal. They wrongly assign an intrinsic value to an accidental characteristic that can never possess it, and do so for selfish reasons.

The patriot loves her homeland with special zeal. She gives its interests extra weight for no reason other than that it is her own. Other countries count for less. She may be indifferent to them or even actively hostile. Often, the other side of patriotism is prejudice and xenophobia. In a similar way, the proud man views the accidents of his character with particular favor. He is not disinterested or impartial. Like the patriot, he fails to see that all human beings must be valued and judged from a neutral point of view that assigns no greater worth to one than to another.

Of course, it is not always wrong to give one's country or one's self preference over others. It depends on the reasons for doing so. A rule that commands individuals to pay special attention to the development of their own abilities or authorizes a country to treat an assault on its homeland differently from attacks on other nations may be justified on disinterested grounds that do not ascribe intrinsic worth to accidents of any kind.[41] What seems wrong about both patriotism and pride is their reliance on this ascription as a justification for preferring one's self to others.

Yet if selfishness can be justified without assuming that the accidents of fortune possess a value of their own, the reverse is true as well. One can love them for their own sake, in a selfless way. The experience of friendship shows this to be so. More important, it suggests that among friends the love of what is given as a piece of fate is a familiar aspect of human fulfillment. But how exactly? The answer will bring us back by a detour to the self-interested love of one's own fate and help us see patriotism and pride in a more favorable light.

Some friends are colleagues; others are social acquaintances or political allies; a few are lovers in the narrow sense of the word. Friends sometimes share a specific goal; others just enjoy each other's company. Often we are particularly close to those in our families. Friendships differ in intimacy and intensity. The field is vast and varied. But all friendships share two characteristics: selflessness and partiality.

Friends may be useful to one another. They may serve each other's needs. But people are friends only if the utilitarian dimension of their relation is accompanied by a selfless concern that the other do well for his or her own sake. Sometimes this is the dominant motif in their relation, sometimes only a minor one. It may be intermittent or constant. But its presence is what makes the relation a friendship rather than something else.

We are also partial to our friends. We care about and for them in a special way. They constitute a small group within a larger whole to whom we owe many legal and moral duties of a more general kind. What makes our friends special is some distinguishing trait they possess. It may be their family connection; passion for food, film, fishing, or travel; sense of humor, physical proximity, or smile. It cannot be their humanity, though, because that is something we all share. Humanity commands universal respect for men and women everywhere but it is never enough to motivate the partiality of the attachment we feel for our friends.

The passions, interests, and physical looks that attract us to our friends are composites of inheritance and choice. How do we feel about the accidents that constitute the first? Not, in most cases, as a stubborn bit of fate with no value of its own, loveable only if it has been shaped by a deliberate act of will. Nor, in general, do we see these accidents as a stage prop of sorts, valuable because they provide the background for a free or autonomous life. *Any* set of endowments meets this requirement. We love our friends because they have the particular traits they do; no others could be substituted for them.

Even this is not quite right. The word *because* suggests that our friends are one thing and their traits another. In reality, there is little difference between the two. Loving our friends selflessly is close if not identical to loving the accidents that make them who they are. The life of friendship is the love of accidents. Without it, friendship does not exist. The combination of selflessness and partiality on which every friendship rests cannot be explained except on the assumption that the inheritance with which our friends construct their quirky lives is loveable for its own sake, like our friends themselves.

Aristotle insisted that having friends is part of a fulfilling life. A man may be happy in other respects, he says, but needs friends for his happiness to be complete. He regarded friendship as a kind of keystone that not only adds to the other goods that contribute to human happiness—a virtuous character, material comfort, and public renown—but holds them in place by enabling their possessor to share these goods with others.[42]

Aristotle's account of friendship remains the best we have. No other philosopher has surveyed the subject in such depth. Still, a modern reader is bound to be dissatisfied with the narrowness of his account. Aristotle's list of virtues is too short and his view of character too confined. By defining the best sort of friendship as that between virtuous men, he misses the ways in which many friendships go beyond and sometimes even against judgments of virtue and vice.

The narrowness of Aristotle's discussion of friendship is ultimately due to the most resistant of his metaphysical prejudices, which he shared with Plato. For both, the individuality of a thing has no ultimate reality of its own. Only its general form is real. This belief shapes every branch of Aristotle's philosophy, including those devoted to the study of human nature. In particular, it influences his treatment of friendship, where it leads to the formalistic conclusion that all friendships must be judged by those between men of exemplary character, in whose admiring reciprocity the universal form of our humanity is brought to perfection.

We no longer share this belief. Individuality is for us something quite real—perhaps the most real thing of all. We attach a high, perhaps supreme value to individuality as such. That we do reflects the profound influence of the Christian revolution in values, which puts the individual at the center of things cosmically, ethically, and aesthetically, upending the classical order of values and preparing the way for our modern one.[43]

One of the countless consequences of this revolution is a dramatic adjustment in our understanding of the nature of friendship. We still believe, as Aristotle did, that a life without friends is woefully incomplete—indeed, barely human at all. But we do not think or say that we love our friends because they live according to a general pattern of virtuous conduct. For us, this is not the whole or even the most important part of friendship. We love our friends as individuals, not as representatives of a type. And because their individuality is inseparable from their inheritance—genealogical, biological, emotional, and intellectual—we love what is given rather than chosen in their hybrid makeup, not as a setting for virtue but on its own account. This feeling is remote from Aristotle's idea of friendship. It is at the center of ours.

For us, too, friendship is the keystone of human happiness. We must have friends to be fulfilled as human beings. But if that is so, then our fulfillment depends on the selfless love of what is accidental in our friends, since this is what makes us partial to them—in the most basic sense, it *is* them. What does this modern understanding of friendship suggest about the self-directed love of the patriotic and proud?

## VI

Patriotism is self-serving in a way that friendship is not. The patriot's selfless devotion to her country is often an important element in her own self-regard. It is also more properly subject to moral review. My personal friendships are morally defeasible too. A friend who misbehaves may lose my respect, and with it my affection, though not always. But political communities are often founded on a commitment to moral values. These are part—not the whole but a conscious and articulate part—of what the relation of citizen to nation is *for*. The demand to justify one's loyalty in light of the values for whose sake the relation exists arises with greater urgency and persistence for a patriot than a friend.

These are important distinctions. Yet friendship and patriotism share something important, and the value of the first, as we commonly experience it, illuminates that of the second.

It is, of course, possible to live without friends. There are anchorites who have no friends and misanthropes who shun them. There are moral athletes who befriend only those who share their beliefs or belong to the same party—a form of loyalty, even unto death, but not of friendship as we ordinarily think of it.

Socrates seems to have had no friends in this sense. He loved young men in general but none in particular.[44] Many readers of Plato's dialogues have been inspired by the life of Socrates, as others have by that of Jesus, who also had followers but no friends. Each seems, in a certain light, to have led a better-than-human existence. Yet neither is a model for a fulfilling *human* life. One reason is that neither includes the partial attachment to a special few that is the essence of friendship as we know it. To live without friends as they did one must be "a beast or a god."[45]

There is an old debate as to whether the best life for a human being is one devoted exclusively or at least preeminently to the nourishment of the best part of the soul or to the cultivation of the whole.[46] Those who take the latter view may be called "humanists" in a specific sense of the word. For them, the human condition is defined by the awkward conjunction of the elements that compose it, not its highest or best or most elevated part alone. In their view, the fulfillment of our humanity requires that our lower, earthly, mortal needs be met together with our higher ones. From this perspective, the need for friends is not something to be shunned or overcome or treated as a stepping stone to something higher, but acknowledged and fulfilled. A life in which the need is ignored or actively repressed is incompletely human. Those who invite us to aspire to a higher station where the dross of human life is left behind are bound to regard friendship as a dangerous temptation.

When we philosophize or pray, we fly "six thousand feet above man and time."[47] But we cannot live at such an altitude, nor should we wish to. The atmosphere is too thin. To keep from flying off into an airless region where only angels can survive, we need to love a few among those with whom we share the earth on account of their peculiar quirks, which from such an elevated perspective seem unworthy of affection. We must have friends to be *grounded*—to be human, for better and worse. Friendship gratifies our need for roots.

Patriotism is like this too. Just as a few are able to make do without friends, others (a greater number perhaps) live without countries to love. Some do so voluntarily. There are ex-pats and cosmopolites who feel no loyalty to any political community at all (though they may be strongly attached to a particular place, like Paul Bowles to Tangier or Bernard Berenson to Florence).[48] Others have been cut off or cast out of the country they love. They form a large and heterogeneous class of exiles, refugees, deportees, and stateless persons.

Among those who have no country, some celebrate their lack of patriotism. Even those who have one sometimes do. They regard with bemusement or disgust the attachment that others, including their fellow citizens, feel to a particular nation rather than, say, the party of humanity or the republic of letters.[49] They are happy to be rid of the distortions and destructive temptations of such narrow prejudices. They are like Socrates and Jesus. They deny that a loving attachment to a specific political community is a vital part of a fulfilling human life, just as these two celebrated exiles from humanity denied that our love of certain human beings, on account of their laughter and looks and the accidental histories we share with them, is a component of such an existence.

This is as much a mistake in the one case as the other. Who (except Socrates and Jesus) thinks that friendship is merely an option, like wearing your hair long, and not an essential part of human happiness? The humanist accepts our divided nature. She embraces our longing to climb and affirms our need for roots. The tension between them is inescapable. Still, she wishes to live nowhere else. We exist in the tension, she says; it is who we are; the yearning to escape it is a form of self-loathing.

In our personal lives, the need for roots is met by the love of a few on account of the idiosyncrasies that set them apart. In politics, it is met by the love of one's country on account of the historical and cultural inheritance that distinguishes it from other nations. A life without patriotism is as incomplete in human terms as a life without friends and for the same reason. It is rootless too—the word we use to describe those who by choice or fate have no country to call their own.

The cosmopolite who insists that patriotism is the enemy of human fulfillment accepts the advice of Socrates, who instructs us to love our friends only as the blurred image of Beauty itself, and of Jesus, who says, "If you come to me but will not leave your family, you cannot be my follower."[50] His counsel is just as inhuman.

Refugees who have lost their home and anxiously seek a new one confirm the strength of the longing for a country to love and its place in a normally fulfilling life. They show that the need for political roots remains even when the roots are cut and demonstrate that the condition of those condemned to live without a country is not a normal or natural one but a diminished existence instead, as much as the life of those who are compelled to live without friends.

Those who have friends and countries to love do not love them unreservedly. Their love is always conditional. It can be shattered or lost. The risk is especially great in the case of countries. Most political associations are based on a shared commitment to ideals. Their dependence on a real or professed allegiance to principles, declared or evolved, makes them especially vulnerable to attack on the grounds that the principles have been ignored or abandoned.

But neither in the case of personal friendship nor that of patriotic devotion does the conditional nature of the love transform its essential nature. It remains the love of someone or something distinctive, loveable not despite but because of its distinction, which is determined in part by an inheritance irreducible to choice. Both sorts of love depend on the paradoxical but familiar fact that the individuality of a person or country may be both intrinsically and conditionally loveable. Our fulfillment as human beings rests on our acceptance of this paradox and willingness to live with it.

The paradox vanishes if we think of inheritance, whether personal or political, merely as an obstacle to choice and view the latter as the sole source of value. It vanishes too, though less completely, if we think of it as an enabling condition of worth only because it provides the frame that freedom needs to be anything at all, yet is of no special value as one particular inheritance rather than another.

On either view, our condition looks less troubled—more of a piece. But we are not "of a piece." We are suspended between sky and earth. Renouncing this unstable in-between in favor of something more steady and stout brings a kind of relief but only at the expense of self-denial— the repudiation of our uniquely awkward position, which, however much we sometimes long to be rid of it, can no more be overstepped than our shadow. The only view of the relation between choice and inheritance that accepts the awkwardness of our situation rather than secretly despising it is one that sees inheritance not as an obstacle, or even an enabling condition, but something intrinsically if conditionally loveable for its own sake.

## VII

And pride? What can be said in its defense?

To view with self-approval one's fidelity to the moral law, especially under difficult or dangerous conditions, is a vital motive to right conduct. The feeling arises through the subordination of personal interest to a law that demands respect for all. The satisfaction of complying with it is the same feeling of respect the law demands toward others directed back toward oneself as a citizen of equal standing in what Kant calls "the kingdom of ends."[51] Far from suggesting, as the word *pride* does, any preference for oneself, the self-respect that accompanies obedience to the moral law depends on the suppression of every preference of this kind.

Something similar is true of the feeling of accomplishment that comes with the completion of a task or the cultivation of a talent. We generally regard this as a healthy form of self-regard. Even here, though, the emphasis tends to be on qualities we associate with agency rather than inheritance—determination, focus, patience, and the like. We are content that people take pride in the hard work they put into developing their gifts but balk at the thought they should be proud of possessing these gifts themselves, which are an accidental by-product of what Rawls calls "the natural lottery."[52] They have no moral value. The moralistic condemnation of pride hangs over our readiness to disparage it even when it reflects the sense of accomplishment we feel at our own industrious self-improvement.

The reasons for caution are obvious.

Pride in one's inheritance is an invitation to condescension and contempt. It is a short step to the belief that those who do not share it stand lower in the scale of human worth. We are not compelled to take this step, but all the aristocratic societies of the past remind us how easy it is.

In addition, as Hobbes argues with great force, pride is a stumbling block to political cooperation. To create a community with the strength to police our common affairs in a way that spares us the worst night-mares of endless controversy and war, "vainglory" must be cabined and controlled.[53] This is why Hobbes calls Leviathan the "king of the Proud"—the only earthly power able to contain the dangerous passion of self-regard.[54]

The Christian religion is on Hobbes's side. It condemns pride as the greatest of all sins—the root of every other. Kant's attack on what he calls "heteronomy" of the will is an abstract reformulation of the same idea.[55] Every moral system other than the true one, he says, rests on the blasphemous belief that our given interests and abilities possess a value of their own. Even Aristotle, who considered pride a virtue—who might even be called the Philosopher of Pride—did not think that a great man loves the accidental peculiarities of his personality, but only those features of it that conform to a general ideal of virtue.[56] Neither the classical defense of pride nor the Christian condemnation of it leaves room for the idea that loving oneself on account of one's inheritance is even a respectable passion, let alone essential to a fulfilling human life.

And yet it is.

Those who feel no affection for the accidents of their psychic constitution suffer from a kind of homelessness analogous to that of the cosmopolite or displaced person. Socrates encourages us to embrace our alienation. I should regard the accidental passions of my mind, he says, and those of the body in which they are housed, as a prison I can escape if I try.[57] Aristotle has a friendlier view of the body but shares Socrates' contempt for the idea that individuality has any value of its own. Augustine's view of the body is less sympathetic (to put it mildly), and his idea of individuality is yoked to that of the will, which, in contrast to our bodily powers, is exactly the same from one person to the next.[58] Kant follows suit.

All these thinkers celebrate an ideal of human fulfillment that puts us at odds with the peculiarities of our fateful endowments. They invite us to view these as a prison, a constraint, a mere condition, and to believe that being fully human means transcending them in some fashion. Whatever form the invitation takes, it reflects a kind of detachment, even self-hatred. Yes, transcendence is a feature of the human condition. It is what sets us apart from other living beings. But what makes us human is not the power of transcendence alone. It is the appearance of this power in a field of accidents as unique and fatefully given for each of us as the bodies that set us apart.

The humanist loves the whole. She does not love either the astonishing power of transcendence or the fatality of the circumstances in which it arises, in isolation from the other, but embraces the heartbreaking tension between them. Rather than flee into the comfort of a philosophy or religion that preaches the virtue of homelessness, she prefers to stay with the human condition as she finds it and to love it as best she can, awkwardly, fallibly, incompletely, rather than loving one part of herself with the illusion of success. For her this means loving who she is, as a constellation of endowments she has neither chosen nor made, *and also* as one who, in thought and feeling, has the power to rise above the world, herself included, and to see it from what religious thinkers call the standpoint of eternity.

This is not a farfetched idea. An example I have used before may help to make it clearer. A carpenter decides to make a table. He has a blueprint in mind. He thinks about the finished table before he starts. He transcends the world in thought. Still, he must build his table from the wood he has, and any wood is bound to have its special knots. If he sees these not as an obstacle to his creativity but as an inspiration for it, he will love the wood he has been given, knots and all. Without them, the table will not be his or he its maker. No other knots will do.

A carpenter who thinks this way about the relation between plan and wood sees himself as a trustee. He is neither master nor slave, but a fiduciary with independent judgment and a duty of care. He has been given certain material on which to impose his plan. His wood has a distinctive personality. He feels bound to bring this out while also realizing his design. These goals are not the same; there is a tension between them. But he cares about both and is prepared to live with the tension. Indeed, more than prepared: the tension defines the challenge and excitement of his work. He exists as a craftsman only within it.

An individual's relation to herself is like this too. She also has been given certain material with which to shape a plan of life. She has even less choice than the carpenter, who can at least pick the wood he wants. The life she makes with her inheritance of looks, appetites, powers, and vulnerabilities is partly a product of choice. It reflects her values and ideals and is modeled on a blueprint of sorts. But it also reveals, for the world to see, the quirks of her personality. This is something of value to her as well. She cares about her plan and her idiosyncrasies too. These can be displayed well or poorly. They may become a source of disappointment or anguish rather than fulfillment and pleasure. But in either case her feelings arise only because she loves her inheritance and feels a fiduciary's loyalty to it.

In the political realm, loyalty of this kind is what we call patriotic devotion. Its personal equivalent is pride. Each is a standing temptation to selfishness and the mistreatment of others. No one should discount the dangers and difficulties involved. Yet if we feel no loyalty to our inheritance, personal and political, we can never love more than a part of ourselves. We can never be at home in our humanity with its exhilarating contradictions.

The radicals of every age—Socrates, Jesus, Robespierre—eliminate the tension by reducing the value of the given to zero. Their reactionary opponents, who also exist in every age, eliminate the tension in the opposite way, by raising the value of the given to an absolute, with which no choice can ever compete.

The humanist accepts the tension and resolves to live in it with no expectation of release. She sees the dangers but prefers to face rather than avoid them for the sake of an anodyne peace. She loves her ideals and longs to realize them on earth. She also loves the inheritance that is, for her, the earth itself.

Walt Whitman's *Leaves of Grass* affirms a humanism of this kind. His poem is an ecstatic celebration of pride. It sings the song of himself—of his peculiar thoughts and feelings, above all those of his bodily appetites.[59] Yet his near-obsessional love of his own idiosyncrasies opens the way to a cosmic appreciation of the dignity—the divinity—of every other human being, each with his or her own foibles.[60] There is a tension between these attitudes—the selfish and the selfless—though there are moments in the poem when it nearly disappears. But the reader knows or feels that without the love of oneself, warts and all, the love of other people is bound to be thin and insecure—to become the bloodless and unreliable respect for persons that defines relations in Kant's kingdom of ends or behind Rawls's veil of ignorance.

For Whitman, this personal truth has a political side. Our democracy, he says, is not just a scheme of distributed powers or an arrangement for protecting the equal rights of its citizens. It is this and more. Its final goal, which lies in the farthest distance, is what he calls an "idiocrasy" in which each of us, "no two alike and every one good," achieves a "perfect individualism" in pursuit of that "special nativity" that makes every human being different from all others on earth.[61]

The goal of American life is to make it possible for each of us to be proud of our accidental inheritance. And because America is as unique among nations as each of us is among human beings, the patriotic devotion of those who love it is more than a commitment to an ideal, though it is certainly that. It is the love of an inheritance too, always a little suspect on account of the dangers it invites, but as essential to being at home politically as pride is to being at home in one's body.

This is Walt Whitman's America. It is not in favor now. The moralists and cosmopolites control the conversation in our colleges and universities and other institutions of high culture. Outside them, and partly in response, the forces of reaction are growing.

These are inhuman alternatives. We should reject them both. If we cannot love what is given to us as an inheritance as well as our chosen ideals, we can never be at home in our restless condition.[62]

Being at home is not the same as being at peace, but it is preferable to the false peace of self-denial. Should we be depressed by the fact that these are our only options? The question makes no sense. Or rather, it makes sense only from an inhuman point of view. Being human means embracing with loyal care, if subject to perpetual and anxious review, the characters and countries in which it is our fate to live. Without a dose, at least, of what Nietzsche calls the love of fate, our lives become mere emblems of humanity or, with the reactionary's exaltation of destiny, something even worse.[63]

# CHAPTER SIX

# Golden Apple in a Silver Frame

## I

In December 1860, Abraham Lincoln was the president-elect. He would not be inaugurated until the following March. By then, seven states had seceded from the Union; four more would soon follow. Waiting to be clothed with the powers of his office, Lincoln faced the greatest crisis the country has ever known.

On December 20, South Carolina became the first state to secede. Two days later, Lincoln wrote to Alexander Stephens, an influential Georgian who would later serve as vice president of the Confederate States of America, hoping to reassure Stephens of his intentions. "I fully appreciate the present peril the country is in, and the weight of responsibility on me," Lincoln wrote. "Do the people of the South really entertain fears that a Republican administration would, directly or indirectly, interfere with the slaves, or with them about the slaves? If they do, I wish to assure you, as once a friend, and still, I hope, not an enemy, that there is no cause for such fears. The South would be in no more danger in this respect than it was in the days of Washington." Lincoln acknowledged that his appeal was likely to fall on deaf ears. "I suppose this does not meet the case. You think slavery is right and ought to be extended, while we think it is wrong and ought to be restricted. That, I suppose, is the rub. It certainly is the only substantial difference between us."[1]

He was right, of course. On December 30, Stephens wrote back defending the Southern position at length. In his view (which the Supreme

Court had affirmed three years before in the *Dred Scott* case), the Constitution guarantees the right of slave owners to bring their slaves into the new territories added since the original compact. He concluded by urging Lincoln to reconsider his position before it was too late. "A word 'fitly spoken' by you now would indeed be like 'apples of gold in pictures of silver.' "[2]

The allusion is to Proverbs 25:11. Stephens could assume that Lincoln knew it. We have no record of Lincoln's reply, but there does survive a short note that he wrote for his own purposes, spurred by Stephens's biblical reference. It is only a fragment but a famous one because it touches on fundamental questions of political and constitutional thought.

> All this [by which Lincoln presumably meant the condition of the United States in 1860 and the division between North and South over the question of slavery] is not the result of accident. It has a philosophical cause. Without the Constitution and the Union, we could not have attained the result; but even these, are not the primary cause of our great prosperity. There is something back of these, entwining itself more closely about the human heart. That something, is the principle of "Liberty to all"—the principle that clears the path for all—gives hope to all—and, by consequence, enterprise, and industry to all.
>
> The expression of that principle, in our Declaration of Independence, was most happy, and fortunate. Without this, as well as with it, we could have declared our independence of Great Britain; but without it, we could not, I think, have secured our free government, and consequent prosperity. No oppressed people will fight, and endure, as our fathers did, without the promise of something better, than a mere change of masters.
>
> The assertion of that principle, at that time, was *the* word, "fitly spoken" which has proved an "apple of gold" to us. The Union, and the Constitution, are the picture of silver, subsequently framed around it. The picture was made, not to conceal, or destroy the apple; but to adorn, and preserve it. The picture was made for the apple—not the apple for the picture.[3]

Gold is more precious than silver; a frame exists for the sake of the object it preserves, not the other way around. It is tempting to conclude that in 1860, on the threshold of war, Lincoln thought of the Constitution as a means to an end and the Declaration the end itself. This seems confirmed by his decision three years later, in the Gettysburg Address, to date the beginning of the American experiment in self-government not from the ratification of the Constitution but from the signing of the Declaration instead.[4] Lincoln's view of the relation between the Constitution and the Declaration was more complex, however.

Lincoln appears to have hated slavery from the time he was a very young man. "If slavery is not wrong," he famously said, "nothing is wrong."[5] This proposition was, for him, a moral absolute. It rested on the principle of human equality enshrined in the Declaration, the polestar of his unwavering belief in the moral injustice of slavery.

Yet Lincoln also revered the Constitution. His view of it differed from that of more radical abolitionists who believed the Constitution had little value apart from its utility as a device for ridding the country of slavery. If it helped, fine; otherwise, they said, discard it. This led some to favor disunion, if that was the price to be paid for living in a country without the moral stain of slavery.[6] Lincoln saw things differently. He cared about the preservation of the Union—not at any cost, to be sure, but as something good in itself. He was not an abolitionist but a qualified unionist who was prepared to tolerate the continuing existence of slavery in the South if that was needed to hold the country together, so long as "the public mind" might "rest in the belief that [slavery] is in the course of ultimate extinction"—the issue at stake in the long-simmering debate over the extension of slavery to the territories, as Lincoln stressed in his letter to Alexander Stephens.[7]

For Lincoln, the preservation of union was an intrinsic good, like that of human equality, and not a mere means for achieving the latter. He viewed the prospective failure of the American adventure in popular rule as a catastrophe in its own right, apart from the spread of slavery. The challenge, as he saw it, was to save these two great goods without sacrificing either to the other. Whether and how to do this was the principal subject of his learned, folksy, passionate debates with Stephen Douglas in the fall of 1858.[8]

The evil of slavery cannot be explained or justified by anything in the Constitution of 1787. For that, we must look to the Declaration of 1776. The principles announced in the Declaration are not uniquely American, however. They are transcendent norms of a moral or theological kind that apply to all people at all times. The teachings of the Declaration are exportable to every corner of the world. The Constitution, by contrast, is a charter of national government whose purpose is to bring a separate and distinctive political community into being. It is a peculiarly American artifact. The union it creates has a local form and binds only those who are party to it. Lincoln knew that disunion would be a disappointment to those everywhere who believed in the possibility of democratic self-rule, but he did not view the survival of his country merely as a means to a cosmopolitan end. He was the humanitarian champion of a universal moral cause and also an American patriot, devoted to the survival of his nation as a distinct political community, one among many, with a character of its own.

As such, he faced a uniquely American dilemma. The states of the North and South were bound together by an act of union that from a moral point of view was a historical accident—a political necessity, perhaps, but one that had no transcendent moral claim on the participants. Why should *this* union, as opposed to any other, matter from the standpoint of moral right and duty? Some abolitionists saw things in this light. They believed the Constitution imposes no independent moral duties at all. Lincoln disagreed. He regarded the fact of union, though contingent, as a circumstance imbued with ethical meaning not unlike the accidental fact of family membership. He saw the division between North and South as a family quarrel and believed with all his heart that the question of slavery had to be resolved within the family circle, not by abandoning it, as secessionists and radical abolitionists both urged. Only one who valued *both* the historical accident of constitutional union *and* the timeless principle of moral equality could have taken the position Lincoln did between these opposing camps.

Before the war, Lincoln put special stress on the first of these two values. In February 1860, only ten months before South Carolina seceded from the Union, he gave a long and lawyerly speech at Henry Ward Beecher's church in New York.[9] Apart from his speech in 1854 on the Kansas-Nebraska Act and his debates in Illinois with Stephen Douglas four years later, Lincoln's Cooper Union Address was the most careful of his many prewar statements on the question of slavery in the territories. Given that Beecher was an outspoken abolitionist, Lincoln might have been expected to stress the Declaration, with its emphasis on the equality of all human beings. Instead, he focused on the language of the Constitution, the views of those who drafted and ratified it, and later acts of Congress in an effort to show, by the most scrupulous historical analysis, that "our fathers, when they framed the Government under which we live," had no intention to bar the federal government from outlawing slavery in any then-existing or later-acquired territory, contrary to what Stephen Douglas claimed and Roger Taney held in the *Dred Scott* case in 1857.[10]

In what can only be called a relentlessly originalist argument, Lincoln demolished the Douglas-Taney position. The remarkable thing is that he took the care to do so. From the standpoint of the Declaration, the constitutional subtleties that Lincoln surveys in his Cooper Union Address seem like a distraction from the issue at hand. The place where slavery exists has no bearing on its wrongness, nor do the views that certain politicians held about it at some time in the past. These matter only from a constitutional perspective. Today, readers of the address are likely to be perplexed, if not bored, by Lincoln's exhaustive treatment of the narrow constitutional question of territorial government. But nothing demonstrates more clearly his prewar commitment to constitutional—as distinct from universal moral—values, including above all the value of union itself.

It may be claimed with some plausibility that Lincoln's view of the relative weight of the values represented by the Declaration and the Constitution shifted during the war. Like many in the North, he came to see victory in double terms, as the restoration of union *and* the abolition of slavery in the states where it already existed. Yet even as the vindication of human equality rose in importance as a war aim, he sought to conduct the war within constitutional bounds.

Whether he succeeded is debatable. Still, even as Lincoln moved toward Gettysburg and a formulation that put the Declaration in a leading position, constitutional values continued to matter to him. His preoccupation with the nice question of the status of the states in rebellion; his decision to tie the Emancipation Proclamation to his constitutional powers as commander in chief (which limited its reach); and his defense of the suspension of *habeas corpus* as an act within his competence under Article II (contrary to what Taney held in *Ex Parte Merryman*): all reflect Lincoln's abiding commitment to constitutional values, even as the suffering and sacrifice of war brought the moral imperative of the Declaration into sharper relief.[11]

It is impossible to say how Lincoln would have conceived the relation between the Declaration and the Constitution in the postwar world of Reconstruction, had he lived to see it. His very last speech, though, delivered just days before his death, suggests a view still deeply attached to constitutional values and the preservation of the union—above all, to the necessity of getting the rebellious states back into what he calls their "proper practical relation" to the federal government—as well as to ful-filling the promise of the Declaration, which by the spring of 1865 had moved beyond the challenge of abolition to that of black enfranchise-ment (on which Lincoln takes a characteristically moderate position).[12]

Where Lincoln's thinking might have gone in the troubled years ahead is anyone's guess, but I think he would have landed somewhere be-tween the radicalism of the 39th Congress and the revanchism of An-drew Johnson and his Southern supporters. It seems likely that he would have continued to view constitutional union and human equality as dis-tinct yet intrinsic goods, whose relation is not unambiguously hierarchi-cal, like that of means to end, but something more complex and fraught. If Lincoln's image of the Declaration as a golden apple "adorned" by the Constitution's silver frame is understood to imply a simple instrumental relation between the two, then it does not reflect the subtlety of his view, either before, during, or after the war, so far as we can guess.

How, then, should we conceive this relation? And how should we re-solve conflicts between the Declaration and the Constitution, if and when they arise? Indeed, what sort of conflicts are these? If the relation is that of means to end, the answer to all these questions is straightforward. The first always yields to the second. A tool that does a poor job of securing the goal for which it was designed must be discarded or rebuilt. But if the Constitution embodies values that are worthy in their own right, the rela-tion between these values and those of the Declaration is harder to define and the challenge of accommodating them considerably greater.

This understates the difficulty. The problem is not merely one of har-monizing the language of these two documents or resolving certain doc-trinal inconsistencies between them. The difficulty lies deeper. The values they reflect are grounded in two different ways of thinking about human nature and the circumstances of political life. One is radical, the other conservative, in a sense to be explained. The challenge of finding their "proper practical relation" is the perennial task of balancing the radical and conservative strains in American government. Viewed in this light, the challenge begins to look almost insuperable—Lincolnian, one might say.

## II

We have read or heard the Declaration of Independence so many times that we know its most famous words by heart. But our familiarity is a lia-bility. It makes it hard for us to hear, let alone to ponder, the rhetorical rhythms that carry the reader in a seesaw movement back and forth from the opening words of the Declaration to its stirring conclusion.[13]

The Declaration begins *in medias res*. It starts in the world of politics and time—in the "course" of "human events." Here, men grapple with the problems of political order, burdened by the past and planning for the future. They do so from a uniquely human vantage point—one caught in time yet able to survey and (in limited ways) direct it. God does not see things from this point of view; nor do our animal friends. Neither lives in time in the awkward and divided way that we do. Our peculiar relation to time is the source of a whole range of distinctly human feelings—regret, for example, and hope, which neither God nor animals feel—and of all the phenomena of political life (commitment, duty, alliance, and betrayal) that preoccupy human beings as they struggle to fashion and preserve what the Declaration calls their "political bands."

The world of politics and time is one of conflicting opinions, where the truth is always in dispute. No political truth can ever possess the finality of a mathematical proof. So long as we remain within this world, partisanship is unavoidable. The possibility of establishing any durable political order therefore requires accommodation to the fact of disagreement— what the first sentence of the Declaration calls "a decent respect to the opinions of mankind."

Having begun with time and opinion, however, the Declaration quickly shifts gears. The second sentence tells us that some "truths" are "self-evident." Self-evidence is a characteristic of mathematical and metaphysical truths. There are no truths of this kind in the ordinary "course" of political debate. If they exist at all, and can be used (in Descartes's phrase) as a "clear and distinct" standard by which to settle our partisan disputes, then we must grasp them from a vantage point that transcends the realm of politics and even that of time.[14]

Self-evidence implies necessity. A self-evident truth (as opposed to an empirical one) cannot not be. This is how God sees all truths and how we grasp certain ones (those of mathematics, for example). If there are self-evident *political* truths, our ability to comprehend them depends on our real but necessarily limited power to see the temporal world of politics from a timeless point of view.

How should we conceive this point of view? The Declaration is ambiguous. The self-evident truths of which it speaks are "Laws of Nature and of Nature's God."[15] Perhaps (as orthodox Christians claim) they are binding because and only because God laid them down. Perhaps (as eighteenth-century Epicureans believed) they are the necessary rules of an eternal, uncreated natural order. Whichever view one takes, however, the laws in question are defined by their immunity to time. They lack the changeability and defeasible partiality that is the essence of the world of politics in which the Declaration takes its start.

After moving from human things to divine ones—from time to eternity—the Declaration shifts gears again and returns to the world of political complaint. The body of the Declaration is a detailed recitation of various wrongs the king of England and his administrators have committed against their North American subjects. This takes the form of a "history." There is no history of the "Laws of Nature and of Nature's God." They are eternally the same. A history takes time to unfold and is never something we can deduce or intuit. There is nothing "self-evident" about it. We *experience* history, and the lessons we draw from it depend on commonsensical norms of evidence and judgment that experience alone supplies. These can be summarized under the heading of "prudence."

Prudence has no place in mathematics or philosophy. By contrast, it is the leading virtue in political life—the one most urgently required of those who hope to form a community with any chance of surviving for even a modest length of time. Prudence "dictates" that when a political community's temporal laws are misaligned with the "Laws of Nature and of Nature's God," only a "long train of abuses and usurpations" justifies the victims in sacrificing the benefits of continued order for the vindication of an eternal truth. The Declaration's principal purpose is to demonstrate that judged by this prudential standard, the king's repeated violation of a transcendent law justifies a radical break in political relations.

The worldly point of view from which this bill of complaints is constructed is reinforced toward the end by an invocation of the "ties" of "common kindred" or "consanguinity" that bind the king to his rebellious subjects. There are no ties of this kind in the world of eternal truths. The latter are timeless and therefore bloodless. Kinship is anything but. It has no philosophical relevance but immense political weight. The Declaration makes a strong appeal to this most temporal of values.

Yet this is not (quite) the final word. In summing up, the Declaration invokes, one last time, the "Supreme Judge of the World" as the arbiter of human "intentions." His verdict is not like that of an earthly judge. It is not a mere opinion or reversible on appeal. It is the truth, beyond politics and time. The signatories take their stand on this transcendent ground, relying on "divine Providence" to weigh the rights and wrongs of history with infallible certainty.

The very last words of the Declaration, though, bring the seesaw back to politics, where the document began. The signers are not theologians arguing an abstract point of natural law or private individuals concerned with the eternal salvation of their souls. They are political actors, "Representatives . . . in General Congress Assembled," embarked on a worldly venture, full of danger and promise, to whose success they pledge their lives, fortunes, and "sacred honor," the last of which exists only in the realm of political action.

The first word of the Declaration is "when." It sounds in the register of time. The last word is "honor." Honor is highest among political goods. But if, rhetorically speaking, the Declaration begins and ends in the realm of politics and time, its most famous passage is the one that proclaims the existence of timeless truths with a transcendent authority and invites the reader to judge the dispute between the colonists and their British masters from a point of view beyond the merely human. When Lincoln described the Declaration as our "apple of gold," it was these eternal truths he had in mind.

It is easy to understand why this particular passage stood out in Lincoln's mind and does in ours. The political realm is one of rights and duties—the right to vote, for example, and the duty to pay taxes. By what standard is their legitimacy to be judged? To say that one political right is founded on another leads to an endless regress. The same is true of duties. Only a right or duty that applies in every case regardless of the conventional and contingent arrangements that human beings devise for themselves can answer the question in a final way. There are, however, no absolute rights or duties in the world of politics. To find them, we must look beyond this world to that of "nature" or "God." Assuming they exist, as the Declaration does, these absolutes necessarily enjoy a moral and epistemic priority over all merely political privileges and obligations. Because they apply in every imaginable situation, it is therefore vastly more important to understand them than to recall the particular grievances that pushed the colonists to revolt in 1776. The Declaration catalogues these grievances at length. But we can forget the catalogue so long as we remember the eternal standards by which these and every other worldly wrong is to be judged.

This much seems obvious. What is less obvious, perhaps, is just how *radical* these standards are.

The first of the Declaration's self-evident truths is the equality of all "men." If we judge things from the standpoint of historical and personal experience, nothing could be less self-evident. Every political regime, from time out of mind, has rested on an unequal distribution of power and authority. Even a republic, or representative democracy, assumes an inequality between electors and elected. Beyond that, it is obvious that human beings not only differ in their talents and abilities but that some have greater gifts than others. These political and natural inequalities cannot be abolished; every attempt to do so has failed. But then what does the equality of all men mean? It does not describe a fact. It states a norm by which existing inequalities are to be judged.

This norm is an abstraction. We reach it by a process of thought. The process starts in the world, with the observation that human beings differ in many ways—this one is tall, that one short; this one black, that one white; this one male, that one female. It then puts these differences aside (this is what abstraction means) in favor of the judgment that the men and women in question are really and truly equal despite the plain differences among them.

Socrates called attention to this process of abstraction in the *Phaedo*, when he asked one of his young interlocutors to tell him whether two sticks were of equal length.[16] The question cannot be answered by measuring the sticks. One will always be shorter than the other even if the difference is not discernible to the eye. Socrates' point is that "equality" cannot be observed. It does not exist in the world. It is an idea we discover only by looking through the superficial inequalities that blanket the face of the world to something unseen beyond it.

The Declaration does more than rely on this abstraction. It raises it to a position of supreme authority. It invites us to devalue what we see on the surface of things by assigning a greater worth to something that can never be seen. This already amounts to a break with ordinary experience—to a revaluation of what we habitually take for granted in our lives (like the prisoners in Plato's Cave, who think the shadows they see on the wall before them are real).[17] The radical promise of the Declaration begins with this break.

It is reinforced by the claim that the unseen equality by which the visible inequalities of the world are to be judged is not of human origin. It is something divine. Human beings are competent neither to create nor to destroy it. To invoke it as a norm is to hold human beings accountable to a standard of which they are not—and cannot be—the authors.

The ever-present possibility of appealing to this standard as a justification for doing or refusing to do something in the world of politics and history puts every political argument on permanent probation, subject to its conformity with an abstraction that exists beyond man and time.

On this view, the realm of political action is more than merely hostage to a higher value. It is a sphere of disappointment and even, perhaps, of sin. If all men are "created" equal, why is there so much inequality in the world? The standard may not be of human origin but our departure from it is. If we have fallen away from God's creation, the fault is ours. We are to blame and ought to pay the price. The Declaration is a work of the high Enlightenment but its implied condemnation of mortal human beings for failing to live by God's law has more than a whiff of the old Puritan spirit that still reverberated in Jonathan Edwards's sermons a generation before (and that defines the pathos of Lincoln's Second Inaugural ninety years later).[18]

Let us pursue this line of thought a step further.

The Declaration's proclamation that all men are created equal is followed by the more specific statement that this equality is one of "unalienable [and therefore humanly indestructible] rights," which is followed in turn by an even more specific enumeration of these rights themselves. The basic one (the Declaration does not say the only one) is the right "to Life, Liberty and the pursuit of Happiness."

There is a straightforward interpretation of these words that limits their reach. Every human being has a right to live and move as he or she wishes and to pursue a conception of happiness of his or her own choosing, within the limits of the law. Equality of rights means that differential barriers may not be put in the way of this pursuit. Later thinkers will call this equality "of opportunity." There is no right, on this view, to a further equality of "outcome"—to equal success in the pursuit of happiness, however one defines it.[19] This commonsensical interpretation of the right is broadly libertarian (or "formalistic," as some call it).

The fact that the Declaration speaks of a right to "pursue" happiness, not to *be* happy, recommends this interpretation.[20] But there is an ambiguity lurking in the language of the Declaration—a crack that in time will become a chasm.

A pursuit can be stymied in different ways. The pursuer may be forcibly prevented from proceeding. Or she may be free to go her way but lack the resources to make meaningful use of her freedom. The point of pursuing anything is to obtain it—that is what the pursuit is for. From this point of view, it makes little difference whether the blockage is the result of an obstruction from without or a limitation from within (a scarcity of resources, including talent, knowledge, and skill). A formalistic view of freedom that insists on this distinction makes little sense so far as the point or purpose of the freedom is concerned. Is there another perspective from which its meaning is better understood?

The Declaration says nothing about this. The question lies in the future. But it is there waiting to be asked. There is a direct line from the Declaration's affirmation of the right to life, liberty, and the *pursuit* of happiness to Franklin Roosevelt's insistence on freedom from want and fear—on the right to *happiness itself.*[21] One might even say—this is the progressive view—that the long, uneven, but steady movement from a formal or libertarian conception of the Declaration's idea of equality to a substantive view of it represents not so much a replacement of the original idea, let alone a repudiation of it, as a fulfillment in twentieth-century terms of what the Declaration promises in the words of the eighteenth.

This is a debatable conclusion. There are libertarians who deny it.[22] What cannot be denied, though, is the Declaration's radicalizing potential. The abstractness of its ideal of equality; its transcendent authority; the implicit condemnation of human beings who fail to respect or redeem it; and the ambiguity of the ideal itself, which invites a limitless process of extension in which existing political arrangements are continually found to fall short in previously unsuspected ways, all combine to put a morally and spiritually irresistible pressure on every worldly state of affairs, which from the point of view of Lincoln's "golden apple" can never be more than a temporary and inadequate compromise with values that lie beyond the furthest horizon of everything human beings are able to accomplish on earth.

The radicalism of the Declaration's standard for measuring rights and duties is reflected in the actions it justifies to ensure the standard is met. Like the standard itself, these actions are not political in an ordinary sense. They are not the result of the normal processes of compromise and conciliation. They interrupt these processes and cause a revolutionary break in the existing political order.

We know the words by heart. "Whenever any Form of Government becomes destructive of these ends [the ones fixed by the eternal laws of nature and of nature's God] it is the Right of the People to alter or abolish it, and to institute new Government" along lines that "seem to them most likely to effect their Safety and Happiness." It is not only their *right* to do this but their "*duty* to throw off such Government, and to provide new Guards for their future security." This is the practical implication of the theoretical truths from which the Declaration takes its compass heading.

The key words are *abolish, throw off,* and *new.* The people may first try to "alter" existing arrangements. "Prudence dictates" that they attempt this first. But the right—the duty—to ensure that the organization of political power conforms to the requirements of the "self-evident" truth that all men are created equal and endowed with certain unalienable rights does not stop there. The full force of the right becomes apparent only when efforts at conciliation fail. Before this point, commonsense and practical judgment guide the aggrieved in their campaign for reform. Beyond it, only revolution remains.

This is the backstop that guarantees the legitimacy of every compromise short of it. Revolution is the criterion by which all reforms are to be measured, in the same way the eternal truth of universal equality is the test by which every human political arrangement must be judged. Like these truths, the ever-present possibility of revolution determines the legitimacy of what happens in the realm of political life, where events are always continuous and bargaining is normal. Revolution is the flashing forth of eternal truths in the familiar ebb and flow of historical time—an eruption of the divine into the human—which is why it is so terrible and awe-inspiring.

Prudence is contextual. It presupposes an already-existing political space—a theater of sorts. Revolution creates; it brings something new into being. It takes the whole of political life as its object and surveys it from a point of view no longer bound by the ordinary "guards" that guide and constrain our political deliberations. In doing so, it reenacts on a lesser scale the divine *fiat* by which God brings the world into existence. It is the most God-like act of which human beings are capable, and though intended to inaugurate a new political regime, can be understood only in theological terms, as the exercise of a power analogous to God's own. By comparison, every ordinary political act looks incommensurably small.

Nothing suggests the theological dimension of the Declaration quite as clearly as the small word *duty,* inserted parenthetically, almost casually, it seems, right before the catalogue of British crimes. To whom is this duty owed? The Declaration does not say. The inference, perhaps, is that the revolutionaries owe it to one another. (The last words of the Declaration support this reading.) But there is another interpretation. If there are eternal truths; if God is their author; if these truths have been insulted or ignored by certain human beings, then others, their victims, have a duty to God to see that things are set right. If they fail to correct them, if they balk at revolution, they disappoint not only their worldly comrades but their transcendent creator as well. This is a failing of a more-than-human kind. No mere political fault can compare with it.

The Declaration does not say this. But the philosopher whose spirit hovers over it does. According to John Locke, we owe our bodies and souls to God, and as God's trustees we have a responsibility to look after them. We have a duty to institute governments for this purpose and to overthrow them when they fail to do what they should. The duty falls equally on all of us because as God's creatures, we stand on a par. To suffer a government that compels us to violate God's command is a crime against God himself.[23]

Like the Declaration, Locke's *Second Treatise on Civil Government* addresses a political question. But it does so from a theological point of view that grounds our political rights and duties in an obligation that transcends them. This is what gives Locke's *Treatise* its radical character. The essence of modern radicalism is its insistence that we judge what happens on earth from the vantage point of heaven—whether Locke's or Lenin's—and put human things aside for the sake of divine ones.

The explicitly theological structure of Locke's argument has disappeared from the Declaration. But the radicalism it inspired in Locke's revolutionary tract lives on in Jefferson's document, with its appeal to transcendent truths and insistence that we have the right—indeed, the duty—to defend them against all merely political inconveniences. The Declaration mentions God in an equivocal way. Locke's God has become something paler, more rational, more Epicurean. But the Declaration of Independence, like the *Second Treatise*, is inspired by a timeless and universal ideal whose absolute priority over all worldly concerns must never be obscured by our temporal hopes or fears and parochial political projects. So long as we look to the Declaration for a sense of national purpose and identity, we are bound to conceive our local, historical, and political vocation in otherworldly terms.

## III

When we turn to the Constitution, we breathe a different air.

To begin with, the words *God* and *Nature* do not appear in the Constitution. Their absence is a clue to its more practical concerns. Its use of the word *equal* is another. In the Declaration, the word refers to a status or condition that is pre-political in both a conceptual and normative sense. The word *equal* appears several times in the Constitution but with a strictly political meaning (as when, for example, Article V declares that "no state, without its consent, shall be deprived of its equal suffrage in the Senate"). There is no hint of a timeless human equality that precedes the arrangements established by the Constitution and sets the standard by which to judge them. (The Fourteenth Amendment brings this transcendent idea of equality into the text of the Constitution itself. It constitutionalizes the language and values of the Declaration of Independence. I shall return to the Fourteenth Amendment in due course.)

The word *right* (so central to the Declaration) appears twice in the original body of the Constitution but with none of the same weight. It is used repeatedly in the ten amendments that were added in 1791—so often that we colloquially refer to them as a bill of "rights." But the insignificance of the word in the unamended Constitution reflects the very different atmosphere in which its drafters worked. They were concerned with questions of institutional design and durability, not the vindication of God-given rights.

The Preamble to the Constitution underscores the difference. Where the Declaration appeals to self-evidence, truth, nature and God, the Preamble places us squarely in the realm of politics and time. The Constitution serves worldly ends ("justice," "defense," "welfare," and "tranquility"); seeks to improve an already existing scheme ("to form a more perfect union"); and aspires to establish a government that will last for ages to come (for "Posterity").

The last is particularly important. It reflects a concern that John Marshall reiterates in several of his greatest opinions and explains his emphasis on the "written-ness" of the Constitution.[24] The timeless laws of nature and of Nature's God are inscribed in our hearts and can be discovered by introspection. A political venture, like the one launched by the Constitution, takes place in time and is therefore vulnerable to forgetfulness. The Framers, and Marshall after them, thought it imperative to memorialize the Constitution in a written document whose fixed words provide a measure of protection against time's amnesiac flood, in the absence of any unwritten tradition with the strength to play this role.

The watchword of the Constitution is not *equal* or *right* but *power.* Each of its first three articles begins with "Power" or "Powers." The Constitution is preoccupied with the problem of power. It mobilizes power for the sake of strength and seeks to manage its dangers.

The consolidation and containment of power was a characteristically Roman obsession. The greatest Roman historians studied its uses and abuses with a connoisseur's eye. So, of course, did Thucydides, but the greatness of the Greeks, as Cicero and other Roman writers note with a mixture of envy and pride, lay in the fields of artistic and philosophical achievement, not that of disciplined practical power. Here is where the Romans excelled.

The Framers studied Roman history closely. They knew the Roman writers well, admired them greatly, and sometimes struck a consciously Roman pose.[25] This was more than a pretentious masquerade. It fit the Framers' peculiarly Roman fascination with the question of power. If the Declaration's invocation of transcendent truths and eternal laws has a Christian provenance, the Constitution's preoccupation with power is inspired by an older tradition of classical writing that remains of interest to those in every age who seek to solve the first problem of political life— that of concentrating power without being destroyed by it.

The critical idea is the one we know as "checks and balances." It is a very old idea. There is an early version of it in Aristotle's *Politics*. Polybius develops it at length in his history of Rome, written in the second century BCE. Montesquieu is generally regarded as its most influential modern exponent.[26] The drafters of the Constitution were intimately acquainted with the idea of checks and balances and subscribed to the theory behind it.

Simply put, the theory is this. All human beings seek power. They want it for moral and material reasons and also for its own sake. They enjoy the experience of exercising dominion over others (what Augustine calls the *libido dominandi*—an appetite he condemned but the Romans accepted and, within limits, admired).[27] Given the chance, those with power will always seek more. Power is expansive. It cannot be otherwise, so long as human nature remains what it is. The only practical remedy is to disaggregate power and distribute it in discrete parcels, each of which must struggle to hold its own against the others.

To do this in a way that does not drastically weaken or paralyze power (for whose sake men form political associations, so that they will have more power together than they do apart), is the great challenge of constitutional design. The Framers of the Constitution met it by devising a complicated system of offices, at once interlocking and competing, so that the occupants of each, in order to do their own work, must depend on the cooperation of others holding different positions and can expect resistance from them in case they overstep their bounds.

The result might be described as a "fractal" division of powers, branching out along two main lines (vertically between the states and the national government, and horizontally among the three main departments of federal power) into ever-finer divisions, each marked by the same combination of cooperative integration and guarded opposition. By joining this scheme of distributed powers to the personal ambitions of those occupying each of its offices, the Framers hoped to ground their structural solution to the danger of concentrated power in the passions of human nature, which can be disciplined but never abolished.[28]

The Framers understood that political power is never (just) physical force. Every meaningful accumulation of power is a function of authority, which depends on others' acceptance of the claim to possess it.[29] Where they do, authority exists; where they refuse to accept the claim or simply ignore it, there may be power but no authority.

The ultimate source of authority in the American system of government is "the People" who "ordain and establish" the Constitution. The limited authority of every officeholder with a specified quantum of power is a function of his or her ability to successfully claim to be acting on behalf of the People. Each is a representative of the People. None (to use the language Hobbes employs) is the "author" of the role he is "authorized" to perform—the playwright of the drama in which he acts his part.[30] The author (to follow the metaphor) is offstage. The People speak once. They "ordain and establish" and then retire. There can be no authority *within* the scheme they create except by appeal to the People, and yet because they stand *outside* the scheme, the propriety of any appeal can never be definitively confirmed. All appeals to the People are, as we say today, "endlessly contestable." The competition among them is as much a source of checking and balancing as the pro forma division of constitutional powers itself.

All this is familiar to every student of American constitutional law. The Constitution's "separation of powers" is as much a part of our national grammar as the "self-evident" truths of the Declaration of Independence. But there is an essential difference between them. If the latter has a radical bent, the former inclines in a conservative direction.

The Declaration begins in the "course of human events" but quickly leaves it for a higher perspective. It surveys the whole of history as God might, with an eye to truths that neither require nor allow for empirical demonstration. The Constitution remains tied to human things. It is an experiment that may or may not succeed—one whose arrangements are hostage to time in a way the self-evident truths of the Declaration are not. The Preamble acknowledges this. Even as it announces something new, it remains connected to the past and future. In offering their novel scheme to the American people, the Framers afterwards claimed to be acting as the agents of an existing political body in a line of continuous and unbroken authority.[31] The claim was dubious but reflects the same temporal point of view as the Constitution itself.

Time means obscurity, uncertainty, the need for judgment and compromise. There is no compromising with the principle of equality or the rights that follow from it. One may decide to wait before insisting on their recognition, but the rights themselves are absolute. The Constitution, by contrast, rests on nothing solider than the tentative and defeasible judgment that the balances it strikes are sensible and will last. It is tethered to time and mutual concession, which can never be entirely principled. The long-term success of the venture it sets underway depends on the risky and fallible appraisal of "things that may be otherwise"—something no self-evident truth can be.[32]

It has sometimes been suggested that the People play a role in the Constitution analogous to the one that God played in earlier systems of government.[33] There is something to this. There is no higher authority, beyond that of the People, to which one may appeal to validate its judgments, just as there is no higher standard by which to measure God's decrees. But the analogy is also a reminder of how profoundly different the Declaration and the Constitution are in this respect.

The God of the Declaration is accessible to reason and conscience. His laws can be grasped and put to work in human affairs. The whole argument of the Declaration rests on the assumption that the weight of divine authority can be employed here on earth to resolve political disputes with incontrovertible finality. By contrast, the People who "ordain and establish" the Constitution never again enter the political world except as a standard to which battling partisans are compelled to appeal but always controversially and inconclusively. Having spoken, the People bequeath their Constitution to its human trustees, who now must labor for as long as the arrangement lasts to work things out for themselves with no prospect of ever being able to settle their disagreements on theological, as opposed to prudential, grounds. The Constitution has no "beyond" whose transcendent authority can be brought down to earth.

The Declaration of Independence was written in the midst of a fierce political fight. But its signers believed that over and above their worldly complaints (the lack of representation; the quartering of troops; the removal of defendants to be tried in foreign courts), they had God on their side. The Declaration promises help from a more-than-merely-human power. It rests on the wonderful, extravagant, enthusiastic hope that right-minded human beings can not only grasp the laws that God proclaims but summon them effectively in aid of their political rights.

The Constitution leaves those who accept it with nothing but themselves—flawed, venal, yet capable, on occasion at least, of acting with a regard for the public good—to make whatever adjustments are necessary to keep their enterprise afloat on the sea of time, without the prospect of divine intervention. If the Declaration is an enthusiastic document with a theological edge, the Constitution is a sober one, reconciled to the vicissitudes of time and the realities of human nature. This is part of what it means to say that the Declaration has a radical soul and the Constitution a conservative heart.

## IV

The Constitution solves the problem of power by dividing it. The natural way to think of this division is in spatial terms. One power (that of the president, for example) is here; other powers (those of the legislative and judicial branches) are there. The result is a system of checks and balances. This may be conceived in mechanical terms, like the springs and gears of a clock; in cosmological ones, like the gravitational balance of the planets; or in more organic terms, like the interplay among the parts of a living body.[34]

But all these images miss an important dimension of the constitutional solution to the problem of maximizing and constraining power. This other dimension is temporal, not spatial. If the Declaration subordinates time to eternity, the Constitution looks to time as a saving force—not as something to be weighed or judged from a point of view beyond it but as a source of hope and help, as well as doubt and disappointment, in human affairs. This is the deepest difference between the Declaration and the Constitution and the ultimate source of the latter's enduring conservatism.

The philosophy of David Hume throws light on the meaning of this difference. There is a striking parallel between Hume's view of the relation between time and authority and the outlook of the Framers. If Locke is the presiding spirit of the Declaration, Hume is in the background of the Constitution. The differences between these two philosophers are reflected in the temper of the documents their ideas inspired.[35]

Locke approached the problems of politics from a religious point of view. His account of the social contract and the rights that it protects is not based on rational self-interest but on our antecedent relation to God. The duties the contract creates arise from those we owe our creator. The latter come first; they exist before and beyond our temporal obligations to other human beings. The priority of religion over politics and of eternity over time is particularly clear in Locke's *Letter concerning Toleration.* For Locke, the good of toleration as a political practice lies in the freedom it gives us to pursue our eternal salvation, which transcends every imaginable advantage of a worldly kind.[36]

Hume did not have a religious bone in his body (not a Christian one, at least).[37] He was a skeptic where Locke was a believer, a bemused observer of human follies where Locke was an ardent participant in the routines of Christian life. But Hume did more than deprecate pious appeals to God and eternity as a touchstone of temporal authority. That was the negative side of his philosophy. He also insisted that the passage of time has a normative value of its own: that time itself can validate, authorize, obligate; that it has the power to confer on the "facts" of life a "value" that commands our respect and obedience. This was Hume's positive teaching about time.

It is at work, for example, in his famous argument that the intellectually insoluble problem of induction (that of justifying future predictions on the basis of past experience) can only be answered by the practical force of custom.[38] The same idea lies behind Hume's solution to the difficulty—which he states with a clarity that has perplexed philosophers ever since—of deriving *ought* from *is.* This cannot be done, Hume says, as a theoretical matter. Only the passage of time and the emergence of practical habits of agreement allow us to bridge the philosophical chasm between values and facts.[39]

Most important, for political purposes, Hume viewed the social contract on which political authority rests as a kind of convention.[40] If we think of it as an agreement, in the way Locke does, an obvious question arises. Why are the parties to the agreement bound to observe its terms? On a contractarian view, this can only be because of a prior agreement, and so on, *ad infinitum,* unless one resorts to God, which Locke was prepared but Hume unwilling to do. This is analogous to the problem of induction and that of deriving values from facts. It too is incapable of solution by reason alone.

The source of the authority of any contractual duty, including those anchored in an "original" social contract, cannot be found, Hume says, in timeless principles that are self-evidently true in the sense the Declaration uses the expression. The only conceivable explanation of their authority is one that ascribes to the passage of time what reason alone denies it: the intrinsic power to validate what lasts, just because it does.

*Why* do conventions bind? Because they have existed for some indefinitely long time. This is true of modest conventions—those concerning modes of dress and speech, for example—but it applies equally to the most basic convention of all, on which our habit of obedience to the law is founded. Just how long a convention must last to be binding will always be a matter of debate, and no convention can put the duties it supports beyond criticism and reform. But these are details. The important point— the one that marks the deepest divide between Hume and Locke—is that the former assigns to routine, habit, convention, and time an inherent authority the latter reserves for the eternal laws of God alone.

This difference is a symptom of the divide between two branches of Enlightenment thought.[41] The Founders were heirs to both and drew on both, one more prominently in the Declaration and the other in the Constitution.

The first of these might be called the "continental" Enlightenment. It had several distinct strands, some more radical than others. Voltaire, Rousseau, Diderot, and Kant are representative figures. Spinoza was perhaps the most thoroughgoing and clear-headed of them all (though his contemporaries regarded him with a suspicion bordering on horror).[42] Despite his English birth and his role in English politics, Locke belongs to this continental Enlightenment too. He was introduced to it during his exile in Holland and brought it back to England when he returned.[43]

The second Enlightenment was the English-speaking one, centered in London and Edinburgh. Burke, Gibbon, Ferguson, Smith, and Hume were among its leading figures. Just listing their names alongside the great champions of Enlightenment in France and Holland is enough to suggest the conservative character of one and the radicalism of the other.

One source of the intellectual and temperamental differences that set the proponents of these two Enlightenments apart is their contrasting attitude toward the normative power of time. Hume invokes this power to cut the Gordian knots of scientific induction, moral judgment, and political obligation. Burke celebrates it even more enthusiastically—at times with theatrical relish. Gibbon's history is a sustained reflection on the vicissitudes of time, which become so moving in his telling only because he takes time as seriously as he does. Nothing distinguishes the great writers of the continental Enlightenment from their English-speaking counterparts as sharply as their disdain for the idea that time hallows what lasts and confers an authority on it that in the continental view can only flow from eternal laws beyond the range of human events.

The Declaration of Independence is animated by the spirit of the continental Enlightenment that Jefferson inherited from Locke. The Constitution is shaped by Hume's belief that time itself has the power to generate allegiance and authority. The Framers were allergic to speed. They designed a constitution that not only divides power but slows it too. Their design is founded on the Humean conviction that what takes time and lasts long has the best chance of capturing the hearts and minds of human beings. Rather than appealing to eternal truths, as the Declaration does, the Constitution employs time as a cure for the distempers of time, including those that come with every attempt to form a lasting association with others whose interests and opinions differ from our own.

# V

The Framers believed the ultimate source of political authority lies in the will of the People. They also believed that the only workable form of democratic government in a community of any size is one that acts indirectly, through elected representatives, an arrangement Madison famously converted from a shortcoming to a strength.[44] The Framers' commitment to democracy was further qualified by what we today regard as unconscionable restrictions on the franchise. Still, even with these limitations, some enduring and others not, the government established by the Constitution is essentially democratic or "popular."

Plato had a dim view of democracy.[45] He saw it as an invitation to theft and extortion. Where the "many" rule, Plato said, they will always be tempted to use their power to take the property of the few and redistribute it more widely. The Framers shared this age-old anxiety.[46] They designed a Constitution that was meant to protect against expropriation by dispersing power in a way that makes it more difficult for a simple majority to take what is not theirs. This might be called the "spatial" side of their solution to the problem of popular rule. But it has another, equally important "temporal" dimension—one that reflects the Framers' belief that the desire of the many to seize the property of the few is the result not of appetite alone but of a blinding short-sightedness that obscures what Tocqueville calls their "interest well understood."[47] The remedy is to decelerate the processes of government in order to create the time needed for more sober reflection.

The longing to have more is a universal human appetite. Often those who feel it act in a calculating way, looking with detached calm for the best way to satisfy their wants. The more intense the longing becomes, however, the more likely it is to cloud one's judgment and obscure the truth that even for those who have the least, the benefits of taking what is not theirs today are more than offset by the danger of having it stolen or confiscated tomorrow—to conceal the advantages of what we call "the rule of law."

The antidote is a cooling-off period: more time to think, weigh, and judge. It is not a surefire cure, but it is the best that human beings can do. For those who hope to create a democracy with any chance of survival, the most promising approach is to mobilize the passage of time as a moderating force against frenzy and in support of sobriety, compromise, and concession.

The Constitution is built on a fear of "mobs."[48] The mob is the danger that haunts every democracy in the same way that tyranny is the threat that lurks behind every government based on the rule of one or a few. But what exactly is a mob?

It is, of course, a large group. Three cannot be a mob. But mere size is not its defining trait. The crowd at a football game is not (yet) a mob. The most striking characteristic of a mob is its impetuosity—its infection by a contagious passion that fuses its members into a mindless fury that overwhelms the voice of reason and deliberation and tempts them to act together outside the established procedures of the law. This is what distinguishes a mob from a conspiracy (which can be a threat to democracy too, though of a cooler and more deliberate sort). If the Framers were especially fearful of mobs, it is because they shared the antipathy, which so many ancient writers expressed, to the excitement, the ecstasy, the thrilling but mind-numbing pleasure of being caught up with others in the reciprocal and reinforcing passions of a "movement" whose members are no longer in control of their feelings, even (perhaps especially) when these are enflamed by a righteous sense of injustice.

The Framers worried about the inevitable clash of class interests. They hoped it might be softened but assumed it can never be settled once and for all. More fundamentally, though, they worried about the loss of self-control to which every mob is prone, whether inspired by material interest or moral conviction—the loss of what the Greeks called *sophrosyne*, a word that suggests, at once, temperance, balance, and stability of character.[49] When this is lost or endangered, the best restorative is time—the chance to cool off and take a more measured view of things— and the best strategy for affording the time that is needed is one of delay. The Constitution is a magnificent scheme of delays.

The requirement that a bill be passed by *both* houses and *then* go to the president for his signature; that in case the bill is vetoed, it *go back* to the legislature for further consideration; the requirement that, in cases of impeachment, there *first* be an indictment and *then* a trial (which moves at a stately pace); the bar against the president entering treaties or making certain appointments *except* with the "advice and consent" of the Senate (a time-consuming process); the *staggering* of elections to the Senate and the *longer* terms of senatorial appointment; the establishment of a vast and open-ended "judicial power," which is always exercised more *slowly* than its legislative and executive counterparts: these are all devices for delay.[50] Taken together, they increase the time needed to make, administer, and test the authority of laws. They are ways of capitalizing on the validating power of time and of strengthening the authority that attaches to what happens gradually, unlike the volatile waves of emotion that inspire the changeable moods of a mob.

This power is the source of all traditional and customary authority. It also strengthens the authority of the more conscious acts of self-government for which the Constitution provides an orderly frame. The ultimate source of this authority lies with the People, but the Constitution they "ordain and establish" creates a system of interlocking delays that clothes what is done in their name with a dignity and legitimacy that the passage of time alone confers. This is a characteristically Roman idea. It lies at the heart of Hume's philosophy and of the English-speaking Enlightenment more generally, and stands in sharp contrast to the Christian radicalism of the continental Enlightenment of which Locke's *Second Treatise* and Jefferson's Declaration are brilliant expressions.

Two further points are worth noting. The first has to do with character.

The Constitution creates incentives for service, on the one hand, and mechanisms of selection on the other, that together are meant to increase the likelihood that those with better characters will want to run for office and be chosen when they do. This is intended to promote the advancement of those best qualified by temperament and training. Democracy means rule by the People. But if popular government is to succeed, those with good characters must be encouraged and helped to play a leading role in it. This is a central theme in the *Federalist* (which acknowledges that a stable government must be designed to work even when men of good character are not "at the helm").[51]

If we pause and ask what "good character" meant to the Founders, the obvious answer is the kind of character they themselves possessed. No doubt this is true. But their idea of character was not frivolous or entirely self-serving. It had behind it—and still does—the authority of a long tradition of philosophical and historical thought reaching back to Aristotle, Plutarch, and Tacitus, among others.

A great deal can be said about this tradition, but one point is relevant here. In the view of Aristotle and those who followed him, a good character takes time to acquire. It is in essence an ensemble of habits.[52] These form slowly. In time, they become a more reliable basis for judgment and action than any rule or principle deduced by thought alone. (The same is true of bad character.)

This is the point where the idea of character touches the Humean conviction that habit, not reason, is the source of the authority that law and morality possess. Both rest on the assumption that, in practical matters at least, time has the power to do what timeless truths cannot. The Framers' belief in the value of delay and their determination to do the most that can be done in a democratic regime to advance the careers of the best spring from the same conservative instinct that mistrusts what is definitive, quick, and transparent in favor of the slowly matured and always somewhat opaque political and personal deposits of time.

The second point concerns judicial review. The Constitution leaves a vital question unanswered—one that touches on the structural coherence of the scheme as a whole. When disputes arise concerning the meaning of the Constitution itself, who has the final authority to resolve them? Or is there perhaps no *final* authority, only competing ones, exercised by those who occupy different positions in the constitutional distribution of powers?[53]

Fifteen years after the ratification of the Constitution, the Supreme Court answered this question. It said that issues of constitutional interpretation are ones of law and therefore "emphatically the province and duty of the judicial department" to decide in an authoritative way.[54]

Others (presidents, legislators, and citizens) remain free to offer their interpretations and to criticize those of the Court. These disagreements sometimes become political controversies that lead, in time, to a change of judicial personnel. The Court always depends, moreover, on the legislative and executive branches to respect and enforce its decrees; it has neither the "will" nor "force" to do so on its own. And of course any judgment the Court renders may be overridden by amending the Constitution itself. In these and other ways, the power of the Court is constrained. It is not the power of an autocratic sovereign free to make law as it pleases.[55]

Still, even with these qualifications, the Supreme Court occupies a position of interpretive authority unique among modern democratic governments. It does so despite the absence of a provision in the Constitution explicitly conferring this power on it. The principle of judicial review, as we have come to call it, is not a constitutional rule at all. It is a *para*-constitutional norm whose entrenchment in American life and law is a consequence of its having been accepted, sometimes grudgingly, for a very long time by others with the authority to speak on behalf of the People from the vantage point of the competing positions they occupy in our constitutional scheme. Its acceptance is a function of the validating power of time and therefore always vulnerable to loss or decay, since whatever acquires authority because it lasts declines or disappears when it ceases to do so.

The authority of the Supreme Court is therefore a variable quantity. It may be greater or less. Today, some think it is ebbing.[56] But if one asks why the principle of judicial review has become such a settled feature of our system of constitutional law despite the absence in the Constitution of any express affirmation of the principle itself, the best answer is that it reinforces the Constitution's strategic use of delay and shares in its Humean appeal.

Giving a court of law the final word regarding the meaning of the Constitution is a further antidote to the dangers of passion and mob rule. Lawsuits take time; they move at a leisurely pace, mindful of procedural requirements that lawyers and judges respect but others often do not. It may be years before a political controversy reaches the Supreme Court for decision, and when it does those who decide it (some, at least) are likely to have been appointed years before. The Court is always out of step with the times. It is permanently old-fashioned.

The justices do not sit as guardians who, like those in Plato's *Republic*, enjoy a privileged access to truths beyond time.[57] We expect their opinions to be reasoned, but the authority of their decisions only partly depends on the reasons that support them. It is also a function of the time the justices have taken to consider the cases that come before them, the deliberateness with which they deliver their opinions, and the continuity of their decisions with others rendered in the past.

This is always subject to challenge. A critic may say that the Court has proceeded with haste or distorted the past for the sake of a present result. Sometimes the critic is right. But the criticism draws strength from the belief that when the Court acts as it should, it moves slowly, cautiously, with a concern to protect the evolved continuities of interpretive judgment—in a spirit of delay, and with due respect for the consecrating power of time that informs the Constitution as whole.

Even the process of judicial appointment reflects this. The drafters made assumptions about the role of character in electoral politics. They believed that temperance, caution, and a devotion to the public good are habits that take time to develop; that those with these qualities will be recognized as outstanding candidates for office; and that, once elected, they will govern with greater wisdom and discernment, not invariably but as a general rule. Today these beliefs seem archaic. Many even find them offensive. There is, however, one striking exception. Those nominated to judicial positions are still expected to be men and women of good character—to have the intellectual and emotional strength to judge dispassionately yet with a human sympathy for those whose fates lie in their hands. This is what we mean by *judicial temperament*, a phrase that signifies a set of habits solidly founded on long experience and training and resilient enough to provide a bulwark against personal advantage and partisan loyalty.[58] If the principle of judicial review represents an extension of the Constitution's preference for protracted processes of deliberation and compromise over both the maelstrom of passion and the certainty of transcendent truths, the presumptive importance of character in the selection of judges, and Supreme Court justices in particular, reflects the lasting appeal of an eighteenth-century ideal of temperament founded on a belief in the normative power of time.

Judicial review is the most conservative feature of our American system of government. This is not only because it is "counter-majoritarian."[59] It is conservative because it assumes that time has the power to confer on human judgments an authority that abstract reasoning alone can never produce. The Constitution as a whole rests on this assumption. The Declaration, by contrast, appeals to self-evident truths and eternal laws. From their perspective, delay is at most a useful tactic but never something good in itself. The ponderous and time-consuming requirements of the Constitution and the informal principle of judicial review must be judged as all tools are. If the Constitution is a poor means for achieving the equality held up by the Declaration as a transcendent ideal, then it needs to be reformed. If judicial review is a stumbling block in the way of vindicating the rights that belong to all of us before and beyond any merely political process, then it should be rejected. Today, when many believe that the Supreme Court has lost its way and is no longer inspired by the passion for equality that shaped the decisions of the Warren Court; when half the country thinks the Court has become a re-actionary dam holding the waters of justice back; when the very idea of the Court as a deliberative body relatively insulated from the passions of political life seems increasingly incredible, and the normal processes of government are crippled by gridlock and partisan loathing: today, the case for viewing the Constitution as a failed tool seems especially strong.[60]

If this view is nevertheless wrong, it is because the Constitution is not a tool whose value is measured by its success in fulfilling the vision of the Declaration. It is because (as Lincoln thought) the work of conserv-ing our union has a worth of its own; because the Constitution embodies conservative values that we cherish for their own sake, just as we do the radical ideals of the Declaration; and because, as a people, we are both Humeans and Lockeans, inspired by two documents, one of which as-signs an authority to time that the other denies it.

How has it happened that the complexity of Lincoln's view of the re-lation between the Declaration and the Constitution has been replaced in the minds of some by the simpler belief that the Declaration's tran-scendent ideal of equality is the end by which the means of the Constitu-tion should be judged? The answer has to do with the issue that prompted Lincoln's observation that the Declaration is our "golden apple" and the Constitution its "frame of silver." It has to do with slavery.

# VI

When the signers of the Declaration of Independence proclaimed that "all men are created equal," they did not have slaves in mind. They were eager to avoid the issue of slavery for the sake of preserving a revolution-ary coalition that included many slaveholders. Even those who opposed slavery for the most part supported a temporizing strategy. They hoped that with a little encouragement, it would disappear in time. The Consti-tution itself adopts this approach. Article I, Section 9 forbids Congress from enacting any law prohibiting the importation of slaves until the year 1808. It is the Constitution's only explicit sunset provision.

Thomas Jefferson described slavery as a debasement of slave and master alike yet thought—hoped—it would eventually wither away on its own. Toward the end of his life, Jefferson lost confidence in this comforting belief, which had helped him live with his intellectual and moral contradictions. The Missouri Compromise filled him with fear. It sounded "a fire-bell in the night," though he never became an outright abolitionist, unprepared to brook postponement or delay.[61]

Lincoln was clearer about the absoluteness of the wrong. Slavery is a crime, always and forever. Yet up to the start of the Civil War and for some time after, he continued to subscribe to Jefferson's temporizing strategy. Slavery need not be extirpated immediately, root and branch, in the Southern states where it then existed. It was enough to be confident of its "eventual extinction." He insisted this was the course the Framers intended.

Unlike Jefferson, Lincoln explicitly tied the wrongness of slavery to the words of the Declaration. Even as he continued to temporize, he found in the Declaration the anchor for his conviction that certain principles possess a transcendent authority independent of all considerations of political expediency. Among these, he said, is the proposition that the equality of all men absolutely forbids the ownership of some by others. Still, for as long as he could, Lincoln sought to straddle the widening space between the Declaration's eternal decrees and the spirit of the Constitution, which promotes delay for the sake of political union.

"And the war came."[62] Lincoln's straddle became unsustainable. Forced to choose sides, he eventually chose abolition—everywhere and without further delay. Lincoln still hoped to preserve the union as well. This remained a goal up to the end of his life. But the Civil War put an end to all strategies that looked to the disappearance of slavery in "the ordinary course of events." The eternal truth that slavery is wrong had now to be affirmed in political time. The affirmation was consecrated in blood.

After the war, the "self-evident truths" of the Declaration were brought into the body of the Constitution itself through the postwar amendments.[63] Many of the amendments' supporters believed these truths to be the end for whose sake the Constitution exists. Others saw things differently. They rejected the idea that the Constitution is merely a means to the advancement of human equality and continued to affirm the inherent worth of its conservative scheme of adjustments and delays. In this sense, the question of how to think about the relation between the timeless ideals of the Declaration and the Constitution's valorization of time was not settled once and for all by the Civil War amendments. They merely gave it a new form. They made it an *intra*-constitutional dilemma—a problem of constitutional interpretation and therefore of constitutional law.

The story of how over the next century the relation between these two documents came to be interpreted in the language of constitutional law can be told in a few broad strokes.

The Thirteenth Amendment abolished slavery. The Fifteenth guaranteed the right to vote "regardless of race, color or previous condition of servitude." The Fourteenth gave the Declaration's principle of human equality an even more expansive constitutional grounding. It spoke in spacious terms of a right to "due process" and the "equal protection of the laws." These open-ended terms invited a process of interpretive expansion that in time led to the application of the principle of equality to a seemingly endless number of issues other than race.

In the decades that followed the ratification of the Fourteenth Amendment, the Supreme Court defused its radical potential where issues of race are concerned. Three famous cases were especially important in this respect. Two of them, *The Civil Rights Cases* (1883) and *Plessy v. Ferguson* (1896), dealt directly with race.[64] The first established a "state action" requirement that made it difficult for federal officials to use the Fourteenth Amendment to prosecute individuals for denying blacks their political and civil rights when the wrongdoers were arguably acting on their own and not as agents of the state. The second held that the amendment's equal protection clause is satisfied by laws that segregate blacks and whites so long as they are treated equally. Together, these two decisions ensured that the South was left free with only minimal federal interference to restore a regime of racial subordination that preserved many of the features of the antebellum order—the new caste system we call "Jim Crow."

The third case was the earliest of the three. Unlike the other two, *The Slaughter-House Cases* (1873) did not explicitly involve race.[65] The decision had doctrinal consequences, though, that, together with the state action requirement and the endorsement of separate but equal, helped to frustrate efforts to impose a new order of racial equality on a recalcitrant South. The most important of these was the Court's narrow reading of the Fourteenth Amendment's provision that no state shall make or enforce any law abridging "the privileges or immunities of citizens of the United States"—a requirement the Court interpreted as applying only to the limited class of protections that attach to federal (as distinct from state) citizenship.[66] The case itself, however, involved a challenge to a Louisiana law not on the grounds that it discriminated on the basis of race but for the very different reason (as the butchers who brought the suit saw it) that it interfered with their pre-political right to pursue a trade of their own choosing.

Justice Miller wrote for a narrow majority. He insisted that the Fourteenth Amendment was intended to protect the rights of recently freed slaves and gave this as a reason for caution in extending its protections to rights of other sorts, including that of free labor. He then proceeded to treat the dispute as a garden-variety example of the ancient problem of determining the limits of a state's police powers when they conflict with the freedom of individuals to work as they wish, and concluded that in the case at hand these limits had not been exceeded.

In dissent, Justice Field insisted that the language of the Fourteenth Amendment applies more broadly than Miller claimed. He enthusiastically embraced its expansive potential, arguing that the Fourteenth Amendment was meant to give the self-evident truths of the Declaration a new anchor in the Constitution itself.[67] Among these truths, he said, is the proposition that every individual has the right to use or sell his labor as he wishes—a right that in Field's view the Louisiana statute at issue in the case impermissibly infringed. Field lost the fight in *The Slaughter-House Cases* but his interpretation of the Fourteen Amendment eventually prevailed. Thirty years later, the Court adopted it in *Lochner v. New York* (1905).[68]

The *Lochner* decision rested on the Lockean belief that we each own our labor-power and have a right to employ it as we wish, free of all but the most necessary restraints. It held that the due process clause of the Fourteenth Amendment provides constitutional protection for this pre-political right. Justice Miller's cramped interpretation of the Fourteenth Amendment in *The Slaughter-House Cases* had softened its radicalism by confining the amendment's affirmation of human equality to the special case of race. Justice Field's broader reading opened the way to what in *Lochner* became (for a time) the orthodox view that the Fourteenth Amendment installs the self-evident truths of the Declaration in the heart of the Constitution itself, at least so far as the right to property is concerned. Whenever this right is challenged, *Lochner* implied, the normal political processes of concession and compromise are to be judged against the standard of a pre-political ideal that transcends time altogether.

Meanwhile, the question of race languished and the country settled into a long night of injustice.

Those who objected to the decision in *Lochner*, as Holmes famously did, believed that the right to property should not be immunized from the give-and-take of political life.[69] They opposed elevating the peremptory spirit of the Declaration to a position of commanding authority in the interpretation of constitutional law for the sake of protecting the right to buy, sell, and work on terms of one's own choosing. In time, their view prevailed. Property lost the special protection it had enjoyed as Locke's favored child. *West Coast Hotel v. Parrish* (1937) put the ghost of *Lochner* to rest.[70] But the spirit of the Declaration, which Field celebrated in his *Slaughter-House* dissent and which animated the decision in *Lochner*, did not vanish from the United States Reports. It migrated.

The seeds of change were planted in the noontime of *Lochner* by Justice James McReynolds in *Meyer v. Nebraska* (1923) and *Pierce v. Society of Sisters* (1925).[71] In these pivotal decisions, the Court unanimously held that the Fourteenth Amendment protects the right of parents to educate their children in the manner they think best. The freedom to do so, McReynolds said, is one we bring with us when we enter political society; it is neither created by law nor can be taken away by it. The argument is familiar from *Lochner*. It reflects the ideals of the Declaration and continues the line of constitutional thought inaugurated by Field's dissent. What makes these two opinions so remarkable is their extension of these ideals to choices that touch on intimate, personal matters as contrasted with the impersonal business of buying and selling.

A long series of further extensions lay ahead: from *Meyer v. Nebraska* and *Pierce v. Society of Sisters* to *Griswold v. Connecticut* (1965), where the Court held that married couples have a constitutionally protected right to use contraceptives; *Roe v. Wade* (1973, since overruled), which declared that for a specified time pregnant women have the right to decide whether to carry their fetus to term; *Lawrence v. Texas* (2003), invalidating sodomy laws across the nation; and *Obergefell v. Hodges* (2015), holding that the Fourteenth Amendment guarantees same-sex couples a right to marry that no state can deny.[72]

Justice McReynolds would have been appalled. Yet the impetus behind this remarkable reinterpretation of the rights protected by the Fourteenth Amendment was founded on the belief, which McReynolds shared, that we possess certain unalienable rights whose higher authority is beyond the power of legislators to construct or dismantle. It was motivated by a commitment to the Lockean ideals of the Declaration of Independence, which became part of our basic law through the adoption of the Fourteenth Amendment, and acquired vastly greater authority when the Court returned at last, in 1954, to the question of racial equality.[73]

*Brown v. Board of Education* did not come out of the blue. A series of Supreme Court decisions prepared the way for it, cautiously challenging the doctrine of separate but equal in the sphere of higher education and gingerly advancing the ideal of racial equality in other areas of law (for example, by outlawing the use of racially restrictive covenants in real estate sales).[74] Other developments beyond the work of the Court exerted pressure in the same direction—most notably, perhaps, the desegregation of the armed forces by presidential order in 1948 and the growing need to blunt the Soviet Union's painfully accurate portrait of American racism.[75]

Still, *Brown* was an earthquake. It declared with startling simplicity that the long-delayed, deeply suppressed question of racial equality would no longer be postponed but was now to be settled once and for all on the basis of the principle of human equality, for whose sake the Civil War had been fought and the post–Civil War amendments adopted. The decision released immense forces that had long been held in suspension by the tension between two great seismic blocks.

Other questions remained—most important, that of implementation. But the impact of *Brown* was as great as it was because the Court said in a brief, unanimous opinion that time was up; that there would be no more delay; that the temporizing strategy for the abolition of slavery and its reincarnation as Jim Crow was at an end; that the day of reckoning had come, and other constitutional subtleties must yield to the transcendent ideals of the Declaration of Independence, now inscribed in the language of the Fourteenth Amendment.

Chief among these subtleties is the separation of powers between the national and state governments—what John Marshall called the "genius" of our federal system.[76] This is one of the Constitution's principal devices for dividing and delaying the exercise of power. The defendants in *Brown* relied upon it. They urged the wisdom of further delay.[77] But against their pleas, *Brown* insisted on the priority of an absolute norm, as Jefferson had done in calling for a revolution to vindicate the colonists' rights after the resources of prudence had been exhausted. *Brown* reenergized the Fourteenth Amendment with the sublime authority of the Declaration, which flows from its demand that we judge all human laws, including the supreme law of the Constitution, from the standpoint of self-evident truths whose compulsory force no rational, conscientious man or woman can deny.

Yet *Brown* did more than merely reaffirm the timeless principles of the Declaration and acknowledge that they had been given constitutional standing in the Civil War amendments. The tension between these principles and the valorization of delay that the Constitution embraces and exploits had been made unbearably sharp by a century of moral neglect in which the country tolerated a system of legal apartheid that mocked the Declaration's paean to human equality. This was an explosive contradiction. *Brown* released its pent-up force. Once discharged, it had a transforming effect on the whole of constitutional law, much of which now had to be rethought and perhaps rebuilt in light of the supremacy of the eternal law of human equality over all merely political arrangements—on the basis of the belief that the Constitution is a form of human government whose purpose is to "preserve" and "adorn" the divine truths of the Declaration.

It is often said that the Warren Court, whose work began with *Brown* and continued into the 1960s under the leadership of a new chief justice, made equality its guiding value.[78] There is a great deal of truth in this. But more fundamentally, the Court recalibrated the balance between the Declaration and the Constitution. It put the first, with its insistence on "the Laws of Nature and of Nature's God," ahead of the second, with its affirmation of the authority-generating power of time. What the Warren Court did and did not do should be understood in this light—as should the conservative reaction against it.

The meaning of this reaction is best explained (if only poorly by many who today call themselves conservatives) as a campaign to restore the values of the Constitution to something like parity with those of the Declaration—to put Hume back into a rough balance with Locke in response to the radicalism of insisting that the Declaration always comes first. The long nightmare of slavery and Jim Crow strengthens the latter judgment. *Brown* gave it enormous prestige. Since *Brown*, the challenge for conservatives has been to show that we are morally and constitutionally compelled to embrace *Brown*'s teaching on race, yet need to be cautious about extending the Lockean values behind it to other areas of life whose complexities, conflicts, and unprincipled alignments recommend a more Humean approach and greater respect for the virtues of delay.

# VII

*Brown* reaffirmed the central principle of the Declaration of Independence with an absoluteness befitting its timeless authority. De jure segregation is unjust everywhere and always. But if the principle of *Brown* is immutable, its enforcement depends on human beings working over time to adjust its simple command to the complexities of political and social life. This is the challenge of implementation. The Court faced it a year later in *Brown II* (1955).[79]

*Brown II* uses a famous formula to capture the tension between transcendent principle and worldly reality. Schools must desegregate "with all deliberate speed."[80] The phrase is meant to acknowledge the unconditional nature of the principle while recognizing that its implementation has to take conditions into account. Some delay is inevitable for practical reasons but will not be countenanced when it is intended to challenge the principle itself.

"All deliberate speed" is of course not the solution to a problem but the description of one. After *Brown*, the Court grappled with it for two decades in a series of cases testing the constitutionality of various school desegregation plans and the authority of the federal courts to design and enforce them.

Where, in the past, a school district has been entirely and explicitly segregated by law and an administratively simple remedy is at hand, the answer is clear. The remedy is constitutional and courts have the power to enforce it (*Green v. New Kent County*, 1968).[81] Where a district has been partly and indirectly segregated as a result of racially motivated siting decisions and school zoning practices, and the remedy is more complex and intrusive, the answer is less clear. It is still yes, but not unambiguously so (*Keyes v. Denver*, 1973).[82] Where the only feasible desegregation plan requires the consolidation of many separate school districts, most of which have never been segregated by law, either directly or indirectly, and the plan involves the very far-reaching use of highly complex techniques, the plan is even farther removed from the simple truth of *Brown* and the clear command of *Brown II*. A court's authority to uphold it against the political will of the people is tenuous and ought to be denied (*Milliken v. Bradley*, 1974).[83]

The doctrinal evolution from *Green* to *Milliken* has its supporters and critics. For the critics, *Milliken* represents the abandonment of the promise of *Brown* and of the special responsibility of the federal courts—the supra-political custodians of supra-political truths—to make sure the promise is kept.[84] They view *Milliken* as a capitulation to the defenders of delay who have grown subtler than the Southern obstructionists who opposed *Brown* in the early 1950s but remain as resistant as their bigoted predecessors to the imperative of racial equality.

Most important, these critics insist that the distinction between de jure and de facto segregation is conceptually indefensible.[85] There is no principled difference, they say, between these two sorts of segregation, only a practical one, which has no intrinsic weight from the standpoint of absolute right and wrong—of justice and injustice as measured by the immutable ideal of human equality. The critics of the Court's retrenchment in its school desegregation decisions take their point of departure from the Declaration of Independence and are buoyed by its radical spirit. They look to *Brown* as its vindication in constitutional law.

Those who view the arc of these decisions more favorably do so in part because they acknowledge the importance of complexities the critics deny—or, more exactly, because they view them not as obstacles to be weighed in instrumental terms but as social and cultural realities with their own moral salience.[86] They assign greater value to the freedom of choice and movement that contributes to de facto segregation. They acknowledge the injustice of the dim prospects that trap many in our inner cities but value the pluck and patience and devotion to their families that motivate those who escape. They value the ideal of the neighborhood school, to the extent it is still attainable. And because they regard all these things as having some worth of their own, they refuse to treat them merely as means to the end of eliminating school segregation root and branch.

They are more content than the radical critics of *Milliken* to allow this contest of values to be settled in a political process; to tolerate compromise and delay; and they are more suspicious of judges who claim the authority to override this process in the name of the Fourteenth Amendment, which gives the courts the footing they need to enforce the transcendent ideals of the Declaration as a positive legal norm. They are more Humean in outlook and less inclined to view the Constitution as a means to a Lockean end.

Since Lincoln, the pre-political truths of the Declaration have always seemed most obviously and urgently applicable to race. This gave *Brown* its tremendous force. But *Brown*'s vindication of the ideal of human equality had an appeal that reached far beyond questions of race. *Brown* raised the ideal to a position of preeminence in constitutional law generally and in doing so decisively shifted the balance between the radicalism of the Declaration and the conservatism of the Constitution in favor of the former. Two other branches of law illustrate this phenomenon. One is the law of voting rights, the other that of reproduction.

The right to vote is first among political rights.[87] It is the right to have a say in the making of laws that will determine what other rights citizens have. It is the right *to be* a citizen—to have a voice in collective self-government. In a democracy that rests on the presumed equality of all its citizens, the right to vote must be distributed equally. Every vote should count the same. This is simple legal logic. Its fundamental axiom is "one man, one vote."

The Supreme Court affirmed the axiom in *Reynolds v. Sims* (1964).[88] In *Reynolds*, the Court invalidated a recently enacted Alabama statute and a proposed amendment to the state constitution that assigned representatives to the two chambers of the state legislature partly or wholly on the basis of territory rather than population. For seven decades, Alabama had failed to reapportion representatives to reflect the demographic shift from countryside to city. Race was an important factor in its failure to do so.

In striking down the statute and proposed amendment, the Court took an exceptionally strong stand. "Legislators represent people," Chief Justice Warren wrote, "not trees or acres. Legislators are elected by voters, not farms or cities or economic interests."[89] The only scheme of apportionment consistent with this view is one that follows as closely as practically possible the numerical approach implied by the principle "one man, one vote." This requires that representatives be distributed on a strictly quantitative basis. The Fourteenth Amendment demands it.

Warren's conclusion is far removed from the Madisonian (ultimately, Humean) idea of effective representation as reflected in the mechanisms of the Constitution. Madison's view rests on the assumption that society is not a collection of independent atoms but of groups with overlapping and distinct interests; that these are organized in different ways, some on the basis of wealth, others of profession, neighborhood, culture, and religion; that the stability of society depends on the widely shared belief that different interest groups have a fair chance to make their case in the public forum; and that the adjustment of these interests takes time and requires compromises of all sorts.[90] To facilitate the process, representation ought not to be structured in a strictly numerical fashion. Other factors (including geography and political affiliation) must be taken into account. "One man, one vote" may be a sensible default but departures from it should be allowed for the sake of a system of government better adjusted to the qualitative complexities that constitute the warp and weft of human life.

This is the way representative government looks to those who take their stand within the "course of human events." If instead one views the political process from the timeless vantage point of the Declaration, the value of these complexities is harder to grasp. The self-evident truths of the Declaration all turn on the equality of individual human beings and their rights as individuals. The Declaration is morally and metaphysically atomistic. And because the truths it affirms are eternally valid, the jockeying of competing interest groups represented in qualitatively different ways is unlikely to appear to be of much value.

The priority that *Brown* assigns the pre-political egalitarianism of the Declaration in the context of race helps to explain the reductive individualism of the Warren Court's most famous apportionment decision a decade later. Like *Brown, Reynolds v. Sims* vindicates a basic human right against the awkward, opaque, unprincipled accommodations of a protracted political process, which have little or no worth when judged by the sharp-edged principle that all men are created equal. It too reflects the triumph of the simple radicalism of the Declaration over the complexity and conservatism of the Constitution. The conservative response began with Justice Harlan's dissent in *Reynolds v. Sims*.[91] The current view that even the most extreme forms of political gerrymandering do not violate the constitutional mandate of "one man, one vote" bears a certain resemblance to Harlan's respect for the complexities of the democratic process, though the rigidity of the conservative position is now as great, and its tone as radical, as the view that it opposes.[92]

The most controversial assertion of the priority of the Declaration over the Constitution, though, has not been in the area of race or representation but in the law of reproductive rights. What lawyers call the principle of "substantive due process" survived the death of *Lochner* and migrated to the realm of intimate life.[93] The seed that was sown in *Meyer v. Nebraska* and *Pierce v. Society of Sisters* became a full-grown plant in *Griswold v. Connecticut*. Eight years later, *Griswold* flowered in *Roe v. Wade*, whose core teaching was refined and restated in *Planned Parenthood v. Casey* (1992).[94] The central idea in this line of cases is easily stated. Every human being has a right to determine how to arrange his or her private relations so long as these do no harm to others. The home is an especially important domain of such relations and within the home, one's body, which we are free to use (or abuse) as we choose, again subject to a general (if vague) prohibition against harming others.

This way of describing the right underscores its affinity to a Lockean way of thinking and emphasizes its pre-political nature, insulating it from political attack. It puts the right to privacy, of which the right to abortion is an offshoot, in the orbit of the Declaration and allows those who defend it to draw on the enhanced prestige that *Brown* conferred on the Declaration as a standard of constitutional law.

When the right in question is the freedom to use contraceptives, engage in consensual sex with other adults, or marry whomever one chooses, the authority of the Declaration and the appeal of Locke are at a maximum. The case of abortion is different. The choice to abort is not self-regarding to the same degree these others are. It directly touches the vital interests of another. At what stage do these interests arise? How much weight should they be given? How long does a woman need to make an informed decision? These are not (just) technical questions. They cannot be answered with a mathematical formula like the trimester scheme of *Roe*, which resembles the numerical test in *Reynolds v. Sims*.[95] They involve intractable moral and spiritual dilemmas.

Those who see things from a Humean perspective believe these dilemmas ought to be left to the political process, with protective guardrails of inexact height, rather than settled by a supra-political Court on the basis of immutable Lockean rights. Some of *Roe's* now-victorious critics view the question of abortion in this light, but others are inspired by a fundamentalism as radical as that of their opponents. They too conceive the question from a Lockean point of view, though the transcendent right they affirm is not that of pregnant women but of the unborn children in their wombs. Like *Roe's* defenders, they are riding the tailwinds of *Brown*, which lifts the wings of all who soar to Jeffersonian heights.

The true constitutional conservatives are those who are committed to *Brown* but resist giving Jefferson's self-evident truths a determinative weight in other areas of law, including the law of reproductive rights, where the truth is anything but self-evident. They are wary of *Brown's* radicalizing potential and determined to restore a more Lincolnian balance between the political moralities of the Declaration and the Constitution. Pressed by radicals on both the left and right, these Humean conservatives have been losing ground for some time. What some describe as the conservatism of the Supreme Court today is not a refutation but a confirmation of this, for its victories have been prepared by the allure over the last half century, in conservative circles at least, of a slogan that is antithetical to Hume's reliance on the valorizing power of time and the Constitution's employment of it to create a system of authority that is built, not broken, by delay. The slogan is "originalism."

# VIII

"Originalism" is a theory of law—or, more accurately, a family of theories, since there is no single orthodox version of it. Developing and defending the theory of originalism has been a cottage industry in American law schools for a very long time; so has criticizing its shortcomings.[96]

Originalism is not, of course, a merely academic phenomenon. It has an established place in public opinion. Many think of it as a "conservative" theory of law—indeed, *the* conservative theory since it has no serious competitors for the title. The fight for and against originalism is widely viewed as the most important philosophical battleground in the perennial contest between conservative and progressive methods of legal, and especially constitutional, interpretation.[97]

Originalism did not begin, however, as much of a theory at all. It lacked the qualities of rigor we associate with the word. In its earliest phase, it can best be described as a loosely framed criticism of the work of the Warren Court, motivated by two related concerns and the need to find a theoretical hook on which to hang them.[98]

The first had to do with what conservative critics of the Court viewed as its illegitimate extension of judicial authority into areas properly left to the political process. The second reflected their dismay at the Court's insistence on the moral and legal priority of a wide range of individual rights in matters involving race, reproduction, voting, and the criminal process. Too often, its critics said, the Court had overstepped the appropriate bounds of judicial review in the name of a theory of human equality whose pre-political truths it took to be beyond the realm of ordinary political debate.

Progressive defenders of the Warren Court had elegant theories to explain their position. John Rawls's *A Theory of Justice* is the leading example.[99] Wanting something to offer in response, the Court's conservative critics landed on originalism. Its fundamental premise is as old as the worry about "judicial activism"—a new term but not a new worry. The originalists of the 1970s and 1980s insisted (as Jefferson had in 1803) that judges should not interpret the law according to their own speculative beliefs but ought to abide by the intentions of those who made the law in the first place as reflected in the words they chose at the time.[100] If judges follow this basic rule, the advocates of originalism claimed, their discretion will be cabined and the political process restored to a position of proper authority.

This simple suggestion raised many questions. One has to do with the meaning of "intent." Whose intent and how expressed? What is the relation between text and context—between words and their public meaning? What if the original intent of those who made the law (in the case of the Constitution, who drafted and ratified it) was to defer to the views of later generations regarding its interpretation?[101] Analogous questions arise in the law of contracts, where "intent" is often similarly ambiguous.

A second and more basic question concerns the authority of past acts of lawmaking to bind those who come later. Are the living obliged to defer to the dead? There are practical reasons for doing so. But are there any moral grounds—and to the extent the Constitution embodies a set of moral beliefs, any constitutional grounds—for such deference?

Ingenious attempts have been made to answer these questions. Their subtlety and sophistication are impressive. But the answers are unconvincing.

Some, in an effort to solve the problem of intent, have gone to such extravagant lengths that the distinction between originalism and its progressive counterpart—what legal scholars call "living constitutionalism"—has all but disappeared.[102] Others have invoked the authority of "history and tradition" as a supplement to past acts of political will, either to explain their meaning or provide independent support for the rule of the dead over the living. In doing so, though, they have merely shifted the debate over the interpretation of intent to the equally intractable question of how best to describe the meaning of complex historical and cultural processes. More fundamentally, they have elided the distinction between will and tradition as sources of moral and political prestige—the first of which rests on the special authority of laws that have been deliberately chosen and the second on that of patterns and practices whose authority depends on the fact that they have not been consciously adopted at all.[103]

These are important, perhaps decisive failings. But originalism has another, deeper defect.

Originalism was invented to give conservatives a theory with which to combat the shortcomings of the Warren Court. It sought to do this by tethering the free-wheeling eternal-present of a speculative egalitarianism to a fixed and binding act performed at a particular moment in the past. But originalism shares with the judicial activism it opposes a similarly negative attitude toward the valorizing power of time. It is not a conservative theory of constitutional law in the Humean sense at all but a radical one that is poorly equipped to provide a fundamental alternative to the progressive Lockean interpretation of the Constitution as a means to transcendent ends.

Originalism stops time in its tracks. That is what it is meant to do—to define the meaning of what happens in the law over time from the perspective of a single extraordinary event that establishes once and for all an inflexible measure of judgment in the same way Jefferson's self-evident truths do. The latter exist outside of time; the originalist's act of founding takes place within it. Jefferson's truths are discernible by reason; the originalist's founding is an assertion of will. But both assign supreme importance to a fixed and unchanging standard whose authority is not established by the passage of time but proof against it. Both elevate the authority of the moment, the instant, the once-and-for-all—the finality of reason or will—and minimize or deny the normative value of adjustment, delay, and habit, which only exist in the extended movement of time. Even when judges with an originalist bent appeal to history and tradition, they use them to shore up their explanation of the meaning of a momentary decision and interpret them with an inflexibility that betrays their hostility to the Humean idea that beliefs, though always subject to critical review, acquire legitimacy only because they last.

For some time, originalism has been the dominant form of constitutional conservatism. In the minds of many, the two are nearly synonymous. But originalism leans in a Lockean, not a Humean, direction. Originalists may support conservative positions—that is debatable—but they certainly do not do so for conservative reasons.

## IX

There is a more promising though underappreciated strain of conservative constitutional thought. It offers a better vehicle for striking the right balance between the absolutism of the Declaration and the Constitution's reliance on the authority of time. It has deep roots in American law but also, like originalism, assumed its modern form in response to the perceived excesses of the Warren Court. Its most articulate champion was a law professor named Alexander Bickel, whose ideas are now mostly forgotten except in academic circles. The demise of the tradition of constitutional conservatism that Bickel represents is a great loss for conservatives and progressives alike.

Bickel was born in Romania in 1924 and moved to America at the age of fourteen, not speaking a word of English. Later he recalled with great affection the Jewish world of his childhood, in Bucharest and then in New York City. Bickel served in the army in the Second World War; attended City College and then Harvard Law School; served as a law clerk to Felix Frankfurter; and was appointed to the Yale Law School faculty in 1956.[104] His best-known book, *The Least Dangerous Branch*, was published in 1962.[105] Bickel wrote several other books and hundreds of articles before his early death from cancer in 1974. His last book, *The Morality of Consent*, appeared posthumously the following year. The title essay contains his most ambitious attempt at a general philosophy of law. In it, Bickel claims that his theory of constitutional interpretation was inspired by the ideas of Edmund Burke and contrasts the spirit of Burke's philosophy with that of John Rawls.[106]

Much of Bickel's writing in the late 1960s and early 1970s was critical of the Warren Court. He enthusiastically supported the *Brown* decision, on which he worked as a law clerk, but had growing doubts about later school desegregation and apportionment cases. He was opposed to affirmative action and thought *Roe* wrongly decided.[107] This is a familiar enough constellation of conservative views. What makes Bickel's work memorable is the distinctive way he defends these views.

The central idea of *The Least Dangerous Branch* is the value of delay in the adjudication of constitutional questions. The Court ought to go slowly, Bickel says. It needs to give itself and the country time to come to an adjustment, especially when the question is explosive and incapable of resolution in a fully principled way (like those concerning integration and abortion). Deference to the other two branches of government and to the political process generally is advisable in most cases.[108]

It is not that there are no absolutes. There are. *Brown* affirms one: no one should ever be denied the right to attend a school, vote, apply for a job, or marry a person of another race because of the color of his or her skin. But absolutes are few and the attempt to identify them should be approached with the humble recognition that one person's self-evident truth is another's transparent falsehood.

This counsels caution and an acknowledgment of the power of time to generate an authority of its own. It calls for the practical, political virtue of prudence rather than a speculative knowledge of pre-political rights.[109] It underscores the need to accept the multiplicity of fundamental values and the intractability of conflicts among them, hence the need to resolve or at least temper these conflicts on political rather than judicial terms. It values conversation over command and the authority of time over that of principles that lie beyond it.[110] Sometimes, as in *Brown*, this inclination must yield to the imperative of a truth beyond time, but when it should is a higher-order judgment that itself must be made on prudential grounds. Nothing, perhaps, matters more than making this judgment wisely, yet there is no transcendent principle to settle the matter. The one who must make the decision cannot escape what Bickel calls the "Lincolnian tension" between prudence and principle.[111]

These were the general ideas that shaped Bickel's reading of constitutional history and his increasingly critical assessment of the work of the Warren Court. His specific judgments followed from them. One need not accept them all to see the value of Bickel's ideas. His early attack on affirmative action, for example, shows an insensitivity to the need for some temporary compromise among the conflicting values involved that is uncomfortably close to the dogmatism he criticizes in other decisions.[112] But to challenge his judgment in these terms is to do so on Bickelian grounds.

Bickel was the champion of time against eternity. He was a defender of constitutional values against those enshrined in the Declaration, not in every case but more often than not. He associated his views with those of James Madison, whose acceptance of the difficulty or impossibility of resolving the most impassioned political conflicts in a principled way; recognition of the need for practical adjustment; and acknowledgment of the virtue of delay Bickel enthusiastically affirmed. These were the starting points of his modern Madisonian theory of constitutional law.

When, at the end of his short life, Bickel sought to trace his theory back to a more fundamental philosophical source, he located it in the thought of Edmund Burke, whose reverence for tradition Bickel greatly admired.[113] This was a mistake. Burke is a dubious inspiration for a conservative theory of American constitutional law. His insistence on the value of a landed nobility and an established church (among other beliefs) puts him at odds with the secular and democratic spirit of the Constitution. A better choice would have been David Hume, the enlightened philosopher of habit and accreted authority. Bickel may have thought he was a Burkean but he was not. He was a Humean whose attachment to the Constitution was motivated by his mistrust of the Lockean radicalism that inspires those who take their cue from the Declaration instead.

Compared with the faux conservatism of the originalist theory of interpretation—with its brittleness and preference for single, decisive moments over extended processes of colloquy, compromise, and delay—Bickel's is the real article. It offers a more encouraging point of departure for those who view the Constitution as a worldly scheme of government founded on consent built slowly over time and value it as a conservative counterweight to the soaring ideals of the Declaration, for whose imperfect realization the Constitution is a home but not a tool: a better way of understanding its role as a protective frame.

The Supreme Court has taken a conservative turn since the end of the Warren Court.[114] Progressives see this as the repudiation of a promise. They say it has no moral or constitutional justification. Conservatives have only the poor theory of originalism to offer in reply. They rightly look ridiculous in the eyes of their opponents.

There is an alternative, though.

*Brown v. Board of Education* was the greatest decision of the twentieth century, but it cast a dangerously long shadow. It invited an extravagant egalitarianism—buoyed by confidence in the eternal rights of man, which the struggle to rid the country of the scourge of racial discrimination had sharpened and emboldened—that demotes the authority of politics and promotes that of the Court in a way that upsets the Lincolnian balance between the Declaration and the Constitution.

Bickel's conservatism helps us understand where and why the post-*Brown* Court went wrong. It offers a genuinely conservative position from which the radicalism of today's Court and of the theory of originalism to which its members sometimes look for support may be seen for what they are—as impostors of conservatism whose fundamentalist and quasi-Lockean views ought to be rejected, in the name of Madison and Hume, by all who see the dangers in a univocal and uncompromising commitment to the ideal of pre-political rights that is part, but only part, of our national inheritance.

Our inheritance is defined by a commitment to the timeless principles set out in the Declaration *and* to a constitutional scheme that valorizes time and encourages trade-offs, conciliations, and sensible balance. There is a lasting tension between them. We are radicals and conservatives at once. This is who we are, uniquely, perhaps, among the nations of the earth. Bickel's philosophy of law offers a better, richer account of this dilemma than the flimsy abstractions of the originalists. Lincoln felt the predicament with physical force yet never tried to escape it. This is what made him a great American as well as a hero to humankind. Bickel invites us to follow his lead.

Occasionally one hears a Bickelian note in the Supreme Court reports. One hears it, for example, with explicit reference to Bickel himself in Justice Breyer's dissent in *Bush v. Gore* (2000) and in more muted tones in Chief Justice Roberts's brief concurrence in *Dobbs v. Jackson Women's Health* (2022).[115] One may even detect it, perhaps, in Roberts's contrasting opinions in *Rucho v. Common Cause* (2019) and *Moore v. Harper* (2023).[116] But for a real constitutional conservatism to live and breathe again, these occasional notes must swell into a chorus, be gathered in a song, loosen their connection to the narrow partisan interests that make them seem so opportunistic, and become, as they once were, a recognized and respected tradition of constitutional thought.

# CHAPTER SEVEN

# The Here and the Hereafter

## I

In the fall of 1801, the Baptists of Danbury, Connecticut, wrote to Thomas Jefferson asking for his help. He had been president for seven months.

At the time, Connecticut still had an established religion.[1] Its laws subsidized and supported the Congregational Church, as they had since 1639. The First Amendment to the federal Constitution forbids any law "respecting an establishment of religion" but was understood to apply to acts of Congress alone. The Baptists therefore had no legal remedy. "What religious privileges we enjoy," they complained, "we enjoy as favors granted and not as inalienable rights." While acknowledging that he was not "the National Legislator," they asked for a word of encouragement from their "beloved President," whose views, they said, "are bound to spread like the radiant beams of the sun" and to shine "through all these States—and all the world—until hierarchy and tyranny be destroyed from the earth."[2]

The Danbury Baptists had reason to hope for a favorable reply. Jefferson was a champion of religious liberty. He was the author of the Virginia Statute for Religious Freedom, on which the language of the First Amendment was modeled, and had courted the Baptists and other minority groups in the election of 1800.

They were not disappointed. On New Year's Day, Jefferson wrote back, enthusiastically praising the words and spirit of the First Amendment.

"I contemplate with sovereign reverence," he told the Baptists, "that act of the whole American people which declared that their legislature should 'make no law respecting an establishment of religion, or prohibiting the free exercise thereof,' thus building a wall of separation" between the realm of political action and that of religious belief.[3]

It is a famous but misleading phrase. Jefferson's "wall" is not what the word implies—a sharp boundary separating two entirely distinct jurisdictions, like the border between the United States and Canada. There is plenty of leakage in both directions.

The town of Greece, New York, may, for example, open its monthly meetings with a prayer, so long as nonbelievers are not made to feel coerced or excluded. The city of Pawtucket, Rhode Island, is permitted to include a crèche in its annual holiday display. The town of Bladensburg, Maryland, may allow a private group to place on public property a large memorial in the shape of a Latin cross honoring soldiers who died in the First World War. The state of New York may lend textbooks to parochial school students. And of course it is unobjectionable that the dollar bill says "In God We Trust" and that every sitting of the Supreme Court begins with the dramatic exclamation, "God save the United States and this honorable Court."[4]

In some of these cases, religion is allowed to make a limited but real appearance in the public square; in others, the state is permitted to put its powers at the disposal of religious belief. By the same token, the claims of religious conscience must sometimes yield to considerations of public safety and health. Except in special circumstances, the consumption of illegal drugs and the sacrifice of animals are forbidden even when they are part of a prescribed religious ritual. The prohibition of polygamy is an even more striking example.[5] If Jefferson's "wall" were really an impermeable barrier between separate, self-contained spheres of authority, none of these transgressions would be allowed.

The fact that they are has caused some to remark on the inaptness of Jefferson's image.[6] It also reminds us that the accommodation of religious and political values cannot be settled once and for all in an axiomatic way. Their reconciliation is an ongoing work of practical adjustment involving concessions on both sides. There is no way to resolve with unambiguous finality our national perplexity as to where the exact line between politics and religion should be drawn.

Still, it seems ungenerous to quarrel with Jefferson's choice of words and not terribly enlightening to observe that questions will always arise regarding the precise thickness and height of his wall. We know what Jefferson meant. We believe, as he did, that politics is one thing and religion another. More important, we believe that separating the two is good for both—that it serves the cause of religion as well as that of the state. The preamble to the Virginia Statute puts it succinctly. On the one hand, "Our civil rights have no dependence on our religious opinions any more than [on] our opinions in physics or geometry." On the other, the establishment of religion "tends only to corrupt the principles of that very Religion it is meant to encourage, by bribing with a monopoly of worldly honours and emoluments those who will externally profess and conform to it."[7]

These are twin evils. Jefferson's wall is meant to protect against both. This is a basic and in some ways distinctively American goal. That the aim of the First Amendment is to shield religion from politics as much as the reverse is the most enduring expression of the paradoxical fact that we are at once a thoroughly secular and earnestly religious people—more so, perhaps, than any other on earth.

## II

The good on the side of politics is secured by the establishment clause. Its purpose has been described many times. Justice O'Connor offers a contemporary statement in her concurrence in *Lynch v. Donnelly*, the Pawtucket crèche case. "The Establishment Clause," she writes, "prohibits government from making adherence to a religion relevant in any way to a person's standing in the political community. . . . Government endorsement or disapproval of religion . . . sends a message to nonadherents that they are outsiders, not full members of the political community, and an accompanying message to adherents that they are insiders, favored members of the political community."[8]

In O'Connor's view (which four other justices shared), the crèche at issue in the *Lynch* case conveyed no religious message at all. It was, she said, just one item in a large display that included "a Santa Claus house, reindeer pulling Santa's sleigh, candy-striped poles, a Christmas tree, carolers, cutout figures representing such characters as a clown, an elephant, and a teddy bear." In the company of these other symbols, the crèche carried only a broad message of holiday cheer. The four dissenting justices thought otherwise. Even amid such an assemblage, they said, the crèche retained its essential religious meaning. The "message of the nativity is that God became incarnate in the person of Christ." This is the fundamental teaching of the Christian religion but not, for example, that of the Jews, whose God "does not unite with human substance on earth."⁹

Despite their sharp disagreement on this question of symbolic interpretation, however, all nine members of the Court accepted without reservation Justice O'Connor's statement of the basic aim of the establishment clause. Expressed in different ways, it has been an article of national orthodoxy since the First Amendment was ratified in 1791.

The critical phrase in her concurrence is "political community." It appears three times. There are, of course, many sorts of community. The members of a family are a community; so are those who speak French, belong to a book club or trade association, or contribute to the Nature Conservancy. Like these others, a "political" community may be large or small, compact or widely distributed. What distinguishes it is not its size or concentration but the goal that unites those who belong to it. A political community exists for the sake of governing its own affairs. This is what political communities are for.

Other communities may be self-governing too (though many, like that of French speakers, are not). But self-government is not the purpose for which they exist. It is incidental to some other goal the community is striving to reach. Likewise, a political community may seek though self-rule to achieve a great variety of ends—the accumulation of wealth, cultural prestige, or military power. But these no more define its existence as a political community than the self-government of a book club or corporation defines its existence as a cultural or economic one.¹⁰

This way of distinguishing political from other communities is very old. According to Aristotle, it is what distinguishes a city, which exists for the sake of self-rule, from a household, whose goal is the raising of children and the satisfaction of need.¹¹ Among the former, he draws a number of further distinctions that reflect the different arrangements that cities adopt in order to rule themselves. He calls these "regimes" or "constitutions."¹² Aristotle's classification of regimes has had enormous influence on our tradition of political thought. Through a long succession of writers, ancient and modern, it was preserved in modified form down to the eighteenth century.

Loosely speaking, the American system of government belongs to the family of regimes that Aristotle calls "democratic." It does not rest on the kingly authority of "one" or the aristocratic command of a "few" but on the popular will of the "many"—on the authority of "the People," regardless of distinctions of birth, wealth, or virtue. It rests on their *in-*distinctness, and hence on their equality.

The American Constitution contains features that are only awkwardly reconciled with the idea that each citizen is equal to every other. The fact that states are equally represented in the Senate means that citizens are not. The acceptance of the para-constitutional principle of judicial review puts further pressure on the idea of democratic equality. Still, the ultimate reservoir of authority from which the Constitution springs is that of an unranked "People," each of whose members possesses an identical quantum of authority—none higher or lower, more lordly or regal, more deserving of deference and respect than any other. Our Constitution is the revisable system of government that "we the People" have framed to regulate the affairs of the democratic community we had already formed, in a notional sense, before the adoption of this or any constitutional scheme.

The principle of democratic equality has both negative and positive implications. The first is that no one may be excluded from a share in the collective work of self-government on account of some characteristic that has no bearing on his or her capacity for reflective participation. This negative conclusion rests on a more elusive positive ideal. If some characteristics, like race and gender, are irrelevant to one's right to participate, which are vital to it? What is the power or capacity that qualifies each citizen to join with others, on equal terms, in fashioning a system of government designed to meet their common and conflicting needs?

Locke calls it by its simplest name. It is, he says, the power of "reason." Kant defines it as "autonomy." John Rawls (who draws on both) describes it as the ability to frame a "plan of life."[13] There are important nuances here. Yet each insists that all and only human beings possess the power in question and that nothing more is needed to qualify for participation in political life. Other characteristics are irrelevant to what Justice O'Connor calls a "person's standing" in the American political community. In addition to race and gender, these include a person's religious beliefs.

For both Locke and Kant, a true understanding of the human condition still rested on the belief that the world was created by an all-knowing God who exists apart from and before it—what today some call the principle of "intelligent design."[14] Among other things, "enlightenment" meant the detachment of the ideal of political equality from every theological premise, including this one. The establishment clause is one of its many expressions. It decouples the right of political participation from any and all religious beliefs, even the bare affirmation of God's existence. Whether we think of a person's religion as an inheritance, an identity, or a set of beliefs, the suggestion that religion is relevant to his or her political standing is as offensive to the establishment clause and the enlightened way of thinking it reflects as the claim that race or gender is relevant in a similar way.

Did the crèche in Pawtucket suggest otherwise? The question divided the Court in *Lynch v. Donnelly*. But all the justices agreed that admission to the American experiment in self-government is on terms of strict equality and that the power of self-rule (of "reason" or "autonomy") no more depends on a person's religious beliefs than on the color of his or her skin. This is the political good secured by Jefferson's wall. It is relatively easy to see and fits with many other values of our dominantly secular culture. It is accepted by those for whom religion is important as well as those who scorn it. If anything, Justice O'Connor's observations about political "standing" are likely to seem boringly obvious to the devout and irreligious alike.

## III

What about the other side of the wall? Why is the separation it commands good for religion as well? There is a familiar answer here too.

The state has the authority to regulate external conduct. "When principles break out into overt acts against peace and good order," it may proscribe them.[15] But the government has no right to dictate which "religious opinions" citizens should hold or to prefer some to others by giving them official sanction and support. The realm of religious belief must be shielded from official interference in order to protect the freedom of these opinions themselves, whose meaning and value for those who hold them is damaged or destroyed when certain beliefs are either required or forbidden by law. Moreover, the truth about those matters to which religious opinions relate "is great and will prevail if left to herself." In religious inquiries, like every other, truth "is the proper and sufficient antagonist to error, and has nothing to fear from the conflict unless by human interposition disarmed of her natural weapons, free argument and debate; errors ceasing to be dangerous when it is permitted freely to contradict them."[16]

These are Jefferson's words from the Virginia Statute for Religious Freedom. They are a classic statement of the argument for the free exercise clause, which protects the good of religion on one side of his wall as the establishment clause does that of politics on the other. Interpretive disagreements will continue to arise. Do Sunday closing laws impermissibly invade the realm of religious freedom? What about a rule requiring male police officers to shave their beards?[17] Still, the good of religious freedom is acknowledged by all the disputants in these cases, just as the political good of disestablishment was taken for granted by both sides in *Lynch v. Donnelly*.

But this is a little too quick. There is an asymmetry in our understanding of these two goods. It is one that conventional views of the First Amendment obscure.

Unless they are theocrats, even the religiously devout agree that the good of our democracy requires the disestablishment of religion. They accept the ideal of political equality and acknowledge that the right of political participation must be independent of religious belief, though they sometimes complain that expressions of religious conviction should be accorded greater respect in public debate.[18] They affirm this ideal while insisting that other goods—more important ones, perhaps—transcend the realm of political life. In this regard, the religious and irreligious see eye to eye. Both care about the good of our democratic institutions and value them from the inside, as participants in the American system of self-rule.

They disagree, however, regarding the good of religion. The religious value this good from the inside too, but those who have no attachment to religion or feel an active hostility toward it see things differently. They may regard the free exercise of religion as an important good but if they do, they value it from the outside. Perhaps they endorse religious freedom because it dampens sectarian conflict and promotes the public peace. Perhaps they value it because they value freedom of thought and expression in general and see no manageable way of distinguishing religious opinions from any other. These are perfectly good reasons for supporting the freedom of religious belief. But they are external reasons, not internal ones. The religious and irreligious may agree that Jefferson's wall protects an important good on this side too, but it is not a good that both embrace *as their own* in the way they do the good of democracy on the other side of the wall.

This asymmetry is part of the meaning of the claim that secularism is today for many a religion of its own. The claim is often made in a hostile spirit by devout believers who object to what they see as attempts to restrict religious freedom in the name of political equality—the effort, for example, to compel bakers and web designers to make customized wedding cakes and websites for gay couples despite their opposition to same-sex marriage on religious grounds.[19] When defenders of the baker and web designer say that in their opponents' view, secularism is a religion, they are objecting, in part, to what they see as an illegitimate recalibration of the balance between political and religious values. But this is not the whole of it. Their objection reflects a deeper concern. It expresses the belief that in their adversaries' eyes, political equality is an intrinsic good but religion is not. In this respect, the devout contend, the playing field is not level.

Their complaint might be put as follows. "We recognize that political equality is a good in itself. But we insist that religion is a good of the same kind too. Religion addresses fundamental questions of human and cosmic importance as vital to our spiritual fulfillment as the protection of equality is to our political well-being. Our opponents either fail to see or refuse to concede this. They view religion from the outside. We see it from the inside—just as we do our membership as citizens in a political community of equals. Our vision is bifocal; theirs is not. Their concessions to religious freedom are always grudging—hence, to those for whom religion matters for its own sake, condescending if not downright insulting. This will continue to be true so long as the champions of political equality refuse to acknowledge the intrinsic good of religion as an essential component of human well-being."

This is not a new complaint. It is as old as the debate over religious freedom itself. The answer is just as old. "We are happy to concede that everyone should be left free to follow his or her spiritual leanings, in whatever direction they wish, consistent with the requirements of public safety. Enforced conformity of practice or belief is a recipe for political chaos and an insult to freedom of conscience. But do not ask us to concede that religion has any value of its own—because it does not. Religion is a province of superstition and enthusiasm, nothing more. It starts from extravagant beliefs that reason cannot support and encourages forms of devotion that reason cannot sustain. Religion is the enemy of enlightenment and though we must, for the sake of peace and the sanctity of conscience, accept that many will continue to be drawn by its irrational allurements, we will never agree that it is good for its own sake, or that the freedom to believe what one wishes about God, or any other chimera, is more than a political convenience of external value only."

This back-and-forth is wearily familiar. It has grown lifeless and stale. What more remains to be said? For those who still have any interest in the subject, the only thing left, it seems, is to decide which side they are on.

I disagree. I enthusiastically embrace the enlightened ideal of political equality and affirm the principle that a person's standing in our democratic community is entirely independent of his or her religious beliefs. I also agree with the devout that religious freedom is valuable for its own sake because religion itself is. They say that God is not a mere opinion but the truth about the world. I concur. But I differ from most who say this in one crucial respect. I believe that the intrinsic value of religion can be demonstrated on enlightened grounds too, and that the enlightened case for religion best explains why the separation of church and state is good for the essential human pursuits on both sides of Jefferson's wall.

My view puts me at odds with the defenders of two other, more familiar positions. It distinguishes me from the secular champions of political equality who view religious freedom as a practical necessity but deny that religion is vital to human fulfillment. It also distinguishes me from those defenders of religious freedom who insist that the transcendent truth of God's existence cannot be demonstrated by reason alone. Still, my view has an eminent predecessor. In the end, I think, it comes closer to Jefferson's own position than either of these other two and might without exaggeration be described as a restatement of his enlightened understanding of the needs of our divided souls.

# IV

To see why, we must ask a question the Supreme Court has rarely considered. What *is* religion? What distinguishes "religious" beliefs from other deeply held convictions of a nonreligious kind? We could ignore the question if the Constitution did not use the word *religion* but spoke instead of personal belief, or ethical commitment, or something of the kind. But it does use the word and singles out religion for uniquely favorable treatment.

The First Amendment assumes that it is peculiarly important to separate religion from politics—more important than to exclude morality from public life, which we neither can nor wish to do.[20] But why? What is it about religion that justifies its special treatment? John Locke had an answer. He explains it at length in his *Letter concerning Toleration*.

Locke believed that the world was brought into being by a providential creator who continues to superintend its affairs. He also believed that

our souls are immortal. Because they are, he says, we have a supreme interest in the fate of our souls in the world to come. That world, unlike
this one, is eternal; it has no beginning or end in time. The short-lived
fortunes we experience as members of a temporal and transient political
community pale by comparison.

In addition, Locke believed that each of us must pursue our eternal
salvation in a "conscientious" way. No one else can decide for us what we
must do or believe here on earth in order to secure a blessed life by
God's side. In particular, the state cannot dictate an answer. It cannot
prescribe an orthodoxy of ideas or practices so far as the fate of our souls
is concerned. No delegation of responsibility is possible; the only authority that matters is one's own.

To be sure, the freedom to believe and to act on one's beliefs is not
absolute. Some religious (or rather, in Locke's view, antireligious) practices may be restricted for reasons of state. This includes the public es-
pousal of atheism. Locke also believed that intolerant sects need not be
tolerated.[21] But the restrictions on religion must be as narrow as possible,
consistent with the preservation of political order. Otherwise, the demands of political life trespass upon our private preparations for the
world to come—a pursuit that eclipses all our busy but ephemeral preoccupations in this life. Any attempt to regulate religion beyond this bare
minimum is bound to be ineffective. Worse, it corrupts the conscientious
search for a path to salvation, which we must each find for ourselves.

Jefferson accepted Locke's view that religious liberty is a fundamental, pre-political ("natural") right but for less orthodox reasons. When re-
ferring to God, Jefferson sometimes uses the word without adornment
or substitutes stock phrases like "the common father and creator of
man."[22] It is doubtful, though, whether he shared even Locke's minimal-
ist version of Christian belief. What is certain is that he did not consider
this or any other orthodoxy to be a condition for asserting one's right to
religious freedom, a privilege he was happy to extend to atheists too.

Jefferson's defense of religious freedom presupposes an idea of religion that is *thinner* than Locke's watered-down theism yet *thicker* than
mere morality. His idea of religion falls between these two limits—
between even the least demanding Christian orthodoxy, on the one hand,
and the most robust secular morality on the other. Jefferson never defines this idea with any precision. It may be he could not. Perhaps he
thought any attempt at clarity was politically unwise. Yet the Virginia
Statute that he drafted and the First Amendment he praised in his letter

to the Danbury Baptists both depend on a view of religion that falls between these upper and lower bounds.

Because most Americans (including Supreme Court justices) have always thought of religion in theistic terms, the pressure to define it has never been terribly great. The question has remained in the background. But we must address it if we want to be able to explain to the champion of reason—someone like Jefferson, perhaps—why she has reason to agree that religion is of value for its own sake and the wall that protects it more than a peacekeeping device.

## V

*United States v. Seeger* is one of the few cases in which the Supreme Court has considered the question directly.[23] Daniel Seeger claimed an exemption from the draft during the Vietnam War. He described himself as a conscientious objector. The Universal Military Training and Service Act excused from combat training and service those who by reason of their "religious training and belief" are conscientiously opposed to participation in war in any form. The act defined religious belief as "belief in a relation to a Supreme Being involving duties superior to those arising from any human relation" but expressly excluded "essentially political, sociological, or philosophical views or a merely personal moral code."[24]

Seeger expressed "skepticism or disbelief in the existence of God" yet insisted that he possessed "a religious faith in a purely ethical creed" and "cited such personages as Plato, Aristotle and Spinoza" in support of his convictions. In weighing his claim, the Court surveyed a wide range of religious beliefs, including all the familiar theistic systems that rest on the idea of God as a personal creator. It made a point of including Hinduism and Buddhism as well. Struggling to define a test for what counts as a religious belief for purposes of the statutory exemption, the Court could only say that a belief passes the test if it "occupies a place in the life of its possessor parallel to that filled by the orthodox belief in God of one who clearly qualifies for the exemption."[25]

The Court ruled unanimously that Seeger met this standard and he received his exemption. As a matter of law, this was enough to decide the case. In theological terms, though, the Court's test is plainly inadequate.

What exactly is the "parallel" to which the Court refers? It does not consist in the sincerity with which a belief is held or the consistency of the actions based upon it. Those who deny the existence of any Supreme

Being are fully capable of sincerity and consistency too. Their lives may be as ethical as those of the most devout, yet they fail the test the Court proposes.

The test makes sense, and can be applied in an intelligible way, only if the words *God* and *Supreme Being* mean *something*—if they are more than rhetorical flourishes intended to underscore the seriousness of a belief. Their meaning must be wider than the familiar "orthodox" conceptions of God. It must be broad enough to include the pantheisms of the East and West, of Buddha and Spinoza. And yet the words cannot be stretched so far as to cover every coherent and commanding system of ethical norms. The dividing line between ethics and religion lies somewhere in between. But until "God" and "Supreme Being" have been given a nonorthodox yet substantive definition, it is impossible to say where this line falls or whether a bespoke system of beliefs like Seeger's "parallels" those that history and convention put squarely on the side of religion.

The Court should not be faulted for failing to undertake this theological task. Its decision in *Seeger* went as far as the case required and made practical, political sense in the charged atmosphere of the Vietnam War. This is all the Court should ever attempt to do where questions of religion are involved.

The members of the Court are ill equipped by training, and ill suited by virtue of the office they hold, to fish in theological waters. America has made do for more than two centuries with a rough *modus vivendi* that strikes an acceptable balance between politics and religion. The Court's responsibility is to preserve this balance, not upset it. If this means it should abstain from theological adventures, that is very much to the good. The Court serves the nation well by keeping its nose out of all such business. It could only do harm by attempting to define with greater precision what "God" and "Supreme Being" mean.

Still, the question is a good—indeed, unavoidable—one, not for the Court, perhaps, but for any speculative observer who wants to understand how religion differs from morality and why the "relation between man and God" that Jefferson's wall protects on one side, as it does the equality of citizens on the other, is a rationally demonstrable component of human fulfillment.

So let us make a fresh start—a "second sailing," as Socrates calls it in the *Phaedo*.[26] Help comes from an unexpected quarter.

In *Planned Parenthood v. Casey*, the Supreme Court affirmed, by a narrow margin, the continuing vitality of what it called the "central idea" in

*Roe v. Wade*, decided nineteen years before and since overruled in *Dobbs v. Jackson Women's Health Organization*. The five justices who voted in *Casey* to uphold *Roe v. Wade* could not agree in all respects, but three of the five joined in a plurality opinion that stood as the opinion of the Court.[27]

A woman's decision whether or not to have an abortion, the plurality said, is one of those "intimate and personal choices a person may make in a lifetime, choices central to personal dignity and autonomy." The freedom to make such choices unburdened by the "compulsion of the State" is a vital part of the "liberty protected by the [due process clause of the] Fourteenth Amendment." Then the plurality added a memorable sentence. "The heart of liberty," they said, "is the right to define one's own concept of existence, of meaning, of the universe, and of the mystery of human life."[28]

The last sentence has had its critics. Justice Scalia mocked it a decade later in his dissent in *Lawrence v. Texas*, calling it "the famed sweet-mystery-of-life passage." It is either an empty rhetorical gesture, he said, or a benign-seeming platitude that undermines the rule of law.[29] Others have been equally harsh. "You'd search in vain," one evangelical critic wrote, "to find a more apt description of our secular age" with its "culture of expressive individualism" or a better statement of the ideal of the "sovereign self" untethered from tradition and God.[30]

The passage has had its admirers too, perhaps most famously Ronald Dworkin. The abortion decision, he wrote a year after *Casey* was decided, touches on questions of a spiritual kind that invite, perhaps compel, reflection on one's place in the cosmic order of things. These are the sort of questions we normally associate with religion, whether organized or not. This observation led him to propose that a woman's right to decide whether to terminate her pregnancy is better lodged in the free exercise clause of the First Amendment than the due process clause of the Fourteenth.[31] It was an extravagant proposal that convinced few on either side of the debate. Yet it is relevant to our inquiry here.

The plurality opinion in *Casey* is overwrought and poorly argued. As a defense of *Roe*, it leaves much to be desired. The "sweet-mystery-of-life passage," in particular, adds little to the argument. It reminds us, though, of a fact about the human condition that is at once utterly familiar and uncannily strange. The most ardent evangelicals and uncompromising secularists have reason to acknowledge it.

If we pay attention to this fact, it will bring us in due course to what the Court in *Seeger* wisely declined to provide: a definition of God and defense of the good of religion that is neither partisan nor empty. To reach it, we have to make a detour through the precincts of philosophy. But if we follow it to the end we will arrive back where we began, at Jefferson's wall, whose function is to help us live with the awkward straddle between what theologians call the "here" and the "hereafter" and to accommodate their inexorable yet incommensurable demands.

# VI

That life is a "mystery" is already striking. A life may be long or short; full of pain or pleasure; ruled by fear or complacency and ease. But none of these makes it distinctively human. The lives of dogs and cats have the same characteristics too. Life is a mystery only for us. It is not a mystery for other animals because they lack the reflective detachment to ask what life means.

When we are puzzled by something, inquire about its meaning, and find an answer that satisfies us, the puzzle disappears. I see a man wearing a large cardboard sign walking up and down the street in front of my apartment. I've never seen such a thing before. I ask a friend what it means. She tells me, "He's been paid to carry an advertisement for a new store." The mystery vanishes.

Mysteries exist only under two conditions. The first is that we be able to ask ourselves about them. What is going on here? What does this mean? The second is that we not yet be able to answer the question we ask. Some puzzles, like the mystery of the man with the sign, are temporary. Others are more lasting. A few are permanent. The mystery of life belongs in this last group.

Many questions, of course, never arise because we never have occasion to ask them. I have never asked myself, for example, whether it will rain tomorrow in Vladivostok. I may go a lifetime without asking this question and an infinite number of others. But the question of the meaning of life is one that none of us can altogether avoid. It is bound to occur to each of us at one time or another, though few perhaps give it sustained thought.

The difficulty of answering the question, moreover, cannot be overcome with further study. Some, of course, claim to have settled the matter definitively. They know the meaning of life and are happy to share it with others. But their security is fragile. The possibility of doubt always remains, for them as well as those they hope to persuade. Even the most confident answer to the question of the meaning of life is vulnerable to being upset by new facts and ideas.

The question is therefore one we can neither avoid nor answer conclusively. We cannot free ourselves from it or put it finally to rest because, as Kant says, it "transcends every faculty of the mind."[32] This makes it a question of a peculiar kind. The peculiarity is a symptom of the human condition. More exactly, it *is* the human condition, and our inability either to decline to consider it or to resolve the puzzle once and for all is no more a fault than the human condition itself is.

For something to puzzle me, I must be able to consider it from a distance. When I ask about the meaning of the man with the cardboard sign, I reflect on his movements from the vantage point of my apartment three stories up. He is there and I am here. He is one human being and I am another.

There are innumerable possible objects of study, some drawn from my inner experience and others from the world outside me. Only a fraction ever become actual objects of speculation for me or anyone else. But all that do presuppose a reflective detachment from the object in question.

With the man in the street or the weather in Vladivostok, the detachment is easy to grasp. It is the separation between my position at a particular place and time and the spatially or temporally distinct position of the object I am studying. I consider the man there from my vantage point here; I ask about the weather tomorrow from my perspective today. In all inquiries of this prosaic kind, my reflective point of view is a position within my life itself.

But the same cannot be true when I ask myself about the meaning of life as a whole. A particular event may trigger this reflection—the death of a parent or birth of a child; a winter sunset; the face of a stranger on the bus; a walk through the Old Masters gallery at the Metropolitan Museum of Art. But whenever and however the question arises, I must be sufficiently detached from my life as a whole to take it as an object of study.

The German word for object is *Gegenstand*. It means "that which stands over against." The man with the cardboard sign is an object in this sense. So are the blinking traffic light down the street and the weather in Vladivostok. But how can life as a whole be an object like these? How can a person be sufficiently detached from the life he or she is living to ask, "What does my life mean?" How is it possible that my whole life be something that "stands over against" me?

The best answer to this question also explains why the question itself can never be answered. There is something mysterious about this. It is part of the meaning of the mystery of life.

# VII

*Transcendence* is the word philosophers and theologians use to describe the detachment that allows us to take life as a whole as an object of wonder and thought.[33] We are always *in medias res*, carried along from one moment to the next by the ceaseless flow of time. Yet we have the power to view our lives from a vantage point that is not confined by the temporal current in which they unfold.

In one sense, we are prisoners of time. None of us can escape its iron law of succession. Yet in another, we do escape it whenever we turn our attention to anything that has a longer life than our own—the Constitution of the United States, for example, or the history of Western civilization, or the cosmic career of the sun. We can think about these and countless other long-lived objects and events only because our thoughts are not constrained by the tiny fragment of time that we actually experience, between the boundary stones of birth and death, but roam widely beyond these.

This is even more striking in the case of thoughts whose objects have no beginning or end in time—that never "come into being or pass away," as Plato puts it.[34] Mathematical objects are the most familiar example. They made a deep impression on Plato. His entire philosophy was inspired by the experience of transcendence that mathematics epitomizes.[35]

Whether you think of mathematical objects as real things or mental inventions, rectangles and cosines and Fibonacci numbers are possible objects of attention only because we are not wholly lost in time like our animal friends. We transcend it in thought—an incomplete but astounding release that defines the uniqueness of the human condition. One of the great achievements of Kant's *Critique of Pure Reason* is its proof (that is not too strong a word) that the possibility of our attending to the most banal thing in the world—the teacup on the table—and inquiring about its provenance—how did it come to be there?—depends on the same transcendence of time that is dramatically apparent in mathematical inquiries like the one Socrates pursues in the *Meno* with the help of an uneducated slave boy.[36]

We are able to ask about the meaning of life as a whole only because we possess the capacity to conceive our lives as an episode within a longer stretch of time, one that goes on indefinitely in both directions. This is what makes us *mortal* beings: not just ones who die, as all living things do, but those for whom death is an object of reflection. Death is inescapable but so is the power that brings it before our minds as an object of thought. We can escape neither. The two together—death and our awareness of it, our imprisonment in time and our transcendence of it—make us who we are.

We might say that human beings have one foot in time and another outside it. This awkward straddle explains how it is possible for us to be arrested by the mystery of life, which troubles no other animal, and to whose exploration all the immense resources of religion, art, and philosophy are devoted. But it also explains why the question of the meaning of life can never be settled in a definitive way.

To see why, we need to probe a little deeper. What is the significance of the difference between being *in* time and being *outside* it? How are things that are conditioned by time related to those that are not? What is the relation between time and eternity?

This is an exceedingly abstract question—the most abstract, perhaps, that one can ask. But it helps us understand the meaning of religion in a Jeffersonian spirit—as a preoccupation defined by no orthodox set of beliefs, even of a modest Lockean kind, yet distinguished from mere morality. And it lays the ground for an enlightened defense of religion, which must be insulated from political demands as strenuously as the political world must be shielded against the force of religious passion.

# VIII

*Eternity* is an intimidating word. Those who are hostile to religion are likely to be suspicious of it. It suggests something ineffable, mysterious, spooky, against which enlightened minds recoil. It also has a totalitarian ring. Eternal goods (whatever they may be) eclipse all mundane values. Those who invoke them as a justification for action do more than challenge specific worldly practices. They threaten to wreck the whole fragile edifice of human accomplishment. But neither the obscurity of the idea nor its dangers (to which I shall return) should discourage us from trying to understand what eternity means, for no picture of the human condition is complete without it.

In fact, the idea of eternity is more familiar than it seems. Or rather, the *ideas*, for there are two distinct ones. The first, which I have hinted at already, is that of time everlasting.

I often think of things that happened before I was born (Thomas Jefferson's letter to the Danbury Baptists, for example). I also think of things that will happen after I die (the distribution of the proceeds of my life insurance policy or, more remotely, the return of Halley's Comet in 2061). These thoughts rest on the innocuous assumption that time extends backward and forward beyond the limits marked by the start and finish of my own existence.

Reflecting on this banal belief leads to another, more interesting one. However far back in time I allow my thoughts to wander, I can always imagine a time before it. The same is true looking forward. The mental picture I have of earlier and later times becomes hazier the farther I go. Beyond a certain point, it is nothing more than the *idea* of a time before or after any I choose to make the object of my attention.

This is the idea of endless time. Events, lives, epochs—vast periods of geological and cosmic change—all take place within the frame of a time without end. They come and go (even those that last for eons), but time itself does not.

Augustine denied that time is everlasting. He said that God brought it into being when he created the world. The creation of the world and of time were for him a single event.[37] Modern astrophysicists say something similar without the theological baggage. In their view, time is inseparable from the second law of thermodynamics. It begins with the explosion that set our expanding, entropic universe in motion.[38] Before the Big Bang, time did not exist.

Yet neither of these views (the theological or scientific) can stop us from asking what was happening before time began. What was God doing before he created the world? What was the state of the universe before the Big Bang got things going? The question is irresistible. We cannot help asking it even if theologians and scientists insist it makes no sense.

The question is irresistible because our curiosity is insatiable. The human longing to know has no limits. If we are told that our desire to understand cannot be pursued beyond a certain point, we may pause and reflect. We may be stymied for a while—for centuries even. We may be warned that curiosity is a vice (this was Augustine's view) and suppress it for the sake of our spiritual health.[39] But no amount of discouragement can root it out for good.

Curiosity always comes back, and when it does—when we ask why something happened—the only possible answer is that it happened because of some earlier state of affairs. Being insatiable, curiosity wonders why this earlier state existed when and as it did. Again, the only possible answer is that it existed because of something that happened before, and so on without limit.

In this way, the limitlessness of human curiosity exposes its dependence on the idea of endless time and therefore of time everlasting. No theological or scientific proscription can erase this idea from our minds or eradicate our dependence on it. We can no more put it aside than stifle our irrepressible longing to know.

The idea of time without end is the bridge to a second and very different idea of eternity. Human curiosity brings us to this second idea as well—rather quickly, in fact.

The explanation of one event by an earlier one only takes us so far. Until the earlier event has been explained, our understanding is incomplete. It rests on an assumption (a condition) that we take for granted but have not (yet) explained. This condition too may be made a subject of inquiry. Limitations of time and energy always compel us to break off at some point. Yet even if we were able to continue forever, our knowledge would still be conditional. That is because every explanation that accounts for the occurrence of one event by pointing to a previous one leaves unanswered the question of why the endless temporal series in which they occur itself exists and connects things as it does. The entire series is contingent: it might not exist or have been otherwise. All ordinary causal explanations rest on an inexplicable condition whose arbitrariness no understanding of antecedent causes can remove. They therefore fall short of satisfying our desire to know—not accidentally, because we have to leave off inquiring into the order of causes in time, but necessarily, because this order itself cannot be explained by anything that happens in time.

Of course one might say, "So much for curiosity. There are some things we shall never understand. The wise person accepts this." But the desire to know is not so easily dismissed or effectively repressed—especially when there is a familiar answer to the question of why the conditional sequence of events in time has the order it does. It is the answer that every philosopher and theologian from Plato to Nietzsche has given.

The answer is that what happens in time is not contingent and therefore inexplicable. It is explained by its relation to something that is not in time at all—to a being, power, or order of reality that exists of necessity and therefore cannot be other than it is. Different thinkers call this reality by different names. Plato calls it "The Form of the Good," Aristotle "The Unmoved Mover." Spinoza calls it "Substance," Nietzsche

"The Eternal Return." Augustine, Aquinas, Avicenna, and Maimonides all call it "God." Kant calls it simply the "Unconditioned."[40]

Whatever name these philosophers give it, its essence is the same. The ultimate ground of explanation to which all of them appeal is defined by its exemption from the dependence and conditionality that constitute the being of everything that exists in time. The expressions "before," "after," and "caused by" have no application to it. In it, our search for explanations comes to an end. Our desire to know is at rest. Here is the timeless, unconditioned ground of all temporal conditions for whose own explanation it is foolish to ask since anyone who understands what it is, sees (as Aquinas says) that its essence is to exist—that its nature lies in the necessity of its being what and as it is.

When we speak of *eternity* as "time everlasting," the word refers to an endless system of relations constituted by the ubiquitous presence of time. But every explanation that rests on these relations is ultimately incomplete. This prompts us to search for one that is not. Our search leads to the idea of an order of reality from which time is absent—that is "eternal" in the sense that its nonbeing is unthinkable. The two meanings of the word are therefore not only different. In a basic sense, they are opposed, yet the first leads irresistibly to the second and is completed by it. The thinkers I have named and countless others like them use the word *eternity* principally in the second, more obscure yet explanatorily deeper sense.

## IX

This is a challenging train of thought. It has carried us far from Jefferson's wall. Before we return to the constitutional question with which we began, several observations are in order.

First, different thinkers have proposed different ideas of the unconditioned ground of time and offered competing interpretations of its relation to what Plato calls the ever-changing world "of sights and sounds."[41] The history of Western metaphysics is a record of their disagreements about the nature of this relation.

Second, the greatest philosophers have also disagreed about whether we can have any direct knowledge or experience of "the eternal and divine."[42] Some (Aristotle, for example) maintain that it is possible for human beings to have such an experience before they die.[43] Many mystics agree, with an exuberance that contrasts with Aristotle's sober account of philosophical ecstasy.[44] Other philosophers insist there can be no such experience so long as we are confined by the temporal limits in which our lives unfold. Kant is a famous example.[45] Still others (like Aquinas) affirm its possibility but postpone the experience until our next life, in heaven with God.[46]

Third, we conventionally classify some of the thinkers I have mentioned as theologians, others as philosophers. Many but not all of those in the first group believe in a personal God beyond the world who creates it from nothing. Augustine and Luther are examples. By contrast, some but not all of those we call philosophers identify God with the eternality of the world itself. Spinoza is the best, because the most extreme, example of thinkers of this second sort.[47]

All these distinctions and disagreements are of interest to those who enter the metaphysical thicket and ask themselves whether there is anything that by its nature cannot not be. We might think of them as path marks that guide the search and suggest alternative routes. One need not assume the truth of any of them to see that they have a heuristic value for inquiring minds.

There are some, of course, who warn us to stay out of the thicket altogether. "There lies fog and illusion. Nothing of value can be gained from such distractions. They only divert our scarce attention from more urgent practical tasks." Hume is the most famous exponent of this view in the English-speaking tradition.[48] Wittgenstein is a later, more complicated example.[49] Yet in denying the value of inquiring into the nature of the unconditioned—in Hume's case, with arguments of exquisite subtlety—the most determined skeptics acknowledge the commanding power of the demand that sets these inquiries in motion. This is the compliment that skepticism pays to metaphysics. Among other animals, there are no skeptics because there are no metaphysicians.

The demand for a knowledge of the unconditioned is part of human nature. Other animals are curious too, but their curiosity always has a finite goal. Ours cannot be satisfied unless or until we reach the changeless ground of change that alone is capable of bringing our investigations of events in time to a close. There will never be universal, stable agreement about the contents of this knowledge. It is beyond our power to settle once and for all. But the demand for it can never be suppressed. It is a feature of the human condition and though a cause of inevitable disappointment is also the source of much of what is most sublime in the distinctively human world we have built on the metabolic foundations of life, as animals swept along by time yet incapable of ridding ourselves of questions that compel us toward eternity.

This is not an eccentric obsession. Philosophy and theology may be the province of a few.[50] Their rigors demand an aptitude and attention that perhaps only a small number possess. But the longing for a knowledge of eternity is as wide as humanity itself. Beyond the cossetted circle of philosophical minds, it takes many popular forms.

The most familiar are those that offer some connection to the eternal and divine through rituals and sacraments that many can enjoy without the sacrifice of energy and sociability that philosophy and theology require. The Eucharist of the Catholic, the Seder of the Jew, the temple offering of the Hindu, and the Wiccan's summer dance are vehicles for many to experience what the philosophical few seek through more arduous methods. They are different paths to the recognition and celebration of a timeless order that puts the whole of time in perspective and explains what happens in it with a finality that nothing that occurs in time can ever possess. All these rituals are expressions of the peculiar but universal human longing to understand the meaning of life, which can no more be satisfied in a single, uniform way than excised from the human heart.

This throws some light, perhaps, on the question of Thomas Jefferson's own religious beliefs. Jefferson was a fierce champion of religious liberty yet he rarely spoke, in public at least, about religious matters. One might assume that while he was committed to the principle of toleration, his own interest in religion was tepid at best, like that of Washington, Madison, and Franklin. But this would be a mistake, for though Jefferson had little use for the orthodoxies of Christian belief, he was irresistibly drawn to abstract questions, metaphysical as well as scientific. He took the search for explanation far more seriously than his fellow Founders did.

Christian explanations terminate in the will of God. Even for a deist, whose orthodoxy is as spare as Christianity allows, this is where explanation bottoms out. A thoroughgoing rationalist like Jefferson can never be content with this account. It leaves things resting in an act of divine creation that reason is not only incompetent to grasp but forbidden to explore. In his private reflections, Jefferson pushed on in search of a better answer to the question of the relation between time and eternity than any the Christian religion can provide.

This led him to Lucretius, whose first-century philosophical poem *De Rerum Natura* translated the ideas of the Greek philosopher Epicurus for a Latin-reading audience and eventually a modern European one.[51]

Jefferson owned several copies of the book and studied it with care. In his private correspondence, he wrote favorably of the thinker, whose views he called "the most rational system remaining of the philosophy of the ancients."[52]

There is no divine will in Epicurus's philosophy and no personal immortality—no superintending providence or afterlife of punishment and reward. In these basic respects, it is incompatible with Christian belief. Many condemned it for this reason. Yet the idea of eternity is as central to Epicureanism as to the Abrahamic religions that stand in such sharp contrast to it.

In Epicurus's view, eternity is an attribute of the world, not of a God beyond it. The world is eternal in both senses of the word. It takes shape and dissolves in an endless series of cosmic adjustments. These all occur in time. The laws that govern them, though, are timeless. They are the changeless ground of change—the unconditioned cause of every causal sequence in the everlasting, spasmodic flux of cosmic motion.

Jefferson was drawn to Epicureanism in part because its materialism is compatible with certain aspects of modern science.[53] But it also satisfied his demand for explanation in a way that Christianity could not. It seemed to him a more rational answer to the question of why what happens in time happens as it does. (That Epicurus's famous doctrine of the "swerve," on which his account of cosmic motion depends, is as inexplicable in its way as the Christian doctrine of creation, and that a really rigorous rationalist can no more accept the one than the other, might have led Jefferson—had he reflected further on the matter—to the still more thoroughgoing rationalism of Spinoza, whose radical views haunted even the most progressive Enlightenment thinkers and made them uneasily aware that they too had stopped short in their search for reasons.)[54]

Still, even if Jefferson went only as far as Epicurus, his attraction to the philosopher's disenchanted naturalism shows several things about him. It reveals the strength of his philosophical curiosity. It suggests that his curiosity took the form of a demand for ever-deeper explanations. And it demonstrates that this demand can only be satisfied—for Jefferson or anyone else with a philosophical spirit—by an explanation that grounds all others in the self-explanatory being of something that exists of necessity, whether we conceive it to be a God beyond the world or the eternal order of the world itself ("Nature" or "Nature's God," as Jefferson ambiguously puts it in the Declaration of Independence).

Jefferson went much farther than most in his search for understanding. He belonged to the philosophic few. Yet he recognized that the boundless desire to know is one that all human beings share and that even those who do not possess his intellectual passion or power are directed toward eternity by their longing to comprehend the mystery of life.

For many, this longing takes the form of religion in the ordinary sense of the word. Jefferson's religion is not theirs, but it is wrong to say he had none. In its widest meaning, religion is the resolve to see things from the standpoint of eternity. In this broad sense it includes the Calvinist preacher, the tolerant deist, the Anglican planter who harries his slaves during the week and takes Communion on Sunday—and Jefferson the enlightened Epicurean.

Most of the time, we do not need this wider idea of religion to settle the questions raised by the practical challenge of maintaining a wall between church and state. We do need it, though, to understand the oddness of Jefferson's position as an outspoken defender of religious freedom who (by contemporary standards) was strikingly irreligious himself. More important, we need it to answer the question, posed by the *Seeger* case, of how to define religion if it cannot be equated with any particular set of beliefs yet is distinct from mere moral conviction. Most important, we need it to explain why religion, like politics, is good in itself and why the wall between them is needed to protect each from the other.

Our digression on eternity makes the explanation surprisingly straightforward.

# X

Let us consider politics first.

Religion must be kept out of politics for the reason Justice O'Connor suggests. Any religious test for membership in the American political community offends the principle of equality on which our democracy rests. But the egalitarian justification for the disestablishment of religion is not the only or even the best one.

Wherever it appears, and whatever form it takes, the preoccupation with eternity is destructive of political life. From the standpoint of the first, the concerns of the second are bound to seem inconsequential. What happens today or next year or in the next five hundred is not just smaller by comparison with what lasts forever or exists outside of time altogether. It is incommensurably smaller. When we look at things under "the aspect of eternity," worldly events dwindle to insignificance.[55]

John Locke makes this point in his *Letter concerning Toleration*.[56] Locke believed in a providential God who distributes rewards and punishments in the eternal life that awaits us after this one. We have the strongest possible interest, he says, in securing the happiness of our immortal souls. It overshadows the interest we take in our physical safety and the security of our possessions. These are the responsibility of the civil authority, whose jurisdiction, though legitimate so far as it extends, touches matters of infinitely less importance.

Locke is right, but the truth of his view does not depend on the particulars of his theology. Let Locke's conception of eternity be replaced by any other—Muslim, Jewish, Buddhist, Platonist, Epicurean, whatever— the same incommensurability remains. The affairs of this world are bound to seem insignificant from the standpoint of eternity, however one conceives it. Who can possibly care about the next election when it is weighed against an order of reality by comparison with which even the end of the American Republic is an inconceivably small event?

The integrity—the existence, really—of any political world, including our American one, is possible only if those who are committed to it take its interests seriously. If they cease to care about its everyday problems because these seem so small in the blinding light of eternity, the political community itself is at risk. This is one reason why the last great pagan defenders of Roman authority feared the spread of a religious cult that taught its adherents to render unto Caesar not in a spirit of civic loyalty but as an expression of their detachment from worldly concerns.[57]

The existence of the sphere of political action depends on an indifference to concerns that are bound to make the work of politics seem a silly diversion from the one thing that really matters. This is the true lesson of Plato's *Republic*, which purports to show how the knowledge of eternity can be brought down to earth and made the ruling principle in an existing political order but is really meant to persuade its readers of the incommensurability between the two and of the utter inconsequence of all political programs when measured against the pursuit of the Good—the uncaused cause of everything that happens in the theater of time, to whose meaningless spectacle we find ourselves riveted, like the stupefied prisoners in Plato's Cave.[58]

Aristotle, who was better disposed than Plato to the pull of political life, puts the point in the following way. The highest branch of philosophy (metaphysics, "those things that come after physics") is concerned with what cannot not be. Its subject is the eternal and divine. The knowledge of eternity demands that we look away from the world of motion, change, and time to their timeless condition or ground. Politics, by contrast, is concerned with what might be other than it is—with possibility, contingency, and the uncertain balance between success and failure. This requires a different kind of knowledge: what Aristotle calls practical wisdom.[59]

Wisdom of this kind depends on experience and reveals itself in a person's ability to assess the strengths and weaknesses of different human beings and the opportunities that various situations present. It is the ability to maneuver effectively in time. Politics, which unfolds in time, demands it.[60] The leader, the statesman, the one who takes a commanding role in political life, is preeminently a person of practical wisdom.

In metaphysics, practical wisdom is out of place. A philosopher pursuing the eternal and divine can only stumble over the sorts of considerations that are vital to a statesman. He has no need of—even actively spurns—the worldly wisdom that is the source of political greatness.

By the same token, the metaphysician's preoccupation is a threat to the agility a statesman requires. It is not an aid to practical wisdom but (in the statesman's view) a dangerous distraction from it. This is part of the meaning of Aristotle's famous observation that it is as ridiculous to expect exactness in political arguments as to give the all-things-considered practical judgments of a politician any weight in mathematical or metaphysical disputes.[61] It is also the message of the ancient story of the Thracian maid who laughed at the philosopher Thales when he fell down a well while studying the stars.[62]

Among English-speaking philosophers, none was more determined to protect politics from philosophy than Edmund Burke. He quotes Aristotle's dictum with approval.[63] Again and again, Burke used his immense rhetorical gifts to attack those he calls political "metaphysicians" who rely on timeless truths like "the rights of man" to remodel the evolved, complex, and only partly principled arrangements of their communities.[64] Burke lacked Aristotle's appetite for philosophy, but he understood the essential difference between theology and politics—between eternity and time—and recognized that a passion for the unconditioned corrupts political life, where everything is conditioned and nothing lasts forever— or indeed for very long. This is an important thread in Burke's conservatism and one of the points that most sharply distinguishes his view of political life from that of the French revolutionaries and those who descend from them.

Toward the end of his life Alexander Bickel declared himself a follower of Burke against the philosophical school represented by John Rawls, whose *Theory of Justice* concludes with the approving remark that those who accept its argument will be able to see and judge the practical task of framing a constitution and enacting laws from the standpoint of eternity.[65] This is exactly what Burke and Bickel reject. The pursuit of eternity, and the disposition to judge things in its light, is in their view not only out of place in political life but corrosive of it. It devalues to nothing the concern with time whose prudent management is the flawed and risky business of those who care about their political communities and are prepared to sacrifice for them, even though, like all human arrangements, they are destined to pass from the face of the earth.

Locke understood this. Aristotle did too. They had very different ideas of eternity, but both saw how dangerous this idea is when let loose in political life and allowed to become an orienting concern in a realm that demands that time be taken more seriously than any conception of eternity allows.

It does not seem too reckless to suppose that Jefferson shared this worry. Jefferson had a philosophical spirit. He took the search for the unconditioned seriously. He was also a hothead, drawn to extremes and sometimes tempted to act on the basis of first principles alone—rigorously, uncompromisingly, in the spirit Burke sharply condemned.[66] As a result he had an intimate knowledge of the dangers this involves. He knew firsthand what damage philosophy and theology can do when they supplant more worldly modes of judgment. His insistence on erecting a wall between religion and politics can perhaps be explained, on the worldly side, as a shield against the philosopher's world-less pursuit of the eternal and divine whose compulsive attraction Jefferson knew from his own experience.

Whether or not this was Jefferson's aim, it explains the establishment clause in a deeper way than Justice O'Connor's correct but superficial appeal to America's egalitarian political values. To reach it, we need to detach the idea of religion from its conventional meaning. We have to define it in more elementary terms—as a response to the human longing to understand the mystery of life, which leads us all, philosophers and nonphilosophers alike, away from time to eternity. This answers the question raised and deflected in *Seeger*. It also explains why the separation policed by Jefferson's wall is essential to the very existence of everything on its political side.

# XI

The same argument explains why the wall is needed to protect religion from the demands of political life.

From the perspective of eternity, all political passions and preoccupations seem laughably small. Even the most durable projects shrink to fleeting eddies in an endless stream. This is how the Roman emperor Marcus Aurelius saw them. Aurelius was a great statesman and general. He was also a philosopher of some distinction. He spent his evenings composing meditations to remind himself of the triviality of all he had done during the day on campaign in the north, fighting to keep the empire's frontiers intact. What do any of these things mean, he writes, when none of them will be remembered in ten thousand years—a stretch of time that itself is but a second in the eternal career of the world?[67]

Politics is nothing but conditions. It is preoccupied with possibilities, not necessities. "If this happens, what will follow?" In politics, the belief that any program, strategy, or alignment of partisan forces cannot not be—that it exists with the necessity of a mathematical proof or metaphysical demonstration—is more than a source of mischief. It is the worst sort of irresponsibility.

From the standpoint of eternity, responsibility means the exact opposite. It means turning away from the tangled world of conditions—of contingencies and commitments—toward the unconditioned, whose essence is to exist, like the self-generating world of Marcus Aurelius or the world-transcending God to whom Locke prayed. For those whose minds are directed toward eternity—which is all of us, at one time or another— the intrusion of worldly concerns is not just a distraction. It is a terrible infidelity—the abandonment of the pursuit of "the one thing needful" for the sake of a child's toy. If it is essential to keep this pursuit out of our everyday practical quarrels, it is equally important to exclude what Jefferson calls "worldly honours and emoluments" from the authentic (an eighteenth-century deist would have said "conscientious") search for the eternal and divine.

That the good of religion requires its separation from politics will seem obvious to the devout, for whom religion is true and its value intrinsic. Some secularists have a hard time seeing things in this light.

They concede that religion should be tolerated but only for practical reasons. But if we understand religion in the way I have defined it, then even the most aggressively enlightened, who scoff at the devout, have reason to acknowledge the internal good of what Jefferson's wall protects on this side too.

A demand for the unconditioned is not a quirk of the pious, peculiar to them alone. It is what Kant calls "a predisposition of our nature."[68] We are rational beings as well as temporal ones. We live in time yet transcend it in thought. Because we do, we are able to see every period of time from the vantage point of an endlessly longer one and thus to ask a question of the strangest and most radical kind. "What explains the entire series of events that constitutes the endless stream of time?" The question is a symptom of our incapacity (in Kant's words) ever "to be capable of being satisfied with what is temporal (since the temporal is always insufficient for the predispositions of our whole vocation)."[69]

Only what exists outside of time can fully satisfy our curiosity. It may be that the knowledge of what does lies beyond our grasp. This was Kant's position. But the curiosity itself is a product of reason—one we can no more disown than escape our hybrid constitution as time-bound, thinking beings.

Whether (to use Kant's terms) one comes to a dogmatic or skeptical conclusion, the pursuit of the question of whether what happens in time is explained by what does not is an ineliminable aspect of "our whole vocation."[70] It must be allowed a privileged and protected space, undistracted by worldly demands, if we are to be all that our humanity invites—indeed, compels—us to be. This is what makes the freedom to pursue the unconditioned an intrinsic good. And because the motive to pursue it is one that arises, as Kant says, from the very nature of reason itself, even a thoroughly disenchanted rationalist has reason to acknowledge that our attraction to the idea of God is a fateful feature of the human condition, a universal and inextinguishable passion, and not just a private belief that we are free to affirm or deny as we choose. She has reason to agree with the pious that religious toleration is more than a *modus vivendi*.

Thomas Jefferson was a little like Marcus Aurelius. He knew the heat of battle but longed for the quiet of his study. He could not wait to get back from Washington to his hilltop in Virginia where he could pursue the search for causes free from political distractions. This led him to Lucretius and the philosophy of Epicurus, in which only a person with a very serious interest in eternity can have any interest at all. Most of his contemporaries understood the meaning of religion in more conventional terms. Jefferson (I like to think) had a deeper view of it. He understood that religion is not doctrine, sacrament, or church. It is the longing for eternity, which springs from the demands of reason itself and whose pursuit is an essential component of human fulfillment.

Jefferson understood the responsibilities of political life and worked hard to meet them. He also heard the call of reason and knew that those who take it seriously are led away from the world and time to the timelessness of what never ends because it cannot not be. Jefferson was a philosopher-statesman. He grasped the intrinsic good of politics and that of religion too, and understood the importance of separating them by a wall for the well-being of both. He was neither a devout believer nor a dismissive secularist who concedes the need to keep religion out of politics but feels no sympathy for it. He was a rationalist for whom the spirit of religion, as opposed to its dogmas and routines, is the irrepressible response to an inexorable human longing.

To explain why religion is good in itself in terms that even the most irreligious can accept, we need an idea of religion closer to Jefferson's own. We need an idea that is not only compatible with reason but founded upon it. No court of law should attempt to define this idea with any precision. But we need it to be content and perhaps even proud that in our dizzyingly secular age America remains what it was in Jefferson's day—among the enlightened nations of the world, the most secular and at the same time most religious.

# CHAPTER EIGHT

# The Sufficiency of Reason

## I

*Metaphysics* was a curse word for Edmund Burke. He uses it frequently to disparage the style of political thought he most despised. According to Burke, responsible political judgment depends on common sense and practical wisdom, not "the nakedness and solitude of metaphysical abstraction."[1] The revolutionaries in France glutted themselves on abstractions like "the rights of man."[2] The result was a wasteland of turmoil and destruction. "In the groves of their academy, at the end of every vista, you see nothing but the gallows."[3]

Some claim to find in Burke's writings a philosophy of sorts. He was a "realist," they say, or a defender of "natural rights."[4] He had a "Christian" view of the world.[5] All this is true, to a degree. No one will dispute that Burke had fundamental beliefs about the world and human nature. But he was not a philosopher. He not only failed to defend his beliefs in a philosophically rigorous way, he was hostile to the enterprise of philosophy itself.

Philosophy may be a harmless amusement for those who gather in the shade, unburdened by the responsibilities of public life.[6] In politics, though, where judgments have consequences that affect the lives and fortunes of real human beings, abstract speculation is to be avoided. One of the leading tenets of Burke's conservatism is that effective and responsible leaders must eschew the weightless pleasures of philosophy for the graver obligation to act in a judicious if sometimes unprincipled way. In politics it is prudence that counts, not theoretical perspicacity.

It is tempting to conclude that for conservatives there is a tension, perhaps even a war, between their views and the pursuit of philosophical rigor. Burke saw things in this light. He seems, in any case, not to have been deeply or lastingly engaged by the pleasures of abstract thought. The closest he came was his early *Enquiry into the Origin of Our Ideas of the Sublime and the Beautiful* (1757).[7] After that, to the end of his life, Burke was preoccupied with practical questions. He left philosophy behind and eventually turned against it with moral disgust.

This was not true of his older contemporary David Hume. Hume was a speculative philosopher—one of the greatest the West has ever known. He was committed to the search for reasoned explanations and had an immense appetite for metaphysics. He was also a conservative in his moral and political views—closer in this respect to Burke than Locke.

There is, moreover, an internal connection between Hume's most abstract philosophical views and his practical conservatism. In his proposed solution to the deepest problems of philosophy, Hume assigns a decisive role to custom or habit, conferring on time and tradition the authority that conservatives like Burke value so highly. A question remains, though. Can the link between Hume's speculative arguments and his conservative beliefs be sustained? Not if one follows the line of thought pioneered by Immanuel Kant.

Kant was Hume's most brilliant and persuasive critic. He sought to show that custom is incapable of meeting the philosophical challenge that Hume presented with such disturbing clarity. Kant insisted that reason can do better. This led him to a moral and political philosophy that depreciates prudence in favor of reason and tradition in favor of rights. More, perhaps, than any other thinker, Kant explained in compellingly rational terms why the abstract laws that Burke deplored as a benchmark of practical judgment are the best—indeed, the only—measure by which to answer the basic questions of moral and political life.

Many have followed Kant's path. For them, the rapprochement between philosophy and politics points in a progressive direction. They reject Burke's condemnation of philosophy as unenlightened and dismiss Hume's philosophically inspired conservatism as insufficiently enlightened. In their view, enlightenment means taking reason seriously, and for those who do, they say, the only legitimate politics is one based on the rigorous and uncompromising egalitarianism that Kant defended with irrefutable arguments and Burke attacked with enthusiastic but mis-guided eloquence. John Rawls is a recent example.[8]

Is there an alternative? Can the rationalism of philosophy be em-braced without reserve and conservatism shown to be compatible with it, even—especially—when the demand for explanation is carried to its fur-thest limits, beyond those Hume and even Kant acknowledged? Is it pos-sible to love philosophy with all one's heart, as Burke did not, yet share Burke's views about the dangers of making "the metaphysic Knight of the Sorrowful Countenance" one's political model?[9] To be a radical in philosophy and a conservative in politics but on deeper, more reliable grounds than Hume provides?

The answer is yes, but the way to it is not immediately obvious. It begins with Hume and leads through Kant to Spinoza.

## II

The sun rises every day. I am certain it will rise again tomorrow. On what is my certainty based? What *entitles* me to it?

The answer is obvious. My predictions about the future are based on my past observations and those of others, back to the beginning of re-corded history. The sun will rise tomorrow because it has risen every day in the past. But by what right do I assume that my observations about the past justify my making predictions about the future? It seems strange to ask such a question; only philosophers do. But a moment's thought is enough to show that the question is a legitimate and difficult one.

Some statements are self-justifying. They carry their own warrant. That the three angles of any triangle add up to two right angles is an ex-ample. I need look no further than the definition or "idea" of a triangle to see that it must be true.

My prediction about the sun is not like this. There is nothing in the definition of "sun" or "rise" or "tomorrow" that guarantees it will. An un-expected turn of events might cause my prediction to fail. Perhaps the earth will be hit by an asteroid that stops it from turning on its axis, so that for half the inhabitants of the earth the sun will never rise again and for the other half it will never set.

I strongly doubt this will happen. But it *might*. That the sun will rise tomorrow is an empirical, not a logical or mathematical claim. Every em-pirical claim is based on evidence from the past that, however solid and convincing, is not irrefutable. It is not secure against an unexpected turn of events in the way mathematical truths are. Again, then, we must ask, by what *right* do we make such claims? What is the basis—the ground or justification—for empirical predictions about the future based on evidence from the past?

The answer is ready to hand. Nature always follows a regular course, even if our knowledge of it is imperfect. Our past observations may have been incomplete. Perhaps we failed to notice the asteroid in our path. But the future always conforms to the past. We can be as confident of the regularity of nature as we are of the truth of any proposition in geometry.

But is this really so? By what warrant do we make this assumption—that nature follows a regular course? Is it not too an empirical judgment, based on our past observations? And if that is so, what justifies it? It is arguing in a circle to say that the empirical truth that nature follows a regular course is based on the more elementary truth that . . . what? Nature follows a regular course?

This is what philosophers call the problem of "induction." David Hume formulated it with a clarity that has never been matched.[10] Philosophers have been struggling with it ever since.

Hume solved the problem by saying that it cannot be solved on rational grounds. There are no arguments that explain why our assumption that nature follows a regular course is itself supported by reasons. We make the assumption, Hume says, as a matter of habit.[11] The habit is real and secure, but it has no rational foundation. It is just a fact of life, without which we most assuredly could not live, but one that has no deeper rationale that is conceptually prior to the habit itself. In this sense, it is a *brute* fact, meaning one that cannot be explained.

This is the heart of Hume's celebrated skepticism. It is reflected in his moral and political philosophy too. Our surest convictions regarding the nature of justice, property, and law rest, he says, on sentiments and conventions whose potency as brute facts is as striking as their inexplicability on the basis of some more elementary principle or reason. Hume's skepticism is a kind of irrationalism—not in the sense that it elevates dark powers or primordial urges, but because it limits the jurisdiction of reason and puts certain questions beyond its power to answer. Ludwig Wittgenstein followed Hume's path two hundred years later. His ideas of a "language game" and "form of life" reflect a similar kind of irrationalism. They are brute facts as well.[12]

Hume's irrationalism is as powerful as it is because he follows the demands of reason to extraordinary lengths. Reason refuses to take things for granted. It insists on an explanation. In principle, the demand has no limits. The simplest and at the same time most radical formulation of the demand is what Leibniz calls the "principle of sufficient reason." For every question, Leibniz says, there must be an answer—a "sufficient" reason—whether we know it or not.[13] This is the confident (some would say prideful) presumption on which philosophy always proceeds. Leibniz gave it a technical name in the seventeenth century, but it has been the motive and guide of philosophical thought since the age of Parmenides and Heraclitus.[14]

Hume is guided by it too. Indeed, he is one of the greatest devotees of the principle of sufficient reason in the whole of our tradition, forever refusing to take things for granted and instead asking for the reason behind them—up to the point where he believes no further explanations are possible. When he finally gives up and falls back on the brute fact of habit, or sentiment, or convention, as the only way of accounting for our deepest convictions, the skeptical conclusion at which he arrives has such extraordinary power because of the strength of his allegiance to the principle of sufficient reason itself. One can doubt all sorts of things. It is easy to be a skeptic. Hume's skepticism is deep because his loyalty to reason is deep. When reason finally runs out for Hume, you know you have come up against a very significant limit.

## III

One of the most famous virtual colloquies in all of Western philosophy is that between Kant and Hume. According to Kant, Hume "awakened" him from his "dogmatic slumbers" and spurred him to the reflections that led to the system of "critical philosophy" that represents Kant's massively influential contribution to Western thought.[15] The meaning of this awakening and the direction it took for Kant are best understood in terms of the principle of sufficient reason.

Early in his career, Kant wrote in the tradition of speculative metaphysics associated with Leibniz and his disciple Christian Wolff.[16] Stimulated in part by Hume, Kant came to two conclusions. The first was that the impossibility of settling the metaphysical questions that had preoccupied him to that point can and must be demonstrated on rational grounds. It must be shown, by reason alone, why these questions can never be answered. The second was that our belief in the regularity of nature, which Hume calls a habit with no principled explanation, also can and must be explained in strictly rational terms.

Kant saw that Hume's skepticism reflected a stronger commitment to reason than his own metaphysical dogmatism. Before Hume jarred him awake, Kant had believed that certain fundamental truths about God and the soul are rationally demonstrable. Hume's remorseless demand for explanations made it clear that this belief is based on convictions whose truth can never be proven—that it rests on faith. It also showed that if, as Hume says, we have no rational explanation for our belief that the course of nature is lawful, then this belief too is a kind of faith based on a habit of unthinking acquiescence.

Kant resolved to make a new beginning. He would see if, embracing Hume's commitment to reason, he could carry Hume's arguments beyond the skeptical conclusions Hume had reached. Might he be able, by redoubling Hume's efforts at explanation, to construct a reasoned account of our belief in the regularity of nature rather than confess defeat by falling back on the irrational idea of habit? Could he do this in moral and political philosophy as well, arriving at a rational justification for our most important duties and rights, rather than concluding, as Hume does, that these have only a sentimental and conventional basis? And might he be able to prove, by a process of reflection that scrupulously abides by the principle of sufficient reason, that the truth about God and the soul—the pillars of Christian belief—is *necessarily* indeterminable?

These questions preoccupied Kant for the rest of his life. His later philosophy revolves around them. The details are forbiddingly complex, but the impetus for his efforts is easily stated. Kant was inspired by Hume's rationalism and thought he could extend it beyond what he considered Hume's defeatist conclusions. Hume was devoted to the principle of sufficient reason but had not carried the search for reasons far enough.

The first point of attack in Kant's campaign to extend the range of explanation was his reexamination of the problem of induction. According to Hume, our empirical judgments all rest on the habitual expectation that nature follows rules—that it is, "by nature," so to speak, law-abiding. The expectation itself is a brute fact. Kant sought to show that it has a rational explanation. He offered a reasoned defense of the habit that in Hume's view is the point at which all reasons bottom out. Kant's strategy employs a form of argument he calls "transcendental."[17]

The term is much older than Kant's use of it. It was a staple of Scholastic theology. For Aquinas and others, *transcendental* refers to a small set of attributes ("unity," "truth," "goodness," and the like) that every being possesses just because it is a being and regardless of all its other more specific characteristics.[18] Kant adopts the term and puts it to novel use.

He starts with the same fact Hume does. It is a fact that we experience the world, draw inferences from what we experience, and make predictions based upon them. These are not logical judgments but empirical ones, subject to later disproof. In this sense they are always contingent. That we make such judgments cannot be disputed. But how is the fact that we do to be explained?

According to Hume, the explanation is a habit that itself is contingent. It might be different or not exist at all. But that is not an adequate explanation from the standpoint of reason. A fully satisfying explanation has to demonstrate that the thing it seeks to explain cannot be other than it is. This is the only kind of explanation that fulfills the demands of the principle of sufficient reason. Every other is only an invitation to further inquiry. Hume's explanation fails this test. It leaves unanswered the question "Why this habit and not some other?" It is not a *rational* explanation. No appeal to a brute fact can be. The only explanation that passes the test is one that shows why Hume's habit is a necessary rather than contingent feature of human experience. This is what Kant seeks to provide.

His explanation is famously difficult. The heart of it (much simplified) is this. Hume not only takes for granted the fact that we experience the world, which even the most radical skeptic cannot doubt. He also assumes that this experience is orderly. This second assumption rests, Hume claims, on a contingent habit. But—says Kant—the orderliness of experience is not something we *add* to it, as a habitual reflex, *after* the experience. It is not an *afterthought*.

What Hume fails to see, according to Kant, is that absent its orderliness, there is no such thing as experience itself.[19] The orderliness of our experience of the world is constitutive of it—of the fact that we have such experience at all—which without it would be ... what? Nothing about which it is possible to speak and therefore even ask a question. That our experience is ordered in accordance with the rule that nature follows a lawful course is a *necessary* precondition for the very *possibility* of the *actual* fact of human experience—Kant's repurposed formulation of the "transcendental" truth that the entire field of experience, and everything in it, has a property that reason can show to be absolutely necessary for the very existence of our experience itself.

This satisfies the principle of sufficient reason in a way that Hume's reliance on habit cannot. It also compels a second conclusion—one demanded by reason as well. If we start, as Hume does, by assuming that our belief in the orderliness of experience must itself be drawn from experience, as every habit is, then the ground of this belief will always be contingent and therefore incapable of satisfying the principle of sufficient reason. To explain the orderliness of experience in a way that satisfies the principle, we are therefore bound to assume that our belief in the order of the world is not drawn from experience but antecedent to it—a belief, to put it crudely, that we "bring" to our encounter with the world rather than "discover" through it.

The antecedence of this belief is a necessary truth, like the proposition that the orderliness of our experience is a precondition for the possibility of our having any at all. Neither the lawfulness of human experience nor the origin of its laws in the "work" we do constructing an antecedent scheme of rules or regularities is a brute fact that we must simply take for granted. The necessity of both can be demonstrated by reason alone.

The rational proof of these truths, and the exploration of the new world of transcendental philosophy they open up, is the arduous, brilliant labor of Kant's *Critique of Pure Reason*. Inspired by a determination to carry the search for reasons farther than Hume thought possible, Kant's *Critique* is an extension—a further vindication—of the principle of sufficient reason that has defined the goal of philosophy from the start.

The application of the principle to the problem of induction occupies the first part of the *Critique* (the "Analytic"). In the second part (the "Dialectic"), Kant attempts to prove that his demonstration of the rational necessity of the orderliness of nature, which depends for its possibility on the scheme of rules we antecedently generate to create this order in the first place, *simultaneously* proves the rational impossibility of ever settling the age-old philosophical debates about the creation of the world and the immortality of the human soul.

The argument again is complex. The central idea is that because each of these rules is a way of ordering *time*, they can in principle have no application to matters concerning the existence of beings (like God and the soul) that must exist outside of time if they exist at all.[20] The very thing that guarantees the orderliness of our temporal experience—that proves the existence of this order to be a transcendental necessity—*thus also* demonstrates that arguments about the existence of atemporal beings (like God and the soul) are necessarily unresolvable, and not merely contingently so.

In later writings, Kant carries his commitment to reason beyond the "theoretical" questions he addresses in *Critique of Pure Reason*. In the same relentlessly rational spirit, he examines the justification for and content of our most important "practical" (that is, moral and political) duties. The starting point here is the idea of freedom or "autonomy"—of our power to be the authors of laws and not merely their passive subjects. The existence or nonexistence of this power might seem to be a question that can never be answered, according to the argument of the "Dialectic." There is, however, a transcendental path to proving the necessity of the idea of freedom as a premise in our moral and political reasoning.[21]

To explain how the orderliness of human experience is possible at all, we are bound to assume in ourselves a spontaneous power of rule or law creation. Reason itself demands this. But if that is true, then we are allowed—indeed, compelled—to assume the existence of this same power when it comes to our moral and political obligations. The power, after all, is the same. If reason requires us to assume its existence in order to solve the theoretical problem of induction, we are equally justified in assuming it when we consider our practical duties, whose meaning is unintelligible except on the assumption that we have the power to freely comply with them or not.

Kant's description of the content of these duties is challenging and controversial. It begins, though, with the same transcendental presumption on which the scaffolding of the "Analytic" of *Critique of Pure Reason* is built and simply exploits its rational necessity in a practical direction. In this way, Kant is able to carry his exuberant rationalism into the "critical" reconstruction of moral and political thought. He seeks to put these too on a rational foundation that forbids us here, as in the realm of speculative philosophy, ever to rest content with brute facts—with habits, sentiments, conventions, and the like—in the way Hume does, both in his moral and political writings and his "abstruse" theoretical ones.[22]

# IV

Hume assumes that our experience of the world is orderly and coherent. This is, for him, a brute fact. Kant goes to great lengths to demonstrate that human experience is *necessarily* lawful—that it *cannot not* be ordered according to laws that Hume ascribes to the contingent force of habit.

A question remains, though. Granted, *if* we have any experience at all, *then* it must be ordered in the way Kant says. But what accounts for the *existence* of our experience in the first place? This is a version of the ancient philosophical question "Why is there something rather than nothing?"[23]

So long as the existence of human experience is unexplained, it remains a brute fact. Perhaps only a madman would deny it. But there is no contradiction in the idea of a world without us and our experience of it, or, for that matter, in the idea of the world's nonexistence. Human experience may be incontrovertibly real. Its reality, though, is contingent. It might not be. The principle of sufficient reason demands that its existence be explained on noncontingent grounds. No other explanation can fully and finally meet the demand.

The Christian tradition, to which Kant still subscribed, in a muted and highly intellectualized way, offers an explanation of this kind.[24] The world exists because God created it. We exist because God chose to make us and to endow us with the souls we need to experience the world and to recognize and adore our creator. It is tempting to think that God might have made a different world or left us out of the one he created. On reflection, though, we see that this is a mistake. God is all-knowing, all-good, and all-powerful. He must have had a sufficient reason for creating this world among all the ones he might have and for putting us in it. Whatever the reason may be, it explains why the world and we exist—not accidentally but deliberately, intelligibly, explicably, necessarily, because God does nothing under duress or by chance, and sees every consequence of all his actions to the end of time.

Leibniz expounded the logic of this Christian argument with unprecedented rigor.[25] There is a tension, though, between the principle of sufficient reason (to which he was strongly committed) and the doctrine of divine creation (which he refused to disown).

Those who believe that God created the world have a way to answer the question of why we exist and experience the world as we do. Our experience is no longer a brute fact. But then what explains God's act of creation? If, as Leibniz supposes, God had his reasons for creating this world and no other, and for creating it rather than abstaining from creation altogether, then *these reasons* ultimately explain why we and the world exist. But in that case, though we are able to carry our search for explanations back beyond God's creative choice, that choice—and God himself—lose the freedom and independence that for Christians is the hallmark of God's transcendent sovereignty. God is now bound in chains of reason. This is a victory for the principle of sufficient reason but a defeat for Christian belief.

Leibniz saw the tension and worried about it. In the end, though, he was unwilling (whether for philosophical or prudential reasons is hard to say) to abandon his Christian scruples—to throw Christianity under the bus of reason. Nor was Kant willing to make the sacrifice.

In the "Dialectic" of the *Critique of Pure Reason*, Kant purports to demonstrate that the question of whether the world is eternal or was created from nothing by a God beyond it is one that human beings are necessarily unable to answer. But he was not indifferent or undecided between these alternatives. At many points in his later "critical" writings, Kant relies on the idea of divine creation to settle some difficult point of moral, political, or aesthetic judgment, and to explain why our empirical discoveries about nature are not only possible in a general way (that is the aim of the "Analytic") but fit into a coherent and ever-improving system of concrete results.[26]

God is everywhere in Kant's later philosophy—the world-transcending God of Christian belief who possesses the power to bring things into being from nothing through a spontaneous and uncompelled ("miraculous") act of will. That God has a will; that he is free to exercise it in whatever way he wishes; and that he has chosen to create *this* world and place us in it are axioms for Kant. Together they explain the existence of human beings and, by implication, of human experience. That we experience the world is therefore no longer a brute fact. We can assign a reason for it. But the reason is God's will, whose freedom guarantees that it itself can never be explained. God's will is the greatest of all brute facts.

Kant declined Hume's invitation to rest the lawfulness of our experience on habit or convention. He tried to carry the demand for explanation beyond the point Hume thought possible. Yet to explain the *existence* of our experience, Kant fell back on an idea of divine freedom that Hume dismissed with cultured bemusement. He may have been a greater rationalist than Hume, but even for Kant, the principle of sufficient reason went only so far.

To find a philosopher who was prepared to carry it still farther, we have to go back from the eighteenth century to the seventeenth. We have to go back to Spinoza.

# V

Spinoza took the search for explanations as far as anyone has or perhaps can. It led him to a God that is *nothing but* explanation and necessity, from whose divine nature the orthodox Christian attributes of freedom and will have been completely expunged.[27]

Spinoza was the terror of Christian Europe, to which Leibniz and Kant both belonged. They found his philosophy profoundly disturbing—hateful, really—because it sharpened to such a painful point the tension between their Christian beliefs and their commitment to philosophical rationalism.[28]

Spinoza was a crux for both. Leibniz's "monadology" and Kant's "critical philosophy" differ in many ways. Yet each is motivated by the desire to follow Spinoza's search for reasons as far as it can possibly go, *consistent with Christian belief.* Both eventually came to an obstacle no Christian can surmount—beyond which religion forbids reason to proceed. Spinoza was able to clear it because, of the three, he alone was unburdened by the dogma of creation that caused the other two to stumble. Clearing it, he pressed on to become the most relentless rationalist the West has ever known and the least inhibited philosopher—philosophy being, in its essence, the search for explanation itself.

Spinoza's philosophy is set out in a book that was published after he died in 1677.[29] It is a formidably difficult work whose contents are arranged in the form of an elaborate geometrical proof—a reflection of Spinoza's confidence in the rational transparency of his very peculiar ideas. Their exact meaning remains a subject of dispute to this day. One thing, however, is clear. From its first word to its last, Spinoza's *Ethics* is animated by his commitment to the proposition that every question has an answer, even if we do not know what it is.

To many, this is bound to seem absurd. What can be more obvious than that we ask many questions that have no answer—those, for example, that Kant explores in the "Dialectic" of the *Critique of Pure Reason,* including the question of whether the world was created by God.

Spinoza's reply is as follows. The fact that we cannot (yet) answer a question does not mean it is unanswerable. It only shows that our reach exceeds our grasp. For it to make sense to ask a question, the one asking it must assume there is an answer that provides the explanation for which he is looking, even if it is one he will never—indeed, can never—find.[30] The point may be expressed in Kantian terms. The availability, in principle, of an answer to the question is a *precondition necessary for the possibility of its intelligibility* and hence of its being a question at all, since if it lacks intelligibility, it is no more a question than experience is experience without the order that makes it possible in the first place.

Further, every answer that appeals to a contingent fact—to something that might be other than it is—can never be more than a temporary holding action. It goads us to ask what explains this contingency itself, and so on, until we arrive at an answer of a noncontingent kind, whose necessity can be demonstrated by reason alone. Every question, no matter how modest, thus rests on the (transcendental) presupposition that were we able to pursue our inquiry for an infinitely long time, we must eventually come to an answer that satisfies our demand for explanation by proving that what we took to be contingent is necessary after all. This wildly extravagant assumption, farfetched as it may seem, alone guarantees the intelligibility of any question we might ask, and therefore the possibility of asking it, since an unintelligible question is no question at all.

Even the most ordinary questions assume the existence of an answer of this kind. Suppose I ask why the snowflake on my sleeve has the unique shape it does. The question makes perfectly good sense. The search for an answer leads me back through an endless succession of contingencies. I shall never conclude my inquiry. But unless I assume that these contingencies together constitute an infinitely long chain whose own existence is not contingent but rationally required, and therefore necessary in a strictly logical sense, the question with which I began loses its footing. It ceases to be an intelligible question. We forget this in our busy pursuit of useful empirical knowledge, yet it remains a metaphysical truth. The explanation for something as trivial and transient as this tiny snowflake must ultimately rest on the necessary existence of something that cannot not be. Spinoza calls it "God or nature."[31]

What can I know about God or nature? I cannot know it through and through, in fine detail. I know that my snowflake was caused by an antecedent event, that by an earlier one, and so on back in an endless sequence of causes and effects. I am compelled to assume that this infinite sequence, taken as a whole, has the same necessity as the most rigorous geometrical proof. I cannot see how this necessity works *in pianissimo*. That is beyond my powers of perception and cognition. I am a questioning being for whom no metaphysical puzzle is off limits, but I am also a finite being confined to an infinitesimally small patch of time and space.[32] My finitude prevents me from comprehending in fact—with my eyes, as it were—the necessity of the natural or divine order that I know, philosophically, is the ultimate ground, cause, and explanation of all my contingent empirical knowledge.

I *can* see, though, that *some* conceptions of God or nature are demonstrably false. The most important of these, for Western philosophy, is the

Christian (more broadly, Abrahamic) idea of God as a free and other-worldly creator. This view is wrong, Spinoza says, for two related reasons.

First, the Christian God possesses a free will. He has the power to create or not as he chooses. But the will is *in principle* inexplicable. This is true whether we think of it as a power of divine or human agents. If the actions of the will are explicable, that can only be because it is constrained to follow the truth, or do the right, or something of the kind. But in that case, its choices are not free but caused. It is no longer a will at all. The idea of God's will is therefore incompatible with the principle of sufficient reason. Strict adherence to this principle requires that we deny the existence of the will, in heaven and on earth.[33] Its inexplicability contradicts the necessitarian premise on which the intelligibility of all our questioning depends. It renders the pursuit of answers senseless from the start.

Second, for a Christian, God is the only being that cannot not exist. The world, by contrast, is contingent. But then how are the two related?

This question must have an answer too. Like every answer, it has to rest, in the end, on a rationally demonstrable truth rather than a contingent one. Christians insist that God is the only being in whom such an answer can be found.

There are two possibilities. One is that God created the world by choice. But that is not a satisfying answer. It brings us right back to the inscrutability of God's will. The second is that God created the world by necessity. But this is no longer a Christian answer.

Moreover, if the world, as well as God, exists by necessity, there is no reason to assume they are distinct from one another. That would be an unnecessary and therefore irrational duplication. The only rational conclusion, therefore, is that God and the world are different names for the same thing. This is the conclusion at which Spinoza arrives.[34] It is the heart of his heresy, as Christians like Leibniz and Kant saw it.

Yet for those who follow Spinoza's remorseless employment of the principle of sufficient reason to the end, the conclusion is unavoidable. If we assume that every question, to be intelligible, must have an answer, and that every answer, to be sufficient, must come to rest in an order of reality that cannot not be, then we find ourselves carried along by the force of the principle itself to the startling discovery that the world is both inherently and infinitely divine, down to the brief career of the snowflake on my sleeve.

No Christian can accept this, but no philosopher can deny it. Leibniz and Kant were great philosophers and professing Christians as well.

Spinoza made it clear they could not be both at once. In the end, each made an intellectual sacrifice for the sake of Christian belief. Yet the example of Spinoza remains an inspiration, or unsettling provocation, for those who see, as he did with such arresting clarity, that the spirit of philosophy demands a commitment to reason that rules out the possibility of a God whose freedom guarantees his unintelligibility and whose separation from the world opens a gap between two kingdoms whose relation either cannot be explained at all, or, if it can, turns God into an unneeded appendage that does nothing the world is unable to do on its own.

Why does the world exist? Why do we exist and have the experience of the world that we do? Why is there something rather than nothing? It is the last question a philosopher can ask. Beyond it, none remain.

A Christian philosopher answers, "We exist by the will of God." Leibniz and Kant both remained within the Christian tradition. They had no other answer. Spinoza had a different one. "We exist," he says, "because we cannot not be." Our existence is one small part of an infinite reality whose existence is absolutely necessary. The Christian explanation of the existence of the world as an effect of God's will ends in a cul-de-sac of unreason. Spinoza's explanation carries reason farther. It is an affirmation of the principle of sufficient reason, and thus of philosophy itself, against the Christian claim that reason must eventually yield to faith—a brute fact whose revelations can never be explained by reason alone.

# VI

What does this exceedingly abstract line of thought have to do with the relation between philosophy and conservatism? We are now in a position to say.

Burke had an allergy to philosophy. He was revolted by the metaphysical excesses of the French revolutionaries. He believed that philosophy is radical by nature. Its demand for explanation and transparency is always excessive. It is at war with the caution and deference to tradition that characterize the conservative point of view.

Burke was right: philosophy *is* radical. There is no rule of inquiry more radical than the principle of sufficient reason, which defines the spirit of philosophy itself. But this principle is not the cause of the tension between philosophy and conservatism. The conflict arises, paradoxically, when the principle is not carried far enough—when the radicalism of philosophy stops short and accepts the unfathomable will of a world-transcending creator as the explanation for why we and the world exist. It is the *Christian* answer to the question of existence that makes the tension acute. When we move beyond Christian metaphysics to the more radical rationalism of Spinoza's conception of the world as necessary, eternal, and one, the tension dissolves.

The Christian picture of the world has two related features that put conservative beliefs on the defensive.

The first is that it compels us to judge the meaning and worth of what happens here on earth from the vantage point of a God beyond it. The world of human beings is only conditionally valuable. Indeed, it only *exists* on a condition—that God freely chooses to bring it into being. Here on earth, things seem to happen in a haphazard and unpredictable way, but in reality they do not. They happen because God wills them. God is the absolute point of view from which the accidents of political life must be judged.

That there *is* such a perspective creates a standing temptation for those who believe in God to think they have the right, and perhaps the duty, to assume it in their political deliberations—to judge themselves and others as God does. From this point of view, the entire world of politics, with its opacities and insecurities, its contingencies and risks, is devalued and a brighter, less equivocal set of understandings substituted for it.

This is the metaphysical perspective from which the leaders of the French Revolution judged the politics of France. They denounced the church and ridiculed the contents of orthodox belief yet continued to view their situation from an otherworldly point of view.[35] Their reactionary archenemy Joseph de Maistre did the same, on the basis of orthodoxy itself.[36] In a gentler way that Americans still respect, Jefferson's Declaration of Independence encourages a similar confidence in the absolute finality of certain world-transcending truths. It too brings the realm of politics before the bar of metaphysics. Locke's Christian God is in the background.

These views all rest on the conviction that the affairs of *this* world must be weighed from the vantage point of *another*, even when the God who once occupied this vantage point has lost his traditional characteristics and been demoted to the simple idea of a transcendent measure of value.[37] Even in its last, most disenchanted phase, the otherworldliness of the Christian religion invites its secularized followers to insist on the priority of the absolute, beyond space and time, over the tangled confusions of political life.

Second, Christianity has a built-in bias against humility, on which the spirit of political conservatism depends. It may seem strange to say this. Is not Christianity a religion of humility? Does it not teach the wickedness of pride and proclaim that the meek shall inherit the earth?[38]

Yes, but: it also teaches redemption at the end of days; a reunion of the saved with their creator; the promise of a consummating knowledge that surpasses all mortal limits. It encourages those who believe in a perfect life to come to act now, in this life, with an eye to what they must do to secure their eternal salvation, and to judge their actions, and those of others, from the vantage point of the heavenly position that is the imagined goal of all their earthly striving.

Now we see through a glass darkly. But one day we shall be enlightened, and when we are, all the contradictions and complexities of this life will appear for what they are: sound and fury without meaning, the absurd bustle of those who love the world too much. Before that blessed day, we should do all we can to see and act with the enlightenment we shall then possess in fullest measure, of which we already have enough to guide us through the darkness of the world.

This can hardly be called humble.

Humility is the awareness of one's limits. The belief—the knowledge!—that these are temporary and shall soon be overcome encourages those to whom redemption has been promised to look with laughter and contempt on all who consider their limitations irremediable. The humility of those who believe them to be fixed and final is based, Augustine says, on ignorance. It reflects their mistaken belief in the sufficiency of worldly things.[39] This is the essence of pride, as Augustine sees it. Christian humility gives it the lie but substitutes for it a new kind of pride—otherworldly, absolute, guaranteed—that makes those who humbly devote themselves to the affairs of the world, stressing the need for caution and compromise as they go, look like children wandering in the dark.

In these two related ways, the metaphysics of the Christian religion unsettles the conservative habits of moderation and doubt, and strengthens the inclination to look for a transcendent point of view from which to weigh our political choices and judge the actions of the fallible human beings who struggle in the arena of practical life. There is indeed a war between conservatism and Christian philosophy. But it is not a war between conservatism and philosophy *tout court*, as Burke sometimes suggests. Spinoza's hyper-rational, non-Christian metaphysics shows why.

In Spinoza's philosophy, there is no *other*worldly point of view from which this one may be judged. There is only one world, this world, "absolutely infinite," the cause of itself, necessarily and not contingently real.[40] No metaphysical proposition could be more radical. Yet its very radicalness eliminates the possibility of acting in this world from the perspective of some other conceptually and morally prior one and gives the virtue of humility the strongest possible support by guaranteeing that the limitations of our condition, which we share with every finite being, can never be surpassed.

We will never, Spinoza says, be welcomed in a heaven that makes all earthly things appear incommensurably small—because there is no such heaven. We will never be saved from our condition. We should therefore not be tempted by the immodest and dangerous thought that we can ever have some world-transcending purchase on our mortal circumstances. We must accept these circumstances and the limits they entail as our permanent condition, and work patiently, deliberately, and with appropriate humility to better ourselves and our fellow human beings—to come closer to the God of the world, in full recognition that our desire to do so can never be fulfilled and that there is no God beyond the world who guides and judges our actions.[41]

These are conservative instincts. Spinoza's philosophy reinforces them by undermining the Christian beliefs that tempt the faithful in a more radical direction. Yet Spinoza arrives at his position not by declaring a limit to reason or curtailing the search for explanations, but by radicalizing philosophy itself—by carrying the search for reasons beyond the point that any Christian philosopher, Kant included, is prepared to go. If we follow philosophy to the end, we come to a view of the world (though Spinoza does not say this) that anchors the conservative affirmation of humility and prudence in a metaphysics that guarantees they can never be displaced by the philosophical commitment to reason—because Spinoza's view of the world, which confirms the place of these conservative virtues in the drama of human life, is the most rational view of all.

In any Christian metaphysics, humility and prudence are at most conditional goods. They can never be more than that, given the absoluteness of the otherworldly point of view from which we are to judge things here on earth. In Spinoza's philosophy, by contrast, these virtues are not subject to dislodgement. They are grounded in the only world there is. Philosophy and conservatism are reconciled. Indeed, more than reconciled, for the second is shown to flow from the first with implacable logic.

Hume was a rationalist. He took the principle of sufficient reason seriously. Because he did, he concluded there was no rational explanation for our conviction that the future must be like the past. He believed it can only rest on custom or habit. This made it easy for him to adopt a moral and political conservatism founded on the assumption that time and tradition have the power to generate norms on their own.

Kant went farther. He demonstrated that the lawfulness of nature is a necessary, not contingent, and constitutive, not inductively derived, feature of all possible human experience. But he could not explain the *existence* of our experience, or of the world, except on the familiar Christian assumption that we and the world are creatures of God, brought into being by a spontaneous and therefore unintelligible act of creation.

At this point, Kant's search for explanations runs out. It ends in a rarified Christian metaphysics that motivates and rewards a spirit of moral and political radicalism. All of Kant's practical writings reflect the disdain for prudence and tradition, and the habit of judging human affairs from an otherworldly point of view, that the Christian religion invites, even compels.[42]

Spinoza went farther still. He carried the search for reasons beyond the point Kant thought possible. In the end, he arrived at a monism that equates the real with the intelligible and the intelligible with the necessary—a metaphysics that is both more rational than Kant's critical philosophy and more hospitable to the conservative virtues Burke admired.

In Spinoza, the most radical philosophy thus proves to be the solidest foundation for the worldly values that Burke thought incompatible with the spirit of philosophy itself. To see why, we have to enter the thicket of metaphysical speculation that Burke was loathe to explore and that Hume, though he loved philosophy dearly, failed to explore far enough. For conservatives who are drawn to Burke and Hume and take their side against the political radicalisms that descend from Kant and Locke, the reward of following Spinoza to the end and of seeing how far the principle of sufficient reason allows us to go is the discovery that metaphysics is not the enemy of conservatism but its most stalwart friend. Like other people, most conservatives have only a modest appetite for philosophy. But for those who are blessed or cursed with a larger one, the discovery that it is possible to be faithful to the spirit of philosophy and a conservative too, not accidentally or through a tactical division of loyalties but integrally, in a rationally defensible way, makes the search for a reply to Burke's contempt for metaphysics—along the path from Hume to Kant and on (or back) to Spinoza—eminently rewarding.

# CHAPTER NINE

# Extravagance and Modesty

## I

"What a remarkable piece of work is man," the chorus in *Antigone* sings.[1] "He knows the language of the tongue" and "thought that has wings."[2] He knows "the passions that create cities."[3] He ventures out with reckless abandon, moved by curiosity and gain. "In the tossed waves of winter he dares the bucking back of the sea when the swells swirl heavy."[4] He remakes the world that other animals merely inhabit. Death alone defeats him. He can do everything but "cure death."[5] There is nothing on earth as astonishing as this extravagant, resourceful, yet mortal animal—and nothing so dangerous.

We are a danger to other living things—"the birds of the air," "the wild beasts of the hills," the "fish from the deep" that we trap in our nets.[6] We are a danger to the earth, the "greatest of the goddesses," our "pliant mother" on whose fertility the work of sowing and reaping depends.[7] Most strikingly, we are a danger to ourselves. Other animals kill their kind from hunger or fear. We murder and enslave other human beings for profit, pride, and pleasure and out of a boundless anxiety for our own future safety, driven by the power of imaginative projection that keeps us in a perpetual state of war, just as it enables us to build cathedrals and write poems that first exist only in the mind.[8] Today, we have it in our power to destroy all life on earth. Whether we do or not is a choice we make every day.[9] Can there be a greater danger?

To escape it once and for all, we would have to suppress the power of imagination that gives our ambitions their "wings" and shatters the limits within which the desires of other animals are safely confined. That would mean giving up all the other things that flow from this power as well— the whole world of human culture that exists only on account of our extravagant longings. Some may think it a reasonable trade, but even if it were, it is beyond our power to make. The only thing other than death that irrevocably constrains our ability to fashion the world according to our fantasies and fears is our powerlessness to renounce this ability itself. We are stuck with our extravagance. It is a fate like death.

And what are the "wings" that we cannot refuse, on which we soar to extravagant heights? "Thought," the poet says, and "language." Among all living things we alone are blessed and cursed with the power to see time from a vantage point beyond it—to study its restless motions even as we are swept along by them. This is the condition of all science and art and of the practical work of foresight and planning on which every distinctively human project depends. Extravagance is another name for transcendence.

To regret it makes no sense. It is who we are. Nor is it possible to be indifferent to the spectacle of human ambition. Any participant in the human adventure is bound to feel a mixture of wonder and fear—of astonishment and pride as well as foreboding and dread. This combination of feelings is the motive for a view of human life that is as old as organized reflection on it. It is the conservative view of life.

The conservative dislikes speed, abrupt change, discontinuities in practice and taste. She is suspicious of large abstractions untethered from habit and custom as a test of character or basis for political action. She feels an instinctive mistrust of enthusiasm, charisma, and utopian dreams. She feels the weight of the past and has a tempered loyalty to it. She favors steadiness and reliability in people and programs. Rigid judgments and partisan polarities run against the grain of her belief that most people are too complicated and most political programs too uncomplicated to be celebrated or reviled as wholly good or bad. She has modest expectations, personally and politically, though her modesty is leavened with a cautious measure of hope; she knows it is almost always possible to do at least a little bit better.

These attitudes and feelings go together. They belong to a recognizable style of judgment and conduct. They constitute the conservative cast of mind. In their private lives, most people are conservatives in this sense much of the time. It is hard to organize a life on any other basis.

Many fewer are philosophical conservatives who oppose their view of life in a principled way to other ideas of human nature and political action. Partly this is because very few people are philosophically inclined in any direction at all but partly it is because the appeal of revolutionary and utopian schemes increases as we move to higher levels of abstraction where the complexities of life are left behind. This is just what the philosophical conservative fears. It moves her to state her position in more explicit terms as a counter to what she sees as her opponents' thrilling but dangerous illusions.

Everyone worries about the dangers of human extravagance, but different people react with varying degrees of anxiety. For some, the boundlessness of human striving seems a constant emergency—a standing threat to the existence of the very world in which the exuberance of art and philosophy and the freedoms of political life are possible at all. They value these things but are especially impressed by the destructive effects of the power from which they arise. Danger is never far from their minds. The modesty they admire as a principle of judgment and action is, for them, a necessary if imperfect antidote to the permanent threat of extravagance—the source of all that is grand and ruinous in human life. Those who feel the danger with particular urgency tend to become conservatives of a principled kind.

## II

It is possible to be a conservative in this broad sense and hold any of a number of different views on matters of social policy: to favor free markets or oppose them; endorse a policy of isolation or one of engagement; believe the wall between church and state should be higher or lower. Each is compatible with modesty and caution, a respect for the past, and a preference for incremental adjustment. There are conservative versions of each.

The relative strengths and weaknesses of these competing views is a subject of endless debate. Concrete judgments of fact and value are always involved, and the specific circumstances matter. Often, though, the contenders also struggle to claim the mantle of conservatism in general. "We are the true conservatives," they say; "our opponents are false pretenders." In most cases, there is little to be gained from trying to resolve these title disputes. They tend to be more nominal than real, and the verdict changes as the circumstances do. There is, however, a genuine distinction of lasting importance that divides the champions of modesty into two opposing camps. It has to do with their attitude toward the phenomenon of human extravagance that motivates their shared preference for continuity and caution. Some of those who fear extravagance love it as well. A few even assign it supreme value. Others are cool to it; they feel no attraction to the boundary-shattering exuberance of human desire or are actively repulsed by it. The philosophies of Burke and Aristotle illustrate the difference.

Burke quotes with approval Aristotle's dictum that one must not expect deductive rigor in political debates, which call for practical judgment instead.[10] He recognized the affinity between their views and correctly understood that Aristotle's emphasis on the value of prudence gives his political philosophy a conservative tenor.

There is much to be said for this judgment. Other aspects of Aristotle's thought confirm it. His earnest attack on Plato's semi-serious proposal that his idealized Guardians hold their wives, children, and belongings in common reveals a more conservative cast of mind. Where Plato discounts the importance of family ties of love and loyalty, Aristotle insists on the ubiquity and value of both.[11] There is also Aristotle's preference for the stable habits of a property-owning middle class and his defense of the virtues of what he calls a "mixed" regime in which different groups or classes each have a limited share.[12] These are all expressions of the spirit of modesty that dominates Aristotle's political thought as it does Burke's own, motivated in each case by a suspicion of abstraction and skepticism about utopian goals.

But here the similarity between these two conservatives ends. For Burke, metaphysical extravagance has no appeal. He is uninterested in the pursuit of ultimate truths. There is nothing to suggest that Burke would suppress philosophy so long as it remains a harmless pastime—a private hobby with no pretension to public authority. But there is also nothing to suggest that he thinks it very important, let alone considers it the noblest of all human activities. Burke and Aristotle both see speculative abstraction as a threat to political order and adopt a conservative stance in response. But Aristotle loves philosophy as the highest of all human pursuits while Burke is at best indifferent and often hostile toward it.

At the beginning of his lectures on metaphysics, Aristotle observes that we are restlessly curious beings. We desire to know, he says, not just for the sake of the practical benefits it brings but for the sheer pleasure of knowing.[13] This is already something extravagant.

Our longing to know for its own sake moves us to search out the causes of things. Why do they happen as they do and not in some other way? The search continues until we arrive at an answer beyond which it is pointless to inquire. We reach the end of our investigations when we see that every other cause is ultimately caused by something that is the cause of itself and therefore self-explanatory.[14]

It is hard to imagine a more extravagant idea. Yet according to Aristotle, our desire to know brings us to it with a compulsive force that cannot be suppressed and will not be satisfied by anything less extravagant. This is the arc of human curiosity. Aristotle traces it in his writings on the soul, the stars, the weather, the parts of animals, and everything that belongs to the study of nature in general—and then even beyond this in the *Metaphysics*, where he examines the fundamental conditions of every inquiry into the cause of the movements we observe in the eternal cosmos we inhabit for a time until we die.

This is remarkable enough. What is even more striking is the portrait Aristotle offers of the philosophical life in the last book of the *Nicomachean Ethics*.[15] Only a few lead lives of this kind. Partly that is because they alone have the freedom and resources to do so; partly it is because only a few experience the curiosity they share with other human beings as an insatiable demand. Still, however exceptional philosophy appears from the standpoint of ordinary life with its prosaic routines, Aristotle insists that those who pursue it lead the most fully human life of all—the one in which the promise of transcendence is realized to the great possible degree. He recognizes that even a philosopher must eat. No human being can sustain the experience of supreme fulfillment for long. Yet while it lasts, he says, the few who have it are indistinguishable from the divine reality that is the goal of their inquiries. They become gods themselves, until the dinner bell rings, and in this ecstatic moment show what it means to be a human being.[16]

Loosed in the political world, philosophy is an invitation to fantasy and turmoil—a source of danger and destruction. It must be kept out of politics at all costs. On this, Aristotle and Burke agree. Yet for Aristotle the extravagance of thinking is also the most loveable thing about us. The modesty it demands in political life sits side by side with the immodesty it invites. If we reject the first, we risk destroying the human world in which thinking and all our other transcendent ambitions can be stably pursued. But if we deny or depreciate the second, we lose sight of what this world is for. This is the dynamic accommodation on which Aristotle's conservatism rests. Burke's is more strident but in a sense less comprehensively human because there is in it no love of the extravagance whose dangers incite his impassioned plea for caution.

## III

There are many Burkean themes in these pages—friendship for the dead; the good of patriotism; the value of delay; the need for a wall between the here and the hereafter. They reflect my distaste for immodesty. And yet there are other themes that make it clear I love extravagance too—the claim that excellence is sovereign among goods; that the existence of God is the truth about the world; and that every question we can ask must have an answer. These are radical claims, especially in a culture dominated by a democratic hostility to the idea of nobility and the disenchanted habit of viewing religion as matter of personal opinion.

Burke had no interest in defending these beliefs or even in exploring them. He was not metaphysically inclined. By contrast, Aristotle puts them at the center of his portrait of the supremely excellent human being—the one who understands that every question about the order of the world is fully answerable because it leads back to an unmoving and changeless reality that cannot not be. This is the extravagant claim at the heart of Aristotle's conservative philosophy. It is the essence of the classical ideal of the human condition, which Aristotle shares with his poetically inspired and more reckless teacher Plato.

I remain attached to this ideal even today, under democratic and disenchanted conditions. It is the inspiration for the radical parts of this book. These are balanced by a repeated plea for modesty in various forms, also inspired by Aristotle, who grasped with particular sobriety the dangers that accompany our ecstatic love of the eternal and divine. Burke recognized the dangers but lacked Aristotle's appetite for metaphysics. I share the appetite—not just because I have the emotional makeup I do (though that is certainly true), but also because I believe, as Tocqueville did, that a view of the human condition that leaves our extravagance out of account or suppresses it for the sake of comfort and peace is an invitation to nihilism and worse.

My conservatism, like Aristotle's, is marked both by a reverence for transcendence and an abiding fear of it. Is this a contradictory position? Only as contradictory as the splendid and dangerous animal it describes—always reaching up to the gods yet threatening to destroy the worldly institutions and traditions he needs to survive.

This is the only honest and inclusive kind of humanism. It is equally opposed to modesty in philosophy and extravagance in politics. It might be called "ecstatic conservatism." Aristotle is its first great proponent. Still, he can only take us so far. There is too wide a gulf between Aristotle's classical ideals and our modern ones for the balance he strikes between extravagance and modesty to remain compelling today.

To begin with, there are the obvious differences: Aristotle's beliefs, for example, that species are immortal, stars never die, women are inferior to men, and some human beings are slaves by nature.[17] We know the first two beliefs are false and reject the last two on ethical grounds. Modern science and morality subvert many of Aristotle's convictions.

Beyond these specific failings, his entire philosophy is characterized by a lack of interest in, or appreciation of, the distinctiveness of individuals as such. There is no suggestion anywhere in Aristotle's writings that for human beings fulfillment includes the attainment and expression of a unique point of view. The reasons lie deep in his metaphysics—in his understanding of the distinction between form and matter and assignment of reality and intelligibility to the first alone. The result is a formalistic conception of identity in which self-realization means the successful exhibition of a form one shares with others of one's kind.[18] Nothing, perhaps, distinguishes Aristotle's view of the human condition so dramatically from ours, for while certain aspects of his account of human flourishing have a perennial appeal, we assign a value to the uniqueness of the individual that Aristotle's metaphysics disallows.

Another and even more important difference follows from this one. Aristotle believes that it is possible for a human being to be completely fulfilled—for a serious young man to become all that his humanity allows, without remainder or residue, and to reach this state before he dies. He adds two caveats: accidents may derail the pursuit of perfection, and even if they do not, no one can sustain it for more than brief periods of time. Still, with these two qualifications Aristotle insists that fulfillment is within our grasp.

This follows from the formalism of his idea of perfection. A form is a shape. It is bounded and finite, like the shape of a circle or square. One can define it exactly and exhaustively so that nothing remains to be known or said about it. If human fulfillment means exhibiting (literally, "filling fully") the requirements of the general definition of humanity in one's own life, then it too can be achieved completely, like a circle drawn according to its proper definition, whose inevitable inexactness is due to material factors that are a matter of indifference so far as the essence of the circle is concerned.

Our view of the human condition is radically different. Modern writers portray it in various ways, but a common theme runs through their different accounts. They all insist that we are necessarily incomplete—that there is a gap we cannot close between longing and fulfillment.[19] This is unthinkable for Aristotle. It violates the cosmic rule that for any desire to be meaningful—indeed, intelligible at all—it must be capable of reaching its goal. This applies to human longing too. The deepest and most irremediable feature of the human condition, as we moderns understand it, is therefore one whose very possibility Aristotle denies as a matter of principle.

Anyone who accepts the modern view is bound to see the extravagance of human longing in a different light—as something more restless, inventive, unstable, anti-authoritarian, and therefore more dangerous than Aristotle supposed. This makes the need for a compensating modesty more urgent. Our acceptance of the chasm between longing and fulfillment intensifies both sides of the equation. Aristotle's calm adjustment of extravagance and modesty (which to our restless modern minds is part of its appeal) is no longer up to the task. Can his ecstatic conservatism be defended on grounds more congenial to modern belief?

# IV

David Hume gives us reason to think it can. Hume disliked enthusiasm in politics and religion. He favored modesty in manners and social arrangements.[20] In these respects, he and Burke thought alike. But Hume was also an ardent philosopher. He shared Aristotle's extravagant passion for thinking, though Hume's philosophy reflects the destabilizing effects of the modern belief that our longing to understand the world can never be fulfilled.

We first encounter the world through perception—most vividly and accurately with our eyes. The things we see confuse us; they are a heterogeneous mass of colors and shapes. According to Aristotle, the confusion is temporary. The world has a permanent and knowable order. Its motions follow a fixed set of laws dictated by the forms of things. We are able to mentally detach these forms from the mass of perceptions in which they are buried and to contemplate them on their own. This is what we mean by thinking.[21] The mind's ability to think allows us to comprehend the intelligible structure of the world at ever higher levels of generality. Eventually, our inquiries come to an end; there is nothing more to know; our longing to understand is fully satisfied.

Hume rejects this view entirely. Experience, he says, begins with perception but never gets beyond it. Our observations of the world are not a portal to timeless truths.[22] We may treat them as such; it is difficult to suppress the temptation to do so. But this is at most a necessary fiction. Our perceptions accumulate in a growing heap that never brings us to a rational understanding of the world as it really is.

The old Aristotelian assumption that they do seems, by comparison, naïve, childish, unduly limiting: it keeps human curiosity penned within a sheltered harbor whose comfort is bought at the price of suppressing the wish to explore the exciting and dangerous sea beyond it. Hume's "empiricism" (this is what philosophers call it) is haunted by disappointment: there can be no end to the gathering of facts, no repose in final knowledge.[23] But it is fired by a thrilling extravagance too—by the same sense of endless adventure that gives every modern account of the human condition its distinctive frisson of discovery and risk, exaltation and belittlement. Aristotle's cosmic rationalism seems by comparison timid and tame. Hume is the more adventurous philosopher.

His counterbalancing insistence on modesty and common sense in practical affairs is no doubt partly temperamental. Hume seems to have been emotionally inclined toward stability, balance, prudence, and caution and repulsed by zeal and intolerance, especially in religion. But his conservativism has a philosophical motive as well. Hume's preference for settled habits of thought and established patterns of conduct is partly a response to a problem created by the extravagance of his own theory of human understanding, which unchains the pursuit of knowledge from the ancient metaphysical assumptions that kept it tethered within a circumscribed orbit.

The problem is that no collection of facts, however large, by itself yields an understanding of the world we perceive. We understand the world when we are able to explain why things happen as they do and to make reliable predictions about the future. Explanation and prediction rely on rules; they cannot do without them. But where do these rules come from? Not from the facts themselves, Hume says. We infer them from the facts but the inference may be mistaken. There can never be a guarantee that it is not. The warrant for the rules we need to explain anything at all must have another source.

Hume's celebrated solution to this puzzle is his conclusion that we accept the otherwise groundless rules that every explanation employs as a matter of custom or habit.[24] There is no basis for them, he says, other than our long-standing acquiescence in their truth. On Hume's view, truth turns out to be a tradition whose authority is based on nothing other than its durability. Like every tradition, this one too is susceptible to change. But it changes slowly and piecemeal and even as it does continues to derive its authority from our habitual acceptance of it. This is a conservative idea—one might even call it *the* conservative idea. One of the most striking features of Hume's philosophy is his importation of this idea from the realm of moral and political thought, where it has always had a home, into the heartland of metaphysics, where he uses it as an instrument of modesty to solve or at least soften the most pressing problem created by the extravagance of his altogether modern account of our endless pursuit of understanding.

# V

We are the inventive animal, full of surprises, changing the world and ourselves as we go. Things may be stable for a while, or seem so. But novelty and disruption cannot be stayed for long. There is delight in this and danger too—discovery and destruction. Those who feel the danger acutely are drawn to the conservative virtues—prudence, caution, gradualism, a suspicion of concentrated power, modesty of expression and demand.

The celebration of these qualities may be joined, though, by an enthusiastic embrace of the extravagance that gives rise to the danger itself. This was Aristotle's position. He loved metaphysics even as he cautioned that it has no place in politics, where men of good character and sound judgment ought to rule.

But Aristotle's metaphysics is insufficiently extravagant, by modern standards at least. It is tempered—pacified, disciplined, rendered less dangerous—by his assumption that our longing to know all that can be known is capable of fulfillment. Once we accept that it cannot, the radicalism of the longing is exposed; its danger grows; we are ejected from the restful possession of Aristotle's divine knowledge and condemned to perpetual, anxious searching instead.

Among modern thinkers who reject the reassuring certainties of Aristotle's metaphysics yet share his enthusiasm for it and share as well his conservative preference for habit and moderation as personal and political values, Hume is one of the most impressive. His commitment to reason is boundless. He demands an explanation of judgments that Aristotle took for granted. He pushes beyond the Pillars of Hercules onto the horizonless sea of empirical science—like Tennyson's Ulysses.[25] And yet despite or perhaps because of his radicalism as a thinker, Hume is especially devoted to the conservative virtues in both private and public life.

Still, even Hume's radicalism has its limits. In the end, he gives up on the search for reasons and falls back on the conservative idea of custom as an answer to the most difficult question his restless reflections provoke. This is not so much a reconciliation of extravagance and modesty as an exhausted truce between them. This is where Kant begins his celebrated attack.

Kant refuses to concede that the laws of human reason rest on nothing but custom or habit. The rules that guide our investigation of the world are not, Kant says, accidental or contingent. They are the necessary ground of all possible experience, and therefore of the experience we actually have.[26] This is a radical idea in comparison to Hume's deference to habit as the basis of all human science. It carries the adventure of reason beyond the limits Hume imposed on it. If Hume's philosophy is more extravagant than Aristotle's, Kant's is more extravagant still.

Yet Kant's more radical idea of the explanatory power of reason has two limits of its own. The first is that reason cannot explain why specific empirical laws (that a body remains in motion or at rest until affected by another body) are not wholly contingent, unlike the necessary laws of experience in general (that every event has a cause). The second is that these necessary laws do not explain why we actually have any experience at all.

Neither of these questions can be answered on the basis of the transcendental arguments of *Critique of Pure Reason*. Yet Kant refuses to simply dismiss them. His devotion to reason is too great. When he returns to them in *The Critique of Judgment*, he answers both by appealing to the Christian idea of creation. The world exists and its fathomless diversity has an order we are able to grasp through an endless process of empirical inquiry *because* it was brought into being by an all-powerful providential God who wants the best for it and us.[27]

This is where the buck stops for Kant. If Hume's rationalism bottoms out in habit, Kant's rests ultimately on the orthodox belief in a creator God who exists before and beyond the world. Both are modern philosophers for whom the disjunction between longing and fulfillment is axiomatic. Both are moved by the extravagant demands of a desire to know that can never come to rest in the tranquility of the old Aristotelian philosophy. If anything, Kant feels this demand more strongly than Hume. But the Christian orthodoxy in which his search for explanation concludes is *at once* a sacrifice of the intellect that puts a damper on metaphysical extravagance *and* the inspiration for a moral and political philosophy that attacks the conservative values of tradition, character, and habit in the name of enlightened citizenship and a cosmopolitan kingdom of ends.[28]

If Kant goes farther than Hume in the search for reasons and causes, his Christian faith, which Hume proudly refuses, leads to a "practical" philosophy in which autonomy, equality, and respect for persons are the keynote themes, rather than the old-fashioned ideas of character, balance, and moderation that Hume embraces in a spirit closer to Aristotle's *Ethics* than Kant's *Critique of Practical Reason*. If the extravagance of Kant's theoretical philosophy is restrained by his acceptance of the dogma of creation, his endorsement of a moral ideal that is hostile to conservatism, both ancient and modern, springs from the same commitment. However brilliant, beautiful, and inspiring Kant's philosophy may be, those who seek a view of human life that is *at once* more metaphysically adventurous *and* more conservative in its moral and political judgments, more ecstatic *and* more cautious, must look elsewhere to find a thinker who feels the thrill of endless vistas, of the inventiveness of the animal who always goes beyond, as well as the need to conserve the world against the risks of our freewheeling adventures by throwing a protective cordon around tradition and habit—yet is free of the Christian prejudice that limits Kant's thinking in both respects.

There are two modern philosophers who fit this description. One is Nietzsche and the other is Spinoza. They may seem an odd pair, but Nietzsche eventually saw the resemblance between them. He called Spinoza his "predecessor."[29] What did these two otherwise very different thinkers share in common?

# VI

That Nietzsche loved extravagance, no one will doubt. He expresses his views with an immodesty that no philosopher has matched. Reading Nietzsche is an intoxicating and dangerous experience.

The substance of Nietzsche's philosophy is wildly extravagant too. From *The Birth of Tragedy* on, he offers an unsparing critique of the most widely shared and unthinkingly accepted values of modern democratic life. His assault on the virtues of Christian morality puts all our conventional norms of equality and human rights on the defensive.[30]

But this is only the negative side of his philosophy. It has a positive side that is equally arresting. Nietzsche's attack on European morality does not end, as some suppose, in a nihilistic cul-de-sac—in the now widely shared belief that we live in a world without meaning. It culminates in a new post-Christian metaphysics: a poetic vision of the world as a single, whole, eternal being, the self-generating ground of its own existence, not unlike Aristotle's pagan cosmos but with the crucial difference that all the individuals in it are graded according to their unique splendor in a way that Aristotle's formalistic idea of excellence rules out.[31] It is an extraordinary proposal—a novel combination of classical and Christian motifs. Nietzsche's obscure idea of the eternal return is its most striking expression.[32] This extravagant thought came to him, he says, in an ecstatic moment walking along the shore of Lake Silvaplana in Switzerland, "six thousand feet above man and time."[33]

But where is the countervailing respect for habit, tradition, and manners that is the mark of every ecstatic conservatism from Aristotle to Hume? The answer is, in Nietzsche's idea of nobility.[34] Like Aristotle, Nietzsche takes the distinction between noble and common souls for granted. He believes in the rank order of men, though unlike Aristotle he understands nobility to mean the fulfillment of an individual destiny rather than conformity to a virtuous type. This destiny is for each of us a fate. We need to freely embrace it—to "love" it as our own.[35] Those who think of Nietzsche as an apostle of freedom are therefore partly right. But the democratic idea that all lives are of equal value because everyone enjoys the same freedom to affirm whatever way of life he or she chooses is for Nietzsche more than a mistake. It is an insult to the idea of nobility: a blasphemy that modern democrats affirm as sacred dogma.[36]

Nobility is a hard-won achievement. It is the result of a long and disciplined devotion to what Socrates called his "daimon," the ruling fate of a person's special endowment and peculiar circumstances in life.[37] It is a kind of habit of educated dignity and poise, acquired through patience and persistence. Like Aristotle, Nietzsche saw nobility as an accomplishment that takes effort and time.

For an individual, the time is the whole of her life.[38] For a people or an institution, it is many lives, bent for generations toward a common goal—the Roman people and the Catholic Church.[39] Disrupters, eccentrics, utopian visionaries of all sorts distract from the work and weaken the discipline required to build anything noble on earth.

Those who want to tear the work down in the name of justice and equality are the enemies of nobility. Their resentful attacks threaten the long-matured works of beauty and power that give human life its supreme value and distinguish it from the humdrum life of animals that never rise above the smothering routines of need. This is Nietzsche's anti-revolutionary judgment. He offers it repeatedly.[40] It is the source of his contempt for all that he finds pedestrian and ignoble in the flatland of modern civilization. His devastating portrait of "the last man" is its most pointed expression.[41]

In this judgment we hear an echo of Burke's own, though Nietzsche expresses his anti-revolutionary sentiments with a violence that even at his most contemptuous Burke never exhibits. It is accompanied, moreover, by a speculative radicalism that has no counterpart in Burke's political writings—one that goes beyond even Kant's relentless rationalism, which is still hobbled by Christian prejudices that no longer inhibit Nietzsche's metaphysical imagination. The result is a philosophy that seems to mark the outermost limits of both extravagance and conservative modesty.

But in fact it does not. We reach these limits in Spinoza, the seventeenth-century Marrano Jew who Nietzsche surprisingly identified as his true philosophical precursor—a mild man with the most extravagant ideas of any philosopher who has ever lived and a correspondingly deep appreciation of the need to conserve the institutions of civilized life against the destructive powers of the time-transcending animal who loves God without limit but as often abuses these powers as puts them to work in the service of its ecstatic calling.

## VII

Spinoza's *Ethics* is composed in the form of a geometrical treatise—a tightly interconnected series of axioms, proofs, and corollaries.[42] Even the passions are analyzed in this passionless style. The serenity of the *Ethics* is light years away from Nietzsche's explosive formulations and delight in giving offense. But the quiet surface of Spinoza's book is merely the public face of a philosophy as radical as Nietzsche's own and in some ways quite similar to it.

For Spinoza too, the world is one, eternal, and divine. There is no God beyond it who creates the world and sustains it in being.[43] The world is the "cause of itself," the source of its own being.[44] It is composed of countless individuals, each of whom constitutes a unique but limited perspective on the world as a whole. Each longs to encompass as much of the world as it can in its representation of it. This longing can never be fulfilled: the world is too great to be captured from any finite point of view. But some individuals make greater progress than others toward this unattainable goal. They are more real and powerful than those whose mastery of the world is less complete—reality and power being for Spinoza, as they are for Nietzsche, equivalent terms. This is the essence of nobility. Its achievement takes time and discipline. Only a few achieve it.[45]

These are the shared premises of Spinoza's theology and the cosmic "perspectivism" that Nietzsche sketched toward the end of his sane life. Each repudiates the Christian belief that the world is one thing and God another. Each affirms a view that more closely resembles Aristotle's pagan metaphysics, with the vital difference that individuality plays a central role in the philosophies of both ("modes" in Spinoza's vocabulary, "perspectives" in Nietzsche's).[46] Each is an original, adventurous, *daring* combination of ancient and modern ideas.

There are two respects, though, in which Spinoza's philosophy is the more radical of the two. One concerns its form and the other its content.

Nietzsche presents his view of the world in images, stories, histories— as a work of art. Spinoza offers his as a demonstration whose conclusions have the force of rational proof. To say, as Spinoza does, that his metaphysics is not only true but provably so strains the reader's credulity beyond Nietzsche's less demanding claim that his picture of the world is an artful representation that may convey a sense of mastery but lacks what Nietzsche says no perspective can ever possess: the ability to secure its dominance once and for all as a truth beyond cavil or dispute.

The greater radicalism of Spinoza's geometrical method is mirrored in the view of the world he employs it to present. Along with the several parallels between his metaphysics and Nietzsche's, there is one striking difference. Spinoza's world, like Nietzsche's, is one and eternal. But it is infinite too. It has no spatial or temporal limits; there are infinitely many individuals within it and each of these can be understood (explained, described, appreciated) in infinitely many ways. The idea of infinity is one of the cornerstones of Spinoza's theology.[47] It has no counterpart in Nietzsche's poetic portrait of the world as an eternal but bounded whole (like Aristotle's finite cosmos). The result is a God even more distant from the finite beings that are "in" it (including all the human ones) than

Nietzsche's self-sustaining world going round in its closed circle. With this, the pathos of striving and failure that characterizes every modern view of the human condition reaches a peak that cannot be surpassed: an extravagance of love and disappointment that expresses in a metaphysically rigorous way the essence of the starstruck, mortal being that Sophocles portrays in his choral song.

The counterpart of this extravagance is a modesty that gives Spinoza's *Ethics*, with its exhilarating theological demands, an unmistakably conservative cast—not unlike Aristotle's *Ethics*, whose enthusiastic portrait of the life of the mind is balanced by a conservative appreciation of practical virtue. This becomes clearer as the reader moves from part 1 of Spinoza's *Ethics* ("Of God") to the fifth and last part ("On Human Freedom"). The focus shifts from the world (from "substance" or "nature") to the place of human beings within it and to the question of how one ought to live.[48] The most fulfilling of all possible lives, Spinoza says, is one devoted to intellectual refinement. He and Aristotle agree in this respect. But Spinoza's judgment regarding the superiority of the *vita contemplativa* is tempered in a way that Aristotle's is not.

Unlike Aristotle, Spinoza insists that the pursuit of knowledge can never come to an end. There is always more to understand about the world than one does at any moment. The wise human being is keenly aware that an infinite gap always remains between what she longs to know and presently does. This introduces a note of modesty into the heart of Spinoza's idea of intellectual virtue. It has far-reaching practical implications.

Because she knows that perfect knowledge lies beyond her grasp, the wise person is mistrustful of those who claim to possess it—especially if they want to impose their ideas on others.[49] She is tolerant of other views even when she knows them to be mistaken and is bemused at the countless forms of superstition in which human beings enslave their minds. Her bemusement is not mean-spirited or hostile. It is accompanied by feelings of friendship and generosity toward those whose lives are lived in comparative darkness—by the wish to do what she can to help them toward greater enlightenment.[50] They are, after all, more like herself than not. Most are deaf to the appeal. They are easily seduced by revolutionary schemes of psychological and political reform. But however thrilling, these programs are all doomed. None can ever be a substitute for the hard work of individual self-mastery. This is a fact of life but not a reason either for despair or disengagement. The wise person reacts to the foibles of her fellow human beings with equanimity and calm, redoubling her efforts to help those she can while recognizing that only a few are ever likely to make significant progress in the life of the mind.

There is, though, one danger wise men and women consider immediate and pressing—the equivalent of a five-alarm fire. In a state of nature, where no political authority as yet exists, everyone is free to do whatever he can. The rule in such a state is that "big fish eat small fish."[51] The creation of a political regime establishes a system of law and order. The big fish now have a duty to abstain from eating the small ones and the small ones a right to complain if they are attacked. The state enforces the one and protects the other. This is the good of politics as Spinoza understands it.[52] Yet however secure any such regime may be, it is always vulnerable to abuse or destruction. We never get out of the state of nature completely. The risk of murder, theft, and enslavement remains. Knowing this, the wise person will be impressed not only by the good of political order but its fragility as well. She will feel the urgency of protecting its hard-won achievements against the forces of ignorance and misguided self-interest that threaten the human world at every moment. She will be suspicious of speculative programs and intolerant crusades that jeopardize the settled framework of civilized life that alone enables us to pursue our loftiest ambitions in relative safety and peace. She will be politically conservative—precisely because her philosophical ambitions are so extravagant.

Spinoza was a champion of religious freedom and toleration. In these respects, he differed from his contemporary Thomas Hobbes.[53] Spinoza was on the liberal side of the ledger. Yet like Hobbes he appreciated the need for social order and the difficulty of sustaining it. He was cautious in his estimate of what human beings are able to accomplish when they act together as a group, partly because he saw how dangerous the love of power is when it takes the form (as it often does) of a longing for wealth and domination, and partly because he understood that the greatest achievements are those we must win on our own as individuals struggling to grasp the implications of the simple proposition that God is "a substance consisting of infinite attributes, of which each expresses eternal and infinite essence."[54]

We may be joined in this pursuit by a few friends, but the task is not a collective one except in the very limited sense that only government can create the security needed for it. The extravagance of our love of power, which is so often blind and self-destructive, puts this fragile accomplishment at risk just as it moves the blessed few to strive toward extraordinary heights of understanding. The result is a blend of caution and enthusiasm that resembles Aristotle's own, recast to reflect the infinitude of human longing—an enlightened conservatism inspired by the exhilarating and terrible discovery that our noblest desires are incapable of satisfaction and therefore both more extravagant than Aristotle supposed and more in need of a compensating modesty to keep them in check.

Spinoza's political conservatism has a parallel in his account of personal virtue. His treatment of the passions is subtler than Aristotle's. It has a psychoanalytic realism that Aristotle's lacks.[55] Yet he too emphasizes the need for discipline and self-control and the cultivation of reliable habits that establish a stable emotional framework at the individual level analogous to the legal one that government provides for whole communities. Here too, the stress is on moderation and calm—on balance, contentment, and peace. The similarity between Spinoza's portrait of the wise man and Aristotle's description of the virtuous one is at many points quite striking, though Spinoza's is enriched by an appreciation of our constant tendency toward self-defeat that gives his account of the human good a distinctively modern appearance with a Freudian look.[56]

Spinoza owned a signet ring engraved with a rose and the Latin word *Caute*, or "caution."[57] The meaning of the word and of Spinoza's choice of it has been a subject of speculation since his death. Perhaps it means "Be careful in expressing your views if others find them disturbing." Spinoza followed this advice to the end of his life. But perhaps it also means "Proceed with modesty and care in cultivating your personal character; in respecting the fragility of political order; and in the ecstatic work of thinking, whose extravagance demands that we proceed with utmost rigor by making sure at every step that we have not been unhinged by the passion for eternity that carries us up and out of the world of human things." If we understand its meaning in this way, it is not at all surprising that Spinoza chose "caution" as his motto. No other word seems better suited to this most modern and enlightened of conservatives, whose philosophy presents an integrated picture of the human being that gives both extravagance and modesty their due—one in which wariness and ecstasy each has its proper place.

# Afterword

Is our public life today different than it was fifty years ago—or a hundred and fifty? Many believe that our divisions are deeper than ever before and our contempt for those with whom we disagree more violent. Both progressives and conservatives warn that we are at a breaking point—that the end of the American experiment is at hand. At times it seems that the only proposition on which all agree is that we have reached a crisis of exceptional, if not unique, proportions.

In one respect, of course, the judgment is exaggerated. It is a result of the myopia from which the living always suffer. A moment's reflection is enough to remind us that we have been in deep trouble before: divided by warring convictions, enflamed by mutually uncomprehending sentiments, speaking—shouting—with a venomous excess that made it seem foolish to hope we would ever be able to "bind up the nation's wounds," as Lincoln put it. However sour the public mood today, are the parties that glare at one another from their entrenched positions more estranged than they were in the spring of 1861, or the winter of 1932, or the summer of 1968? Is the sting of their words sharper than the calculated slanders that John Adams and Thomas Jefferson hurled at one another in 1800 and that have been a staple—often entertaining if rarely edifying—of every presidential campaign since? It is easy to forget the passions of the past in the obliterating heat of those that now consume us.

Yet in another respect, the belief that there is something uniquely dangerous about the present moment is altogether true. The danger has to do with time, whose power both to destroy and to heal has always been a preoccupation of thinkers and politicians in the conservative tradition.

On the one hand, time undoes all our human works. It disfigures every building, corrupts every institution, and slackens every norm of behavior—sometimes slowly, sometimes swiftly but always implacably. Nothing in our human world—or in the natural world, insofar as we are now its guardians too—can survive for long without attention and care. We are engaged in an endless program of upkeep. There is no escape from it so long as we remain subject to time's sovereign power. Conservatives in particular stress our duties of trusteeship and remind us that if we do not meet them, we become something less than fully human—the short-lived "flies of a summer" with no past, no future, no heritable world at all.

But if time has the power to dissolve and destroy, it has the power to heal as well. This is a conservative theme too. Time gives us the chance for second thoughts, conciliation and compromise, and the blessing of forgetfulness, which cools tempers even when it does not extinguish them altogether. This is the virtue of time—its positive side, which must be mobilized to meet its resistless negative power. Those who understand this recognize that time is the most powerful ally we have in the unending struggle to preserve our human world against the depredations of time. The American system of government exemplifies this strategy. It is a system of artful delays that is meant to give us the time we need to reach the kind of checkered and often unprincipled agreements that alone can carry us through from one age to another in an ongoing project of repair and renovation that would otherwise be impossible in a nation so large and diverse.

This is what today seems unprecedentedly fragile. The structure of our government has not changed. But it has been overtaken by technologies of communication that are shrinking the time we need to reflect, revise, calm down, and take a sober second look. Ideas are now communicated with lightning speed to a global audience. The time between thinking and speaking—to everyone everywhere all at once—is disappearing. The result is thoughtlessness, incaution, and the lowering of barriers to the immediate expression of feeling, which is always rawer before time dulls its edge. Our divisions today may not be any wider than they were before—in some respects, they are the same divisions—but the shrinking of time in our digitalized lives gives our disagreements an urgency and immediacy that make conciliation and adjustment look like a fool's errand.

We all have reason to worry about this, but conservatives should be especially concerned. That is because they place great weight on the saving power of time in politics, culture, and human life generally. It is as if they had been deprived of their most important asset in the centuries-old campaign, which began with Edmund Burke, to explain and defend the conservative point of view.

What are conservatives to do? The first thing is to remind us of what we share in common, progressives and conservatives alike.

Most important is our commitment to the broad ideals of the Enlightenment. These include political equality, religious toleration, and scientific rationality. Interpretations of these differ but within a wide consensus regarding their value and vital contribution to the civilization we call home. There are outliers who flatly deny one or another of these ideals, but they have little chance of persuading the rest of us to abandon them. Especially at a moment of such angry division, it is important to recall that beneath the turmoil of our day-to-day battles, which we fight from the moment we wake up and check our phones until we collapse with exhaustion at night, there is wide and stable agreement about the values that form the core of the civilization we hold dear and have a common duty to protect.

But if conservatives are better equipped to explain why the acceleration of communication compromises the power of time as a saving force, the invocation of the enlightened ideals that unite nearly all of us puts conservatism on the defensive and makes it less congenial to many. It gives progressivism a field advantage.

The reason is that these ideals invite an unwarranted extension that to unwary eyes looks natural if not inevitable. Their immense appeal encourages the belief that equality is not only a political good but the highest good of all; that tolerance is imperative because God is merely a belief; and that the past has no authority of its own, as science assumes and insists. In each case, the extension shares the attraction of the ideal from which it derives. It seems justified and improving—the progressive elaboration of an uncontested axiom of thought. But this is a destructive illusion, for these extensions are not merely unsupported by reason or experience. Each strikes at something vital to our humanity—at our love of excellence, attunement to eternity, and friendship for the dead, without which, as Burke warned, we become less than fully human or no longer human at all.

The depreciation of these three dimensions of human longing and fulfillment are the ruling prejudices of our age. They are *arrogant* prejudices. Each celebrates our self-sufficiency as the highest of all goods and views every form of dependency as a mortal threat to it. One applauds our freedom from the commanding attraction of greatness and beauty, which call us up and out of ourselves to something higher and finer and more discriminating. Another denies our need for a connection to an order of reality that surpasses everything we can accomplish in the register of time. The third casts a pall over the affection we feel for our now-departed companions in the adventure of life, without whose company our world shrinks to a lonely point.

Those who believe that our prejudices are true—as true as the ideals from which they draw unearned prestige—think they are elevating our humanity by making it more self-sufficient. But the reality is the reverse. Their elevation is a diminution. It scorns the dependencies that make us human in the first place and does so with a confidence that is shocking to those whose idea of the human condition is at once more circumspect and ennobling.

It falls to the conservative to remind us of the saving power of time in an age that threatens to dissolve it. It falls to the conservative to recall the human values our enlightened biases conceal or deny. Today, true conservatism means countering the arrogance of our most pervasive prejudices with something humbler: a view of the human condition that has no date-stamp on it, one that invites us to remember and to cherish our ageless dependencies, which from a progressive point of view seem merely like fetters but whose humbling parameters alone make possible every form of human greatness, every human glory, every human love worthy of the name.

This is true conservatism. It takes time to expound and time to consider. Will it get the hearing it deserves in the rush and clatter of our speed-addled age?

# Notes

## Chapter One. Our Prejudices

1. Thomas Jefferson to James Madison, September 6, 1789, in *The Papers of Thomas Jefferson*, vol. 15, ed. Julian P. Boyd (Princeton: Princeton University Press, 1958), 392.
2. Aristotle, *De Anima*, in *The Complete Works of Aristotle*, ed. Jonathan Barnes (Princeton: Princeton University Press, 1984), 415b1.
3. Frank Kafka, *Diaries*, 10.1 (January 10, 1920), in *The Diaries of Franz Kafka*, ed. Ross Benjamin (New York: Knopf Doubleday, 2022), 585 (e-book). See also Hannah Arendt, *The Human Condition* (Chicago: University of Chicago Press, 1958), 248.
4. Alexis de Tocqueville, *Democracy in America*, trans. Harvey C. Mansfield and Delba Winthrop (Chicago: University of Chicago Press, 2002), 3.
5. Tocqueville, *Democracy in America*, 475 (Democratic peoples "rush at equality as at a conquest, and they become attached to it as to a precious good someone wants to rob them of. The passion for equality penetrates all parts of the human heart; there it spreads, and fills it entirely"). See also *Democracy in America*, 3 ("Among the new objects that attracted my attention during my stay in the United States, none struck my eye more vividly than the equality of conditions").
6. Tocqueville, *Democracy in America*, 304–6 ("Oppression has with one blow taken from the descendants of the Africans almost all the privileges of humanity!"), 307–25 (Indians "have not only withdrawn, they are destroyed"), 573–76 ("Although in the United States the woman scarcely leaves the domestic circle and is in certain respects very dependent within it, nowhere does her position seem higher to me").
7. Tocqueville, *Democracy in America*, 224.
8. Tocqueville, *Democracy in America*, 631 ("These same opinions are spreading more and more in Europe. . . . These ideas take root and grow as conditions

become more equal and men more alike; equality gives birth to them, and they in their turn hasten the progress of equality"), 636 ("When equality develops in a people that has never known freedom or that has not known it for a long time, as is seen on the continent of Europe, the old habits of the nation come to be combined suddenly and by a sort of natural attraction with the new habits and doctrines").

9. As a presidential candidate, Donald Trump boasted, "There's nobody who has done so much for equality as I have." "Verbatim: Donald Trump Calls Himself Crusader for Equality," *New York Times*, March 1, 2016, https://archive.nytimes.com/www.nytimes.com/live/super-tuesday-2016-elections/verbatim-donald-trump-calls-himself-crusader-for-equality/index.html.

10. The American Constitution's notoriously demanding amendment process generally requires the consent of two-thirds of both houses of Congress and three-fourths of all state legislatures. U.S. Constitution, Article V. The French Constitution empowers the Constitutional Council to review proposed legislation for constitutionality. Constitution de la Ve République, Articles 61–62. The German Constitution bans political parties that threaten democracy. Grundgesetz für die Bundesrepublik Deutschland [Constitution] 2014, Article 21.

11. Owen Fiss, *Why We Vote* (New York: Oxford University Press, 2024), 67.

12. Tocqueville, *Democracy in America*, 675.

13. Tocqueville, *Democracy in America*, 604 ("Men equal in rights, in education, in fortune, and to say it all in a word, of similar condition, necessarily have needs, habits, and tastes barely unalike. As they perceive objects under the same aspect, their minds naturally incline toward analogous ideas, and although each of them can diverge from his contemporaries and make his own beliefs for himself, in the end, without knowing it and without wishing it, all meet each other in a certain number of common opinions"), 606 ("In all times when conditions are equal, general opinion puts an immense weight on the mind of each individual; it envelops it. . . . As all men resemble each other more [they become incapable of] discovering anything that elevates him very much above them and distinguishes him from them").

14. Tocqueville, *Democracy in America*, 615.

15. Aristotle, *The Nicomachean Ethics*, trans. Robert C. Bartlett and Susan D. Collins (Chicago: University of Chicago Press, 2012), 1098a13–16 ("We posit the work of a human being as a certain life, and this is an activity of soul and actions accompanied by reason, the work of a serious man being to do these things well and nobly, and each thing is brought to completion well in accord with the virtue proper to it").

16. Tocqueville, *Democracy in America*, 116 ("In that part of the American continent, the population therefore escapes not only the influence of great names and great wealth, but of that natural aristocracy that flows from enlightenment and virtue. No one there exercises the respectable power that

men accord to the memory of an entire life occupied in doing good before one's eyes").

17. For example, Joseph de Maistre, *Considerations on France*, trans. and ed. Richard Lebrun (Cambridge: Cambridge University Press, 1995), 39 ("Notice again how crime forms the foundation of the entire republican edifice: this word 'citizen,' which they have substituted for the old forms of courtesy, is addressed to the vilest of humans"), 58–61 (predicting the failure of the French Revolution's "chimerical system of deliberation and political construction by abstract reasoning"); de Maistre, *Etude sur la souveraineté* (Lyon, 1884), 437 ("Monarchy entails *as much* and maybe even *more liberty* and *equality* than any other government"); Friedrich Nietzsche, *Twilight of the Idols*, in *The Anti-Christ, Ecce Homo, Twilight of the Idols, and Other Writings*, ed. Aaron Ridley and Judith Norman (Cambridge: Cambridge University Press, 2005), sec. 37 (" 'Equality' [a certain factual increase in similarity that the theory of 'equal rights' only gives expression to] essentially belongs to decline: the rift between people, between classes, the myriad number of types, the will to be yourself, to stand out, what I call the pathos of distance, is characteristic of every strong age").

18. Some recent thinkers have sought to reassert the importance of character vis-à-vis that of duty. See Iris Murdoch, *The Sovereignty of Good* (London: Routledge, 1970), 89 ("A philosophy which leaves duty without a context and exalts the idea of freedom and power as a separate top-level value ignores this task and obscures the relation between virtue and reality. We act rightly 'when the time comes' not out of strength of will but out of the quality of our usual attachments and with the kind of energy and discernment which we have available"); and Bernard Williams, *Shame and Necessity* (Berkeley: University of California Press, 1993), 41 ("What people miss, I suspect, is a 'will' that has these two features: it is expressed in action, rather than in endurance, because its operation is supposed itself to be a paradigm of action; and it serves in the interest of only one kind of motive, the motives of morality. In particular, it serves in the interest of duty").

19. Michael Walzer, *Spheres of Justice: A Defense of Pluralism and Equality* (New York: Basic Books, 1984), 320–21. My view overlaps with Walzer's in some ways but not in others.

20. Tocqueville, *Democracy in America*, 52 ("There is in fact a manly and legitimate passion for equality that incites men to want all to be strong and esteemed. This passion tends to elevate the small to the rank of the great; but one also encounters a depraved taste for equality in the human heart that brings the weak to want to draw the strong to their level and that reduces men to preferring equality in servitude to inequality in freedom").

21. Tocqueville, *Democracy in America*, 428–33 (on a democratic people's taste for literature and the arts), 439–43 (on Americans cultivating the arts), 450 (on the literary industry).

22. Tocqueville, *Democracy in America*, 441 (noting that in democracies "excellent workers who penetrate to the furthest limits of their profession are formed; but they rarely have the occasion to show what they know how to do: they are carefully sparing in their efforts; they keep themselves in a skillful mediocrity that judges itself and that, though being capable of reaching beyond the goal it proposes for itself, aims only at the goal it reaches for"), 678–82 ("I believe that it is easier to establish an absolute and despotic government in a people where conditions are equal than in any other, and I think that if such a government were once established in a people like this, not only would it oppress men, but in the long term it would rob each of them of several of the principal attributes of humanity").

23. See Susan Sontag, "Fascinating Fascism," *New York Review of Books*, February 6, 1975 ("In [Riefenstahl's] *Triumph of the Will*, the document [the image] not only is the record of reality but is one reason for which the reality has been constructed, and must eventually supersede it"); Murdoch, *Sovereignty of Good*, 33 ("Words are the most subtle symbols which we possess and our human fabric depends on them. The living and radical nature of language is something which we forget at our peril. . . . The most essential and fundamental aspect of culture is the study of literature, since this is an education in how to picture and understand human situations").

24. Murdoch, *Sovereignty of Good*, 97–100.

25. Woodrow Wilson, "What Is Progress?" in *The New Freedom* (New York: Doubleday, 1913) (e-book), 34 ("Men through many thousand years never talked or thought of progress. They thought in the other direction. Their stories of heroisms and glory were tales of the past. The ancestor wore the heavier armor and carried the larger spear. 'There were giants in those days.' Now all that has altered. We think of the future, not the past, as the more glorious time in comparison with which the present is nothing"); Walter Lippmann, *Drift and Mastery* (New York: Henry Holt, 1914), 299 ("So long as tradition is a blind command it is for our world an evil and dangerous thing. But once you see the past merely as a theater of human effort, it overflows with suggestion"). See also Ryan D. Doerfler and Samuel Moyn, "The Constitution Is Broken and Should Not Be Reclaimed," *New York Times*, August 19, 2022, https://www.nytimes.com/2022/08/19/opinion/liberals-constitution.html (lamenting that constitutions "inevitably orient us to the past and misdirect the present into a dispute over what people agreed on once upon a time, not on what the present and future demand for and from those who live now").

26. Max Weber, *Economy & Society*, trans. Keith Tribe (Cambridge, MA: Harvard University Press, 2019), 354–74.

27. Exodus 19:5–6 ("Now then, if you will obey Me faithfully and keep My covenant, you shall be My treasured possession among all the peoples. . . . These are the words that you shall speak to the children of Israel"); John 1:1 ("In the beginning was the Word, and the Word was with God, and the

Word was God"); Quran 18:27 ("Recite what has been revealed to you from the Book of your Lord. None can change His Words, nor can you find any refuge besides Him").

28. Galileo Galilei, *Dialogue concerning the Two Chief World Systems*, trans. Stillman Drake (New York: Modern Library, 2001), 125.

29. In France, Auguste Comte (1798–1857) demanded a science of politics equipped to reorganize society along strictly rational lines. Auguste Comte, "Plan of the Scientific Work Necessary for the Reorganization of Society," in *Early Political Writings*, ed. H. S. Jones (Cambridge: Cambridge University Press, 1998), 47 ("Politics must today rise to the rank of the sciences of observation" and apply their discipline to "the spiritual reorganization of society"). In America, the engineer Frederick W. Taylor (1856–1915) championed a scientific approach in industrial management that came to be known as Taylorism. Frederick Winslow Taylor, *The Principles of Scientific Management* (New York: Harper, 1911), 7 ("The best management is a true science, resting upon clearly defined laws, rules, and principles, as a foundation" and "The fundamental principles of scientific management are applicable to all kinds of human activities, from our simplest individual acts to the work of our great corporations, which call for the most elaborate cooperation").

30. Max Weber, *Politics as a Vocation*, trans. H. H. Gerth and C. Wright Mills (New York: Oxford University Press, 1946), 4.

31. See Hannah Arendt's juxtaposition of Tocqueville and Marx in *Between Past and Future: Six Exercises in Political Thought* (New York: Viking, 1961), 77 ("Where a genuine interest in political theory still survived it ended in despair, as in Tocqueville, or in the confusion of politics with history, as in Marx. For what else but despair could have inspired Tocqueville's assertion that 'since the past has ceased to throw its light upon the future the mind of man wanders in obscurity'? This is actually the conclusion of the great work in which he had 'delineated the society of the modern world' and in the introduction to which he had proclaimed that 'a new science of politics is needed for a new world.' And what else but confusion—a merciful confusion for Marx himself and a fatal one for his followers—could have led to Marx's identification of action with 'the making of history'?"); Michael Burawoy, "Marxism as Science: Historical Challenges and Theoretical Growth," *American Sociological Review* 55, no. 6 (1990): 775, https://doi.org/10.2307/2095745.

32. For "standing reserve," see Martin Heidegger, "The Question concerning Technology," in *The Question concerning Technology and Other Essays*, trans. William Lovitt (New York: Harper & Row, 1977), 17.

33. See Steven Smith, *Reclaiming Patriotism in an Age of Extremes* (New Haven: Yale University Press, 2021), 46 (describing the 1619 Project as a rewriting of history "to make slavery and anti-black racism the core of the American experience from the very beginning"—a narrative that "views our founders

as either hypocrites or knaves" and "denies or diminishes the efforts of generations of Americans [to end slavery]"). Compare Alasdair MacIntyre, "Is Patriotism a Virtue?" (Lindley Lecture, University of Kansas, March 26, 1994), 4 ("Patriotism is one of a class of loyalty-exhibiting virtues [that is, if it is a virtue at all] other members of which are marital fidelity, the love of one's own family and kin, friendship, and loyalty to such institutions as schools and cricket or baseball clubs. All these attitudes exhibit a peculiar action-generating regard for particular persons, institutions or groups, a regard founded upon a particular historical relationship of association between the person exhibiting the regard and the relevant person, institution or group"). MacIntyre carefully diagnoses what he calls the "liberal moralist" objection to patriotism. See 7 ("For the impersonal moral standpoint, understood as the philosophical protagonists of modern liberalism have understood it, requires neutrality not only between rival and competing interests, but also between rival and competing sets of beliefs about the best way for human beings to live. Each individual is to be left free to pursue in his or her own way that way of life which he or she judges to be best; while morality by contrast consists of rules which, just because they are such that any rational person, independently of his or her interests or point of view on the best way for human beings to live, would assent to them, are equally binding on all persons. Hence in conflicts between nations or other communities over ways of life, the standpoint of morality will once again be that of an impersonal arbiter, adjudicating in ways that give equal weight to each individual person's needs, desires, beliefs about the good and the like, while the patriot is once again required to be partisan").

34. Max Weber, "Science as a Vocation," in *The Vocation Lectures*, trans. Rodney Livingstone, ed. David Owen and Tracy B. Strong (Indianapolis: Hackett, 2004), 30 ("Our age is characterized by rationalization and intellectualization, and above all, by the disenchantment of the world. Its resulting fate is that precisely the ultimate and most sublime values have withdrawn from public life. They have retreated either into the abstract realm of mystical life or into the fraternal feelings of personal relations between individuals").

35. David Torrance, "The Relationship between Church and State in the United Kingdom," House of Commons Library, September 14, 2023, https://commonslibrary.parliament.uk/research-briefings/cbp-8886/; Steven Erlanger, "France Enforces Ban on Full-Face Veils in Public," *New York Times*, April 11, 2011, https://www.nytimes.com/2011/04/12/world/europe/12france.html; U.S. Constitution, amendment I ("Congress shall make no law respecting an establishment of religion, or prohibiting the free exercise thereof"). On the prohibition against the establishment of religion in the United States, see *Engel v. Vitale*, 370 U.S. 421 (1962) and *School District of Abington Township, Pennsylvania v. Schempp*, 374 U.S. 203 (1963). See also *Goldman v. Weinberger* 475 U.S. 503 (1986) and *Kennedy v. Bremerton School District*, 597 U.S. ___ (2022).

36. Although religion remains a powerful force in American life, attendance and affiliation are declining. As of 2020, according to the Pew Research Center, 30 percent of Americans did not affiliate with any religion at all. Pew estimates that the percentage of religiously unaffiliated Americans will grow to between 34 and 52 in the next half century. Pew Research Center, *Modeling the Future of Religion in America*, September 2022, https://www.pewresearch.org/religion/2022/09/13/modeling-the-future-of-religion-in-america/. Generation Z attends formal religious services far less often than previous generations. Daniel Cox, "Generation Z and the Future of Faith in America," *Survey Center on American Life*, March 24, 202, https://www.americansurveycenter.org/research/generation-z-future-of-faith/. Religion nevertheless continues to be attractive to many as a source of solace and comfort. See Clare Ansberry, "The Surprising Surge of Faith among Young People," *Wall Street Journal*, April 24, 2023, https://www.wsj.com/articles/the-surprising-surge-of-faith-among-young-people-42422obd. There is also strong historical precedent for the periodic revival of flagging religious institutions. See Robert Putnam, *The Upswing: How America Came Together a Century Ago and How We Can Do It Again* (New York: Simon & Schuster, 2020) (e-book), 148–69.

37. Weber, "Science as a Vocation," 30.

38. Charles Taylor, *A Secular Age* (Cambridge, MA: Harvard University Press, 2007), 20.

39. Immanuel Kant, *Critique of Pure Reason*, trans. Paul Gruyer and Allen W. Woods (Cambridge: Cambridge University Press, 1998), Bxxx.

40. Kant, *Critique of Pure Reason*, A584/B612.

41. Tocqueville, *Democracy in America*, 18 ("I undertook to see, not differently, but further than the parties; and while they are occupied with the next day, I wanted to ponder the future").

42. Jerry Z. Muller, "The Conservative Case for Abortion," *New Republic*, August 21, 1995, https://newrepublic.com/article/91305/the-conservative-case-abortion; Robert Shrimsley, "The Conservative Crisis of Capitalism," *Financial Times*, July 12, 2023, https://www.ft.com/content/2c103989–6883–4b34–9b47–560779e6bc4c; Nadine Strossen, "Religion and the Constitution: A Libertarian Perspective," *Cato Supreme Court Review* (2005–6), https://www.cato.org/sites/cato.org/files/serials/files/supreme-court-review/2006/9/strossen.pdf.

43. Adam Smith, *An Inquiry into the Nature and Causes of the Wealth of Nations* (London: W. Strahan, 1776).

44. Friedrich A. Hayek, *The Road to Serfdom*, ed. Bruce Caldwell (Chicago: University of Chicago Press, 2007), 95–96 ("The more complicated the whole, the more dependent we become on that division of knowledge between individuals whose separate efforts are coordinated by the impersonal mechanism for transmitting the relevant information known by us as the price system"); George Stigler, "The Economics of Information," *Journal of Political Economy* 69, no. 3 (June 1961): 213.

45. John Stuart Mill, *On Liberty*, ed. Edward Alexander (Ontario: Broadview, 1999), 52 ("The only purpose for which power can be rightfully exercised over any member of a civilized community, against his will, is to prevent harm to others. His own good, either physical or moral, is not a sufficient warrant. He cannot rightfully be compelled to do or forbear because it will be better for him to do so, because it will make him happier, because, in the opinion of others, to do so would be wise, or even right. . . . The only part of the conduct of anyone, for which he is amenable to society, is that which concerns others. In the part which merely concerns himself, his independence is, of right, absolute. Over himself, over his own body and mind, the individual is sovereign"), 54 ("The principle requires liberty of tastes and pursuits; of framing the plan of our life to suit our own character; of doing as we like, subject to such consequences as may follow; without impediment from our fellow-creatures, so long as what we do does not harm them even though they should think our conduct foolish, perverse, or wrong").

46. Friedrich A. Hayek, *Law, Legislation, and Liberty* (Chicago: University of Chicago Press, 1978), 9 ("Given this information, he will be able to use his knowledge of the circumstances of his environment to select his immediate aim, or the role from which he can hope for the best results. It will be through this choice of immediate aims, for him merely a generalized means for achieving his ultimate ends, that the individual will use his particular knowledge of facts in the service of the needs of his fellows; and it is thus due to the freedom of choosing the ends of one's activities that the utilization of the knowledge dispersed through society is achieved"); George Priest, "The Common Law Process and the Selection of Efficient Rules," *Journal of Legal Studies* 6, no. 1 (January 1977): 81 (arguing that the "common law process incorporates a strong tendency toward efficient outcomes" as a result of market forces).

47. Karl Marx and Friedrich Engels, *Communist Manifesto*, ed. Eric Hobsbawm (London: Verso, 1998), 34–35 ("Constant revolutionizing of production, uninterrupted disturbance of all social conditions, everlasting uncertainty and agitation distinguish the bourgeois epoch from all earlier ones. All freed, fast-frozen relations, with their train of ancient and venerable prejudices and opinions, are swept away, all new-formed ones become antiquated before they can ossify. All that is solid melts into air, all that is holy is profaned, and man is at last compelled to face with sober senses, his real conditions of life, and his relations with his kind").

48. David Hume, "Of Commerce," in *Essays, Moral, Political and Literary*, ed. Eugene Miller (Indianapolis: Liberty Fund, 1985) part 2, 263–64 ("This perhaps is the chief advantage which arises from a commerce with strangers. It rouses men from their indolence; and presenting the gayer and more opulent part of the nation with objects of luxury, which they never before dreamed of, raises in them a desire of a more splendid way of life

than what their ancestors enjoyed. And at the same time, the few merchants, who possess the secret of this importation and exportation, make
great profits; and becoming rivals in wealth to the ancient nobility, tempt
other adventurers to become their rivals in commerce. Imitation soon dif-
fuses all those arts; while domestic manufactures emulate the foreign in
their improvements, and work up every home commodity to the utmost
perfection of which it is susceptible. Their own steel and iron, in such laborious hands, become equal to the gold and rubies of the Indies"); David
Hume, "The Natural History of Religion," in *Hume: Dialogues concerning
Religion and Other Writings*, ed. Dorothy Coleman (Cambridge: Cambridge
University Press, 2007), 133 ("Those who undertake the most criminal and
most dangerous enterprises are commonly the most superstitious, as an ancient historian remarks on this occasion. Their devotion and spiritual faith
rise with their fears"); Adam Ferguson, *An Essay on the History of Civil Society*
(Indianapolis: Liberty Fund, 2011), 173 ("Man, under this measure of corruption, although he may be bought for a slave by those who know how to
turn his faculties and his labour to profit; and although, when kept under
proper restraints, his neighbourhood may be convenient or useful; yet is
certainly unfit to act on the footing of a liberal combination or concert with
his fellow-creatures: His mind is not addicted to friendship or confidence;
he is not willing to act for the preservation of others, nor deserves that any
other should hazard his own safety for his").

49. Edmund Burke, *Reflections on the Revolution in France*, ed. Frank M. Turner
    (New Haven: Yale University Press, 2003); Edmund Burke, *An Appeal from
    the New to the Old Whigs* (London: J. Dodsley, 1791); Edmund Burke, *Letter
    to a Noble Lord* (London, 1796).

50. Burke, *Reflections*, 81.

51. Burke, *Reflections*, 74; see also 68 ("Where trade and manufactures are want-
    ing to a people, and the spirit of nobility and religion remains, sentiment
    supplies, and not always ill supplies, their place; but if commerce and the
    arts should be lost in an experiment to try how well a state may stand with-
    out these old fundamental principles, what sort of a thing must be a nation
    of gross, stupid, ferocious, and, at the same time, poor and sordid, barbari-
    ans, destitute of religion, honour, or manly pride, possessing nothing at
    present, and hoping for nothing hereafter?").

52. Burke, *Reflections*, 67 ("Nothing is more certain, than that our manners, our
    civilization, and all the good things which are connected with manners and
    with civilization, have, in this European world of ours, depended for ages
    upon two principles; and were indeed the result of both combined; I mean
    the spirit of a gentleman, and the spirit of religion"); Ian Harris, "Burke and
    Religion," in *The Cambridge Companion to Edmund Burke*, ed. David Dwan
    and Christopher J. Insole (Cambridge: Cambridge University Press, 2012),
    103 (Burke "emphasized the social benefits of Christianity, rather than its
    truth").

53. Burke, *Reflections*, 32 ("You would have had a free constitution; a potent monarchy; a disciplined army; a reformed and venerated clergy; a mitigated but spirited nobility, to lead your virtue, not to overlay it; you would have had a liberal order of commons, to emulate and to recruit that nobility; you would have had a protected, satisfied, laborious, and obedient people, taught to seek and to recognize the happiness that is to be found by virtue in all conditions; in which consists the true moral equality of mankind, and not in that monstrous fiction, which, by inspiring false ideas and vain expectations into men destined to travel in the obscure walk of laborious life, serves only to aggravate and embitter that real inequality, which it never can remove; and which the order of civil life establishes as much for the benefit of those whom it must leave in an humble state, as those whom it is able to exalt to a condition more splendid, but not more happy").

54. The distinction between a "natural aristocracy" grounded in "virtue and talents" and an "artificial aristocracy founded on wealth and birth" is emphasized by Thomas Jefferson in his correspondence with John Adams. Thomas Jefferson to John Adams, October 28, 1813, in *The Adams-Jefferson Correspondence*, ed. Lester J. Cappon (Chapel Hill: University of North Carolina Press, 1988), 388.

55. Thomas Jefferson to John Adams, October 28, 1813, in *The Adams-Jefferson Correspondence*, 388.

56. Burke, *An Appeal from the New to the Old Whigs*, 51 ("Prudence is not only the first in rank of the virtues political and moral, but she is the director, the regulator, the standard of them all"); Burke, *Reflections*, 53 ("The body of the community, whenever it can come to act, can meet with no effectual resistance; but till power and right are the same, the whole body of them has no right inconsistent with virtue, and the first of all virtues, prudence").

57. Each of the Abrahamic religions features some version of this view. Dante, for example, vividly depicts the hollowness of life without God. He implies that even the most virtuous nonbeliever is condemned to Limbo, the first circle of hell, where the eternal distance from God is itself a supreme punishment. They suffer an "untormented sadness, the passive state of those who dwelled apart," and "without hope ... live on in desire" of salvation. Dante Alighieri, *The Inferno*, trans. John Ciardi (Oxford: Oxford University Press, 1996), 27–28. The Tanakh likewise disputes "the sufficiency of worldly goods." Ecclesiastes 2:1–2 ("I said to myself, 'Come now, I will mix with joy and experience pleasure,' and behold, it too was vanity. Of laughter, I said, 'It is mirth' and concerning joy, 'What does it accomplish?' "). The Quran suggests that the apostate will suffer divine punishment. Quran 88:22–24 ("You are not 'there' to compel them 'to believe.' But whoever turns away, persisting in disbelief, then Allah will inflict upon them the major punishment"). Contemporary writers echo the theme. See, for example, Simon Jacobson, *Toward a Meaningful Life: The Wisdom of the Rebbe*

*Menachem Mendel Schneerson* (New York: HarperCollins, 1995) (e-book), 288–97 ("By understanding G-d as the essence of absolute reality, we come to the awesome realization 'There is none else besides Him.' Or, even more simply, 'There is none else.' From the perspective of an absolute reality, there is truly nothing else. . . . We are the generation that will complete the process of bringing to consciousness G-d's presence in the world. Let us finally raise the curtain that has shrouded G-d's presence for so long"); Rod Dreher, "Re-sacramentalizing My Life," *American Conservative*, January 25, 2016 ("We live in a world in which we have lost the reflexive sense of God's presence in all things—what the Evangelical theologian Hans Boersma calls 'sacramental ontology.' All Christians used to believe in this. We began to lose this vision in the 13th and 14th centuries, and it is all but gone now. We won't start to recover spiritually and morally until we begin to recover this ancient Christian vision to some significant degree"); Ayatollah Murtadha Mutahhari, *Goal of Life* (Qom, Iran: Bethat Islamic Research Center, 1982), 23 ("They believe that there is one truth and that is God. They consider other things shadows of the truth. In their opinion everything is an attribute of God. If we die without recognizing the truth we would have died in infidelity, ignorance, darkness and absolute unawareness").

58. Niccolò Machiavelli, *Discourses on Livy*, trans. Harvey C. Mansfield and Nathan Tarcov (Chicago: University of Chicago Press, 1996), 34–35 ("Whoever considers well the Roman histories sees how much religion served to command armies, to animate the plebs, to keep men good, to bring shame to the wicked"); Thomas Hobbes, *Leviathan*, ed. J.C.A. Gaskin (Oxford: Oxford University Press, 1998), 74–75 (The purpose of religion is "to make those men that rel[y] on [it], the more apt to obedience, laws, peace, charity, and civil society").

59. Harris, "Burke and Religion," 103.

60. G. K. Chesterton, *Orthodoxy* (1908; repr., London: Bodley Head, 1927); C. S. Lewis, *The Screwtape Letters* (London: Geoffrey Bles, 1942); Jacques Maritain, *Integral Humanism: Temporal and Spiritual Problems of a New Christendom*, trans. Joseph W. Evans (New York: Charles Scribner's Sons, 1968).

61. Pierre Duhem, *Le système du monde: Histoire des doctrines cosmologiques de Platon à Copernic* (The System of the World: A History of Cosmological Doctrines from Plato to Copernicus) (Paris: A. Hermann, 1914); Francis Oakley, "Christian Theology and Newtonian Science," *Church History* 30, no. 4 (December 1961).

62. Pierre Duhem, *Essays in the History and Philosophy of Science*, trans. and ed. Roger Ariew and Peter Barker (Indianapolis: Hackett, 1996), 175–77 ("A century elapsed between the condemnations pronounced by Etienne Tempier [277] and the editing of the Traité du ciel et du monde by Oresme [377] and within that time, all the essential principles of Aristotle's physics

were undermined and the great controlling ideas of modern science formulated"); Francis Oakley, "Christian Theology and the Newtonian Science: The Rise of the Concept of the Laws of Nature," *Church History* 30, no. 4 (December 1961): 449 ("There can remain little room for doubt either that the voluntarist conception of natural law attained a wide currency in the sixteenth and seventeenth centuries, or that it was directly descended from the similar theory hammered out by the nominalist theologians in the years after the condemnations of 1277. It was conceived both with a juristic and a scientific sense, and, being the result of a crucial shift in the direction of the 'simplified view of nature' which was later to be adopted by Galileo, Descartes and Newton, was eminently compatible with this view"). See also John Maynard Keynes, "Newton, the Man" (speech delivered by Geoffrey Keynes, Trinity College, Cambridge, July 16, 1946) ("Newton was not the first of the age of reason. He was the last of the magicians, the last of the Babylonians and Sumerians, the last great mind that looked out on the visible and intellectual world with the same eyes as those who began to build our intellectual inheritance rather less than 10,000 years ago").

63. Newton viewed God as the " 'Lord God,' *pantokrator,* or 'Universal Ruler' " who decreed the laws of nature. See Isaac Newton, *Principia Mathematica,* 2nd ed. (Cambridge, 1713), General Scholium. In an earlier unpublished treatise, Newton emphasized the unknowability of God's power. *De Gravitatione et Equipondo Fluidor,* in *Unpublished Papers of Isaac Newton,* ed. A. Rupert Hall and Marie Boas Hall (Cambridge: Cambridge University Press, 1962), 138 ("It is hardly given to us to know the limits of the divine power, that is to say whether matter could be created in one way only, or whether there are several ways by which different beings similar to bodies could be produced"). See also Samuel Clarke and Gottfried Leibniz, *The Leibniz-Clarke Correspondence,* ed. H. G. Alexander (Manchester: Manchester University Press, 1956).

64. For example, the Catholic Church maintains the compatibility of Catholic theology with the theory of evolution and the Big Bang hypothesis. John Paul II, "Message to the Pontifical Academy of Sciences," *Quarterly Review of Biology* 72, no. 4 (December 1997), 381–83 ("There is no conflict between evolution and the doctrine of the faith regarding man and his vocation, provided that we do not lose sight of certain fixed points"); Pius XII, "Discourse of His Holiness Pope Pius XII given on 3 December 1939 at the Solemn Audience Granted to the Plenary Session of the Academy," in *Discourses of the Popes from Pius XI to John Paul II to the Pontifical Academy of the Sciences, 1936–1986* (Vatican City: Pontificia Academia Scientarium, 1986), 82 ("It seems that science of today, by going back in one leap millions of centuries, has succeeded in being witness to that primordial Fiat Lux when, out of nothing, there burst forth with matter a sea of light and radiation, while the particles of chemical elements split and reunited in millions of galaxies").

## Chapter Two. Bullied Pulpit

1. Herodotus, *The Histories*, trans. Robin Waterfield (Oxford: Oxford University Press, 1998), book I, chaps. 131–40; Tacitus, *Germania*, trans. Harold Mattingly (London: Penguin Classics, 2010), chaps. 7–27.

2. Charles de Montesquieu, *The Spirit of the Laws*, ed. Anne Coller, Basia Carolyn Miller, and Harold Samuel Stone (Cambridge: Cambridge University Press, 1989); Giambattista Vico, *New Science*, trans. Dave Marsh (London: Penguin Books, 2000); Alexis de Tocqueville, *Democracy in America*, trans. Harvey C. Mansfield and Delba Winthrop (Chicago: University of Chicago Press, 2002); Adam Ferguson, *An Essay on the History of Civil Society* (Cambridge: Cambridge University Press, 1996); J. G. Herder, *On Social and Political Culture*, trans. F. M. Barnard (Cambridge: Cambridge University Press, 1969).

3. Hermann Broch, *The Death of Virgil*, trans. Jean Starr Untermeyer (New York: Pantheon Books, 1963).

4. Broch, *The Death of Virgil*, 312.

5. Broch, *The Death of Virgil*, 312.

6. Marcus Tullius Cicero, *De Finibus Bonorum et Malorum*, trans. H. Harris Rackham (Cambridge, MA: Harvard University Press, 1931).

7. Cicero, *De Finibus Bonorum et Malorum*, book I, chaps 2–4.

8. Cicero, *De Finibus Bonorum et Malorum*, book III, chap 2.

9. Virgil, *Aeneid*, trans. Allen Mandelbaum (New York: Bantam Classics, 1981), book II.

10. Lucretius, *On the Nature of Things*, trans. Martin Ferguson Smith (Indianapolis: Hackett, 2001); Stephen Greenblatt, "In Search of Lucretius," in *The Swerve: How the World Became Modern* (New York: Norton, 2012).

11. Edward Gibbon, *The History of the Decline and Fall of the Roman Empire*, ed. David Womersley (London: Penguin Books, 1994), chaps. 23, 24.

12. Hannah Arendt, "The Crisis in Culture," in *Between Past and Future: Six Exercises in Political Thought* (New York: Viking, 1961), 212.

13. Aristotle, *The Nicomachean Ethics*, trans. Robert C. Bartlett and Susan D. Collins (Chicago: University of Chicago Press, 2012), 1152a30–33; see also John McDowell, *Mind and World* (Cambridge, MA: Harvard University Press, 1996), 84.

14. Paul Oskar Kristeller, "The Modern System of the Arts," in *Renaissance Thought and the Arts* (Princeton: Princeton University Press, 1990); Larry Shiner, *The Invention of Art: A Cultural History* (Chicago: University of Chicago Press, 2001).

15. Marcel Duchamp, *Fountain*, 1917, porcelain, Tate Modern, London (replica); James Joyce, *Ulysses* (Cambridge: Cambridge University Press, 2022).

16. Erich Auerbach, *Mimesis: The Representation of Beauty in Western Literature*, trans. Willard R. Trask (Princeton: Princeton University Press, 1968); G.W.F. Hegel, *Introductory Lectures on Aesthetics*, trans. Bernard Bosanquet (London: Penguin Books, 2004).

17. Immanuel Kant, *Critique of the Power of Judgement*, trans. Paul Guyer (Cambridge: Cambridge University Press, 2001), 5:203–5.

18. Hannah Arendt, "Tradition and the Modern Age," in *Between Past and Future*, 20–21; Thorstein Veblen, *The Theory of the Leisure Class* (Oxford: Oxford University Press, 2009); Marcus Tullius Cicero, *On the Orator*, trans. E. W. Sutton and H. Rackham (Cambridge: Loeb Classical Library, 1948), book II, 13.57; Aristotle, *Politics*, trans. C.D.C. Reeve (Indianapolis: Hackett, 1998), 1334; Hannah Arendt, *The Human Condition* (Chicago: University of Chicago Press, 2019), 14.

19. Arendt, "The Crisis in Culture," 217.

20. Fréderic Elsig, "Connoisseurship and Art History: Reflections on a Problematic Relationship," *ARS* 42, no. 1 (2009): 109.

21. Aristotle, *Nicomachean Ethics*, 1177a–b.

22. Plato, *Apology*, in *The Collected Dialogues of Plato*, ed. Edith Hamilton and Huntington Cairns (Princeton: Princeton University Press, 1961), 21b–23c; Plato, *Euthyphro*, in *The Collected Dialogues*, 15c–16a; Plato, *Greater Hippias*, in *The Collected Dialogues*, 286a–e.

23. John Ruskin, *The Stones of Venice* (Boston: Da Capo, 2003).

24. Anthony Ashley Cooper Shaftesbury, *Characteristics of Men, Manner, Opinions, Times* (Cambridge: Cambridge University Press, 2018); Edmund Burke, *A Philosophical Inquiry into the Origin of Our Ideas of the Sublime and Beautiful* (London: George Bell and Sons, 1889); Kant, *Critique of the Power of Judgement*.

25. Roosevelt Montás, "Why the Core Matters for a New Generation," *Chronicle of Higher Education*, November 16, 2021; Justin Stover, "There Is No Case for the Humanities," *American Affairs* 1, no. 4 (2017); "Liberal Education at Chicago," University of Chicago College, February 8, 2024, http://collegecatalog.uchicago.edu/thecollege/liberaleducationatchicago/.

26. Zelda Popkin, "Finer Things of Life," *Harper's Magazine* 164 (1932): 602–11.

27. Tocqueville, *Democracy in America*, chaps. 1, 3, and 4 (introductory chapters on geography, history, and government), 121 (discussion of habits, mores, and opinions), 295 (the "principal goal" of American democracy).

28. Tocqueville, *Democracy in America*, 525 (respect for the practical), 403–6 (impatience with philosophy), 506–9 (material enjoyments), 198–99 (experience as measure of truth), 489–91 (Americans joining groups), 448 (lack of reverence for aristocratic learning), 433 (lack of reverence for tradition), 587–88 (love of change), 482–83 (individualism), 479–81 (tension between equality and freedom), 243 (refuge in majority opinion).

29. Tocqueville, *Democracy in America*, 482–83.

30. Tocqueville, *Democracy in America*, 433–38.

31. John Dewey, *The Public and Its Problems* (Athens: Ohio University Press, 1954); Louis Brandeis, *Brandeis on Democracy*, ed. Philippa Strum (Lawrence: University Press of Kansas, 1995); *New State Ice Co. v. Liebmann*, 285 U.S. 262 (1932), 262.

32. See generally Hans-Georg Gadamer, *Truth and Method*, trans. Joel Weinsheimer and Donald G. Marshall (London: Bloomsbury, 2013), especially 3–39.

33. Tocqueville, *Democracy in America*, 489–92.

34. Tocqueville, *Democracy in America*, 535–38 (mildness of manners), 544–45 (sympathy across social boundaries), 278–81 (religious toleration).

35. Friedrich Nietzsche, *Thus Spoke Zarathustra*, trans. Walter Kaufmann (London: Penguin Books, 1978), sec. 18.

36. Tocqueville, *Democracy in America*, 239; Hannah Arendt, *The Origins of Totalitarianism* (Cleveland: Meridian Books, 1962), 305–25.

37. Jeremy Bentham, *The Rationale of Reward* (London: John & H. L. Hunt, 1825), 206 ("pushpin is as good as poetry"). For a contemporary expression of this view, see Joseph Margolis, "Robust Relativism," *Journal of Aesthetics and Art Criticism* 35, no. 1 (1976): 37–46.

38. Tocqueville, *Democracy in America*, 506.

39. Clare McAndrew, *The Survey of Global Collecting, 2023* (Basel: Art Basel & UBS, 2023).

40. Tocqueville, *Democracy in America*, 519.

41. Alan S. Kahan, *Alexis de Tocqueville* (London: Bloomsbury, 2009).

42. Tocqueville, *Democracy in America*, 504–5.

43. Tocqueville, *Democracy in America*, 492.

44. Herbert Croly, *The Promise of American Life* (Princeton: Princeton University Press, 2014), 490–558; William Reilly, "A Higher Education Playbook for Strengthening Democracy: What Institutions Can Do," *Times Higher Education*, March 28, 2022; Nancy Kranich, "Libraries and Democracy Revisited," *The Library Quarterly* 90, no. 2 (2020); John F. Kennedy, "Remarks at a Closed Circuit Television Broadcast on Behalf of the National Cultural Center," Washington, DC, recorded November 29, 1962 ("Moreover, as a great democratic society, we have a special responsibility to the arts, for art is the great democrat calling forth creative genius from every sector of society, disregarding race or religion or wealth or color").

45. Plato, *Republic*, trans. G.M.A. Grube (Indianapolis: Hackett, 1992), 439d–444b; Aristotle, *Nicomachean Ethics*, 1102a–1103a; Cicero, *De Finibus Bonorum et Malorum*, book III, chap. 75.

46. Jacob Klein, *A Commentary on Plato's Meno* (Chapel Hill: University of North Carolina Press, 1979), 114–15; Hans Jonas, *The Phenomenon of Life: Towards a Philosophical Biology* (Evanston: Northwestern University Press, 2001), 157–74.

47. Marilyn Stoksad and Michael W. Cothren, *Art History* (London: Pearson, 2014), 8–11; Helen Gardner, *Art through the Ages* (Boston: Cengage Learning, 2015), 14–29; H. W. Janson, *History of Art* (Upper Saddle River, NJ: Prentice Hall, 2011), 1–17.

48. Aristotle, *Metaphysics*, trans. Hugh Lawson-Tancred (London: Penguin Books, 1999), book I.

49. Sybil Milton, "Art in the Context of Auschwitz," in *Art and Auschwitz*, ed. David Mickenberg, Corinne Granof, and Peter Hayes (Evanston: Northwestern University Press, 2003).

50. Broch, *The Death of Virgil*, 418.

51. The Metropolitan Museum of Art, "The Met Welcomed More Than 7 Million Visitors in Fiscal Year 2019," Met press release, July 10, 2019.

52. Walt Whitman, "Mannahatta," in *The Complete Poems*, ed. Francis Murphy (London: Penguin Books, 2005); Walt Whitman, "Crossing Brooklyn Ferry," in *The Complete Poems*.

53. Andy Warhol, *Brillo Boxes*, screenprint and ink on wood, 1964, Philadelphia Museum of Art; Chuck Close, *Mark*, acrylic on gessoed canvas, 1978–79, private collection.

54. Kant, *Critique of the Power of Judgement*, 5:338.

55. See, for example, "Why Be a Liberal Arts Major?" University of Nebraska Omaha College of Arts and Sciences, October 27, 2022, https://www.unomaha.edu/college-of-arts-and-sciences/academic-advising-center/choosing-a-major/liberal-arts.php.

56. Sarah Kaplan, "The Rise and Demise of the Much-Loathed SAT," *Washington Post*, July 28, 2015; *Regents of Univ. of California v. Bakke*, 438 U.S. 265 (1978), 316.

57. 27 Liberal Arts College Presidents, "Liberal Arts Colleges to Keep Prioritizing Diversity," *Inside Higher Ed*, May 11, 2023; Bryan Van Norden, "Western Philosophy Is Racist," *Aeon Magazine*, October 31, 2017; Anna Bernard, *Decolonizing Literature* (Hoboken, NJ: Wiley, 2023); Rachel Spence, "Feminism's Question for the Western Canon," *Financial Times*, August 26, 2021; Katy Waldman, "The Canon Is Sexist, Racist, Colonialist, and Totally Gross. Yes, You Have to Read It Anyway," *Slate Magazine*, May 24, 2016; Caché Owens-Velásquez, "Tangible Strategies for Decolonizing the Classroom," Global Racial and Social Inequality Lab, University of New Hampshire, 2024, https://cola.unh.edu/global-racial-social-inequality-lab/tangible-strategies-decolonizing-classroom.

58. Darren Walker, "Museums Need to Step into the Future," *New York Times*, July 26, 2019.

59. Holland Cotter, "In 'African Origin' Show at Met, New Points of Light across Cultures," *New York Times*, January 6, 2022.

60. "Diversity, Equity, Access, and Inclusion," Morgan Library & Museum, last modified 2024, https://www.themorgan.org/about/deai.

61. James Rondeau, "Our Commitment to Racial Justice and Equity," Art Institute of Chicago, June 3, 2020, https://www.artic.edu/articles/841/our-commitment-to-racial-justice-and-equity.

62. Anthony Tommasini, "To Make Orchestras More Diverse, End Blind Auditions," *New York Times*, July 16, 2020.

63. Tocqueville, *Democracy in America*, 517.

64. Tocqueville, *Democracy in America*, 500.

65. Pew Research Center, *In U.S., Decline of Christianity Continues at Rapid Pace* (Washington, DC, 2019).

66. U.S. Department of Education, *Digest of Education Statistics, 2021* (Washington, DC, 2021); Claire Gaudini, *Generosity Unbound: How American Philanthropy Can Strengthen the Economy and Expand the Middle Class* (New York: Broadway, 2010).

## Chapter Three. The Sovereignty of Excellence

1. Robert Nozick, *Anarchy, State, and Utopia* (Chicago: Basic Books, 1974).

2. John Rawls, *A Theory of Justice*, rev. ed. (Cambridge, MA: Belknap Press of Harvard University Press, 1999); Elizabeth S. Anderson, "What's the Point of Equality?" *Ethics* 109, no. 2 (1999): 287–337; Ronald Dworkin, *Sovereign Virtue: The Theory and Practice of Equality* (Cambridge, MA: Harvard University Press, 2000); Teresa Bejan, "What Was the Point of Equality?" *American Journal of Political Science* 66, no. 3 (July 2022): 604–16.

3. Alexis de Tocqueville, *Democracy in America*, trans. Harvey C. Mansfield and Delba Winthrop (Chicago: University of Chicago Press, 2002), vol. 1, part 2, chap. 1.

4. Immanuel Kant, *Groundwork of the Metaphysics of Morals*, in *Immanuel Kant: Practical Philosophy*, trans. and ed. Mary Gregor (Cambridge: Cambridge University Press, 1996), 4:395.

5. Harry Frankfurt, "Equality as a Moral Ideal," *Ethics* 98, no. 1 (1987): 21–43.

6. Frankfurt, "Equality," 21.

7. Rawls, for example, argues that the distribution of "primary goods" should deviate from strict equality only when doing so will improve the position of the least well-off. Rawls, *A Theory of Justice*, 54–55, 78–81.

8. Sen and Nussbaum have developed this approach in a series of works beginning with Sen's Tanner Lectures. Amartya Sen, "Equality of What?" in *The Tanner Lectures on Human Values*, ed. Sterling M. McMurrin (Salt Lake City: University of Utah Press and Cambridge University Press, 1980). Other contributions include Amartya Sen, *The Idea of Justice* (Cambridge, MA: Harvard University Press, 2009); Amartya Sen, *Development as Freedom* (New York: Anchor Books, 1999); Martha Nussbaum, *Creating Capabilities: The Human Development Approach* (Cambridge, MA: Harvard University Press, 2011); and Martha Nussbaum, *Women and Human Development: The Capabilities Approach* (Cambridge: Cambridge University Press, 2000).

9. Nussbaum, *Creating Capabilities*, 17–45.

10. Nussbaum, *Creating Capabilities*, 115.

11. On the broadest meaning of "power," see Baruch Spinoza, *Ethics*, in *The Collected Works of Spinoza*, trans. Edwin Curley (Princeton: Princeton University Press, 1994), E4 A, E5.

12. Karl N. Llewellyn, *The Bramble Bush: The Classic Lectures on the Law and Law School* (Oxford: Oxford University Press, 2008), 112.

13. Kant, *Groundwork*, 4:436.
14. Aristotle, "De Anima," in *The Complete Works of Aristotle: The Revised Oxford Translation*, ed. Jonathan Barnes, vol. 1 (Princeton: Princeton University Press, 1984), ii 4, 416b9–11.
15. Kant, *Groundwork*, 4:413.
16. P. F. Strawson, "Persons," in *Individuals: An Essay in Descriptive Metaphysics* (London: Methuen, 1959), 87–116.
17. Immanuel Kant, *Critique of Pure Reason*, trans. Paul Gruyer and Allen W. Wood (Cambridge: Cambridge University Press, 1998), A137–47/B176–87.
18. Alexander Pope, *An Essay on Man*, ed. Tom Jones (Princeton: Princeton University Press, 2016), 56.
19. Rawls, *A Theory of Justice*, 118–23.
20. Rawls, *A Theory of Justice*, 80.
21. Rawls, *A Theory of Justice*, 221–27.
22. Plato, *Republic*, trans. G.M.A. Grube (Indianapolis: Hackett, 1992), 514a.
23. Plato, *Republic*, 516a.
24. Aristotle, *De Anima*, in *The Complete Works of Aristotle: The Revised Oxford Translation*, ed. Jonathan Barnes, vol. 1 (Princeton: Princeton University Press, 1984), 430a:10–25.
25. Aristotle, *Metaphysics*, in *The Complete Works*, vol. 2, XII, 1072a.
26. Aristotle, *Politics*, in *The Complete Works*, vol. 2, 1254b16–21.
27. Augustine, "On the Free Choice of the Will," in *On the Free Choice of the Will, On Grace and Free Choice, and Other Writings*, trans. and ed. Peter King (Cambridge: Cambridge University Press, 2010), 2.I.3.5–7.
28. Plato, *Protagoras*, in *The Collected Dialogues of Plato*, ed. Edith Hamilton and Huntington Cairns (Princeton: Princeton University Press, 1961), 352a–359a.
29. Aristotle, *The Nicomachean Ethics*, trans. Robert C. Bartlett and Susan D. Collins (Chicago: University of Chicago Press, 2012), 1150b19–1150b28.
30. Augustine, *Confessions*, trans. F. J. Sheed (New York: Sheed & Ward, 1943), 32.
31. Kant, *Groundwork*, 4:394; Immanuel Kant, *Critique of Practical Reason*, trans. and ed. Mary J. Gregor (Cambridge: Cambridge University Press, 2015), 5:29–30, 5:63, 5:79.
32. Kant, *Groundwork*, 4:439.
33. Charles Norris Cochrane, *Christianity and Classical Culture: A Study of Thought and Action from Augustus to Augustine* (Oxford: Oxford University Press, 1940), 113.
34. Kant, *Groundwork*, 4:430.
35. Augustine, "On the Free Choice of the Will," 55–61; John 8:6–7; John 14:6; Luke 19:1–10.
36. Augustine, *The City of God against the Pagans*, trans. and ed. R. W. Dyson (Cambridge: Cambridge University Press, 1998), book 22, chap. 30.
37. Immanuel Kant, *Religion within the Boundaries of Mere Reason*, trans. J. W. Semple (Edinburgh: Thomas Clark, 1838), 48–50.
38. Kant, *Groundwork*, 4:447.

39. Kant, *Critique of Pure Reason*, A508–9/B 536–37.
40. Kant, *Critique of Pure Reason*, Bxiii–xxii; Edward Westermarck, *Ethical Relativity* (London: Kegan Paul, Trench, Trubner, 1932), 59; Wilcomb E. Washburn, "Cultural Relativism, Human Rights, and the AAA," *American Anthropologist* 89, no. 4 (1987): 939–43.
41. John Rawls, *Political Liberalism* (New York: Columbia University Press, 1996), 174.
42. Sigmund Freud, *Three Essays on the Theory of Sexuality*, trans. James Strachey (New York: Basic Books, 2000).
43. Friedrich Nietzsche, *The Will to Power*, trans. Walter Kaufmann and R. J. Hollingdale, ed. Walter Kaufmann (New York: Random House, 1967), sec. 267.
44. Friedrich Nietzsche, *Beyond Good and Evil*, in *Beyond Good and Evil / On the Genealogy of Morality*, trans. Adrian Del Caro (Stanford: Stanford University Press, 2014), sec. 2.
45. Aristotle, *Metaphysics*, 982a20–982b10.
46. Gregory Nagy, *The Best of the Achaeans: Concepts of the Hero in Archaic Greek Poetry* (Baltimore: Johns Hopkins University Press, 1979), 17.
47. Aristotle, *Metaphysics*, 1042b8–1043a11; Aristotle, *Nicomachean Ethics*, 1177b26–1860.
48. Homer, *The Iliad*, trans. Robert Fagles (New York: Penguin Books, 1990).
49. Tacitus, *The Annals*, trans. A. J. Woodman (Indianapolis: Hackett, 2004), 11.22.2–4 ("In ancestral times this had been a reward of excellence, and it was lawful for all citizens who trusted their good qualities to seek magistracies"); Ovid, *Metamorphoses*, trans. Stanley Lombardo (Indianapolis: Hackett, 2010), 13.440 ("As much as the general exceeds the soldier, so much greater am I than you"); Virgil, *Aeneid*, trans. Frederick Ahl (Oxford: Oxford University Press, 2007), 340 ("Does he still grieve now for his lost mother, and does his father's / Fame, does Aeneas inspire him to old-fashioned courage, a real man's / Greatness of soul, does the thought that his uncle was Hector inspire him?").
50. Plato, *Euthyphro*, in *The Collected Dialogues*, 178c.
51. Plato, *Republic*, 514a—517c.
52. Plato, *Republic*, 519d—520c.
53. Aristotle, *Physics*, in *The Complete Works of Aristotle*, vol. 1, 206b13–206b16; Aristotle, *Metaphysics*, 1045b28–1046a4.
54. Aristotle, *Physics*, 194b16–199b32.
55. Plato, *Gorgias*, in *The Collected Dialogues*, 452a.
56. Terence Irwin, *Plato's Ethics* (New York: Oxford University Press, 1995), 68; Michael Beresford Foster, *Political Philosophies of Plato and Hegel* (New York: Russell & Russell, 1965), 48.
57. Plato, *Republic*, 443d.
58. Aristotle, *Nicomachean Ethics*, 1097b23–1098a16.
59. Augustine, *The City of God*, 153–265.

60. Sophocles, *Antigone* 331, trans. Nicholas Rudall (Chicago: I. R. Dee, 1998), 22.

61. Homer, *The Iliad*; Homer, *The Odyssey*, trans. Robert Fagles (New York: Penguin Classics, 1997), 455–67.

62. Thucydides, *History of the Peloponnesian War*, trans. Richard Crawley (London: J. M. Dent; New York: E. P. Dutton, 1910), book 5, chaps. 84–116.

63. Plato, *Apology*, in *The Collected Dialogues*, 42a.

64. Nietzsche, *Beyond Good and Evil*, sec. 167 ("Every elevation of the type 'man' has hitherto been the work of an aristocratic society—and so it will always be: a society which believes in a long scale of orders of rank and differences of worth between man and man needs slavery in some sense or other. Without the pathos of distance such as develops from the incarnate differences of classes, from the ruling caste's constant looking out and looking down on subjects and instruments and from its equally constant exercise of obedience and command, its holding down and holding at a distance, that other, more mysterious pathos could not have developed either, that longing for an ever-increasing widening of distance within the soul itself, the formation of ever higher, rarer, more remote, tenser, more comprehensive states, in short precisely the elevation of the type 'man,' the continual 'self-overcoming of man,' to take a moral formula in a supra-moral sense").

65. Martin Heidegger, *Pathmarks*, trans. and ed. William McNeill (Cambridge: Cambridge University Press, 1998), 252 ("Human beings do not decide whether and how beings appear, whether and how God and the gods or history and nature come forward into the clearing of being, come to presence and depart. The advent of beings lies in the destiny of being. But for humans it is ever a question of finding what is fitting in their essence that corresponds to such destiny; for in accord with this destiny the human being as ek-sisting has to guard the truth of being").

66. Martin Heidegger, *Being and Time*, trans. John Macquarrie and Edward Robinson (New York: Harper Perennial, 2008), 167 ("If Dasein discovers the world in its own way [*eigens*] and brings it close, if it discloses to itself its own authentic Being, then this discovery of the 'world' and this disclosure of Dasein are always accomplished as a clearing away of concealments and obscurities, as a breaking up of the disguises with which Dasein bars its own way"); Martin Heidegger, *The Origin of the Work of Art* in *Poetry, Language, Thought*, trans. Albert Hofstadter (New York: Harper & Row, 1971), 53 ("In the midst of beings as a whole an open place occurs. There is a clearing, a lighting. Though of in reference to what is, to beings, this clearing is in a greater degree than are beings. This open center is therefore not surrounded by what is; rather, the lighting center itself encircles all that is, like the Nothing which we scarcely know").

67. Heidegger, *Being and Time*, 377 ("Temporality is the primordial 'outside-of-itself' in and for itself. We therefore call the phenomena of the future, the character of having been, and the Present, the 'ecstases' of temporality").

68. Heidegger, *Being and Time*, 185 ("With equal primordiality the understanding projects Dasein's Being both upon its 'for-the-sake-of-which' and upon significance, as the worldhood of its current world. The character of understanding as projection is constitutive for Being-in-the-world with regard to the disclosedness of its existentially constitutive state-of-Being by which the factical potentiality-for-Being gets its leeway").

69. Martin Heidegger, *The Fundamental Concepts of Metaphysics: World, Finitude, Solitude*, trans. William McNeill and Nicholas Walker (Bloomington: Indiana University Press, 1995), 184 ("The main points of our approach are encapsulated in three theses: [1.] The stone is worldless; [2.] The animal is poor in world; [3.] Man is world-forming").

70. Hannah Arendt, *The Human Condition* (Chicago: University of Chicago Press, 1958), 188.

71. Plato, *Republic*, 508c.

72. Juan P. Lewis, "Did Varro Think That Slaves Were Talking Tools?" *Mnemosyne* 66 (2013): 643.

73. G.W.F. Hegel, *Phenomenology of Spirit*, trans. A. V. Miller (Oxford: Oxford University Press, 1977), 111–19.

74. Genesis 1:27 ("So God created man in his own image, in the image of God created he him"); Thomas Aquinas, *The "Summa Theologica" of St. Thomas Aquinas*, trans. Fathers of the English Dominican Province (London: R&T Washbourne, 1911), II-II Q25 A3.

75. Kant, *Groundwork*, 4:435.

76. Kant, *Critique of Practical Reason*, 5:77.

77. Jonathan Schell, *The Fate of the Earth* (New York: Knopf, 1982).

78. Heidegger, *Fundamental Concepts*, 184.

79. Immanuel Kant, *Practical Philosophy*, trans. and ed. Mary J. Gregor (Cambridge: Cambridge University Press, 1999), 5:82.

80. Aristotle, *Rhetoric*, in *The Complete Works*, vol. 2, 1407b.

81. Ross Douthat, "The Americanization of Religion," *New York Times*, December 21, 2022, https://www.nytimes.com/2022/12/21/opinion/america-religion-christianity.html.

82. Aristotle, *Nicomachean Ethics*, 1175a28–1179a33; Arendt, *The Human Condition*, 16; Hannah Arendt, *The Life of the Mind: Thinking and Willing*, vol. 2 (New York: Harcourt Brace Jovanovich, 1978).

83. Erich Auerbach, *Mimesis: The Representation of Reality in Western Literature*, trans. Willard R. Trask (Princeton: Princeton University Press, 1968), 436.

84. Bernard Williams, "Moral Luck," in *Moral Luck: Philosophical Papers, 1973–1980* (Cambridge: Cambridge University Press, 1981), 20–39; Daniel Callcut, "What Are We? On Paul Gauguin, Authenticity and the Midlife Crisis: How the Philosopher Bernard Williams Dramatised Moral Luck," *Aeon*, June 2018, https://aeon.co/users/daniel-callcut; Ramachandra Guha, *Gandhi: The Years That Changed the World, 1914–1948* (New York: Vintage, 2019) (describing, among other things, Gandhi's use of his grand-nieces to test his celibacy).

85. Barry Targan, "Harry Belten and the Mendelssohn Violin Concerto," *Esquire*, July 1, 1966, https://classic.esquire.com/article/1966/7/1/harry-belten-and-the-mendelssohn-violin-concerto. I am grateful to Paul Kahn for bringing this expression to my attention.

86. The poetry of Emily Dickinson, for example, was only published after her death. Todd Millicent Bingham, *Ancestors' Brocades: The Literary Debut of Emily Dickinson* (New York: Harper & Brothers, 1945). Likewise, Vincent van Gogh achieved acclaim only posthumously. Hans Luijten, *Jo van Gogh-Bonger: The Woman Who Made Vincent Famous*, trans. Lynne Richards (London: Bloomsbury, 2022).

87. Hans-Georg Gadamer, *Truth and Method*, trans. Joel Weinsheimer and Donald G. Marshall (New York: Continuum, 2004).

88. Nietzsche, *Beyond Good and Evil*, sec. 72 ("What someone is begins to reveal itself when his talent diminishes—when he ceases to show what he can do. Talent is also finery; finery is also a hiding place"), sec. 89 ("This tyranny, this arbitrariness, this strict and grandiose stupidity has trained the spirit; slavery, it seems, in the cruder and finer sense of the word, is also an indispensable means of spiritual discipline and cultivation"); secs. 172–73 ("Slave morality is essentially the morality of utility"); sec. 132 ("People are punished best for their virtues"); sec. 151 ("Having a talent is not enough: we must also have your permission for it—right? My friends?"); sec. 207 ("He is a tool, a piece of slave, even if certainly the most sublime kind of slave, but in himself he is nothing"); sec. 257 ("Every enhancement so far in the type 'human being' was the work of an aristocratic society . . . a society that believes in a long ladder of rank order and value-difference between one person and another and in some sense requires slavery"); sec. 265 ("There might be a sublime way of letting gifts from above descend as it were upon oneself, and thirstily drinking them up: but for this art and gesture the noble soul has no talent").

89. Spinoza, *Ethics*, E5 P41 S1.

90. Anthony T. Kronman, *Confessions of a Born-Again Pagan* (New Haven: Yale University Press, 2016), 555.

91. Rawls, *A Theory of Justice*, 3.

92. Søren Kierkegaard, *Either/Or: A Fragment of Life*, trans. Alastair Hannay (London: Penguin Books, 1992), 290–91.

93. William Hazlitt, "On Coriolanus," in *Characters of Shakespeare's Plays* (Cambridge: Cambridge University Press, 2009), 60.

94. Rainer Maria Rilke, *Duino Elegies*, trans. A. Poulin Jr. (Boston: Houghton Mifflin, 1977), 5.

95. Martin Heidegger, "What Are Poets For?" in *Poetry, Language, Thought*, trans. Albert Hofstadter (New York: Harper & Row, 1971), 94–139 (discussing Rilke).

96. Walt Whitman, "Memories of President Lincoln," in *Leaves of Grass* (Philadelphia: David McKay, 1891), 255–76 (collecting the poems "When Lilacs

Last in the Dooryard Bloom'd," "O Captain! My Captain!" "Hush'd Be the Camps To-day," and "This Dust Was Once the Man").

97. Walt Whitman, *Democratic Vistas: The Original Version in Facsimile* (Iowa City: University of Iowa Press, 2010).

## Chapter Four. Can We Be Friends with the Dead?

1. For biographical details, see Maurizio Viroli, *Niccolò's Smile: A Biography of Machiavelli* (New York: Hill & Wang, 2002).

2. Niccolò Machiavelli, *The Prince*, 2nd ed., trans. Harvey C. Mansfield (Chicago: University of Chicago Press, 2010); Niccolò Machiavelli, *Discourses on Livy*, trans. Harvey C. Mansfield and Nathan Tarcov (Chicago: University of Chicago Press, 1998).

3. Machiavelli, *The Prince*, 4.

4. Niccolò Machiavelli to Francesco Vettori, December 10, 1513, in *The Prince*, 109–10.

5. Numa Denis Fustel De Coulages, *The Ancient City: A Study on the Religion, Laws, and Institutions of Greece and Rome* (Kitchener: Batoche Books, 2001), 17.

6. Virgil, *Aeneid*, trans. Frederick Ahl (Oxford: Oxford University Press, 2007), 1.220, 1.305, 1.378, 4.393, *inter alia*.

7. *Aeneas, Anchises, and Ascanius*, Borghese Gallery, https://borghese.gallery/collection/sculpture/aeneas-anchises-and-ascanius.html.

8. Hannah Arendt, "What Is Authority?" in *Between Past and Future: Six Exercises in Political Thought* (New York: Viking, 1961), 121.

9. Aristotle, *Nicomachean Ethics*, ed. Roger Crisp (Cambridge: Cambridge University Press, 2000), 1166a.

10. Thomas Jefferson to James Madison, September 6, 1789, in *The Papers of Thomas Jefferson*, vol. 15, ed. Julian P. Boyd (Princeton: Princeton University Press, 1958), 392.

11. Edmund Burke, *Reflections on the Revolution in France*, ed. Frank M. Turner (New Haven: Yale University Press, 2003), 29–31.

12. See, for example, Aimee Ortiz and Johnny Diaz, "George Floyd Protests Reignite Debate over Confederate Statues," *New York Times*, June 3, 2020, https://www.nytimes.com/2020/06/03/us/confederate-statues-george-floyd.html; Nicholas Fandos, "House Votes to Purge Confederate Statues from the Capitol," *New York Times*, June 29, 2021, https://www.nytimes.com/2021/06/29/us/politics/house-confederate-statues-vote.html.

13. Burke, *Reflections*, 30.

14. Samuel Scheffler, *Why Worry about Future Generations?* (Oxford: Oxford University Press, 2020); Derek Parfit, "Future People, the Non-Identity Problem, and Person-Affecting Principles," *Philosophy & Public Affairs* 45, no. 2 (September 2017).

15. Burke, *Reflections*, 81.

16. Burke, *Reflections*, 82.
17. On cathedral building, see John Ruskin, "The Nature of the Gothic," in *The Works of John Ruskin*, ed. E. T. Cook and Alexander Wedderburn, 39 vols. (London: George Allen, 1903–12), 10:245. On constitutional interpretation, see Paul W. Kahn, "The Question of Sovereignty," *Stanford Journal of International Law* 40, no. 2 (Summer 2004): 269–70; and Jed Rubenfeld, *Freedom and Time: A Theory of Constitutional Self-Government* (New Haven: Yale University Press, 2001).
18. Michael Spence, "Job Market Signalling," *Quarterly Journal of Economics* 87, no. 3 (August 1973).
19. *Hamer v. Sidway*, 124 N.Y. 538, 545 (N.Y. Ct. Apps. 1891) (consideration consists "either in some right, interest, profit or benefit accruing to the one party, or some forbearance, detriment, loss or responsibility given, suffered or undertaken by the other"); *Allegheny Coll. v. National Chautauqua County Bank of Jamestown*, 246 N.Y. 369, 373 (N.Y. Ct. Apps. 1972) ("A classic form of statement identifies consideration with detriment to the promisee sustained by virtue of the promise").
20. Aristotle, *Nicomachean Ethics*, 1162a, 1166a.
21. John Rawls, *A Theory of Justice*, rev. ed. (Cambridge, MA: Belknap Press of Harvard University Press, 1999), 118.
22. Rawls, *A Theory of Justice*, 256.
23. Abraham Lincoln, "First Inaugural Address, March 4, 1861," in *Abraham Lincoln: Speeches and Writings, 1859–1865*, ed. Don E. Fehrenbacher (New York: Literary Classics of the United States, 1989), 221.
24. Leonard Lyons, "Lyons Den," *Daily Defender*, November 4, 1958.
25. Sigmund Freud, "The Ego and the Id," in *The Standard Edition of the Complete Psychological Works of Sigmund Freud*, ed. James Strachey, vol. 19 (London: Hogarth, 1953), 55; Walt Whitman, "Song of Myself," in *Leaves of Grass*, ed. Sculley Bradley and Harold W. Blodgett (New York: Norton, 1973), 88.
26. Erich Auerbach, *Mimesis: The Representation of Reality in Western Literature*, trans. Willard R. Trask (Princeton: Princeton University Press, 1968), 198–202; Anthony T. Kronman, *Confessions of a Born-Again Pagan* (New Haven: Yale University Press, 2016), 843.
27. Freud, "Unconscious," in *Standard Edition*, vol. 14, 166; Freud, "Repression," in *Standard Edition*, vol. 14, 145.
28. Sigmund Freud, *Civilization and Its Discontents*, trans. and ed. James Strachey (New York: Norton, 1962), 16–18.
29. Jonathan Lear, *Freud*, 2nd ed. (New York: Routledge, 2015), 216.
30. Freud, "Studies on Hysteria," in *Standard Edition*, vol. 2, 301.
31. Sigmund Freud, *The Interpretation of Dreams: The Complete and Definitive Text*, trans. and ed. James Strachey (New York: Basic Books, 2010), 553 n. 1; Hans W. Loewald, "Therapeutic Action of Psychoanalysis," in *Papers on Psychoanalysis* (New Haven: Yale University Press, 1980), 248–49.

32. John Toland, *Adolf Hitler: The Definitive Biography* (New York: Anchor, 1991).

33. Ramachandra Guha, *Gandhi Before India* (London: Penguin Books, 2013).

34. Robert A. Caro, *The Years of Lyndon Johnson*, 4 vols. (New York: Knopf, 1982–2012).

35. Ray Monk, *Robert Oppenheimer: A Life inside the Center* (New York: Anchor, 2014).

36. Edward Gibbon, *The History of the Decline and Fall of the Roman Empire*, ed. David Womersley (New York: Penguin Books, 1994), chaps. 22–23.

37. For example, Tobias Hoenger, *Muhammad Asad: A Mediator between the Islamic and the Western World: An Interreligious Discourse* (Munich: Grin, 2010).

38. Friedrich Nietzsche, *Beyond Good and Evil* (New York: Vintage Books, 1989), sec. 155.

39. Walt Whitman, "Song of Myself," 35.

40. William B. Yeats, "Byzantium," in *The Collected Poems of W. B. Yeats*, ed. Richard J. Finneran (New York: Macmillan, 1989), 248.

41. Immanuel Kant, *The Groundwork of the Metaphysics of Morals*, in Immanuel Kant, *Practical Philosophy*, trans. and ed. Mary Gregor (Cambridge: Cambridge University Press, 1996), 4:399.

42. Aristotle, *Nicomachean Ethics*, 1155a.

## Chapter Five.  Character and Country

1. Plato, *Republic*, trans. G.M.A. Grube (Indianapolis: Hackett, 1997), 327a–328d.

2. Plato, *Republic*, 336b–338c.

3. Plato, *Republic*, 368c–369b.

4. Plato, *Republic*, 473c–e.

5. M. B. Foster, *The Political Philosophies of Plato and Hegel* (Oxford: Oxford University Press, 1968), 2–3.

6. Aristotle, *The Nicomachean Ethics*, trans. Robert C. Bartlett and Susan D. Collins (Chicago: University of Chicago Press, 2012), 1095b14–22; Jean-Jacques Rousseau, *The Social Contract and The First and Second Discourses*, ed. Susan Dunn (New Haven: Yale University Press, 2002), 164; Jeremy Bentham, "Article on Utilitarianism," in *The Collected Works of Jeremy Bentham: Deontology Together with a Table of the Springs of Action and Article on Utilitarianism*, ed. Amnon Goldworth (Oxford: Oxford University Press, 1983), 309.

7. John Rawls, *A Theory of Justice*, rev. ed. (Cambridge, MA: Belknap Press of Harvard University Press, 1999), 30.

8. Augustine, "On the Free Choice of the Will," in *On the Free Choice of the Will, On Grace and Free Choice, and Other Writings*, trans. and ed. Peter King (Cambridge: Cambridge University Press, 2010), 21 (1.12.26.86).

9. For an elaboration of these themes, see M. B. Foster, "The Christian Doctrine of Creation and the Rise of Modern Natural Science," *Mind* 43, no. 172 (October 1934).

10. Lionel Trilling, *Sincerity and Authenticity* (Cambridge, MA: Harvard University Press, 1973); Martin Heidegger, *Being and Time*, trans. John Macquarrie and Edward Robinson (New York: Harper Perennial, 2008), 68.

11. Max Weber, *Economy and Society*, trans. Ephraim Fischoff et al. (Berkeley: University of California Press, 1978), 215, 227–28.

12. Aristotle, *Nicomachean Ethics*, 1103a33–34.

13. Aristotle, *Nicomachean Ethics*, 1103b23–25.

14. Aristotle, *Nicomachean Ethics*, 1098a.

15. Plato, *Gorgias*, in *The Collected Dialogues of Plato*, ed. Edith Hamilton and Huntington Cairns (Princeton: Princeton University Press, 1961), 509e; Plato, *Meno*, in *The Collected Dialogues*, 87c; Aristotle, *Nicomachean Ethics*, book VII, chap. 4.

16. Plato, *Republic*, 621d.

17. Heraclitus, "Fragment B 119," in *Early Greek Philosophy*, ed. Jonathan Barnes (London: Penguin Books, 1987), 62.

18. Immanuel Kant, *The Groundwork of the Metaphysics of Morals*, in *Practical Philosophy*, trans. and ed. Mary Gregor (Cambridge: Cambridge University Press, 1996), 4:397.

19. Kant, *Groundwork*, 4:390.

20. Aristotle, *Politics*, in *The Complete Works of Aristotle: The Revised Oxford Translation*, ed. Jonathan Barnes, vol. 2 (Princeton: Princeton University Press, 1984), 1279a–b.

21. Aristotle, *Politics*, 1252b; Karl Marx, *Capital*, trans. Ben Fowkes, vol. 1 (London: Penguin Books, 1992), part 3, chap. 7, sec. 1.

22. Hannah Arendt, *On Revolution* (London: Penguin Books, 2006), 162.

23. Polybius, *The Rotations of Polities*, in *The Histories*, trans. W. R. Paton, vol. 3 (London: Loeb Classical Library, 1992).

24. *Federalist* No. 1 (Alexander Hamilton) in *The Federalist*, ed. Jacob E. Cooke (Middletown: Wesleyan University Press, 1961); "The National Convention: September 21, 1792, Debate," in *Readings in European History*, ed. J. H. Robinson (Boston: Ginn, 1906), 2:446–50; V. I. Lenin, *The State and Revolution* (London: British Socialist Party, 1919).

25. Foster, "The Christian Doctrine of Creation and the Rise of Modern Natural Science," 463–64.

26. Thomas Hobbes, *Leviathan*, ed. J.C.A. Gaskin (Oxford: Oxford University Press, 1996), 7.

27. Paul W. Kahn, *Legitimacy and History: Self-Government in American Constitutional Theory* (New Haven: Yale University Press, 1993); Paul W. Kahn, *Origins of Order: Project and System in the American Legal Imagination* (New Haven: Yale University Press, 2019).

28. Walt Whitman, *Leaves of Grass* (1891–92 ed.), in *Walt Whitman: Complete Poetry and Collected Prose*, ed. Justin Kaplan (New York: Viking, 1982), 494; H. L. Mencken, *The American Language* (New York: Knopf, 1984).

29. Steven Smith, *Reclaiming Patriotism in an Age of Extremes* (New Haven: Yale University Press, 2021).

30. Paul W. Kahn, *Political Theology* (New York: Columbia University Press, 2012).

31. Kant, *Groundwork*, 4:436.

32. Kant, *Groundwork*, 4:397.

33. Kant, *Groundwork*, 4:432.

34. Abraham Lincoln, "The Gettysburg Address," in *Collected Works of Abraham Lincoln*, ed. Roy P. Basler (New Brunswick: Rutgers University Press, 1953).

35. Shailer Matthews, "The Moral Value of Patriotism," *Biblical World* 52, no. 1 (July 1918).

36. Homer, *The Iliad*, trans. Richard Lattimore (Chicago: University of Chicago Press, 2011), VI:486–89.

37. Aristotle, *Metaphysics*, in *The Complete Works*, vol. 2, book Z; Aristotle, *Physics*, in *The Complete Works*, vol. 1, book II.

38. Michael J. Sandel, *Liberalism and the Limits of Justice* (Cambridge: Cambridge University Press, 1998), 11; Bernard Williams, "The Makropolous Case," in *Problems of the Self* (Cambridge: Cambridge University Press, 1973); Martin Hägglund, *This Life: Secular Faith and Spiritual Freedom* (New York: Pantheon Books, 2019).

39. Smith, "Patriotism and Loyalty," in *Reclaiming Patriotism in an Age of Extremes*; Alasdair MacIntyre, "Is Patriotism a Virtue?" in *Patriotism: Philosophical and Political Perspectives*, ed. Igor Primoratz and Aleksandr Pavkovic (London: Routledge, 2002).

40. Kant, *Groundwork*, 4:402; Immanuel Kant, *Critique of Practical Reason*, trans. and ed. Mary J. Gregor (Cambridge: Cambridge University Press, 2015), 5:77.

41. Stephen Nathanson, "Patriotism, War, and the Limits of Permissible Partiality," *Journal of Ethics* 13, no. 4 (2009); Igor Primoratz, "Patriotism: A Two-Tier Account," in *The Ethics of Patriotism: A Debate* (Oxford: Wiley & Sons, 2015).

42. Aristotle, *Nicomachean Ethics*, 1155a.

43. Anthony T. Kronman, *Confessions of a Born-Again Pagan* (New Haven: Yale University Press, 2016), 89–91.

44. Plato, *Symposium*, in *The Collected Dialogues*, 182b; Plato, *Charmides*, in *The Collected Dialogues*, 154b; Plato, *Republic*, 328a–b.

45. Aristotle, *Politics*, 1253a29–30.

46. Aristotle, *Nicomachean Ethics*, 1178a.

47. Friedrich Nietzsche, *On the Genealogy of Morals and Ecce Homo*, trans. Walter Kaufmann (New York: Vintage Books, 1989), sec. 295.

48. Frederic Tuten, "Paul Bowles in Tangiers," *Paris Review*, February 21, 2023; Michael Rocke, *The Biblioteca Berenson at Villa I Tatti* (Cambridge: Cambridge University Press, 2016).

49. Diogenes Laërtius, "Diogenes," in *Lives of the Eminent Philosophers*, vol. 2, trans. R. D. Hicks (Cambridge: Loeb Classical Library, 1925), 24; Martha C. Nussbaum, "Patriotism and Cosmopolitanism," *Boston Review*, October 1, 1994.

50. Plato, *Symposium*, 210e–212b; Luke 14:26.

51. Kant, *Groundwork*, 4:433; Kant, *Critique of Practical Reason*, 5:83.

52. Rawls, *A Theory of Justice*, 64.

53. Hobbes, *Leviathan*, 65–67.

54. Hobbes, *Leviathan*, 212.

55. Kant, *Groundwork*, 4:433; Kant, *Critique of Practical Reason*, 5:43.

56. Aristotle, *Nicomachean Ethics*, 1123a.

57. Plato, *Phaedo*, in *The Collected Dialogues*, 81e.

58. Augustine, "On the Free Choice of the Will," 43–44 (2.6.14.57–2.7.18.71).

59. Whitman, *Leaves of Grass*, 1.

60. Whitman, *Leaves of Grass*, 56, 62; Kronman, *Confessions of a Born-Again Pagan*, 1027–28.

61. Kronman, *Confessions of a Born-Again Pagan*, 44.

62. Benjamin Storey and Jennifer Silber Storey, *Why We Are Restless: On the Modern Quest for Contentment* (Princeton: Princeton University Press, 2021).

63. Friedrich Nietzsche, *The Gay Science*, trans. Walter Kaufmann (New York: Vintage Books, 1974), sec. 276.

## Chapter Six. Golden Apple in a Silver Frame

1. Abraham Lincoln to Alexander H. Stephens, December 22, 1860, in *Collected Works of Abraham Lincoln*, ed. Roy P. Basler (New Brunswick: Rutgers University Press, 1953), 4:201.

2. See *Causes of the Civil War*, https://civilwarcauses.org/ahs-al.htm.

3. "Fragment on the Constitution and the Union," in *Collected Works of Abraham Lincoln*, 4:168–69.

4. Abraham Lincoln, "The Gettysburg Address," in *Collected Works of Abraham Lincoln*, 7:17–23.

5. Abraham Lincoln to A. G. Hodges, April 4, 1865, in *Collected Works of Abraham Lincoln*, 7:281.

6. William Lloyd Garrison, "Editorial in 'The Liberator,'" in *A Library of American Literature for the Earliest Settlement to the Present Time*, ed. Charles L. Webster, vol. 6 (New York: Charles L. Webster, 1892), 222–23.

7. "'A House Divided': Speech at Springfield, Illinois," June 16, 1858, in *Collected Works of Abraham Lincoln*, 2:465.

8. "First Debate with Stephen A. Douglas, at Ottawa, Illinois," August 21, 1858, in *Collected Works of Abraham Lincoln*, 3:1–37; Harry V. Jaffa, *Crisis of*

*the House Divided: An Interpretation of the Issues in the Lincoln-Douglas Debates* (Chicago: University of Chicago Press, 2009).

9. "Address at Cooper Institute, New York City," February 27, 1860, in *Collected Works of Abraham Lincoln*, 3:522–50.

10. *Dred Scott v. Sandford*, 60 U.S. (19 How.) 393 (1857).

11. "First Inaugural—Final Text," March 4, 1861, in *Collected Works of Abraham Lincoln*, 4:264; "Emancipation Proclamation," January 1, 1863, in *Collected Works of Abraham Lincoln*, 6:28–31; "Proclamation Suspending Writ of Habeas Corpus," July 5, 1864, in *Collected Works of Abraham Lincoln*, 7:425–27.

12. "Last Public Address," April 11, 1865, in *Collected Works of Abraham Lincoln*, 8:399–405.

13. Michael P. Zuckert, *The Natural Rights Republic: Studies in the Foundation of the American Political Tradition* (South Bend: University of Notre Dame Press, 1996).

14. René Descartes, *Meditations on First Philosophy*, trans. Michael Moriarty (Oxford: Oxford University Press, 2008), 59.

15. Matthew Stewart, *Nature's God: The Heretical Origins of the American Republic* (New York: Norton, 2014).

16. Plato, *Phaedo*, in *The Collected Dialogues of Plato*, ed. Edith Hamilton and Huntington Cairns (Princeton: Princeton University Press, 1961), 58b–58e.

17. Plato, *Republic*, trans. G.M.A. Grube (Indianapolis: Hackett, 1992), 514a.

18. Jonathan Edwards, *Sinners in the Hands of an Angry God* (Philadelphia: Presbyterian Board of Publication, 1920); Abraham Lincoln, "Second Inaugural Address," in *Collected Works of Abraham Lincoln*, 8:333.

19. Keith Joseph and Jonathan Sumption, *Equality* (London: John Murray, 1979), 32.

20. William Graham Sumner, *What Social Classes Owe to Each Other* (New York: Harper & Bros., 1883).

21. Franklin D. Roosevelt, "Four Freedoms," speech delivered on January 6, 1941, https://www.archives.gov/milestone-documents/president-franklin-roosevelts-annual-message-to-congress.

22. *Grutter v. Bollinger*, 539 U.S. 306, 378 (2003) (Thomas, J., dissenting).

23. John Locke, *Second Treatise*, in *Two Treatises on Government and A Letter concerning Toleration*, ed. Ian Shapiro (New Haven: Yale University Press, 2003), secs. 4, 123, 222.

24. *Marbury v. Madison*, 5 U.S. (1 Cranch) 137 (1803); *McCulloch v. Maryland*, 17 U.S. (4 Wheat.) 316 (1819).

25. Thomas E. Ricks, *First Principles: What America's Founders Learned from the Greeks and Romans and How That Shaped Our Country* (New York: HarperCollins, 2020); Garry Wills, *Cincinnatus: George Washington and the Enlightenment* (New York: Doubleday, 1984), 20.

26. Aristotle, *Politics*, in *The Complete Works of Aristotle: The Revised Oxford Translation*, ed. Jonathan Barnes, vol. 2 (Princeton: Princeton University Press, 1984), 1287b23; Polybius, *The Histories*, trans. W. R. Paton (London: Heineman,

1923), III, 291; Charles de Secondat, Baron de Montesquieu, *The Spirit of the Laws*, trans. and ed. Anne M. Cohler, Basia Carolyn Miller, and Harold Samuel Stone (Cambridge: Cambridge University Press, 1989), 157.

27. Augustine, *The City of God against the Pagans*, trans. and ed. R. W. Dyson (Cambridge: Cambridge University Press, 1998), 12.22, 13.1–3.

28. *Federalist* Nos. 47–51 (James Madison), in *The Federalist*, ed. Jacob E. Cooke (Middletown: Wesleyan University Press, 1961).

29. Max Weber, "The Three Types of Legitimate Rule," in *Economy and Society*, trans. and ed. Guenther Roth and Claus Wittich (Berkeley: University of California Press, 1978), 215–16.

30. Thomas Hobbes, *Leviathan*, ed. Edwin Curley (Indianapolis: Hackett, 1994), 101–5.

31. *Federalist* No. 40 (James Madison).

32. Aristotle, *The Nicomachean Ethics*, trans. Robert C. Bartlett and Susan D. Collins (Chicago: University of Chicago Press, 2012), 1139b19–1139b35.

33. Paul W. Kahn, *Political Theology: Four New Chapters on the Concept of Sovereignty* (New York: Columbia University Press, 2012).

34. David Wootton, *Power, Pleasure, and Profit: Insatiable Appetites from Machiavelli to Madison* (Cambridge, MA: Belknap Press of Harvard University Press, 2018), 134–54.

35. Hume's influence on the Constitution is well documented. He corresponded with Benjamin Franklin, was invoked by Alexander Hamilton during the Federal Convention, and left a deep impression on the thought of James Madison. John M. Werner, "David Hume and America," *Journal of the History of Ideas* 33, no. 3 (1972): 439–56; Douglass Adair, " 'That Politics May Be Reduced to a Science': David Hume, James Madison, and the Tenth Federalist," *Huntington Library Quarterly* 20, no. 4 (1957): 343–60.

36. John Locke, *An Essay in Toleration*, in *Two Treatises on Government and A Letter concerning Toleration*, ed. Ian Shapiro (New Haven: Yale University Press, 2003), 211–54.

37. David Hume, *An Enquiry concerning Human Understanding*, ed. Peter Millican (Oxford: Oxford University Press, 2007), sec. X.

38. Hume, *Enquiry*, 18.

39. David Hume, *A Treatise of Human Nature*, ed. David Fate Norton and Mary J. Norton (Oxford: Clarendon, 2007), 302.

40. Hume, *Treatise*, 355.

41. J.G.A. Pocock, *Barbarism and Religion*, Vol. 1: *The Enlightenments of Edward Gibbon, 1737–1764* (Cambridge: Cambridge University Press, 2004), 68–69.

42. Jonathan Israel, *A Revolution of the Mind: Radical Enlightenment and the Intellectual Origins of Modern Democracy* (Princeton: Princeton University Press, 2010), 70–71.

43. Richard Ashcraft, *Revolutionary Politics and Locke's Two Treatises of Government* (Princeton: Princeton University Press, 1986), 489–90.

44. *Federalist* No. 10 (James Madison).

45. Plato, *Republic*, 563e—564a.
46. Paul J. Larkin Jr., "The Original Understanding of Property in the Constitution," *Marquette Law Review* 100, no. 1 (Fall 2016): 47–48; *Federalist* No. 54 (James Madison) ("Government is instituted no less for the protection of the property than of the persons of individuals").
47. Alexis de Tocqueville, *Democracy in America*, trans. Harvey C. Mansfield and Delba Winthrop (Chicago: University of Chicago Press, 2002), 502–3.
48. *Federalist* Nos. 8, 9 (Alexander Hamilton); *Federalist* No. 55 (James Madison).
49. "Sophrosynē," in *Oxford Dictionary of Philosophy*, ed. Simon Blackburn (Oxford: Oxford University Press, 2005), 345.
50. U.S. Constitution, Article I, Sections 2, 3, and 7; Article II, Section 2; Article III.
51. *Federalist* No. 10 (James Madison); *Federalist* No. 51 (James Madison) ("As there is a degree of depravity in mankind which requires a certain degree of circumspection and distrust: So there are other qualities in human nature, which justify a certain portion of esteem and confidence. Republican government presupposes the existence of these qualities in a higher degree than any other form. . . . Were the pictures which have been drawn by the political jealousy of some among us, faithful likenesses of the human character, the inference would be that there is not sufficient virtue among men for self-government; and that nothing less than the chains of despotism can restrain them from destroying and devouring one another").
52. Aristotle, *Nicomachean Ethics*, 1103b7–1103b26.
53. Keith E. Whittington, *Political Foundations of Judicial Supremacy: The Presidency, the Supreme Court, and Constitutional Leadership in U.S. History* (Princeton: Princeton University Press, 2009); "Speech at Springfield, Illinois," June 26, 1857, in *Collected Works of Abraham Lincoln*, 2:399–410.
54. *Marbury v. Madison*, 5 U.S. (1 Cranch) 137, 177 (1803).
55. Alexander M. Bickel, *The Least Dangerous Branch: The Supreme Court at the Bar of Politics*, 2nd ed. (New Haven: Yale University Press, 1986), 199.
56. William W. Taylor III, "How the Supreme Court Is Destroying Its Own Legitimacy," *Alliance for Justice*, January 25, 2023, https://afj.org/article/how-the-supreme-court-is-destroying-its-own-legitimacy; Spencer Bokat-Lindell, "Is the Supreme Court Facing a Legitimacy Crisis?" *New York Times*, June 29, 2022, https://www.nytimes.com/2022/06/29/opinion/supreme-court-legitimacy-crisis.html; Daniel Epps and Ganesh Sitaraman, "How to Save the Supreme Court," *Yale Law Journal* 129, no. 148 (2019); Tara Leigh Grove, "The Supreme Court's Legitimacy Dilemma," *Harvard Law Review* 132, no. 8 (2019): 2240–76.
57. Learned Hand, *The Bill of Rights* (Cambridge, MA: Harvard University Press, 1958), 73.
58. Stephen L. Carter, *The Confirmation Mess: Cleaning Up the Federal Appointments Process* (New York: Basic Books, 1995).

59. Bickel, *The Least Dangerous Branch*, 16.
60. Stephen I. Vladeck, "Just How Hypocritical Are the Supreme Court's Conservative Justices Willing to Be?" *New York Times*, March 13, 2023, https://www.nytimes.com/2023/03/13/opinion/supreme-court-conservatives-standing.html; Louis Michael Seidman, "The Long, Troubled History of the Supreme Court—and How We Can Change It," *Nation*, June 20, 2022, https://www.thenation.com/article/society/supreme-court-dangerous; Ian Millhiser, "The Importance of Staying Angry at the Supreme Court," *Vox*, July 8, 2023; Aziz Rana, *The Constitutional Bind: How Americans Came to Idolize a Document That Fails Them* (Chicago: University of Chicago Press, 2024).
61. Thomas Jefferson to John Holmes, April 22, 1890, in *The Papers of Thomas Jefferson*, vol. 15, ed. J. Jefferson Looney (Princeton: Princeton University Press, 2018), 550–51.
62. "Second Inaugural Address," March 4, 1861, in *Collected Works of Abraham Lincoln*, 8:323.
63. Eric Foner, *The Second Founding: How the Civil War and Reconstruction Remade the Constitution* (New York: Norton, 2019); Bruce Ackerman, *We the People*: Volume 2: *Transformations* (Cambridge, MA: Belknap Press of Harvard University Press, 2000).
64. *Civil Rights Cases*, 109 U.S. 3 (1883); *Plessy v. Ferguson*, 163 U.S. 537 (1896).
65. *Slaughter-House Cases*, 83 U.S. (16 Wall.) 36 (1873).
66. *Slaughter-House Cases*, 74–75.
67. *Slaughter-House Cases*, 83–131 (Field, J., dissenting).
68. *Lochner v. New York*, 198 U.S. 45 (1905); D. J. Brewer, *Protection to Private Property from Public Attack: An Address Delivered before the Graduating Classes* (New Haven: Hoggson & Robinson, 1891); Owen M. Fiss, *Troubled Beginnings of the Modern State, 1888–1910* (New York: Macmillan Reference, 1994).
69. *Lochner v. New York*, 65–74 (Holmes, J., dissenting).
70. *West Coast Hotel Co. v. Parrish*, 300 U.S. 379 (1937).
71. *Meyer v. Nebraska*, 262 U.S. 390 (1923); *Pierce v. Society of Sisters*, 269 U.S. 510 (1925).
72. *Griswold v. Connecticut*, 381 U.S. 479 (1965); *Roe v. Wade*, 410 U.S. 113 (1973); *Lawrence v. Texas*, 539 U.S. 558 (2003); *Obergefell v. Hodges*, 576 U.S. 644 (2015).
73. *Brown v. Board of Education of Topeka*, 347 U.S. 483 (1954).
74. *Shelley v. Kraemer*, 334 U.S. 1 (1948).
75. Richard Kluger, *Simple Justice: The History of Brown v. Board of Education and Black America's Struggle for Equality* (New York: Vintage, 2004); Mary L. Dudziak, *Exporting American Dreams: Thurgood Marshall's African Journey* (Princeton: Princeton University Press, 2012).
76. *Gibbons v. Ogden*, 22 U.S. (9 Wheat.) 1 (1824), 195.
77. Brief for the Board of Education of Topeka, Kansas, on the Questions Propounded by the Court, *Brown v. Board of Education of Topeka*, 347 U.S. 483

(1954), 1953 WL 78287, at *2–3 ("The public interest, including the interest of negro children in Topeka, equity, and practical considerations require that termination of segregation in the elementary schools of Topeka shall be permitted to be accomplished in a gradual and orderly manner").

78. Geoffrey R. Stone and David A. Strauss, *Democracy and Equality: The Enduring Constitutional Vision of the Warren Court* (New York: Oxford University Press, 2020); Owen Fiss, "Another Equality," *Issues in Legal Scholarship* 20 (2004): 1, 17; Philip B. Kurland, "Egalitarianism and the Warren Court," *Michigan Law Review* 68, no. 4 (1970): 629–82.

79. *Brown v. Board of Education II*, 349 U.S. 294 (1955).

80. Justin Driver, *The Schoolhouse Gate: Public Education, the Supreme Court, and the Battle for the American Mind* (New York: Vintage, 2018), 256; Robert B. McKay, "With All Deliberate Speed: A Study of School Desegregation," *New York University Law Review* 31 (1956): 991.

81. *Green v. County School Board of New Kent County*, 391 U.S. 430 (1968).

82. *Keyes v. School District No. 1, Denver, Colorado*, 413 U.S. 189 (1973).

83. *Milliken v. Bradley*, 418 U.S. 717 (1974).

84. Fiss, "Another Equality," 11–12.

85. M. R. Glass, "From Sword to Shield to Myth: Facing the Facts of De Facto School Segregation," *Journal of Urban History* 44, no. 6 (2018): 1197–226.

86. R. Shep Melnick, "Desegregation, Then and Now," *National Affairs* 58 (Winter 2024), https://www.nationalaffairs.com/publications/detail/desegregation-then-and-now ("Those who attack *Milliken* fail to acknowledge the likely political consequences of a contrary ruling").

87. Owen M. Fiss, *Why We Vote* (Oxford: Oxford University Press, 2023), 1–3.

88. *Reynolds v. Sims*, 377 U.S. 533 (1964).

89. *Reynolds v. Sims*, 562.

90. *Federalist* No. 9 (Alexander Hamilton); *Federalist* No. 10 (James Madison); Peter H. Schuck, "Against (and for) Madison: An Essay in Praise of Factions," *Yale Law and Policy Review* 15 (1997): 553; Keith E. Whittington, "Constitutional Theory as Political Science," in *Constitutional Theory: Arguments and Perspectives* (Newark, NJ: LexisNexis, 2007); Cass R. Sunstein, "Interest Groups in American Public Law," *Stanford Law Review* 38, no. 1 (1985): 29–87; Frank H. Easterbrook, "The State of Madison's Vision of the State: A Public Choice Perspective," *Harvard Law Review* 107, no. 6 (1994): 1328–47; Christopher H. Achen and Larry M. Bartels, *Democracy for Realists: Why Elections Do Not Produce Responsive Governments* (Princeton: Princeton University Press, 2016); Hans Noel, "The Coalition Merchants: The Ideological Roots of the Civil Rights Realignment," *Journal of Politics* 74, no. 1 (2012).

91. *Reynolds v. Sims*.

92. *Rucho v. Common Cause*, 588 U.S. ___ (2019).

93. Erwin Chemerinsky, "Substantive Due Process," *Touro Law Review* 15, no. 4 (1999): 1501–34.

94. *Planned Parenthood v. Casey*, 505 U.S. 833 (1992).

95. *Roe v. Wade.*

96. Ilan Wurman, *A Debt against the Living: An Introduction to Originalism* (Cambridge: Cambridge University Press, 2017); Jack M. Balkin, *Living Originalism* (Cambridge, MA: Belknap Press of Harvard University Press, 2014); Erwin Chemerinsky, *Worse Than Nothing: The Dangerous Fallacy of Originalism* (New Haven: Yale University Press, 2023).

97. Ari Shapiro, "Conservatives Have 'Originalism'; Liberals Have . . . ?" *NPR*, June 23, 2009, https://www.npr.org/2009/06/23/105439966/conservatives-have-originalism-liberals-have.

98. Johnathan O'Neill, *Originalism in American Law and Politics: A Constitutional History* (Baltimore: Johns Hopkins University Press, 2005), 67–93.

99. John Rawls, *A Theory of Justice*, rev. ed. (Cambridge, MA: Belknap Press of Harvard University Press, 1999).

100. Thomas Jefferson to James Madison, May 25, 1810, in *The Papers of Thomas Jefferson*, vol. 2: *16 November 1809 to 11 August 1810*, ed. J. Jefferson Looney (Princeton: Princeton University Press, 2005), 416–17 ("His twistifications in the case of Marbury, in that of Burr, & the late Yazoo case, shew how dexterously he can reconcile law to his personal biasses").

101. H. Jefferson Powell, "The Original Understanding of Original Intent," *Harvard Law Review* 98, no. 5 (March 1985): 885; John O. McGinnis, "Were the Founders Themselves Originalists?" *Harvard Journal of Law and Policy* 46, no. 1 (Winter 2023): 1; Richard H. Fallon Jr., "The Chimerical Concept of Original Public Meaning," *Virginia Law Review* 107, no. 7 (November 2021): 1421–98.

102. Balkin, *Living Originalism.*

103. *New York State Rifle & Pistol Association, Inc. v. Bruen*, 597 U.S. 1 (2022); Sherif Gergis, "Living Traditionalism," *New York University Law Review* 98, no. 5 (November 2023): 1477–555.

104. Abraham S. Goldstein, "Memorial Service: Remarks of Abraham S. Goldstein," in *Alexander Mordecai Bickel, 1924–1974* (New Haven: Yale Law School, 1975), 1–3.

105. Alexander M. Bickel, *The Least Dangerous Branch: The Supreme Court at the Bar of Politics* (Indianapolis: Bobbs-Merrill, 1962).

106. Alexander M. Bickel, *The Morality of Consent* (New Haven: Yale University Press, 1975), 4–23.

107. Nicholas Lemann, "Can Affirmative Action Survive?" *New Yorker*, July 26, 2021 (noting that Bickel cowrote an amicus brief against affirmative action); Bickel, *The Morality of Consent*, 27–29, Brief of the Anti-Defamation League of B'nai B'rith Amicus Curiae, *DeFunis v. Odegaard*, 416 U.S. 312 (1974).

108. Bickel, *The Least Dangerous Branch*, 37, 252.

109. Bickel, *The Least Dangerous Branch*, 125–26, 133; Anthony T. Kronman, "Alexander Bickel's Philosophy of Prudence," *Yale Law Journal* 94, no. 7 (June 1985): 1567–616.

110. Bickel, *The Least Dangerous Branch*, 156, 216, 240; Robert A. Burt, *The Constitution in Conflict* (Cambridge, MA: Belknap Press of Harvard University Press, 1992).

111. Bickel, *The Least Dangerous Branch*, 65–72.

112. Lemann, "Can Affirmative Action Survive?"; Nina Totenberg, "The Painful DeFunis Case Raises the Specters of Racism and Anti-Semitism," *New York Times*, April 14, 1974.

113. Alexander M. Bickel, "Constitutionalism and the Political Process," in *The Morality of Consent*, 3, 11–25.

114. Brandon Bartels, "It Took Conservatives 50 Years to Get a Reliable Majority on the Supreme Court. Here Are 3 Reasons Why," *Washington Post*, June 29, 2018, https://www.washingtonpost.com/news/monkey-cage/wp/2018/06/29/it-took-conservatives-50-years-to-get-a-reliable-majority-on-the-supreme-court-here-are-3-reasons-why; Maxwell L. Stearns, "Standing at the Crossroads: The Roberts Court in Historical Perspective," *Notre Dame Law Review* 85, no. 3 (2008): 875–964.

115. *Bush v. Gore*, 531 U.S. 98 (2000); *Dobbs v. Jackson Women's Health Organization*, 597 U.S. 215 (2022).

116. *Rucho v. Common Cause*; *Moore v. Harper*, 600 U.S. 1 (2023). In *Rucho*, Chief Justice John Roberts held that federal courts cannot review cases of partisan gerrymandering, while in *Moore v. Harper* he rejected the Independent State Legislature theory, which argued that state legislatures can establish election laws without any judicial review by state courts.

## Chapter Seven. The Here and the Hereafter

1. Kelly Olds, "Privatizing the Church: Disestablishment in Connecticut and Massachusetts," *Journal of Political Economy* 102, no. 2 (1994): 27.

2. Danbury Baptist Association, "To Thomas Jefferson from the Danbury Baptist Association," in *The Papers of Thomas Jefferson*, vol. 35, ed. Barbara B. Oberg (Princeton: Princeton University Press, 2008), 407.

3. Thomas Jefferson, "To the Danbury Baptist Association," in *The Papers of Thomas Jefferson*, vol. 36, ed. Barbara B. Oberg (Princeton: Princeton University Press, 2010), 258.

4. *Town of Greece v. Galloway*, 572 U.S. 565 (2014); *Lynch v. Donnelly*, 465 U.S. 668 (1984); *American Legion v. American Humanist Association*, 588 U.S. ___ (2019); *Board of Education v. Allen*, 392 U.S. 236 (1968).

5. *Employment Division v. Smith*, 494 U.S. 872 (1990); *Church of the Lukumi Babalu Aye, Inc. v. City of Hialeah*, 508 U.S. 520 (1993); *Reynolds v. United States*, 98 U.S. 145 (1879).

6. Daniel L. Dreisbach and John D. Whaley, "What the Wall Separates: A Debate on Jefferson's 'Wall of Separation' Metaphor," *Constitutional Commentary* 208, no. 16 (1999): 627.

7. Thomas Jefferson, "A Bill for Establishing Religious Freedom," in *The Papers of Thomas Jefferson*, vol. 2, ed. Julian P. Boyd (Princeton: Princeton University Press, 1950), 545–53.

8. *Lynch*, 687–88; Carl H. Esbeck, "Differentiating the Free Exercise and Establishment Clauses," *Journal of Church and State* 42 (2000): 311.

9. *Lynch*, 671, 708 n. 14

10. Carl Schmitt, *The Concept of the Political*, rev. ed., ed. George Schwab (Chicago: University of Chicago Press, 2007), 25–26.

11. Aristotle, *Politics*, in *The Complete Works of Aristotle: The Revised Oxford Translation*, ed. Jonathan Barnes, vol. 2 (Princeton: Princeton University Press, 1984), 1252b.

12. Aristotle, *Politics*, 1279a–b.

13. John Locke, *Two Treatises of Government and a Letter concerning Toleration*, ed. Ian Shapiro (New Haven: Yale University Press, 2003), 124; Immanuel Kant, *The Groundwork of the Metaphysics of Morals*, in Immanuel Kant, *Practical Philosophy*, trans. and ed. Mary Gregor (Cambridge: Cambridge University Press, 1996), 4:453; John Rawls, *A Theory of Justice*, rev. ed. (Cambridge, MA: Belknap Press of Harvard University Press, 1999), 80–81.

14. Michael Behe, *Darwin's Black Box* (New York: Free Press, 1996).

15. Jefferson, "A Bill for Establishing Religious Freedom," 2:548.

16. Jefferson, "A Bill for Establishing Religious Freedom," 2:548.

17. *McGowan v. Maryland*, 366 U.S. 420 (1961); *Kelley v. Johnson*, 425 U.S. 238 (1976).

18. Marco Rubio, "Speech on Faith and Family" (speech given in Orlando, Florida, May 17 2022), https://www.rubio.senate.gov/transcript-rubio-speech-on-faith-and-family/.

19. *Masterpiece Cakeshop, Ltd. v. Colorado Civil Rights Commission*, 584 U.S. ___ (2018), 1–2, 6, 9, 11; *303 Creative LLC v. Elenis*, 600 U.S. ___ (2023); Mary Eberstadt, "The Zealous Faith of Secularism," *First Things*, January 2018; Patrick Deneen, "A Secular Age?" *American Conservative*, September 3, 2014.

20. U.S. Constitution, Article VI, clause 3; Ronald Dworkin, *Freedom's Law: The Moral Reading of the American Constitution* (Cambridge, MA: Harvard University Press, 1996), 2.

21. Locke, *Two Treatises of Government and A Letter concerning Toleration*, 241–42.

22. Thomas S. Kidd, *Thomas Jefferson: A Biography of Spirit and Flesh* (New Haven: Yale University Press, 2022), 107.

23. *United States v. Seeger*, 380 U.S. 163 (1965).

24. *United States v. Seeger*, 165.

25. *United States v. Seeger*, 165–66.

26. Plato, *Phaedo*, in *The Collected Dialogues of Plato*, ed. Edith Hamilton and Huntington Cairns (Princeton: Princeton University Press, 1961), 99e4–100a3.

27. *Planned Parenthood of Southeastern Pa. v. Casey*, 505 U.S. 833 (1992); *Roe v. Wade*, 410 U.S. 113 (1973); *Dobbs v. Jackson Women's Health Organization*, 597 U.S. ___ (2022).

28. *Planned Parenthood of Southeastern Pa. v. Casey*, 851.

29. *Lawrence v. Texas*, 539 U.S. 558, 588.

30. Joe Carter and Collin Hansen, "Anthony Kennedy's 'Sweet Mystery of Life' and the Self's Impossible Demands," *Gospel Coalition*, June 29, 2018, https://www.thegospelcoalition.org/article/anthony-kennedys-sweet-mystery-life-selfs-impossible-demands.

31. Ronald Dworkin, *Life's Dominion* (New York: Knopf, 1993), 161–66.

32. Immanuel Kant, *Critique of Pure Reason*, trans. Paul Gruyer and Allen W. Woods (Cambridge: Cambridge University Press, 1998), Avii.

33. Hans Jonas, *The Phenomenon of Life* (Evanston: Northwestern University Press, 2001), 23; J. N. Findlay, *The Transcendence of the Cave* (Abingdon, UK: Routledge, 1967), 117; Martin Heidegger, *The Metaphysical Foundations of Logic*, trans. Michael Heim (Bloomington: Indiana University Press, 1984), 168, 214.

34. Plato, *Republic*, trans. G.M.A. Grube (Indianapolis: Hackett, 1992), 527b.

35. Plato, Theaetetus, in *The Collected Dialogues*, 143d–148e; Jacob Klein, *Commentary on the Meno* (Chicago: University of Chicago Press, 1998), 57.

36. Plato, *Meno*, in *The Collected Dialogues*, 82b–85e.

37. Augustine, *Confessions*, trans. Henry Chadwick (Oxford: Oxford University Press, 2009), 482.

38. B. Hartle and S. B. Hawking, "Wave Function of the Universe," *Physical Review D* 28, no. 12 (1983).

39. Hans Blumenberg, "The 'Trial' of Theoretical Curiosity," in *The Legitimacy of the Modern Age* (Cambridge, MA: MIT Press, 1983).

40. Plato, *Republic*, 454c–d, 508a–c; Aristotle, *Metaphysics*, in *The Complete Works*, book 12; Baruch Spinoza, *Ethics*, in *The Collected Works of Spinoza*, trans. Edwin Curley (Princeton: Princeton University Press, 1994), book 1; Friedrich Nietzsche, *The Gay Science*, trans. Walter Kaufmann (New York: Vintage Books, 1974), sec. 341; Augustine, *Against Julian*, in *The Fathers of the Church*, vol. 35 (Washington, DC: Catholic University of America Press, 1957); Avicenna, *The Metaphysics of the Healing*, trans. Michael E. Marmura (Provo: Brigham Young University, 2005); Thomas Aquinas, *Summa Theologiae*, I Q3; Maimonides, *Guide of the Perplexed*, 2 vols., trans. Shlomo Pines (Chicago: University of Chicago Press, 1965); Kant, *Critique of Pure Reason*, Bxx.

41. Plato, *Republic*, 475d.

42. Aristotle, *De Anima*, in *The Complete Works*, 415a31–32.

43. Aristotle, *The Nicomachean Ethics*, trans. Robert C. Bartlett and Susan D. Collins (Chicago: University of Chicago Press, 2012), 1177a.

44. Max Weber, *The Sociology of Religion*, trans. Ephraim Fischoff (Boston: Beacon, 1993), 171. For a satirical account of ancient mysticism, see Apuleius,

*The Golden Ass*, trans. E. J. Kenney (London: Penguin Books, 1998), book 11.

45. Kant, *Critique of Pure Reason*, Avii.

46. Thomas Aquinas, *Summa Theologica*, I Q12.

47. Baruch Spinoza, *Ethics*, in *The Collected Works of Spinoza*, trans. Edwin Curley (Princeton: Princeton University Press, 1994), part I (Concerning God); Michael Della Rocca, *Spinoza* (Abingdon, UK: Taylor & Francis, 2008), 77.

48. David Hume, *An Enquiry concerning Human Understanding* (Oxford: Oxford University Press, 2007), 7, 116.

49. Ludwig Wittgenstein, *Tractacus Logico-Philosophicus*, trans. C. K. Ogden (London: Routledge, 2001), 89.

50. Weber, *The Sociology of Religion*, 124; Leo Strauss, *Persecution and the Art of Writing* (Chicago: University of Chicago Press, 1988).

51. Lucretius, *On the Nature of Things*, trans. Martin Ferguson Smith (Indianapolis: Hackett, 2001); Stephen Greenblatt, "In Search of Lucretius," in *The Swerve: How the World Became Modern* (New York: Norton, 2012).

52. Thomas Jefferson, "To Charles Thomson," in *The Papers of Thomas Jefferson*, ed. J. Jefferson Looney (Princeton: Princeton University Press, 2012), 9:340–41.

53. Thomas Jefferson, "To John Adams," in *The Papers of Thomas Jefferson*, 9:193–97.

54. Matthew Stewart, *Nature's God* (New York: Norton, 2015); Jonathan Israel, *Radical Enlightenment: Philosophy and the Making of Modernity, 1650–1750* (Oxford: Oxford University Press, 2002).

55. Spinoza, *Ethics*, E2p44c2; Thomas Nagel, "The Absurd," *Journal of Philosophy* 68, no. 12 (1971): 720, 727.

56. Locke, *Two Treatises on Government and A Letter concerning Toleration*, 242.

57. Edward Gibbon, *The History of the Decline and Fall of the Roman Empire*, ed. David Womersley (London: Penguin Books, 1994), chaps. 15, 23.

58. Plato, *Republic*, 621d.

59. Aristotle, *Nicomachean Ethics*, 1144b14–17.

60. J.G.A. Pocock, *The Machiavellian Moment: Florentine Political Thought and the Atlantic Republican Tradition* (Princeton: Princeton University Press, 2016), 3–4.

61. Aristotle, *Nicomachean Ethics*, 1141b.

62. Plato, *Theatetus*, 174a; Hans Blumenberg, *The Laughter of the Thracian Woman*, trans. Spencer Hawkins (London: Bloomsbury, 2015).

63. Edmund Burke, "Speech on Conciliation with America," in *On Empire, Liberty, and Reform*, ed. David Bromwich (New Haven: Yale University Press, 2000), 121.

64. Edmund Burke, *Reflections on the Revolution in France*, ed. Frank M. Turner (New Haven: Yale University Press, 2003), 49.

65. Alexander Bickel, *The Morality of Consent* (New Haven: Yale University Press, 1975), 3; Rawls, *A Theory of Justice*, 514.

66. Thomas Jefferson, "To William Short," in *The Papers of Thomas Jefferson*, ed. John Catanzariti (Princeton: Princeton University Press, 1992), 12:14–15; Thomas Jefferson, "To Diodati," in *The Papers of Thomas Jefferson*, ed. Julian P. Boyd (Princeton: Princeton University Press, 1958), 15:325–26; Thomas Jefferson, "To Washington," in *The Papers of Thomas Jefferson*, 15:328–332.

67. Marcus Aurelius, *The Meditations*, trans. G.M.A. Grube (Indianapolis: Hackett, 1983), book III, sec. 10.

68. Kant, *Critique of Pure Reason*, Bxxxiii.

69. Kant, *Critique of Pure Reason*, Bxxxiii.

70. Kant, *Critique of Pure Reason*, Axiii, Bxxxv, B23.

## Chapter Eight. The Sufficiency of Reason

1. Edmund Burke, *Reflections on the Revolution in France*, ed. Frank M. Turner (New Haven: Yale University Press, 2003), 7.

2. Burke, *Reflections*, 55.

3. Burke, *Reflections*, 66.

4. For the first view, see David Armitage, "Edmund Burke and the Reason of State," *Journal of the History of Ideas* 61, no. 4 (2000): 617. For the second, see Russell Kirk, "Burke and Natural Rights," *Review of Politics* 13, no. 4 (1951): 441; Bruce P. Frohnen, "Burke's Defense of Natural Rights and the Limits of Political Power," *The University Bookman* (blog), The Russell Kirk Center, October 18, 2020, https://kirkcenter.org/essays/burkes-defense-of-natural-rights-and-the-limits-of-political-power/.

5. Martin Loughlin, "Burke on Law, Revolution, and Constitution," *Giornale di storia constituzionale* 29 (2015): 50.

6. Plato, *Phaedrus*, in *The Collected Dialogues of Plato*, ed. Edith Hamilton and Huntington Cairns (Princeton: Princeton University Press, 1961), 230a–c.

7. Edmund Burke, *A Philosophical Enquiry into the Origin of Our Ideas of the Sublime and Beautiful*, ed. James T. Boulton (Notre Dame: Notre Dame University Press, 1993).

8. John Rawls, *A Theory of Justice*, rev. ed. (Cambridge: Belknap Press of Harvard University Press, 1999), sec. 40, especially 253.

9. Burke, *Reflections*, 7.

10. David Hume, *A Treatise of Human Nature*, 2nd ed., ed. L. A. Selby-Bigge (Oxford: Clarendon, 1975), book 1, part 3, sec. 6; David Hume, *An Enquiry concerning Human Understanding*, 2nd ed., ed. Eric Steinberg (Indianapolis: Hackett, 1993), sec. 4.

11. Hume, *An Enquiry concerning Human Understanding*, 5.1.5.

12. Ludwig Wittgenstein, *Philosophical Investigations*, trans. G.E.M. Anscombe (Oxford: Basil Blackwell, 1986), 5.

13. Gottfried Wilhelm Leibniz, "Principles of Nature and Grace, Based on Reason," in *Philosophical Essays*, trans. and ed. Roger Ariew and Daniel Garber (Indianapolis: Hackett, 1989), 209.

14. Michael Della Rocca, *The Parmenidean Ascent* (Oxford: Oxford University Press, 2020).

15. Immanuel Kant, *Prolegomena to Any Future Metaphysics*, ed. Gary Hatfield (Cambridge: Cambridge University Press, 1997), 10, 134.

16. For details, see Ernst Cassirer, *Kant's Life and Thought*, trans. James Haden (New Haven: Yale University Press, 1981).

17. Immanuel Kant, *Critique of Pure Reason*, trans. and ed. Paul Guyer and Allen W. Wood (Cambridge: Cambridge University Press, 1998), A11–13.

18. Jan Aertsen, *Medieval Philosophy and the Transcendentals: The Case of Thomas Aquinas* (New York: Brill, 1996).

19. Kant, *Critique of Pure Reason*, A95–99.

20. Kant, *Critique of Pure Reason*, A137–47, A453–55.

21. Immanuel Kant, *The Groundwork of the Metaphysics of Morals*, in *Practical Philosophy*, trans. and ed. Mary Gregor (Cambridge: Cambridge University Press, 1996), 4:447–48; Immanuel Kant, *Critique of Practical Reason*, in *Practical Philosophy*, trans. and ed. Mary Gregor (Cambridge: Cambridge University Press, 1996), 5:47–48.

22. Hume, *An Enquiry concerning Human Understanding*, sec. 1.

23. Leibniz, "Principles of Nature and Grace, Based on Reason," 209.

24. Immanuel Kant, *Religion within the Boundaries of Mere Reason*, ed. Allen Wood and George di Giovanni (Cambridge: Cambridge University Press, 2018).

25. Gottfried Wilhelm Leibniz, *Theodicy: Essays on the Goodness of God, the Freedom of Man, and the Origin of Evil*, ed. Austin Farrer, trans. E. M. Huggard (La Salle, IL: Open Court, 1985).

26. See, for example, Immanuel Kant, *Critique of Practical Reason*, trans. and ed. Mary Gregor (Cambridge: Cambridge University Press, 2015), 5:113–14; Immanuel Kant, *Critique of Judgment*, trans. Werner S. Pluhar (Indianapolis: Hackett, 1987), sec. 62.

27. Michael Della Rocca, *Spinoza* (New York: Routledge, 2008), 2.

28. Jonathan Israel, *Radical Enlightenment: Philosophy and the Making of Modernity, 1650–1750* (Oxford: Oxford University Press, 2001), 162–63.

29. Baruch Spinoza, *Ethics*, in *The Collected Works of Spinoza*, trans. Edwin Curley (Princeton: Princeton University Press, 1994).

30. Spinoza, *Ethics*, 1a4. See also Della Rocca, *Spinoza*, 5 n. 2.

31. Spinoza, *Ethics*, 4p4.

32. Baruch Spinoza to Henry Oldenburg, November 20, 1665, letter 31, in *Spinoza: Complete Works*, trans. Samuel Shirley, ed. Michael L. Morgan (Indianapolis: Hackett, 2002), 846.

33. Spinoza, *Ethics*, 1p32c2.

34. Spinoza, *Ethics*, 1p14; William Charlton, "Spinoza's Monism," *Philosophical Review* 90, no. 4 (1981); Andreas Schmidt, "Substance Monism and Identity Theory in Spinoza," in *The Cambridge Companion to Spinoza's Ethics*, ed. Olli Kostinen (Cambridge: Cambridge University Press, 2009), 79.

35. Emmet Kennedy, *A Cultural History of the French Revolution* (New Haven: Yale University Press, 1989), 344; Jack R. Censer and Lynn Hunt, *Liberty, Equality, Fraternity* (University Park: Pennsylvania State University Press, 2001), 92–94.

36. Joseph de Maistre, *St. Petersburg Dialogues; or, Conversations on the Temporal Government of Providence*, trans. and ed. Richard A. Lebrun (Montreal: McGill-Queen's University Press, 1993), 148. See also Joseph de Maistre, *Considerations on France*, trans. Richard A. Lebrun (Montreal: McGill-Queen's University Press, 1974), 45.

37. Friedrich Nietzsche, *The Gay Science*, trans. Walter Kaufmann (New York: Vintage, 1974), sec. 108.

38. Matthew; Mark; Luke; John; Augustine, *The City of God against the Pagans*, trans. and ed. R. W. Dyson (Cambridge: Cambridge University Press, 1998).

39. Augustine, *The City of God*, 632.

40. Spinoza, *Ethics*, 1p14.

41. Spinoza, *Ethics*, 5.

42. Immanuel Kant, "An Answer to the Question: What Is Enlightenment?" in *Kant: Political Writings*, ed. H. S. Reiss (Cambridge: Cambridge University Press, 1991); Kant, *Groundwork*, 4:443.

## Chapter Nine.  Extravagance and Modesty

1. Sophocles, *Antigone*, trans. Nicholas Rudall (Chicago: I. R. Dee, 1998), 331.

2. Sophocles, *Antigone*, 355–56.

3. Sophocles, *Antigone*, 357.

4. Sophocles, *Antigone*, 332–33.

5. Sophocles, *Antigone*, 362.

6. Sophocles, *Antigone*, 341–43.

7. Sophocles, *Antigone*, 337–38.

8. Thomas Hobbes, *Leviathan*, ed. J.C.A. Gaskin (New York: Oxford University Press, 1998), 1.13.4 ("And from this diffidence of one another, there is no way for any man to secure himself so reasonable as anticipation; that is, by force, or wiles, to master the persons of all men he can so long till he see no other power great enough to endanger him: and this is no more than his own conservation requireth, and is generally allowed").

9. Jonathan Schell, *The Fate of the Earth* (New York: Knopf, 1982), 219 ("We are indeed fated by our acquisition of the basic knowledge of physics to live for the rest of time with the knowledge of how to destroy ourselves. But we are not for that reason fated to destroy ourselves. We can choose to live").

10. Edmund Burke, "On Moving His Resolutions for Conciliation with the Colonies," March 22, 1775, in *Select Works of Edmund Burke* (Carmel, IN: Liberty Fund, 1999), 1:166 ("Man acts from adequate motives relative to his interest; and not on metaphysical speculations. Aristotle, the great master of

reasoning, cautions us, and with great weight and propriety, against this species of delusive geometrical accuracy in moral arguments, as the most falla-
cious of all sophistry"); Aristotle, *The Nicomachean Ethics*, trans. Robert C.
Bartlett and Susan D. Collins (Chicago: University of Chicago Press, 2012),
1094b–1095a; Edmund Burke, "Appeal from the New to the Old Whigs"
(1791), in *The Writings and Speeches of Edmund Burke*, ed. P. J. Marshall, Donald Bryant, and William Todd (Oxford: Oxford University Press, 2015), 4:81
("Prudence is not only the first in rank of the virtues political and moral, but
she is the director, the regulator, the standard of all"); Harold Laski, *Political
Thought in England from Locke to Bentham* (London: Williams & Norgate,
1920), 237 ("Nothing was more alien from Burke's temper than deductive
thinking in politics"); Ioannes Chountis, "Justice and Charity: The Role of
Aristotelianism and Anglicanism in Edmund Burke's Thoughts and Details
on Scarcity," *European Journal of the History of Economic Thought* 29 (2022): 6;
David Anthony Breglia, "The Presence of Aristotle in the Thought of Edmund Burke and Alasdair MacIntyre: Their Response to the Enlightenment
and Modern Liberal Conception of Community and Virtue" (MA diss.,
University of Windsor, 1997).

11. Aristotle, *Politics*, in *The Complete Works of Aristotle: The Revised Oxford Translation*, ed. Jonathan Barnes, vol. 2 (Princeton: Princeton University Press,
1984), 1261a.

12. Aristotle, *Politics*, 1295b ("Since then it is admitted that what is moderate or
in the middle is best, it is manifest that the middle amount of all of the good
things of fortune is the best amount to possess. . . . surely the ideal of the
state is to consist as much as possible of persons that are equal and alike,
and this similarity is most found in the middle classes; therefore the middle-
class state will necessarily be best constituted in respect of those elements of
which we say that the state is by nature composed"); Aristotle, *Politics*,
4.1293–1294a.

13. Aristotle, *Metaphysics*, in *The Complete Works of Aristotle: The Revised Oxford
Translation*, ed. Jonathan Barnes, vol. 2 (Princeton: Princeton University
Press, 1984), 980a ("All men by nature desire to know. An indication of this
is the delight we take in our senses; for even apart from their usefulness
they are loved for themselves").

14. Aristotle, *Metaphysics*, 1072b ("That a final cause may exist among unchangeable entities is shown by the distinction of its meanings. For the final
cause is (a) some being for whose good an action is done, and (b) something
at which the action aims; and of these the latter exists among unchangeable
entities though the former does not. The final cause, then, produces motion
as being loved, but all other things move by being moved").

15. Aristotle, *Nicomachean Ethics*, X.7.1177a–1177b.

16. Aristotle, *Nicomachean Ethics*, X.7.1177b ("But a life of this sort would ex-
ceed what is human. For it is not insofar as he is a human being that a person will live in this way, but insofar as there is something divine present in

him. . . . So if the intellect is something divine in comparison to the human being, the life in accord with this intellect would also be divine in comparison to the human life").

17. Aristotle, *Posterior Analytics*, in *The Complete Works of Aristotle: The Revised Oxford Translation*, ed. Jonathan Barnes, vol. 1 (Princeton: Princeton University Press, 1984), 92b4–8; Aristotle, *On the Motion of Animals*, in *The Complete Works of Aristotle: The Revised Oxford Translation*, ed. Jonathan Barnes, vol. 2 (Princeton: Princeton University Press, 1984), 699b22 ("Now we suppose that the heavens are of necessity impossible to destroy and to dissolve"); Aristotle, *Politics*, 1259b–1260a ("The male is by nature fitter for command than the female. . . . Silence is a woman's glory"), 1255a ("Some men are by nature free, and others slaves, and … for these latter slavery is both expedient and right").

18. Aristotle, *Metaphysics*, 1028b ("The question which was raised of old and is raised now and always, and is always the subject of doubt, viz. what being is, is just the question, what is substance?"), 1029a ("And so form and the compound of form and matter would be thought to be substance, rather than matter"), 1049b ("To all such potency, then, actuality is prior both in formula and in substantiality"), 1050a ("Matter exists in a potential state, just because it may come to its form; and when it exists actually, then it is in its form. And the same holds good in all cases, even those in which the end is a movement. And so, as teachers think they have achieved their end when they have exhibited the pupil at work, nature does likewise. For if this is not the case, we shall have Pauson's Hermes over again, since it will be hard to say about the knowledge, as about the figure in the picture, whether it is within or without. For the action is the end, and the actuality is the action").

19. Michel de Montaigne, *Essays*, in *The Complete Essays of Montaigne*, trans. and ed. Donald Frame (Stanford: Stanford University Press, 1943), 675 ("[Passion] lives still after satiety, and it is possible to prescribe neither constant satisfaction nor end: it goes always beyond what it possesses"); Thomas Hobbes, *Leviathan*, ed. J.C.A. Gaskin (New York: Oxford University Press, 1998), 66 ("So that in the first place, I put for a general inclination of all mankind a perpetual and restless desire of power after power, that ceaseth only in death").

20. David Hume, *A Treatise of Human Nature*, 2nd ed., ed. L. A. Selby-Bigge (Oxford: Clarendon, 1975), 3.3.1 (Describing "modesty and … social manners" as "artificial virtues" with "the tendency of qualities to the good of society"); David Hume, "Essay on Modesty and Impudence," in *Essays Moral and Political and Literary*, ed. Eugene Miller (Indianapolis: Liberty Fund, 1985), 3; David Hume, "Of Superstition and Enthusiasm" (essay 10), in *Essays Moral, Political, and Literary*, 77 ("Enthusiasm being founded on strong spirits, and a presumptuous boldness of character, it naturally begets the most extreme resolutions; especially after it rises to that height as to inspire

the deluded fanatic with the opinion of divine illuminations, and with a contempt for the common rules of reason, morality, and prudence"); Hume, "That Politics May Be Reduced to a Science" (essay 3), 27 ("For my part, I shall always be more fond of promoting moderation than zeal").

21. Aristotle, *De Anima*, in *The Complete Works of Aristotle: The Revised Oxford Translation*, ed. Jonathan Barnes, vol. 1 (Princeton: Princeton University Press, 1984), 429a13–18 ("If thinking is like perceiving, it must be either a process in which the soul is acted upon by what is capable of being thought, or a process different from but analogous to that. The thinking part of the soul must therefore be, while impassible, capable of receiving the form of an object; that is, must be potentially identical in character with its object without being the object. . . . Since everything is a possible object of thought, mind, as Anaxagoras says, in order to dominate, that is, to know, must be pure from all admixture . . . it follows that it too, like the sensitive part, can have no nature of its own, other than that of having a certain capacity. Thus that in the soul which is called mind [by mind I mean that whereby the soul thinks and judges] is, before it thinks, not actually any real thing").

22. David Hume, *An Enquiry concerning Human Understanding*, in *An Enquiry concerning Human Understanding and Other Writings*, ed. Stephen Buckle (Cambridge: Cambridge University Press, 2007), 12.1.16 ("Bereave matter of all its intelligible qualities, both primary and secondary, you in a manner annihilate it, and leave only a certain unknown, inexplicable something, as the cause of our perceptions; a notion so imperfect, that no sceptic will think it worth while to contend against it").

23. David Hume, *A Treatise of Human Nature*, 1.3.6 ("There is no object, which implies the existence of any other if we consider these objects in themselves, and never look beyond the ideas which we form of them. Such an inference wou'd amount to knowledge [and] there can be no impossibility of that kind"); Hume, *An Enquiry concerning Human Understanding*, 7.1.1, p. 60 ("The finer sentiments of the mind, the operations of the understanding, the various agitations of the passions, though really in themselves distinct, easily escape us, when surveyed by reflection; nor is it in our power to recall the original object, as often as we have occasion to contemplate it").

24. Hume, *An Enquiry concerning Human Understanding*, 5.2.21 ("Here, then, is a kind of pre-established harmony between the course of nature and the succession of our ideas; and though the powers and forces, by which the former is governed, be wholly unknown to us; yet our thoughts and conceptions have still, we find, gone on in the same train with the other works of nature. Custom is that principle, by which this correspondence has been effected; so necessary to the subsistence of our species, and the regulation of our conduct, in every circumstance and occurrence of human life"); Hume, *A Treatise of Human Nature*, 1.1.7 ("If ideas be particular in their nature, and at the same time finite in their number, 'tis only by custom they can become general in their representation").

25. Alfred, Lord Tennyson, "Ulysses," in *Poems* (Boston: W. D. Ticknor, 1842), 59–61 ("For my purpose holds / to sail beyond the sunset, and the baths / of all the western stars, until I die").

26. Immanuel Kant, "Prolegomena to Any Future Metaphysics," in *Prolegomena to Any Future Metaphysics That Will Be Able to Come Forward as Science with Selections from the Critique of Pure Reason*, ed. Gary Hatfield (Cambridge: Cambridge University Press, 2004), sec. 27 ("I am very far from taking these concepts to be merely borrowed from experience, and from taking the necessity represented in them to be falsely imputed and a mere illusion through which long habit deludes us; rather, I have sufficiently shown that they and the principles taken from them stand firm *a priori* prior to all experience, and have their undoubted objective correctness").

27. Immanuel Kant, *Critique of the Power of Judgment*, ed. Paul Guyer (Cambridge: Cambridge University Press, 2000), sec. 68, 5:381 ("The expression 'an end of nature' is already enough to preclude this confusion so that there is no mix-up between natural science and the occasion that it provides for the teleological judging of its objects and the consideration of God, and thus a theological derivation"); *Critique of the Power of Judgment*, sec. 86, 5:447.

28. Immanuel Kant, *The Groundwork of the Metaphysics of Morals*, in *Practical Philosophy*, trans. and ed. Mary Gregor (Cambridge: Cambridge University Press, 1996), 4:441; Immanuel Kant, "Doctrine of Method," in *Critique of Pure Reason*, trans. and ed. Paul Guyer and Allen Wood (Cambridge: Cambridge University Press, 1998), 2.2 ("This systematic unity of ends in this world of intelligences, which, though as mere nature it can only be called the sensible world, as a system of freedom can be called an intelligible, i.e., moral world [*regnum gratiae*] also leads inexorably to the purposive unity of all things that constitute this great whole, in accordance with universal laws of nature").

29. Friedrich Nietzsche to Franz Overbeck, Sils-Maria, July 30, 1881, in *Selected Letters of Friedrich Nietzsche*, trans. and ed. Christopher Middleton (Indianapolis: Hackett, 1996).

30. Friedrich Nietzsche, *Beyond Good and Evil*, ed. Rolf-Peter Horstmann and Judith Norman (Cambridge: Cambridge University Press, 2002), secs. 260, 46 ("From the beginning, Christian faith has been sacrifice: sacrifice of all freedom, of all pride, of all self-confidence of the spirit; it is simultaneously enslavement and self-derision, self-mutilation"); Friedrich Nietzsche, *Human, All Too Human*, trans. R. J. Hollingdale (Cambridge: Cambridge University Press, 1986), sec. 116 ("The everyday Christian cuts a miserable figure; he is a man who really cannot count to three, and who precisely on account of his spiritual imbecility does not deserve to be punished so harshly as Christianity promises to punish him").

31. Friedrich Nietzsche, "The Will to Power," in *Writings from the Late Notebooks*, trans. Rüdiger Bittner (Cambridge: Cambridge University Press, 2003,) note 38[12] (June–July 1885), 38–39 ("And do you know what 'the

world' is to me? Shall I show you it in my mirror? This world: a monster of force, without beginning, without end … as force everywhere, as a play of forces and force-waves … an ocean of forces storming and flooding within themselves, eternally changing, eternally rushing back, with tremendous years of recurrence … from the play of contradiction back to the pleasure of harmony, affirming itself even in this sameness of its courses and years, blessing itself as what must eternally return, as a becoming that knows no satiety, no surfeit, no fatigue—this, my Dionysian world of eternal self-creating, of eternal self-destroying, this mystery world of dual delights, this my beyond good and evil, without goal, unless there is a goal in the happiness of the circle. … *This world is the will to power—and nothing besides!* And you yourselves too are this will to power—and nothing besides!!").

32. Friedrich Nietzsche, *The Gay Science*, trans. Josefine Nauckhoff, ed. Bernard Williams (Cambridge: Cambridge University Press, 2001), 4.341.

33. Friedrich Nietzsche, *Ecce Homo*, in *The Anti-Christ, Ecce Homo, Twilight of the Idols, and Other Writings*, ed. Aaron Ridley and Judith Norman (Cambridge: Cambridge University Press, 2005), sec. 123.

34. Nietzsche, *Beyond Good and Evil*, sec. 154 ("The noble type of person feels that he determines value, he does not need anyone's approval. … He knows that he is the one who gives honor to things in the first place, he creates values"); Nietzsche, *Human, All Too Human*, sec. 493 ("Nobility of mind consists to a great degree in good-naturedness and absence of distrust, and thus contains precisely that which successful and money-hungry people are so fond of looking down on and laughing at").

35. Nietzsche, *The Gay Science*, sec. 157.

36. Friedrich Nietzsche, *On the Genealogy of Morality*, ed. Carol Deithe and Keith Ansell-Pearson (Cambridge: Cambridge University Press, 2006), sec. 10 ("The beginning of the slaves' revolt in morality occurs when *ressentiment* itself turns creative and gives birth to values: the *ressentiment* of those beings who, denied the proper response of action, compensate for it only with imaginary revenge. … Nor should one fail to hear the almost kindly nuances which the Greek nobility, for example, places in all words that it uses to distinguish itself from the rabble").

37. Plato, *Apology*, in *The Collected Dialogues of Plato*, ed. Edith Hamilton and Huntington Cairns (Princeton: Princeton University Press, 1961), 31c–d, 40a.

38. Alexander Nehamas, *Nietzsche: Life as Literature* (Cambridge, MA: Harvard University Press, 1985), 194 ("When it comes to life, the 'character' and the 'author' [for Nietzsche] are one and the same").

39. Nietzsche, *The Anti-Christ*, in *The Anti-Christ, Ecce Homo, Twilight of the Idols, and Other Writings*, secs. 60–61 ("What stood as *aere perennius*, the *imperium Romanum*, the most magnificent form of organization ever to be achieved under difficult conditions, compared to which everything before or after has just been patched together, botched and dilettantish. … The *imperium*

*Romanum* that we know, that we are coming to know better through the history of the Roman provinces, this most remarkable artwork in the great style was a beginning, its design was calculated to prove itself over the millennia, nothing like it has been built to this day, nobody has even dreamed of building on this scale, *sub specie aeterni!*—This organization was stable enough to hold up under bad emperors: the accident of personalities cannot make any difference with things like this"); Nietzsche, *Human, All Too Human*, sec. 69 ("The Catholic Church, and before it all the cults of antiquity, had command of the whole domain of the means by which man is transported into unfamiliar states ... the inner world of the sublime, affected, tremulous, contrite, expectant states was born in man principally through the religious cult; that of it which still remains in the soul was, in the days of its germination and growth, tended and cultivated by it").

40. Nietzsche, *Beyond Good and Evil*, sec. 164 ("People who are more alike and ordinary have always been at an advantage; while people who are more exceptional, refined, rare, and difficult to understand will easily remain alone, prone to accidents in their isolation and rarely propagating. Immense countervailing forces will have to be called upon in order to cross this natural, all-too-natural *progressus in simile*, people becoming increasingly similar, ordinary, average, herd-like—increasingly *base!*"), sec. 169 ("People with deep sorrows reveal this fact about themselves when they are happy: they have a way of grasping hold of happiness, as if they wanted to crush or suffocate it, out of jealousy").

41. Friedrich Nietzsche, *Thus Spake Zarathustra*, part 1, sec. 5, ed. Adrian Del Caro and Robert Pippin (Cambridge: Cambridge University Press, 2006), 9–10.

42. See Baruch Spinoza, *Ethics*, in *The Collected Works of Spinoza*, trans. Edwin Curley (Princeton: Princeton University Press, 1994), E1p15c2.

43. Spinoza, *Ethics*, 1.P30 ("A true idea must agree with its object (by A6), that is (as is known through itself), what is contained objectively in the intellect must necessarily be in Nature. But in Nature (by P14C1) there is only one substance, namely, God").

44. See Spinoza, *Ethics*, 1.P29 ("By *natura naturans* we must understand what is in itself and is conceived through itself, or such attributes of substance as express an eternal and infinite essence, that is, God, insofar as he is considered as a free cause").

45. Spinoza, *Ethics*, 5.P42 ("But all things excellent are as difficult as they are rare").

46. Spinoza, *Ethics*, 1.D5 ("By mode I understand the affections of a substance, or that which is in another through which it is also conceived"); Nietzsche, *On the Genealogy of Morality*, sec. 87 ("Let us be more wary of the dangerous old conceptual fairy-tale which has set up a 'pure, will-less, painless, timeless, subject of knowledge' [and acknowledge] there is *only* a perspectival seeing, *only* a perspectival 'knowing'; the *more* affects we are able to put into words about a

thing, the *more* eyes, various eyes we are able to use for the same thing, the more complete will be our 'concept' of the thing, our 'objectivity' ").

47. Spinoza, *Ethics*, 1.D6 ("By God I understand a being absolutely infinite, that is, a substance consisting of an infinity of attributes, of which each one expresses an eternal and infinite essence").

48. See, for example, Spinoza, *Ethics*, 5.P10 ("So long as we are not torn by affects contrary to our nature, we have the power of ordering and connecting the affections of the body according to the order of the intellect").

49. Baruch Spinoza, *Theological-Political Treatise*, ed. Jonathan Israel (Cambridge: Cambridge University Press, 2007), 20.6 ("The true purpose of the state is in fact freedom"), 20.14 ("Freedom of judgment must necessarily be permitted and people must be governed in such a way that they can live in harmony, even though they openly hold different and contradictory opinions").

50. Spinoza, *Ethics*, 4.P35 ("What we have just shown is also confirmed by daily experience, which provides so much and such clear evidence that this saying is in almost everyone's mouth: man is a God to man").

51. Spinoza, *Tractatus Theologico-Politicus*, 16.2.

52. Spinoza, *Tractatus Theologico-Politicus*, 16.5.

53. Spinoza, *Tractatus Theologico-Politicus*, 18.14 ("The most tyrannical governments are those which make crimes of opinions, for everyone has an inalienable right over his thoughts"); Hobbes, *Leviathan*, 251 ("We have no ... obligation to give ear to any doctrine, farther than it is conformable to the Holy Scriptures ... from which, by wise and learned interpretation, and careful ratiocination, all rules and precepts necessary to the knowledge of our duty both to God and man, without enthusiasm, or supernatural inspiration, may easily be deduced").

54. Spinoza, *Ethics*, 1.D6.

55. Stuart Hampshire, *Spinoza* (London: Penguin Books, 1952), 105–6 ("Spinoza is ... nearer to modern psychology than to the commonplace psychology of his contemporaries"); Anthony Kronman, *Confessions of a Born-Again Pagan* (New Haven: Yale University Press, 2016), 616 (contrasting Spinoza's account of the passions with "Aristotle's jumbled psychophysics").

56. See Kronman, *Confessions*, 760.

57. Rebecca Goldstein, " 'Betraying Spinoza,' " *New York Times*, June 18, 2006.

# Acknowledgments

The greatest privilege of teaching at the Yale Law School is the opportunity it affords to study and work with such brilliant, curious, and resourceful students. I wish to record my debt to five in particular. Arshan Barzani, Jonathan Feld, Eli Lee, and Ben Zolf spent endless hours helping me track down obscure sources and put them in respectable form. Adam Flaherty led the team with determination and flair. He has been a vital interlocutor throughout his three years at the law school.

To my supportive editors at Yale University Press, Jennifer Banks and William Frucht, I owe a special debt of thanks. Jennifer and Bill encouraged me at the start and then read the manuscript with sympathy and critical detachment. The errors that remain are mine. They always are. But I would like to think there are fewer of them on account of Jennifer's and Bill's keen editorial eyes.

I owe thanks as well to Robin DuBlanc, my superb copyeditor.

My greatest debt is to my family and to my wife Nancy above all. For years, my children have cheerfully accepted my distractions and tolerated my ideas even when they drifted far from theirs. Nancy is my contrarian muse—always inspiring, never fully agreeing, a loving critic without whose companionship I could do nothing at all, this included.

# Index